Democracy's Arsenal

Democracy's Arsenal

Creating a Twenty-First-Century Defense Industry

Jacques S. Gansler

The MIT Press
Cambridge, Massachusetts
London, England

For information about special quantity discounts, please email special_sales@mitpress.mit.edu.

This book was set in Sabon by Toppan Best-set Premedia Limited. Printed and bound in the United States of America.

Library of Congress Cataloging-in-Publication Data

Gansler, Jacques S.
Democracy's arsenal : creating a twenty-first-century defense industry / Jacques S. Gansler.
    p.   cm.
Includes bibliographical references and index.
ISBN 978-0-262-07299-1 (hardcover : alk. paper)
1. Defense industries—Technological innovations—United States. 2. Research, Industrial—United States. 3. Military-industrial complex—United States. I. Title.
HD9743.U6G36 2011
338.4'735500973—dc22

                                                          2010036043

10 9 8 7 6 5 4 3 2

To Leah, for her love and support

And to Gillian, Douglas, Christine, and their children: may they live in a secure and peaceful future world.

Contents

List of Figures

List of Tables

Preface

President Dwight D. Eisenhower's famous 1961 warning to beware of the "military industrial complex" was followed by a statement that the United States could not have won World War II without the defense industry. Joseph Stalin similarly stated that the allies could not have won the war without the U.S. defense industry. America's security in the twenty-first century depends on a variety of factors, but one of them is the strength and relevance of the industrial base that supports its security.

A major transformation of the defense industrial base is critical to make it strong, responsive, and relevant to the needs of twenty-first-century national security. This book focuses on defining the required transformation and describing how to make it happen. This is my fourth book on the defense industry, and in many ways, this is a life's work.

My first book (which grew out of my PhD thesis), *The Defense Industry* (MIT Press, 1980), focused on the cold war defense industry. It emphasized the period of the post-Vietnam era and appeared prior to the large buildup in defense expenditures that occurred during Ronald Reagan's administration toward the end of the cold war. My second book, *Affording Defense* (MIT Press, 1989), examined the end of the Reagan buildup through the year that the Berlin Wall (1989) came down. At that time, everyone was expecting a decline in the defense budget and was trying to figure out how to get an adequate and relevant security posture with fewer dollars. Finally, my third book, *Defense Conversion* (MIT Press, 1995), described the state of the industry in what was then known as the post-cold war period. It was a low point in defense budgets (people were looking for a peace dividend after the end of the cold war), and defense firms were trying to figure out how they would survive. Many were looking to diversify, if possible, into the commercial world. It was an era of great defense-industry consolidation, and many firms left the defense business. In fact, much of the current structure of the industry today is the result of that consolidation era and the events that followed it.

From 1980 to today, there have been dramatic changes in the world. In the first decade of the twenty-first century, we experienced the horrendous terrorist events of September 11, 2001; the subsequent wars in Iraq and Afghanistan; dramatic changes in technology, industrial consolidation, economics, and geopolitics; industrial and technological globalization; an explosion in annual defense budgets; and $100 billion in annual defense budget supplementals. These dramatic changes demand a rethinking of the future national security posture of the United States, the supporting industrial base, and the ways that we can effectively and efficiently achieve that needed industrial transformation.

This book describes that vision, relates it to the nation's twenty-first-century national-security needs, and, because the government is the sole buyer in this unique market, discusses the changes that are needed within the government to realize this vision through the transformation of the national-security industrial base.

The required changes (both in government and in industry) can be expected to face severe institutional and political resistance, but I believe that the future security of the world depends on the success of this transformation. And it is toward that objective that I undertook to write this book.

Acknowledgments

The author is greatly indebted to and appreciative of his University of Maryland associates William Lucyshyn, Caroline (Dawn) Pulliam, and Alyssa Rodriguez, who helped significantly with the manuscript and figures (particularly Bill Lucyshyn, who spent hours helping with the textual wording and content). They all provided invaluable help and support throughout the entire process of producing this book. Without them, it never would have happened.

Additionally, I am deeply appreciative of the MIT Press, which has done a wonderful job of both editing and publishing my prior three books, as well as this one. It has been great working with them.

1

The Challenge

The Twenty-First-Century Setting

America's rise to a position as the world's lone superpower (in terms of its economic, political, and military position) began at the beginning of the twentieth century.[1] President Theodore Roosevelt expanded U.S. reach globally, U.S. industry experienced enormous growth and reinvented itself to win World War II, the Berlin wall fell, and the Soviet Union collapsed. The twentieth century has been called "America's century." But politicians, scholars, and world observers seem to agree that the twenty-first century will be very different from the twentieth century. Perhaps the wake-up call was September 11, 2001. The terrorist attacks on that day ended the historic view that America's oceans would protect it and led people to rethink the strategic security environment. With the subsequent anthrax attacks in Washington and the global spreading of SARS, people recognized that a more holistic view of security is required. It needs to include worldwide terrorism and global health pandemics (manmade and natural) as well as weapons proliferation, rogue nuclear states, energy dependence, insurgencies within nations (which could easily spread), mass migration, regional conflicts, access to resources (such as water and critical materials), links between international crime and security (for example, narcoterrorism), many geopolitical issues (such as regime stability and the reconstruction of unstable regimes), worldwide economic collapse, and cybersecurity (against attacks on military and civilian infrastructures). Homeland security has become a far higher national priority than it was in the past, and it needs to cover the full spectrum—infrastructure and financial-system protection, missile defense against long-range nuclear-tipped missiles launched by rogue nations, or even an accidental launch from a nation equipped with nuclear warheads and a missile-delivery capability.

The twenty-first century will have far greater uncertainty than the cold war era had. In that bipolar world, both the United States and the Soviet Union were led by rational actors who recognized the destructive power that each adversary possessed. This was sufficient to deter any aggressive nuclear actions. For both sides, the need was primarily to continue to invest in maintaining a strong conventional and nuclear force, and this large and balanced deterrence worked to prevent World War III. However, when facing a multipolar world (for example, one with many anti-American Islamic fundamentalists), deterrence has little value. As a *Washington Post* headline stated, we now face "A Scary World."[2]

In this twenty-first century world of rapid and unpredictable changes in technology, geopolitics, economics, and the military, two things stand out as essential for America's future security. First, a strong U.S. economy is needed to pay for the full range of twenty-first-century security needs. This means a growing economy, balanced government budgets, a fully employed and skilled workforce, a strong dollar, a positive trade balance, and energy independence. As Paul Kennedy warned in his 1987 book *The Rise and Fall of Great Powers: Economic Change and Military Conflict from 1500 to 2000*,[3] states need wealth to obtain military power, and they need military power to acquire and protect their wealth. But he also notes that over the long term, a nation that devotes too many of its resources to the military rather than to the growth of its economy is likely to weaken its national power. This is the challenge that America faces in the twenty-first century. With limited resources for security (so that enough are available for social needs, investments for growth, and so on), how can the multiplicity of potential twenty-first-century security threats be addressed?

The answer to this question lies partially in the second major security consideration for the twenty-first century. Most of the current threats—terrorism, pandemics, weapons proliferation, regional conflicts, energy, environment, scarce resources, and even cyber security—need to be addressed through international cooperation. In this multipolar, globalized world, the emphasis cannot be on unilateral action or isolationist, protectionist policies. Instead, it must be on multinational, cooperative actions that are taken in the interests of each individual nation involved but with the recognition that individual interests are best served by mutual actions.

Although many people (including some members of the U.S. Congress) continue to argue that America can maintain its position in the twenty-first century by continuing to do what it did in the twentieth century, the overwhelming opinion is that this is a period of dramatic change that requires a new way of thinking. For example, when three prior U.S. presidential national security advisers met in 2007 (representing both Republican and Democratic perspectives), Henry Kissinger stated, "The International System is in a period of change like we haven't seen for several hundred years" and is caused by the declining power of nation states, the radical Islamic challenge to historic notions of sovereignty, and the drift of the center of gravity of international affairs from the Atlantic to the Pacific and the Indian Oceans.[4] Zbigniew Brzezinski stated that a global awakening is taking place: "The world is much more restless. It's stirring. It has aspirations which are not easily satisfied. And if America is to lead, it has to relate itself somehow to these new, lively, intense political aspirations, which make our age so different from even the recent past."[5] He went on to say that the United States should tell the world that it wants to be a part of the solutions to the world's problems and that it will engage with other nations to solve the world's problems. Finally, Brent Scowcroft stated that "In this new, very different world, traditional measures of strength don't really apply so much. It's a world where most of the big problems spill over national boundaries, and there are new kinds of actors. . . . we must convince the world that we want to cooperate with them (for our own benefits)" and that we want to be part of the solutions to the world's problems.[6]

Solving these worldwide security problems (such as terrorism, weapons proliferation, rogue nuclear nations, and regional insurgencies) or even avoiding the potential of conflict with a future peer military competitor cannot be viewed primarily as a military effort but must first be addressed as an interagency activity (within the United States government) and as a multinational effort. The U.S. State Department must be a major player in this effort; along with the Director of National Intelligence and the Departments of Defense, Homeland Security, Energy, and Treasury. This will not be an easy step (given the large federal bureaucracies that are involved), but it is a necessary one if the United States is to be in a strong national security position throughout the twenty-first century.

In the twentieth century, it took a long time for the Department of Defense to realize how critical it was for the military services to act jointly and not individually. Modern technology—including information and communication technology, long-range weapons, and space systems—required the army, navy, air force and marines to operate in an integrated fashion. This became formalized in the mid-1980s with the Goldwater-Nichols legislation, which introduced institutional changes and personnel incentives that encouraged integrated, multiservice activities. Additionally, in the twenty-first century, institutional incentives will be required to ensure smooth and effective interagency operations. Fortunately, the first steps in this direction are beginning to appear. In 2008, the State Department appointed a deputy commander to the new Africa Command (AFRICOM), and similar steps are underway for the Southern Command (SOUTHCOM) (which deals with problems such as the drug trade from South and Central America) and for the European Command (EUCOM). Finally, consistent with the uncertainty and lack of predictability associated with the wide variety of potential security concerns in the twenty-first century, the bureaucracy will need to be able to respond much more rapidly and agilely than it has in the past. Because bureaucracies are not known for their responsiveness, institutional changes and new incentives are necessary. As each new event occurs around the world, there will not be time for six to nine months of bureaucratic staffing for response decisions. In addition, those decisions will have to be made in a multinational environment, which complicates the difficulty of achieving a rapid and effective response. Even in the twentieth century, fast and effective decision making was difficult in both the United Nations and the North Atlantic Treaty Organization.

In the multipolar, global environment of the twenty-first century, it is critical that other nations (whether allies or adversaries) respect America (something that, in many areas, was lost during the early days of the twenty-first century). These nations must also be convinced that America will stand behind its commitments (since much of everyone's future security will depend on mutually agreed-to actions). In the United States, these global issues must be thoroughly understood by the U.S. Congress (where politics tends to be a local issue). Cynics often state that "Congress is a leading trailing indicator." Thus, in the interest of protecting America's twenty-first-century security, this area will require strong leadership within the Congress. America cannot solve the problems of terrorism, disease, proliferation of weapons of mass destruction, and mass genocide on its own, and it cannot solve these problems simply by spending more and more money on its military. It must address them with a strong national economy, effective international relations, and a strong but affordable national security posture. This strong national security posture will require a combination of military might and soft power (which, as Joseph S. Nye states, rests on three resources of a nation—"Its culture, its political values, and its foreign policies; all of which must be seen as admired, shared, legitimate, and deserving of support").[7] Military and economic resources can put a nation in a position to have others help support its agenda. Yet even with this combination of soft and hard power, the nation has difficult choices to make in achieving an affordable national security posture for the twenty-first century.

The United States' security cannot be addressed simply by spending more and more on defense. The national budget has many other pressing demands—paying for the rising costs of Medicare and social security (driven by an aging population), paying for universal medical insurance coverage, improving America's education system, upgrading the deteriorating national infrastructure (including bridges and roads), and paying for the huge debt that was incurred in 2009 to counter the financial meltdown. In fact, in fiscal year 2009 (even as expensive wars in Iraq and Afghanistan were underway), President Barack H. Obama proposed a 12 percent reduction in the defense budget, which was the first reduction since 1996. And with the expected continued pressures on the budget and the likely elimination of a large, annual emergency wartime supplemental budget, the Department of Defense soon would face a fiscal crisis. The clear challenge is how to achieve an effective twenty-first-century national security posture within an affordable budget.

Achieving the Required Government and Industry Transformations

The literature suggests that it takes two things to achieve a culture change[8]—(1) recognition of a crisis and (2) leadership that has a vision of the change and is devoted to its implementation. Unlike the periods when the Soviet Union launched its *Sputnik* satellite, when the Berlin Wall fell, and when the events of September 11, 2001, occurred, no precipitous event has triggered a widespread recognition of the need for change. Even more than a decade's worth of warnings were not sufficient to reverse the large institutional resistance coming from the Congress, military, defense industry, and labor unions. These all prefer to continue with the status quo—high defense expenditures to maintain the current defense-industry production of predominately twentieth-century weapons to keep the factories full and to sustain the employment on those projects—even if it does not meet the security needs of the twenty-first century and is increasingly unaffordable.

In October 1998, when I was the under secretary of defense, I observed that the Department of Defense was not taking full advantage of commercial and globalized technologies.[9] It was not adequately addressing the skill base of its aging workforce, was not taking advantage of the potential military and economic benefits of industrial globalization, and was producing increasingly higher-cost traditional weapons systems instead of shifting to technologies and systems that were applicable to twenty-first century warfare. This cry was repeated by many observers during the first decade of the twenty-first century. By 2005, the Defense Science Board, an independent advisory board, observed that the defense industry's independent research and development (R&D that is funded by the firms and not by the Department of Defense) was declining significantly; that resources needed to be shifted from weapons platforms (such as ships, planes, and tanks) to information and systems thinking; that there would be few long production lines in the future; that there was considerable excess capacity in major weapons' production facilities (which the government was paying for); and that there was inadequate industrial planning for the likely future of the defense industry as its customers moved toward twenty-first century equipment and systems.[10] At that time, the industry's response was "If our customers are still asking for old systems, we can't and don't want to convince them to change. It is not in our business interest for them to change." Industry also observed that various government policies, practices, and laws were preventing them from moving toward newer systems and lower-cost purchases. In the following year (2006), many people recognized this need for change. Jeffrey Record stated, "Hostile countries, once a primary threat to U.S. security, have been replaced by rogue states, failed states, and non-state actors."[11] He went on to say that we can no longer expect that America's conventional military superiority can meet the needs of the nontraditional conflicts of the twenty-first century. Finally, he observed that although the Quadrennial Defense Review of 2006 called for expanded special operations forces, "it requested no increases in overall U.S. ground force levels, and stands pat on all major Cold-War legacy weapons systems."[12]

By 2007, even some military leaders were beginning to see this need for a cultural change. The chief of naval operations, Admiral Michael Mullen (later made chair of the Joint Chiefs of Staff) directed his service to craft a national maritime strategy "to address the challenges posed by globalization."[13] He asked that this strategy address the "profound changes affecting technology, economics, security relationships and other arrangements," as well as "energy competition" in the twenty-first century.[14] But although a mismatch—between the needs of a twenty-first-century security environment versus the budgets, policies, and weapons that were actually being implemented—was beginning to be recognized, the coming fiscal crisis and the need for change were still unacknowledged. In reality, the external security world was changing dramatically. Although a new, holistic national-security perspective was required (including a Department of Homeland Security, greatly increased intelligence, and coalition operations), a decade of dramatic budget growth after September 11, 2001, allowed a difficult choice—whether to move toward twenty-first-century security needs or to sustain the continued investments in twentieth-century equipment—to be deferred. The assumptions were that budgets would remain high; that after the conflicts in Iraq and Afghanistan ended, the military would reset its equipment back to where it was prior to the conflicts (by purchasing updated versions of the old equipment as replacements); and that there would not be a shift to a modern, twenty-first-century force at lower budget levels. In fact, it was time for people to be reminded of one of Abraham Lincoln's famous statements: "The dogmas of the quiet past are inadequate to the stormy present. The occasion is piled high with difficulty, and we must rise with the occasion. As our case is new, so we must think anew and act anew."[15]

One person who recognized the coming fiscal crisis and spoke about it through-out the country was David M. Walker, the comptroller general of the United States and head of the U.S. Government Accountability Office (GAO). He stated that "creating the required future U.S. warfare capability, and thus protecting our national security, must be done by improving how the Department, including all of its various component parts, does business; in order to support and sustain our posi-tion as the world's preeminent military power within current and expected resource levels."[16] This resource constraint is the driving force that could cause the needed cultural change as the demands for social expenditures in other areas (including Medicare, social security, education, infrastructure, and medical research) demand the removal of both the $100 billion annual budget supplementals and also the high levels of annual defense expenditures. At that point, the difficult choices must be made, and that pressure, with appropriate leadership, can result in a twenty-first century shift of the U.S. security posture and resource allocations.

By 2010 it was clear that the DoD budget (which, including "supplementals," was over $700 billion) was bound to decline; and that significant change (to address "affordability") was required. Defense Secretary Robert Gates then took the lead[17] in convincing the DOD that there was no choice—change was required. The Services would have to reflect this in their future force planning, weapons requirements, budget, acquisition practices, and so on.

2

The Defense Industry in Perspective

Historic Overview

When people think about the U.S. defense industry, two thoughts come to mind—that it builds the best weapons systems in the world and that it played a major role in winning World War II. In fact, the war-production output of U.S. industry (primarily converted commercial plants) led to its being called the "arsenal of democracy."[1]

The defense industry is a major sector of the U.S. economy, but because it has essentially a single buyer (the Department of Defense), has a small group of major suppliers (essentially an oligopoly in each sector), and is controlled by government laws and regulations, it is not a normal market. In this uniquely structured market, the government (as the sole buyer and the regulator) plans and controls the conditions that should lead to an efficient, effective, and responsive industrial structure that satisfies the wide-ranging needs of the Department of Defense, taxpayers (in terms of affordability), and the laws of the nation (in its ethical behavior).

For economists, a first-best solution is a totally free-market set of conditions. Therefore, a market in which the government creates the conditions for the desired performance is considered a second-best solution. This situation still requires the maximum use of competitive market forces, but the government has the responsibility for being mindful of this market's unique conditions (a regulated market with only one buyer and only a few suppliers in each sector).

An examination of the history of America's need for military equipment reveals that many of the characteristics of today's defense industry owe their origin directly to the historic evolution of this portion of the U.S. economy.[2] Nine features stand out, and each can contribute to the corrective actions that are necessary for the industry to perform at its best in the twenty-first century.

1. The Cyclical Nature of Defense Procurements

Beginning with the revolution, the United States has built up its defense production as required for a war, and as soon as the conflict was over, producers essentially disbanded and returned to normal commercial operations. Each time, the approach taken was that this would be "the last war, and no future military would be required." After the War of 1812, on October 29, 1816, the *Connecticut Courant* reported that "William H. Crawford, Secretary of War, is appointed by the President of the United States to be Secretary of the Treasury, in place of Mr. Dulles, who resigned. We have not heard who is to succeed Mr. Crawford in the War Department. As the business of that office is not now very urgent, it is possible the vacancy may not be immediately filled." Between World War I and World War II, the industry was totally dismantled. Even during the long period of the cold war (1947 to 1991), when a sustained level of expenditures was maintained because of continued concerns about the Soviet Union, there were still wide variations in the expenditures and in the size of the defense industry being sustained (figure 2.1). And during the twenty-year period from 1977 to 1996, industry employment had up-and-down cycles with swings of almost 2 million people—from peaks, including indirect employment, of around 3.5 million (in 1987) to valleys of around 1.6 million (in 1977) (table 2.1).

After each conflict in the second half of the twentieth century—Korea, Vietnam, and the cold war—the public expected (and received) a large peace dividend, and

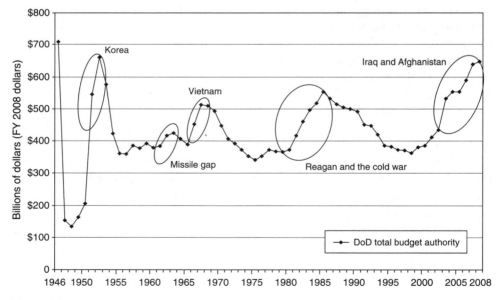

Figure 2.1
Defense budgets, 1946 to 2008. *Source:* Adapted from Steven M. Kosiak, "Historical and Projected Funding for Defense: Presentation of the FY 2008 Request in Tables and Charts," Center for Strategic and Budgetary Assessments (CSBA), June 7, 2007.

Table 2.1
Employment in the defense industry, 1977 to 1996

	1977	1987	1996
Directly related	930,000	1,997,000	1,180,000
Indirectly related	722,000	1,548,000	943,000
Total	1,652,000	3,545,000	2,123,000

Source: Monthly Labor Review, July 1998.

significant defense-budget swings followed. After the cold war, the defense budget plummeted by over $100 billion, and more than 60 percent of that came out of defense procurements (dollars that go directly to the defense industry). Such large cycles create significant inefficiencies, and actions should have been taken to minimize their effects. However, there has been little industrial-base planning (by either government or industry) to minimize the negative effects of widely varying demands for military equipment.

2. The Lack of Industrial-Base Structural Planning

The U.S. civilian economy is built on a strong assumption of the benefits of free-market operation and has long been averse to industrial planning, even in the defense sector. Nonetheless, in this unique market, such planning is required.

Planning involves various structural considerations—such as the number of firms in a given sector, the ability of the government to create competition, and the mix of government and private facilities ownership and workforce—that can result in greater efficiency and effectiveness in terms of equipment performance and costs and in terms of industry responsiveness to changing demands. Given the data shown in figure 2.1 about the cyclical nature of the defense budget and recognizing how the twenty-first century started out (with the terrorists attacks of September 11, 2001), it is likely that defense-industry production will have peaks and valleys and will need to respond to those fluctuations. Yet even during the period of the cold war, when around 5 percent of the gross domestic product of the United States was spent on maintaining the defense industrial base, there was still little industrial planning. The group that had done planning during World War II (the Office of War Mobilization) was abolished immediately after the war. President Harry S. Truman created the cabinet-level Office of Defense Mobilization for the Korean War; and when Dwight D. Eisenhower became president, the office was reduced from cabinet rank in favor of a market approach. Finally, in 1991, the United States had an emergency mobilization division within the Federal Emergency Management Agency (FEMA), but this was subsequently eliminated. Today, an existing executive order (12656) says that FEMA is still responsible for industrial planning (it is now part of the Department of Homeland Security), yet there have been no interagency mobilization exercises since 1991.[3]

Planning for the next conflict as though everything will be the same as the prior one is foolish. The technologies of the twenty-first century are different, the threats are different, the warfighting is different, the equipment needed is different, and in many cases, even the industrial structure is different. This can be seen by comparing the lists of the major military suppliers in World War II with those in 2006 (table 2.2).

While the WWII list is made up of commercial suppliers that converted their production lines for defense use, the 2006 list includes primarily defense suppliers (that may also have some commercial divisions, such as Boeing has). The changing nature of the industry, the evolving technology for warfare, and the uncertain needs for the next set of demands make planning for the future of the defense industry difficult and help to explain why little of it has been done.

The Defense Production Act (which was initiated in September of 1950 and has been renewed periodically up to today) is intended to allow (and encourage) the Department of Defense (DoD) to plan for potential production surges in time of war. It also permits the president to allocate critical materials to defense (as required) and to demand greater output from manufacturers for defense (establishing

Table 2.2
Top defense contractors, World War II and 2006

World War II*	2006**
Bethlehem Steel	Lockheed Martin
Chrysler	The Boeing Company
General Motors	Northrop Grumman
Ford Motor	General Dynamics
Studebaker	Raytheon Company
Wright Aeronautical	Halliburton Company
Dow Magnesium	L-3 Communication
Curtis Wright	BAE Systems PLC
Packard Motors	United Technologies
Sperry Gyroscope	Science Applications International

Notes: *Some of the largest defense contractors during World War II; **the top ten contractors in 2006 ranked by the dollar value of the awards they received.
Source: R. Elberton Smith, *The Army and Economic Mobilization,* The Department, 1991, OSD, http://sizdapp.dmdc.osd.mil/procurement/historical_reports/statistics/p01/FY2006/top100.htm.

Table 2.3
Department of Defense government production and repair facilities, fiscal year 2006

Category	Government civilians	Military	Contract personnel	Operations and maintenance (millions of dollars)
Air logistics centers	21,100	216	500	$5,025
Army depots	15,400	17	2,850	$3,831
Naval aviation depots	10,900	106	683	$1,868
Naval shipyards	25,000	1,655	616	$3,736
Marine depots	1,700	11		$496
Ammo plants	2,000	5	18	$275
Arsenals	3,050	5	53	$502
Approximate totals	69,150	2,014	4,700	$15,733

Notes: Civilian personnel numbers are rounded to the nearest 100. Contract personnel are based on telephone reports from each facility and are not comprehensive. Funds do not include cost of military personnel (which are not available for all facilities) or working capital funds (WCF). For those facilities for which data are not reported, however, WCF in aviation reports equal or exceed the operations and maintenance funding levels.

Source: Based on Department of Defense reports to Congress and contained in Defense Science Board, *Task Force Report on Defense Industrial Structure for Transformation*, July 2008, p. 25.

priorities over commercial demands). Additionally, one of the major planning levers that the government has in this area is determining what portion of the defense industrial base should be in the public sector and what portion in the private sector. For example, many public-sector shipyards (for overhaul and repair), many public-sector aircraft maintenance depots (which, by law, must perform at least 50 percent of all aircraft maintenance work), and numerous government arsenals are still in existence (table 2.3).

In any industrial-base structural planning, these public versus private-sector facilities and the amount of government ownership (even in those facilities operated by the private sector) need to be evaluated.

3. A Lack of Preparedness for the Next Time

The Persian Gulf War (August 2, 1990, to February 28, 1991) was the first time that Scud ballistic missiles were fired at U.S. troops, and Patriot surface-to-air missile systems were needed to shoot them down. Since the Scud attacks were unexpected, the military had inadequate numbers of Patriot systems, and many had to be ordered quickly. Since planning for the Patriot systems had anticipated the need for possible surges, based on prior experiences with expendable weapons systems, U.S. plants had adequate production capacity to build the missiles. But individual parts were required to increase the Patriot production rate, and surge planning had not included the parts. There was an eighteen-month delay in obtaining these parts. Clearly, planning for surge production of these systems had been inadequate.

Until World War I, the Minuteman model of mobilizing manpower in response to war was the nation's planning approach. After World War II, planning anticipated large surges in the production of ships, planes, and tanks. But in Iraq, when roadside bombs started destroying unarmored vehicles, there was an instant demand for armor, which (because it had not been planned for) took years to satisfy. The industries that build the ships, planes, and tanks might be reluctant to change their traditional, end-item-focused preparedness model, and the military might be slow to modify traditions that are built around these platforms. But twenty-first-century preparedness planning needs to address unexpected demands with flexibility and responsiveness. The good news is that preparing for such emergencies is relatively inexpensive and can significantly affect response times when a crisis occurs. (In the case of the Patriot missiles noted above, ordering the long-lead parts in advance of the increased rate of production would have made them available for a surge requirement at very little added cost, since the parts could be used in later years' production if there had been no surge demand.)

4. The Lack of Actual Industrial Responsiveness

In all of its wars, the United States has been able to mobilize men much more rapidly than it has been able to equip them. Today, because of the sophistication of the equipment, the lead times are far longer. Thus, in spite of America's increased overall industrial strength, when unexpected events—such as air attacks on Pearl Harbor, the launching of *Sputnik*, the terrorist attacks of September 11, 2001, and roadside bombs in Iraq—occur, we have often been prepared for the prior event but not for the unexpected new one. And the bureaucracy is structured so that its officials think about the events that they are prepared for, not about the events that might happen (the "surprises").[4]

5. The Lack of an Industrial Base to Match Changing Needs

Flexibility in restructuring and in responding to changing demands will be essential for the defense industrial base in the twenty-first century. It must be focused on items that will be needed in a crisis, including unmanned vehicles, precision weapons, enhanced intelligence equipment, spare parts, and protection for people and equipment. What makes this planning particularly difficult is the rapidly changing nature of technology in the twenty-first century (both in the commercial world and in the military world, which must adapt to the changing technology that is used by adversaries). Since the military is always ready to fight the last war, its industries have also tended to be similarly prepared to build equipment for the last war.

6. The Importance of Science, Technology, and Research and Development

After World War II, Vannevar Bush helped the nation to recognize that science and technology would shape its future growth, competitiveness, and security. The National Science Foundation was established, budgets were increased for research and development (R&D), and university programs were stimulated. When the Soviet Union launched its *Sputnik* satellite in 1957, there was a second surge of emphasis on science and technology. Several agencies were established—the National Aeronautics and Space Administration (NASA), the Advanced Research Projects Agency (ARPA) (within the Department of Defense), and the Defense Science Board (an outside advisory board)—that were aimed at eliminating future technological surprises. During the four and a half decades of the cold war, America's national security strategy was based on technological superiority, and the quality of U.S. weapons systems was counted on to overcome the large quantity of Soviet systems. This recognition of the importance of R&D was matched by significant increases in defense spending, in federal R&D investments, and in basic research at the National Science Foundation and within the DoD. After the anthrax attacks in the fall of 2001, funding increased for the National Institutes of Health to counter biological warfare. Importantly, U.S. defense R&D investments have been of value not only to the nation's defense posture but also to U.S. worldwide industrial competitiveness and have led to jet engines, communication satellites, the early exploitation of semiconductors, the Internet, and huge advances in computing.

7. Significant Differences among Industries in the Defense Industrial Base

Primarily because of their historic evolution, the various sectors of the industrial base (such as ship building, aircraft construction, and munitions manufacturing) are significantly different today. During the American Revolution, for example, ship construction and artillery-piece manufacturing were performed in the private sector, and guns and munitions came mostly from government arsenals. As is still true today, politics have often played a key role in determining the structure of the industry. When Henry Knox wrote to George Washington in April 1794 about the construction of the first six American warships, he said that ship building should be distributed geographically ("It is just and wise to proportion . . . benefits as nearly as may be, to those places or states which pay the greatest amount to its support").[5]

These public and private mixes continued as the defense industry grew. For example, the government owned thirty-seven military arsenals in 1846 and forty-seven by 1859. Because the government owned six navy shipyards (on the Atlantic Coast), the majority of naval ships were built in public yards, but small arms shifted mostly to the private sector (for example, Colt and Remington), with some still coming from the Springfield Armory. During disarmament periods (for example, between the two world wars), the DoD tried to maintain its own facilities; and since there was little market in the private sector, most army equipment (such as guns, tanks, and munitions) came from the six government arsenals. The aircraft industry has been the exception. It started and remained in the private sector (except for the maintenance depots).

The industry is also tiered. Major subcontractors (for jet engines, computers, and radars, for example) often work for different prime contractors, but they are increasingly being integrated vertically into the primecontractor's organization through acquisitions. At the lower tiers, a large number of small suppliers produce parts and materials (such as castings, forgings, and semiconductors) (figure 2.2). Finally, a growing sector of the industry is in the service business.

The majority of defense equipment used to come from commercial industries that converted to war production and returned to commercial operations at the end of the war. In the years immediately after World War II, however, a specialized defense industry grew to meet emerging DoD technological needs (such as jet propulsion for fighter aircraft, microwave radars, missiles, fire control computers, and other unique or predominantly military equipment). Today, most lower-tier

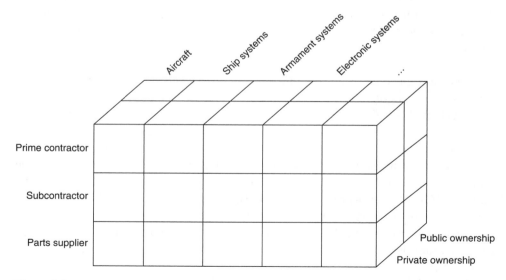

Figure 2.2
The composition of the defense industrial base

elements (subsystems and parts) have a great deal in common with the commercial sector, but most defense goods still come from defense-unique facilities because of government-imposed business practices that force separation.

8. The Consolidation of Defense Firms

After each rapid, wartime buildup and then rapid sell-off, a few large firms take an increased percentage of the defense business. For example, the federal government made large capital investments in plants and equipment in World War II but sold off those holdings after the war at attractive prices to the few firms that happened to be at the location of these facilities. At that time, 250 of the nation's largest firms acquired more than 70 percent of the plants sold.[6] In a number of other cases of World War II facilities, the government maintained ownership, but the companies that colocated with them took over management. This happened at the large aircraft plant in Texas where Lockheed Martin is now building the F-35. The greatest of these consolidations occurred at the end of the cold war, when the top fifty firms merged to become the top five. Because modern defense technologies (both in R&D and in production) are sophisticated and require large capital investments and because large programs are declining, the possibility of further consolidation has raised considerable concerns about the reduction or even elimination of competition (at both the prime contractor level and the subsystem level). In many ways, this concentration, particularly in terms of vertical integration, is counter to the direction that global commercial firms have been moving. No longer is the Henry Ford model of auto production ("steel in, auto out") prevalent in the commercial world. Rather, the trends have been toward outsourcing to competitive suppliers whose core competence is associated with the individual subsystems, parts, or services. With such outsourcing, the commercial firm can remain competitive.

9. The False Perception of Autarchy

Many people think of defense as a problem that can be considered in a closed domestic economic system. The facts indicate the contrary. This reality of multi-national involvement began in the revolutionary period and continues today. In the American Revolution, of the 2,347,000 pounds of gun powder available to the army before the Saratoga campaign, over 90 percent was manufactured from imported raw materials or provided in powder shipments from Europe.[7] Today every weapon system built by the United States contains foreign parts, and many are based on foreign designs. This trend is growing as a result of the globalization of both technology and industry.

The challenge for the twenty-first century is taking advantage of the positive features of the trends (such as the emphasis on R&D and the reality of globalization) while addressing and compensating for features that historically have resulted in ineffective or inefficient performance for the benefit of the nation's security (including potential vulnerabilities from foreign sources).

Defense Spending and the Economy

The total defense expenditures of the United States far exceed those of any other nation. By the middle of the first decade of the twenty-first century, the U.S. defense annual budget of $441.5 billion (an amount that excludes two major items—more than $100 billion of annual defense budget "supplementals" that have been needed to cover the war in Iraq and Afghanistan and also the Department of Energy's budget for nuclear weapons) was a good bit more than the combined military spending of all of the world's other 192 countries.[8] Even countries that have significant defense expenditures (including China, Russia, the United Kingdom, France, Germany, Italy, Israel, Saudi Arabia, South Korea, and Iran) pale in comparison. Not only does the DoD budget dwarf defense expenditures in these other countries, but the distribution of these dollars is also significant. For example, although the U.S. procurement of weapons considerably exceeds that of all of Europe combined, the difference in research and development expenditures is even more extreme. The U.S. R&D is typically three to four times as large as all of Europe combined.

Moreover, the Department of Defense has more than 3 million employees and more than sixty thousand buildings. It operates in 130 countries, has $3.4 trillion in assets and liabilities,[9] and supports an industrial base with the direct labor of over 4 million people. It also has a huge indirect effect on the economy that provides goods and services to the over 7 million government and industry employees, plus their retirees and dependents.

Although the historic trends through World War II were for the United States to disarm after each major conflict, in over forty years of the cold war and continuing into "the long war on terrorism" of the twenty-first century, there has been a sustained level of significant defense expenditures, which is expected to continue in the coming years.

But defense budgets are not intended to cover a single regional conflict. U.S. troops are literally spread around the world (table 2.4).

In addition, the national security budget of the United States must include the basic defense budget, the supplementals that are added to pay for any emergency needs of the Department of Defense (this category includes approximately $170 billion in 2007 for Iraq and Afghanistan), the Department of Homeland Security (approximately $40 billion per year), and the nuclear weapons and naval reactors that are included in the Department of Energy's budget (approximately $17 billion per year). The budget should also include portions of the overall intelligence budget, which once was estimated to be $50 billion to $60 billion a year[10] but in

Table 2.4
U.S. global military commitments, June 2007

CENTCOM	EUCOM	PACOM	SOUTHCOM
Iraq, 169,000	Germany, 75,603	Korea, 40,258	Guantanamo, 75,603
Afghanistan, 20,000	Italy, 13,354	Japan, 40,045	Honduras, 413
Djibouti, 200	Spain, 1,968	Australia, 200	Canada, 147
Egypt, 384	United Kingdom, 11,801	Philippines, 100	Ecuador, unknown
Kyrgyzstan, 1,000	Kosovo, 1,700	Diego Garcia, 491	Afloat, 120,666
Georgia, 21	Bosnia, 2,931	Singapore, 196	
Qatar, 3,432	Turkey, 1,863	Thailand, 113	
Bahrain, 1,496	Belgium, 1,534	Afloat, 16,601	
Saudi Arabia, 291	Portugal, 1,016		
Afloat, 592	Netherlands, 722		
	Macedonia, 104		
	Afloat, 2,534		

2009 was publicly (by the director of national intelligence) put at $75 billion[11] (covering 200,000 people in the DoD and the CIA). Much of this is hidden in a variety of budgets (including within DoD's budget). Various estimates are given for total national security annual expenditures, but by fiscal year 2008, one estimate was $720 billion to $735 billion (which would raise the percentage of gross national product devoted to national security to a range of 5.7 percent for fiscal year 2008).

During the first decade of the twenty-first century, supplemental defense budgets were used to pay for wars in Iraq and Afghanistan. Each year during this period, the supplementals grew, and as the wars continued, supplementals began to exceed $100 billion a year, and in some cases multiple supplementals were required. By fiscal year 2009, the president submitted a budget with a $70 billion initial supplemental. In theory, the purpose of a supplemental is to pay for unexpected expenditures that arise during a fiscal year but were not anticipated at the time that the budget was submitted. As the supplementals began to be expected, however, they became a significant percentage of the armed services' budget plans. When these $100 billion supplementals disappear, the Defense Department will likely face a fiscal crisis. At that point, paying for twenty-first-century systems (versus historic platforms) will become a reality. (Even with the large increases in the post-9/11 defense budgets, by 2010, each of the services was claiming that it was over $20 billion per year short—even with supplementals.) During this period, the nation did not convert its civilian economy to a wartime footing, as it had always done prior to the cold war era, and instead depended on the defense industry for its security needs.

The macroeconomic question of whether large defense expenditures, without conversion of the civilian economy, have positive or negative effects on the U.S. economy is related to whether these expenditures stimulate growth or lead to inflation. Unfortunately, this question has no easy answers. There are experts and data that support both sides of the argument, and the answer seems to depend on overall national economic conditions, the alternative expenditures or fiscal policies that the military is compared to, the economic and social objectives of the policies, and the structure of and the conditions within the defense industry itself.

Because millions of jobs are generated, directly and indirectly, through defense expenditures and hundreds of billions of defense dollars are poured into the economy annually, many look to defense policy as a possible stimulus for the overall economy and for employment in defense-related areas. But comparing the effects of such defense spending with the effects of other government fiscal or monetary alternatives can be misleading. For example, defense expenditures may be a more effective stimulant than expenditures in other areas of government because defense is more capital intensive[12] and thus creates a greater economic multiplier for the dollars invested. However, a tax cut might be an even more effective stimulant (this depends on the form of the cut and the state of the economy at the time of the cut). Similarly, the public-policy objective of the economic stimulant is important. Creation of jobs may be an objective, for example, but the defense sector affects hard-core unemployment very little because of its high skill requirements and high salaries. One analysis (by Wassily Leontief and Marvin Hoffenberg) has shown that, per dollar, military expenditures generate half as many jobs as, but 20 percent more salary dollars than, civilian government expenditures.[13] There are other theories of the macroeconomic effects of defense expenditures (some, for example, consider its effect on the stock market),[14] but a statement by former Federal Reserve chair Arthur Burns provides a good summary: "If the defense sector has stimulated economic development in some directions, it has retarded growth in others."[15] Nonetheless, it is easier for Congress to make expenditures for national security than for almost any other category, which often makes defense spending the obvious candidate for economic stimulation whenever the need arises, particularly in periods of perceived national-security crises.

Perhaps the most important long-term effect of defense spending on the U.S. economy has been in civilian benefits from defense R&D. Because the Department of Defense uses technological superiority as its differentiating strategy, it continuously pushes state-of-the-art performance in a wide variety of areas that have significantly affected the U.S. economy. The DoD's need for small, high-performance electronics led it to be a first buyer (and therefore stimulant) for the semiconductor

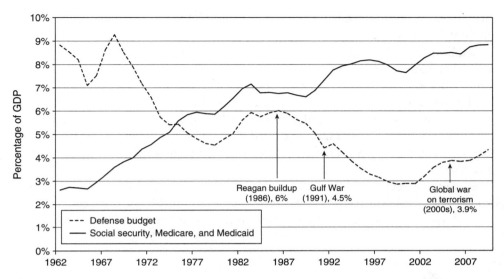

Figure 2.3
The DoD budget and mandatory expenditures (social security, Medicare, and Medicaid) as a percentage of gross domestic product. *Source:* Budget of the United States Government (historical table), *CIA World Factbook* (Washington, DC: U.S. Government Printing Office, 2007).

industry. Its need for worldwide communications led to the communications satellite industry. Other examples include jet engines, the Internet, and the Global Positioning System (GPS). In all cases, these R&D expenditures were done for military needs but benefited the entire national economy. Nonetheless, the purpose of defense expenditures is not economic stimulation, economic growth, or employment (or politics) but must be justified on the basis of the nation's national security needs.

It is instructive to consider defense expenditures as a function of gross domestic product (figure 2.3). Even during the cold war, when the defense budget was maintained above its historic, peacetime low levels and when GDP rose significantly, the share of GDP allocated to defense continued an overall decline—even during the Vietnam War and the Reagan buildup at the end of the cold war. Perhaps surprisingly, given the large expenditures for the Iraq and Afghanistan wars, that overall decline continued. By 2007, total defense expenditures represented only 4.4 percent of the country's gross domestic product.

Based on analyses published by the Government Accountability Office, the United States will not be able to increase its GDP fast enough to satisfy the demands of future defense expenditures, other discretionary needs, repayment of the debt (which by 2017 is estimated to exceed the annual defense budget),[16] and mandatory entitlement programs (such as social security, Medicare, and Medicaid, which, combined, are projected to grow from around 8 percent of GDP in 2000 to about 25 percent of GDP in 2080).

Additionally, although the United States spends overwhelmingly more than all the other nations in the world combined and certainly more than any individual one, many nations' defense expenditures exceed those of the U.S. as a percentage of their gross domestic products (figure 2.4). Yet many other countries (such as the United Kingdom, Australia, and Japan) spend a much smaller percentage of their GDP on national security than the United States does. Nonetheless, on a per-capita basis, in 2008 the U.S. defense budget ($2,000 per person) was second only to Israel's ($2,300 per person).[17]

Despite the recurring hope that peace will break out, history and current worldwide trends do not leave much reason for optimism in this area. Instead, we need to look closely at how the Defense Department spends its money and what can be

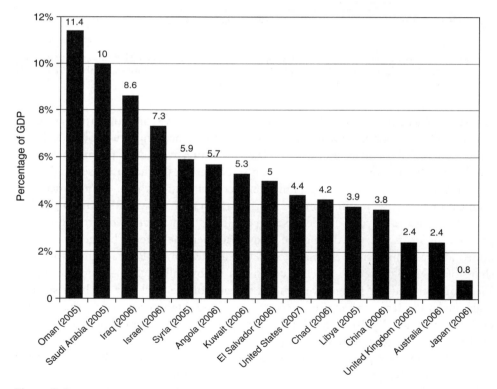

Figure 2.4
Rough comparisons: Defense spending as a percentage of gross domestic product. *Source:* Budget of the United States Government (historical table), *CIA World Factbook* (Washington, DC: U.S. Government Printing Office, 2007).

done to achieve significant reductions without loss of national security. Most of the total DoD budget is divided approximately equally among the army, navy, and air force (with the air force usually slightly higher because of the high costs of individual aircraft and aircraft maintenance, particularly jet engines). The army is far less capital-intensive than the air force, and the major share of the army's costs goes to personnel. The marines are also primarily personnel-intensive, and the Marine Corps' totals tend to be almost an order of magnitude lower than the other services because of its small size. Finally, within the total dollars is a category called "defense wide," which tends to be almost half the level of any one of the three big services and includes the various joint activities across the Department of Defense (such as the Joint Logistics Agency, the Defense Information Systems Agency, and the Ballistic Missile Defense Agency). The distribution among the four services varies from year to year, and as the services move toward more twenty-first-century types of conflicts (such as regional and irregular warfare), personnel numbers are likely to increase for the army and marines. Additionally, in a declining budget environment, it will be increasingly difficult to pay for the large capital costs of navy ships and manned air force aircraft.

The best indicators for trends in DoD budgets are the various categories of expenditures. As defined in the budget process and in order of dollar values, these categories include (1) operations and maintenance (O&M), (2) personnel, (3) procurement, (4) research, development, testing, and evaluation (RDT&E), and (5) other.

Operations and Maintenance

During the long period of the cold war and continuing into the twenty-first century, the DoD's operations and maintenance (O&M) budget (in constant fiscal year 2005 dollars) has grown significantly—from $50 billion a year to around $150 billion a year[18] (and this recent figure does not include large supplemental budgets that go primarily to operations and maintenance for the Iraq and Afghanistan conflicts). This overall increase reflects the costs of operating, supporting, and maintaining complex equipment and the high operating tempo of the conflicts in Iraq and Afghanistan. Rising fuel costs also play a significant role here and reflect the high operating tempo and the high fuel consumption of ships, planes, and tanks. In fiscal year 2008, the Department of Defense spent $15 billion for oil.[19]

As military equipment ages, operations and maintenance costs rise (which has been occurring at a rate of 10 to 14 percent a year), and even if budgets remain level, the DoD will use an increasing share of its resources for O&M. It will not be able to buy new equipment, resulting in a death spiral—as older and older equipment costs more and more for O&M and as less and less money is available to purchase new equipment.

Personnel   From 1945 to 1979, military personnel costs rose gradually with inflation and cost-of-living adjustments (even with the increases for the all-volunteer services). During the large Reagan buildup in the 1980s (at the end of the cold war), however, costs began to skyrocket, with accelerated pay raises as Congress mandated various personnel-related programs (such as the TRICARE military health plan, health care for reservists, and survivor benefits programs) (figure 2.5).

One of the most dramatic personnel cost increases is health care for active and retired military and their families. By 2005, the United States was spending overall $2 trillion annually on health care[20] (this equaled 16 percent of the country's gross domestic product). This represents a doubling of health care's percentage of the GDP from 1975 to 2005, and U.S. health spending is predicted to be nearly 20 percent of GDP by 2016.[21] Military health care and pension costs are also soaring, particularly as the recruits and officers who have formed the volunteer armed forces after the Vietnam War retire and age. This is particularly true for the costs associated with TRICARE, which covers health care for 9 million military beneficiaries.[22] Because of increases in enrollment, benefits, and general medical inflation, TRICARE costs more than doubled from fiscal year 2001 to fiscal year 2005. As of 2005, 42 percent of its budget went for active-duty personnel and their dependents, and the rest went for retirees and their dependents (with medical costs tending to rise significantly with age).

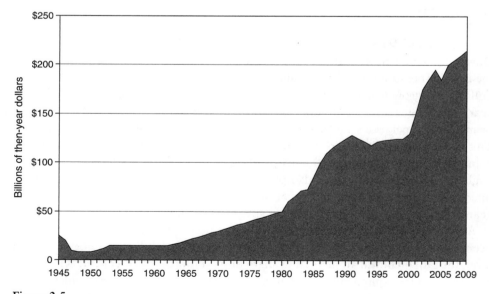

Figure 2.5
Annual military personnel costs, 1945 to 2009. *Source:* Department of Defense, "Green Book," fiscal year 2009.

The rising costs of health care are a growing concern for the overall DoD budget. In discussing the army's fiscal year 2007 budget, U.S. Army Chief of Staff, General Peter Schoomaker, stated that he is "very concerned about the rising human capital costs."[23] He observed that the cost of the regular army has gone up 60 percent since 2001, and the cost of the army reserves has gone up 100 percent—driven primarily by health care requirements. Similarly, Tina Jonas, the comptroller of the Department of Defense, observed that military pay went up 75 percent between 2001 and 2008[24] and Jonas within that escalation health care for the DoD rose by 125 percent in the same time period.[25]

Finally, not all of the costs of DoD health care appear in the DoD budget. In fiscal year 2007, for example, of the total of $93 billion that military health care costs required, $42 billion was covered by the DoD, $31 billion was in the budget of the Department of Veterans Affairs, and $20 billion was in the Department of the Treasury's budget (for retirees).

The all-volunteer services are becoming increasingly expensive. In the presence of extended conflicts (as in Iraq and Afghanistan), benefits (including retention bonuses, hazardous-duty pay, and increased retirement and family benefits) are the major cause of large personnel costs increases, even as the size of the force is declining in many areas.

Procurement

The DoD's total investment account has two parts—procurement (the buying of production systems) and research, development, testing, and evaluation (RDT&E) (the investment in next-generation systems) (figure 2.6).

As shown in figure 2.6, the procurement account builds up dramatically during some cycles (particularly in periods of conflicts) and then declines rapidly thereafter (a "procurement holiday"). In recent times, there was a huge drop in the immediate post–cold war period. From 1989 to 1996 in constant fiscal year 2007 dollars, the overall DoD budget authority declined by about $125 billion, and almost half of this decline came out of the procurement account. In constant 2007 dollars, it dropped from $108.8 billion to $50.6 billion. From 1996 through 2009 (fourteen years), the Pentagon saw the longest buildup in defense budget authority since the 1822 to 1837 period (sixteen years).[26] As can be seen in figure 2.6 (in FY 2007 dollars), the procurement account grew from $50.6 billion in 1996 to $81.3 billion in 2005 (even excluding the supplemental increases), with the biggest period of growth occurring after the terrorists attacks of September 11, 2001, and during the wars in Iraq and Afghanistan. During this buildup from 2001 to 2006, the major weapons programs' total costs (as reported to Congress in the "Selected Acquisition Reports") rose from $700 billion to $1.4 trillion, while the actual quantities being procured declined (reflecting increasing unit costs).

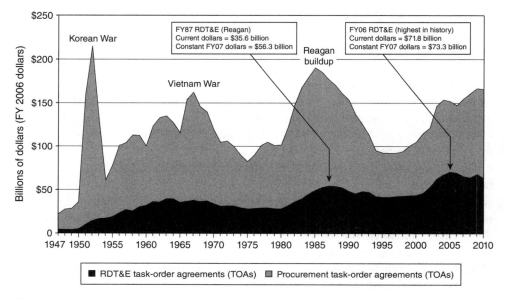

Figure 2.6
Defense investment: Procurement and research, development, testing, and evaluation (RDT&E), 1947 to 2010. *Source:* Office of the Under Secretary of Defense (Comptroller), "National Defense Budget for FY '07" (*Green Book*), March 2006.

So in the early twenty-first century, the quantities of military equipment have declined, while the total dollars for purchasing them have gone up dramatically. The M-1 tank, for example, costs about three times as much as the M-60 tank that it is replacing (excluding inflation and assuming one-for-one replacement). Its performance is dramatically superior (perhaps even three times as good). On a one-for-one replacement basis, therefore, it could be argued that it is worth the money, but it still costs three times as much. If the United States wants to keep the same number of tanks, then it has to triple its procurement expenditures. Similar cost growths have occurred for navy ships and for air force fighter planes. If the air force wanted to maintain its force at a constant size—say, sustain twenty-three tactical fighter wings from 1995 to 2005—then it would have had to purchase approximately 110 aircraft each year. It actually purchased an average of twenty-one aircraft per year.[27] As a reference point, the United States bought about 3,000 tactical military aircraft per year in the 1950s, about 1,000 per year in the 1960s, and about 300 per year in the 1970s. The trends in quantities of military equipment are clear. Norman R. Augustine projected these curves in 1983[28] for fighter planes. He has observed that if the trend continues (and it has, at least through the most modern of the fighter planes, the F-22), then by 2054, the Department of Defense would be using its full aircraft-purchasing power to buy one airplane each year (which he said would have to be shared by the services). It would be a fabulous airplane, and its performance would far exceed that of any today; but numbers do matter. In fact, some argue that total force effectiveness is proportional to numbers squared and is only linearly proportional to individual weapons' performance.[29] To keep total force effectiveness constant while unit costs rise, counting on increases in weapon performance is not sufficient. It is necessary to continue to keep reasonable numbers of these high-cost systems—which is unaffordable (unless the unit costs can be reduced).

Research, Development, Testing, and Evaluation

As is shown in figure 2.6, the long-term direction of the research, development, testing, and evaluation (RDT&E) account has been upward, with the most dramatic increases occurring in the period from 1996 to 2007 (a period when, in constant 2007 dollars, the RDT&E account increased from $42 billion to $65.4 billion). But within this overall account, there has been a shift toward the costs of full-scale weapons development and away from long-term research. This shift has been driven by an enormous increase in the complexity of the weapon systems that continuously expand the state of the art in each area. If the top line of the defense budget becomes significantly constrained, then the shift from the long-term to the short-term might become even greater. Thus, the United States' ability to maintain its long-term technological superiority might be in jeopardy if it does not invest significantly in long-term research.

Budget trends in the post–cold war era are considered in table 2.5, which compares personnel and inventory numbers for 1988 and 2007.

What these figures show is that the large buildup in the defense budget after September 11, 2001, did not reverse the declines in either personnel or

Table 2.5
Defense trends, 1988 to 2007

	1988	2007
Active-duty personnel (thousands)	2,209	1,406
Reserve and guard personnel (thousands)	1,158	843
Civilian personnel (thousands)	1,090	702
Active in-commission ships	573	236
Army divisions (active)	20	10
Air Force fighter/attack (total active inventory)	3,027	1,619

Source: "National Defense Budget Estimates for FY2006," April 2007, *AFA Almanac*, http://www.history.navy.mil/branches/org9-4c.htm.

major equipment that took place immediately after the cold war. The increased dollars paid for much more expensive equipment and for the much higher costs of the all-volunteer force, but reductions in quantity, in both personnel and equipment, were significant.

In any discussion of defense spending and the economy, it is essential to recognize that the driving factor behind the nation's future security is its economic strength. Without strong growth in the economy and an acknowledgment of the other growing demands on resources (such as social security and Medicare), resources will not be available for investment in the nation's security. Without such resources, the personnel and equipment needed to provide high levels of national security will no longer be affordable. There is a need for a parallel track: first, find and implement ways to reduce the costs of national security itself, and second, find and implement ways to strengthen the U.S. economy through dual-use investments in security and economic growth.

The importance of the interrelationship between security and the economy was perhaps best summarized by Gary Hart when he wrote, "Our economic cloak is the basis of our strength, and our strength is the basis for our world leadership."[30] Our military and our political capabilities are critical, but they must be based on our economic strength as a nation. This interdependency between military strength and economic strength is a frequent reference point in this book.

The Cold War and Post–Cold War Years

For more than five decades—from 1947 to 1998—the United States and the Soviet Union stared down each other with huge military establishments and nuclear warheads. Throughout this "cold war" period, the perceived tactical threat (for example, from a sudden buildup and then attack by Russian troops through the Fulda Gap in Germany) led the United States to modernize its military forces at a very high rate (thus providing strong financial support and an "order book" for the continuation of the large defense industry). For example, in fiscal year 1985, the U.S. Department of Defense requested (and Congress authorized) more than 900 aircraft, fifty intercontinental ballistic missiles, twenty-three naval ships, 2,000 tanks and armored personnel carriers, more than 5,000 guided missiles, and 72,000 unguided rockets.[31] At that time, the nation had (depending on how they are counted) twenty to fifty major defense contractors.

In addition, particularly in the last decade of the cold war, the world was going through an information revolution. The commercial world experienced this in the form of the rapid spread of the Internet in the 1990s. For the military, the effects were seen in precision weapons, precision sensors, and the integration of these through a "network of sensors and shooters" (through an integrated command, control, and communications system). Although budgets and military operations still focused on the historic mass-on-mass encounters with traditional weapons, a strong push was being made to superimpose on that model the information revolution and its potential for greatly enhanced military capability, through the application of these information-enabled force multipliers.

In the mid-1980s, a series of what the press called "waste, fraud, and abuse scandals" had two significant effects on the Department of Defense. Some of these abuses involved illegal actions (the "ill wind" scandal happened when a senior navy official entered into improper contractual relations with a contractor), and other abuses involved bad accounting and acquisition practices that resulted in overpriced spare parts and commercial items (such as a $600 toilet seat, $427 hammers, and a greatly overdesigned coffee pot that could survive intact in an air force aircraft crash). To investigate these problems, in 1985 the Congress created the Blue Ribbon Commission on Defense Management (known as the Packard Commission, after the chair, David Packard, cofounder of Hewlett-Packard and a former deputy secretary of defense). Rather than assigning blame, this commission examined the root causes of these waste, fraud, and abuse scandals in the defense acquisition process, looked at the structural changes (in organizations, chains of command, and weapons requirements) that were necessary, and made a number of important recommendations that were subsequently implemented in the Goldwater-Nichols Department of Defense Reorganization Act of 1986. These recommendations included the following:

- An undersecretary of defense for acquisition would have responsibility for the research, development, procurement, testing, and support of all weapon systems. The title was later expanded to undersecretary of defense for acquisition, technology, and logistics.

- An acquisition executive in each of the services would report directly to the undersecretary of defense for acquisition and to the relevant service secretary.

- Program executive officers would report to the service acquisition executive and would oversee the various program managers in a given area.

- A vice-chair of the Joint Chiefs of Staff (at a four-star general officer level) would insert joint authority into the requirements process (by chairing a Joint Requirements Oversight Council that would review and approve all requirements) and would represent the users of the military equipment (the combatant commanders) in the requirements process (rather than having that process driven totally by the military services).

• For future promotion to a flag officer position (general or admiral), a candidate would have to have served in a joint (that is, multiservice) position (a large incentive to improve multiservice planning and operations).

The Packard Commission also recommended that some significant changes be made to federal procurement law, including reducing the use of unique military specifications (to allow greater reliance on commercial items) and enhancing program stability through the use of baselining requirements, milestone budgeting, and multiyear procurements (for selective systems). Many of these acquisition suggestions were implemented within the DoD when William Perry (who had been a member of the Packard Commission) became secretary of defense in 1994.

During this cold war period, Congress implemented a significant set of related actions. Some were quite broad, such as the Competition in Contracting Act (1984) (which encouraged more competition) and (consistent with the Packard Commission's recommendations) the Federal Acquisition Reform Act (1995) (which encouraged greater use of commercial items). It also implemented a requirement to add 6,000 more auditors and mandated the maximum price that the government would pay for a toilet seat ($660). This began a series of legislative actions that were intended to "ensure that there would be no mistakes." Thus, through detailed regulation Congress attempted to remove much of the management judgment that is required for effective and efficient buying of weapon systems. Unfortunately, the only way to be absolutely sure that no mistakes are made is (1) do nothing or (2) take no risks (which means always being behind and spending as much as possible to cover every possible contingency). Neither of these choices is desirable.

Finally, in addition to addressing the scandals, Congress also realized that the services needed to work together more closely. In speeches that he delivered October 1 to 8, 1985, Senator Barry Goldwater said, "The inability of the military Services to work together effectively has not gone unnoticed" and noted that there was an "inability of the Joint Chiefs of Staff to provide useful and timely advice . . . as advocates for joint interests in budgetary matters."[32] In this same period, Senator Sam Nunn stated, "The Joint Chiefs of Staff failed to consistently provide useful and timely military advice to the senior civilian leadership. . . . the Joint Chiefs generally operate under an informal rule requiring unanimous agreement prior to the rendering of advice. As a result, their advice is often muddled and tends to protect the Service's interests."[33] Finally, the 1983 invasion of the Caribbean island of Grenada demonstrated the need for interservice unification of the command, control, and communication systems and for more realism in joint exercises, particularly regarding communication.[34] So the Packard Commission's emphasis on jointness in the requirements process and in military career advancements was strongly supported on Capitol Hill.

Post–Cold War Years[35]

In 1989, the Berlin Wall fell, and in 1991, the Soviet Union collapsed. The ten years from 1991 to 2001 became known as the post–cold war years. The future was simply unknown. At the same time, dramatic changes were taking place in the defense industry, including five clear trends—defense budget cuts, industrial consolidation, changes in security concerns, globalization, and outsourcing of government work.

1. Defense Budget Cuts

The post–cold war collapse of the defense budget was its most significant drop since the end of World War II. As would be expected, the quantities of equipment procured in the ten-year period from 1985 to 1995 dropped dramatically (table 2.6).

This dramatic drop in the quantities of ships, planes, and tanks being procured resulted in an enormous buildup in excess capacity in the defense industry (both in facilities and personnel), and this large overhead had to be absorbed in the few systems that were being built, thus raising their unit costs dramatically. Yet as budgets fell, the platform quantities were shrinking much more rapidly than their unit costs were rising. For example, from 1990 to 1999, aircraft quantities shrunk by 69 percent, but their unit costs rose by 32 percent. Similarly, the quantity of ships shrunk by 84 percent, but their unit costs rose by 50 percent. With tracked combat vehicles (tanks), quantities shrunk by 90 percent, and unit costs rose by 54 percent. As noted above, the Defense Department was in a death spiral. Its equipment was aging and wearing out (from simultaneous training and worldwide deployments), but the DoD could not afford to replace the older systems because budgets were falling and unit costs were rising. In addition, the DoD was facing increasing maintenance costs because its equipment was old and worn out and the costs of spare parts were rising (the air force's costs per flying hour went up over 40 percent in seven years). In response, industry shifted much of its focus from production of weapons systems to support, upgrades, and services since those were

Table 2.6
Procurement of major systems

	1985	1990	1995
Ships	29	20	6
Aircraft	943	511	127
Tanks	720	448	0

Source: Loren Thompson, National Security Studies, Georgetown University, April 21, 1995.

the areas where the remaining dollars were primarily going (from 1997 to 1999, the dollars in these areas increased from 26 percent of DoD awards to 51 percent).[36]

At the end of the cold war, Russia and a number of the other former Soviet Union states still had large arsenals (particularly of strategic nuclear weapons). It was considered highly desirable to find ways (through negotiations known as cooperative threat reductions) for both the United States and the former Soviet Union states to reduce their strategic weapons stockpiles and the means of their delivery (1,846 Russian and 846 U.S. ballistic missiles were literally sawed apart). This was a highly stabilizing effort, but because of the financial instability of many of these former Soviet states, reduction costs had to come from the U.S. DoD budgets. This meant a further lack of money for orders (for the replenishment of weapons) to the U.S. defense industry and U.S. nuclear weapons' establishments.

2. Industrial Consolidation

As the Department of Defense faced the high costs of maintaining the many excess aircraft plants, shipyards, and missile plants that were languishing because of a greatly reduced demand, government defense leaders began to encourage defense-industry consolidations. The best-known call for consolidation came in 1993, when then Deputy Secretary William Perry announced (at the famous Last Supper with industry senior executives) the need for defense-industry consolidation. He also stated that the government would subsidize this behavior by allowing consolidation costs to be reimbursed as overhead costs—as long as the savings to the government could be clearly projected and as long as competition was still maintained within each sector of the industry.

Given declining DoD procurements and their negative effects on the industry, there was great rejoicing in the industry over the opportunity to consolidate. This enthusiasm was matched by Wall Street (where investors made millions on each major defense-industry merger or acquisition). The merger wave began in the late 1980s but accelerated enormously as the defense budget plummeted in the 1990s (figure 2.7).

Figure 2.7 shows some major acquisitions by five large defense contractors, but these five firms absorbed over fifty previous entities. These mergers and acquisitions occurred both horizontally (such as the McDonald Douglas and Boeing combination in the aircraft industry or the Hughes and Raytheon combination in the missile industry) and also vertically (such as Lockheed's acquisition of Loral and Northrop's acquisition of Westinghouse). Within a decade, many major defense suppliers and many more major subcontractors had been consolidated into a handful of dominant defense firms. (From 1993 to 1999, the number of top defense suppliers went from thirty-six to eight, and from 1994 to 1997, the volume of defense merger and acquisition dollars increased from $2.7 billion to $31.2 billion.)[37] The defense

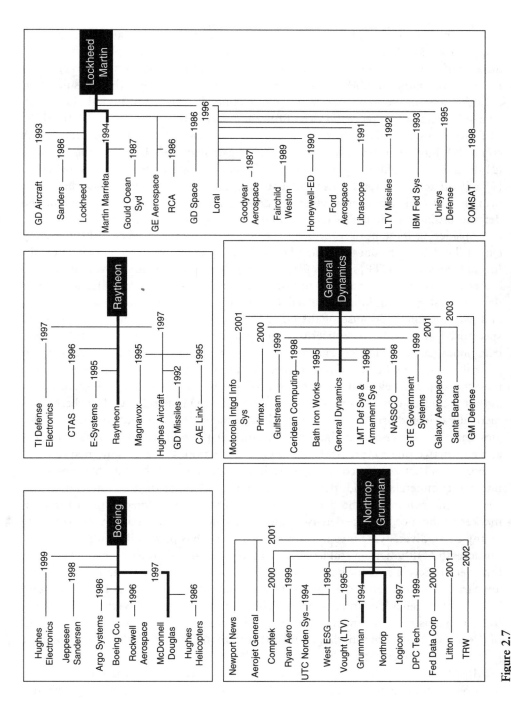

Figure 2.7
Defense-industry consolidation, 1986 to 2001. *Source:* Adapted from "A Blueprint for Action," Aerospace Industry of America Association (AIAA), Defense Reform 2001 Conference, February 14 and 15, 2001, Washington, DC.

industry borrowed to make these acquisitions, and its debt level also rose dramatically—from $15 billion in 1993 to $43 billion in 1999. For example, in the second quarter of 2000, Lockheed Martin had a debt-to-equity ratio of 175 percent as a result of the large number of acquisitions that it made during the consolidation period,[38] and its bond ratings were plummeting. In this same period, Lockheed Martin's bond rating fell from A to BBB-, and Raytheon's went from AA to BBB-.

During this consolidation orgy, a defense firm had several strategic choices. It could (1) buy up other firms to take a larger share of the shrinking market, (2) diversify by building up a commercial business along with its defense business, (3) sell off many of its defense elements (for the high cash value that they were bringing in) and focus on a narrower defense area, or (4) simply get out of the defense business (if it had a large amount of commercial business).

Considering these options in inverse order, a significant number of firms simply exited the defense business. In the high-technology companies, these included California Microwave, GTE, Hughes Electronics, IBM, Lucent, Magnavox, Phillips, and Texas Instruments. In the large industrial companies, there were Allegheny, Teledyne, Chrysler, Eaton, Emerson, Ford, General Electric (except jet engines), Tenneco, and Westinghouse. Because of the complexity of government rules (ranging from specialized accounting to concerns about propriety rights), many technology-rich companies (such as Hewlett Packard, 3-M, and Corning) declined to participate in critical research and development projects of the Defense Department, even though they continued to sell their commercial products to the DoD. Many observers (this author included) were disappointed when the defense industrial base lost these commercially oriented firms (because of the loss of their often more advanced technologies and their lower-cost design orientation), but these firms saw defense business as unattractive due to low profits, excessive regulation, and shrinking markets.

For firms that countered the defense-budget declines by shifting their resources into the commercial world, the record is spotty.[39] Because of the significant differences in the cultures of the defense and commercial environments (particularly in marketing, finance, and the defense engineering emphasis on maximum performance at any cost), diversifying into the commercial world has proven difficult and largely unsuccessful (although several firms have been successful at converting).[40] In general, the overall success rate (of both commercial and military mergers and acquisitions) appears to average around 35 percent, but it has been significantly higher (around 70 percent) when a few firms attempted conversion in areas that were closely related to their mainstream businesses. For many defense firms, as William Frickes, head of Newport News Shipbuilding, told the author in March 1998, "Quite bluntly, [commercial diversification] has not worked!"

Most firms chose the mergers and acquisitions route as either the acquirer or the acquiree. Although the rationales for this approach (including synergism, greater capital availability, more market power, and greater economies of scale) seem appealing, the empirical data on mergers and acquisitions demonstrate are that they have been largely unsuccessful.[41] The difficulty of absorbing different corporate cultures and the lack of management knowledge of the new businesses have proven to be extreme barriers to the desired twenty-first-century characteristics of the consolidated defense firms. (In fact, a McKenzie study[42] of mergers and acquisitions by defense firms showed an 80 percent "unsuccessful acquisitions" record.) Nonetheless, the Government Accountability Office (GAO) found that, as a result of the defense industry consolidations that took place, the Department of Defense saved more than $2 billion in three years.[43]

Consolidating plant activities (both within a firm and across acquired firms in the same business) was an obvious area for potential savings. But most firms chose not to make the plant-consolidation moves—for political reasons (they wanted to satisfy local employment issues), for reasons of optimism (they hoped that budgets would return to high levels and their plants could again operate at full capacity), and for reasons of pessimism (they feared that they would incur significant costs in moving and consolidating the facilities, even though many costs would have been covered in allowable overhead expenses against their defense contracts). Most firms chose not to make the plant-consolidation moves. Lockheed Martin continued to build its new F-22 fighter aircraft in Georgia while building its new F-35 fighter aircraft in Texas; Boeing continued to build aircraft in Missouri, Washington, and California; Northrop Grumman built ships in Mississippi and Virginia; and General Dynamics built ships in Maine and Connecticut. Keeping these plants running at low volume was not as efficient as integrating these operations, but consolidation was politically difficult and was usually not done. There were some exceptions, however, in which the benefits to the government were realized. For example, Raytheon consolidated its missile production in its facility in Tucson, Arizona, and the Defense Department saw weapons' price reductions of up to 25 percent, thus saving the Department of Defense over $2 billion on long-term missile productions.[44] Because the prices paid to the producer are based on their costs for each year, the firms shared very little in the benefits realized from these savings and therefore had inadequate incentives to achieve the benefits from the consolidations.

One adverse affect of consolidation was the restructuring of the industry by size—a few large firms and a significant number of small firms (which were being supported largely by mandated set-asides for small businesses). The increasing disappearance of the midsized firms was notable because formerly they often represented competition for some of the larger firms. The industry was being bifurcated by the acquisition or loss of the midsized firms, which were absorbed by the few remaining large firms or which left the defense sector because they were unable to compete. This was particularly true in the service sector. From 1995 to 2004, the value of the federal service-industry contracts going to midsized firms shrank from 44 percent to 29 percent, and those contracts going to midsize firms in the critical information and communications technology services sector shrank from 29 percent to 13 percent. In both cases, the shrinkage occurred primarily when large firms took over that share of the business.[45]

The defense-industry consolidations had a major negative effect on employment. From 1990 to 1995, defense-industry employment fell by a half million people.[46] These large layoffs in the defense sector and the growing technology boom in the civilian sector (particularly in information-technology areas) led to severe declines in the numbers of graduating engineers seeking employment in defense. In 1990, graduating technology students listed aerospace and defense as their third most popular career discipline, but by 1998, this choice had slipped to number seven in their rankings, being replaced by telecommunications, Internet, biotechnology, and other similar disciplines in the commercial field.[47] In addition to losing new technologists, many skilled workers from the defense industry were leaving to join the growth industries of the commercial market.

With declining budgets and the considerable excess capacity that existed in defense plants, there were significant reductions in capital expenditures by the defense industry. Perhaps even more important for the long term, there was also a significant reduction in company-sponsored independent research and development (IR&D). From 1994 to 1999, for example, the percentage of sales spent on IR&D by defense firms dropped from 4.1 percent to 2.9 percent, and since sales were declining rapidly, total IR&D was a smaller percentage of a smaller number, i.e., an adverse "multiplying factor."[48]

Perhaps surprisingly, during this period of dramatic defense budget reductions and driven by the consolidations that Wall Street tends to favor, defense stock prices actually soared. Between the last quarter of 1990 and the first quarter of 1998, defense stocks produced a return of 664 percent, which compares favorably to 324 percent for that period for Standard and Poor's 500 Index.[49]

By the end of this defense budget down cycle, there was growing concern within the Department of Defense about the trends that were appearing in the defense industry.[50] First, there were growing concerns that in many sectors of the defense industry, the number of firms had been reduced to only two or three major firms in each critical area of defense needs and that there was the threat of going down to one. Second, after the period of Wall Street exuberance over the merger and acquisition activities of defense firms, several firms were not meeting their earnings expectations (for a number of reasons), and their stock prices began to plummet. Third, many firms that had the choice were leaving the defense sector and going to the commercial area, thereby increasing the isolation of the defense sector from the rapid advances of commercial technology and from the exploding market growth in the commercial technology sector. Finally, outmoded export-control policies and practices continued, and many believed that the defense sector should and could remain autarkic—a self-sufficiency that was clearly counter to the needs and realities of the growing focus on coalition warfare and industrial globalization. Steps had to be taken to address these four areas.

First, in terms of competition, the Defense Department, the Justice Department, and the Federal Trade Commission were increasingly concerned about the declining number of firms that were available for competition in the defense sector. Even so, they allowed the consolidations due to the shrinkage in available business and the uniqueness of the defense market structure (a monopoly buyer and a small number of oligopoly suppliers that fought fiercely for the few, infrequent, and declining numbers of major procurements). The regulators reasoned that if the only customer (the DoD) was satisfied with the limited competition and if the cost of maintaining additional potential suppliers was prohibitive, then they would not object to the consolidations on antitrust grounds. The DoD assured them (as Secretary Perry had stated) that it would allow consolidations only if they reduced costs to the DoD and if adequate competition will still exist after the mergers and acquisitions. It was noted that there had always been fierce competition for DoD's aircraft engines, even when only two suppliers (General Electric and Pratt & Whitney) dominated the U.S. defense business (and with Rolls-Royce of England available if needed). Thus, it was agreed that two or three competitors would be adequate for competition in each critical sector and that the shrunken defense market could not support more than that. As the shrinkage continued, the Department of Defense began to monitor more carefully priority, critical technologies and to create protection (or watch) lists to monitor loss of U.S. technological leadership and the adequacy of U.S. suppliers (by 2005, nine critical sectors were being tracked).

Eventually, the consolidation of defense firms would have to come to an end since the government would not allow consolidation from two firms to one (from a duopoly to a monopoly) in any critical defense sector. This was demonstrated by both the Defense Department and the Justice Department when they would not allow General Dynamics (which had already bought the Electric Boat nuclear submarine facility) to buy the Newport News Shipbuilding facility—which was the only other shipyard capable of building nuclear submarines. The remaining choice for the major defense firms was often to buy up lower-tier defense suppliers (the subsystem and critical-component firms). However, when there was a threat that two suppliers were at the point of going to only one supplier in any critical subtier sector, the government again had to step in—as when it stopped the proposed Lockheed Martin and Northrop Grumman merger (not so much because of anti-competitive considerations at the prime contractor level but because of the threat of creating monopoly suppliers at the lower tiers and because of vertical-integration considerations).[51] This proposed merger helped to make visible a growing concern regarding vertical integration. If one prime contractor owned or acquired the only (or even the acknowledged best) supplier of a critical subsystem, then it would be at a significant competitive advantage against other prime contractors, which would not (as the result of the merger or acquisition) have access to that subsystem supplier on future large weapon-system bids. The prime contractors that were proposing the merger or acquisition of the lower-tier supplier usually argued that their acquired subsystem division would be a merchant supplier to anyone bidding against their parent firm. This argument was not felt to be credible. Nonetheless, perhaps surprisingly, the military services often favored the merger of the two remaining suppliers since they believed that this would result in less overhead to be carried (in spite of the empirical evidence that the lack of competition results in rising prices). In the end, they argued that they "could not afford to carry both suppliers."[52] Nonetheless, the services' positions on these issues often had to be overridden by the office of the secretary of defense in combination with the Justice Department or Federal Trade Commission, based on long-term antitrust arguments.[53]

Because fewer and fewer new defense programs were being initiated during this downturn, the small number of remaining firms in a given sector often attempted to team to ensure that they would get at least part of each program (since a competitive loss might mean that they might have to wait a decade or more for the next big opportunity). For example, when the navy was planning to purchase a new destroyer,[54] Lockheed Martin Corporation, Bath Ironworks, and Ingalls Shipbuilding put together what they categorized as the dream team (with Lockheed being the systems integrator and the only two shipyards in the destroyer business providing their expertise). The navy favored this dream team, and it was strongly supported by the congressional delegations from each of these industry suppliers. The office of the secretary of defense, however, insisted that competition between the two shipyards must take place so that the DoD would benefit from the innovations and lower costs that come from competition. The navy subsequently agreed that it benefited significantly from the competition.

Wall Street's immediate reaction to these events—the slowing down of the merger and acquisition trend, the industry's low profits, and the high debt problems in the industry—was a severe erosion in the defense firms' stocks. Lockheed Martin's stock price declined from nearly $60 per share in mid-1998 to under $20 in the closing days of 1999; Boeing lost a third of its market value between April and September of 1998; Raytheon's stock plummeted 43 percent in one day during the fall of 1999; and Northrop Grumman ended the decade trading at $59 a share, far below the $139 it reached in early 1998.[55] By the end of the decade, the financial condition of the defense industry was of increasing concern. As the *Wall Street*

Journal commented in December 1999, "Some of the Defense Industry's biggest players, including Lockheed Martin and Raytheon, are struggling. Eight years of consolidation has left these companies with large debt loads, low stock prices, and weak earnings. Pentagon and industry officials have questioned whether these weakened giants can make the necessary research investments to maintain a U.S. technological edge."[56]

Both Congress and the DoD realized that significant steps were required to slow down the mergers and acquisitions. Also of concern were the health of the industry and the growing separation of the commercial and military markets. To address the former of these issues, the DoD continued to pursue its acquisition reforms and significantly stepped up its business reforms (which were aimed at ensuring a healthier defense industry while still maintaining the benefits of competition). Additionally, there was widespread recognition that the cuts in procurement had gone too far, so the budget began to rise. In 2000, there was a significant upturn in the price of defense stocks (for example, Newport News increased 81 percent, Boeing 58 percent, Lockheed Martin 46 percent, Northrop Grumman 46 percent, General Dynamics 33 percent, and Raytheon 29 percent—in a period when the Standard and Poor's 500 went down by 6 percent and the NASDAQ went down by 23 percent). Additionally, the White House, under Vice President Al Gore, conducted a review of government business (known as the National Performance Review) with an eye toward efficiency, responsiveness, and transparency. This review emphasized simplifying the government's acquisition procedures and relying more on the commercial marketplace. Under DoD Secretary William Perry, these themes began to be implemented within the Pentagon (led by a new organization, created by Secretary Perry, with a deputy undersecretary of defense for acquisition reform). Congress also recognized the importance of trying to bring commercial firms into defense business, and it passed legislation streamlining procurement and the increased use of commercial products. Legislation such as the Federal Acquisitions Streamlining Act (FASA) and the Federal Acquisition Reform Act (FARA) emphasized the procurement of commercial items by the Department of Defense.

These initiatives were continued under Secretary of Defense William Cohen's leadership. The "revolution in business affairs" emphasized the use of commercial best practices, reductions in the size of the DoD infrastructure, and increased use of contracting for DoD services (of a "non-inherently governmental" nature) from the private sector. These growing concerns about the structure of the defense industry led to a series of studies by the independent Defense Science Board, including a 1997 study of vertical integration and a 1998 study of globalization. The secretary of defense's office also issued a series of policy statements—for example, on an anti-competitive teaming policy (1999), a subcontractor competition policy (1999), and a future competition policy statement (2000)[57]—all indicating that the number of competitors in the defense industry had shrunk to such a low level that the Department of Defense could no longer afford a laissez-faire policy.

3. Changes in Security Concerns

As the post–cold war era evolved, military planning began to shift toward identifying regional conflicts and preparing for them. There also was a growing recognition (particularly in the United States, which continued to emphasize advanced technology) that the information age would lead to dramatic changes in military operations and in the kinds of equipment that support these operations (this was termed "the revolution in military affairs"). These changes include

- Precision weapons (one precisely guided missile can replace hundreds of bombs or artillery shells),
- Stealth technology (a single plane can sneak up on a target; when many non-stealthy planes approach a defense system, only a few can pass through),
- Unmanned systems (these include ground, air, and sea unmanned vehicles),
- Netcentric operations-linking distributed sensors and shooters via a command, control and communication "net" (this can achieve a large force-multiplier effect with low-cost equipment by gaining the benefit of many multiple, data-fused sensors and precision shooters),
- Improved command and control systems (these have been enhanced by the information revolution),
- Improved navigation capability (this has been enhanced by the widespread use of the satellite-based global positioning system).

Nonetheless, shrinking defense budgets and institutional resistance to change (by the military, industry, Congress, and labor unions) have posed a dilemma for the Department of Defense. If production lines were to be maintained with fewer dollars, then choices needed to be made about whether old systems should be bought or a shift should be made to new ones. For two years in a row, the air force did not budget money for a remotely piloted aircraft (the Global Hawk), even after Israel dramatically demonstrated the benefits of such unmanned vehicles for long-term reconnaissance. When faced with a choice between buying traditional, high-performance fighter planes or buying new unmanned systems, the air force opted for the former. The program had to be put back into the budget by the office of the secretary of defense (overruling the air force in that case).

In this period, a significant culture change in organization and equipment was required to prepare for warfare in the twenty-first century. But the lessons of history show that, in the absence of an acknowledged crisis, bringing about culture change in a short period of time is difficult.

4. Globalization

Even before the cold war ended, the commercial world was operating in a global market—in terms of both production and consumption. Commercial firms were going offshore to find the best parts, lower-cost and high-skilled labor, foreign markets, and even twenty-four-hour-a-day worldwide operations (using modern communication and information technology). But the defense industry resisted globalization for a variety of reasons, including fear of vulnerability to foreign sources, concerns about technology leakage to potential adversaries, potential domestic-labor arguments (as advocated by both U.S. unions and Congress), and an historic perspective that believed that the defense industry was different and needed to remain autarkic (that is, self-sufficient).

Nonetheless, technology spread globally, and more and more U.S. commercial industries operated on a global basis. Even with institutional resistance, the Defense Department was receiving more equipment that was built with international participation. All U.S. weapons systems, for example, contained some offshore parts (such as semiconductors from Japan and precision glass from Germany). At the parts-supplier level, these purchases were being driven primarily not by lower costs but by the higher performance of these foreign sources. Studies have been done to show that despite the industry's growing dependency on these foreign parts, there was not a corresponding U.S. vulnerability—depending on the number of potential suppliers and the number of countries in which they were located (particularly if a potential U.S.-based supplier was available as a fall-back alternative). There also was no violation of the Buy American Act (since that applies only to end items, not to subcontracts or parts). Significant legislative barriers continued to discourage such foreign purchases, however. For example, many special-interest legislative rules barred the purchase of items such as anchor chains, specialty metals, and clothing from offshore sources. Other legislative trade barriers existed, as well, such as not applying the exemption for foreign sales tax credit (which applies to commercial items) to defense items and having a cumbersome, time-consuming bureaucratic process for the export licensing of items that were purchased offshore and then resold or sent back for repair. By early 2001, at the end of the post–cold war decade, the total purchases of foreign parts at the subcontractor level amounted to significantly less than 1 percent of the total defense budget for that year.[58]

Despite concerns about the need for the U.S. defense industry to maintain an autarkic position, two arguments have been raised (with little effect) to counter them. The military argument is that from a geopolitical perspective, the United States would probably not enter any future military operation without a coalition of allies. So with a battlefield that is made up of interconnected, distributed sensors and shooters from multiple countries, it is in the United States' interest to ensure that each country in the coalition has the best possible technology (which, at that time, usually was U.S. technology). To achieve maximum military effectiveness, therefore, all equipment needed be designed and tested to be interoperable among the coalition partners. In Kosovo—where full interoperability was not the case— U.S. and Dutch planes flew next to each other, and yet they could not communicate in a secure mode because of export-control restrictions on the technology, which greatly reduced their effectiveness and increased their mutual vulnerability. Critical U.S. military technology needed to be shared with our allies, and (by the end of the 1990s) this was increasingly recognized by both the U.S. State and Defense Departments; leading the White House to announce in early 2001 a new policy (the Defense Trade and Security Initiative) on increased technology sharing with our allies. One condition for this U.S. technology sharing with our allies was that those allies needed to implement strict controls over further third-party transfers of the technology.

The other more traditional argument for greater multinational considerations in the defense industrial structure is economic. When the United States and European countries cut their defense budgets, they should share development costs on new weapon systems and have common production lines to achieve economies of scale. Consistent with the globalization trends seen in commercial industries and the rapid global spread of technology in the information age, the major defense industrial firms (on both sides of the Atlantic) aggressively entered each other's markets—often in transatlantic partnerships and frequently through acquisitions. The most notable of these was the aggressive acquisition program that BAE Systems (the dominant defense firm in the United Kingdom) undertook in the United States. First, it bought Tracor and then Sanders, two highly sensitive defense electronics firms. Even though the U.S. defense budget was shrinking, it still was far larger than that of any other nation, which made U.S. acquisitions highly desirable (especially when their stock prices were low). As BAE Systems made known its strategic desire to have a major share in the U.S. defense industry, it became an attractive purchase for U.S. investors. As a result, even though BAE's headquarters was located in London, the company had a large percentage of its employees in the United States, and at any given point, a majority of its stockholders could be U.S. citizens. Many firms from outside the United States began buying into the U.S. market or setting up U.S. production facilities. They were subject to significant government regulation of foreign purchases of U.S. defense firms (for example, under the 1988 Exon-Florio amendment, which required a detached, multiagency review) and to a requirement to establish special security arrangements (for example, U.S. subsidiaries needed to have a majority of U.S. citizens sitting on their board of directors).

During the post–cold war U.S. budget decline, U.S. defense firms began to emphasize foreign military sales. The firms were looking for markets that could help them maintain their existing production lines of the state-of-the art weapons that had been built up for the cold war. Since many other countries wanted the best available weapons and since it was in the best interests of the U.S. military to see that these production lines were maintained (with the support of Congress and labor unions), foreign military sales (FMSs) began to be pursued even prior to the end of the cold war. From 1987 to 1993, America's annual foreign military sales grew from $6.5 billion to $32 billion. Additional out-year sales were ensured when, during the 1992 presidential campaign, President George H. W. Bush approved F-16 fighter plane sales to Taiwan, F-15 fighters to Saudi Arabia, and M1-A1 tanks to Kuwait and the United Arab Emirates. Other countries (including Russia, Britain, Germany, and France) also pursued the international market (particularly the growing market in the Middle East oil states). By 1992, the United States had captured 60 percent of the FMS market, and by 1993, 70 percent.[59] In many cases, arms sales to one country often necessitated sales to another country in the same region to return the balance of forces and provide stability.

Increasingly, U.S. firms were required to provide significant (often over 100 percent) offsets for military equipment sales. In Boeing's sale of airborne warning and control systems (AWACS) to Britain, for example, Boeing was forced to agree to spend $1.30 on parts and labor in Britain for every $1 in revenue that it received from the AWACS sale, and it later struck a similar deal with France.[60] In such cases, Boeing, the prime U.S. contractor, is basically giving away large sales of the future business of U.S. parts and subsystem suppliers, but Boeing argued that it could not have gotten the sale without such offsets. Unfortunately, the long-term effects of offsets on the U.S. economy and the global economy are often less clear.

Controlling the sales of advanced conventional weapons (and nuclear weapons) requires multinational cooperation (as has been shown in the nuclear nonproliferation arena). Only a few countries design and produce advanced major-weapons systems. In 1993, the United States, United Kingdom, France, Germany, Russia, and China accounted for 99.3 percent of all exported tanks in service that year.[61] With so few countries involved, U.S. policy could have led to controls being placed on many types of foreign military sales. However, a defense-industry restructuring strategy would have had to been developed by the DoD in order to maintain a viable defense industry without counting on such sales. Unfortunately, this was not the initial focus of the U.S. government in the early years of the post–cold war era.

5. Outsourcing of Government Work

The final significant defense-industry structural change for the cold war and post– cold war years was outsourcing. Given the Department of Defense's budget cuts, the military had the choice of either maintaining its existing infrastructure (and having less warfighting equipment) or shifting its resources significantly toward warfighting needs and cutting back dramatically on infrastructure. To maintain as much as possible of the force structure and equipment, the military cut back dramatically in other areas. For example, between 1990 and 2000, the acquisition workforce was cut by 300,000 government employees,[62] causing large reductions in many significant management and support functions. The Defense Contract Management Agency was cut in half in that time period.

Because some infrastructure and support functions still needed to be maintained, the DoD followed the path that large commercial firms were following. The DoD began to outsource a significant share of its noncore work (that is, work that was not inherently governmental). In the commercial world, this outsourcing was done with both domestic and offshore sources, and in defense, it was limited largely to domestic firms.

As the defense budget declined in the post–cold war period, the Pentagon began to take advantage of this outsourcing trend by directly outsourcing or competing (public vs. private) work in areas being done by government workers, but that were "not inherently governmental" (such as back-office operations). By the time that the government's civilian workforce was cut by 40 percent, this alternative became more and more attractive to senior Pentagon officials. It also fit in nicely with Vice President Al Gore's efficiency and effectiveness management push (in the National Performance Review), and when President George W. Bush was elected in 2000, it was one of his top five management initiatives. Recognizing an opportunity for a new, large potential market, the defense industry began to push for increased outsourcing of all government work that was not inherently governmental.

As the DoD downsized and outsourced and as military operations increased (for example, in Bosnia), demands for industry support increased at home and with defense contractors who were working in combat areas (for example, by 2007 there were about 190,000 contractors in the Iraq and Afghanistan combat areas). These conditions introduced new industry issues, such as whether the contractors were covered by the Geneva Conventions on prisoners of war, whether they were allowed to be armed, and whose control they were under (the contracting officers or the local combat commander).

The driving trends in the post–cold war U.S. defense industry—the collapse in the defense budgets, the resultant industry consolidations, the changes in the nature of warfare, the shift toward globalization (in technology, economics, and industry), and the changing roles of the public and private sectors—were causing dramatic structural changes in the nature of the defense industry. But on September 11, 2001, a new era began.

After September 11, 2001

In the post–cold war decade, much was written about the changed new world, but the events of September 11, 2001, and their aftermath truly changed the world. The United States found itself at a crossroads, with the need for change obvious to many but with many institutions still resisting change. When Secretary of Defense Donald Rumsfeld came into office, for example, he stated (prior to the terrorist attacks) that there was an obvious need to transform the posture of American security to recognize the changes that were taking place in technology, potential threats, and geopolitics. But because he could not convince the military of this need, the planning (for example, in force structures and equipment) continued to reflect essentially what had been set up for the cold war. The argument was that if we prepared for the big war, all other requirements would simply be lesser cases, and the nation would be fully prepared. But many objective observers felt that dramatic shifts were needed in resources, force structures, planning, and equipment. Fighting terrorism on an international basis was going to require cooperation among nations, and as regional issues became more significant, they would require multinational cooperation (for geopolitical reasons) and a multiagency perspective within the United States (including the State Department, the Defense Department, the Homeland Security Department, and the intelligence community). From a force-structure perspective, a conflict such as that in Iraq and Afghanistan would depend heavily on land forces—army, marines, and special operations forces—that were trained for irregular warfare. The most useful airborne elements were the lower-cost, unmanned reconnaissance and surveillance systems. Yet even after five years into the Iraq and Afghanistan conflicts, when the Pentagon did a *Quadrennial Defense Review* (in February 2006), while it did recommend added expenditures for special operations forces, foreign-language training, and cultural awareness (all things needed for twenty-first-century operations), it requested no increase in the overall U.S. ground-force levels and "stands pat, on all major Cold-War-legacy weapons systems."[63] As former DoD Secretary William Perry and Harvard professor Ashton Carter pointed out in a 2007 article,[64] "to a remarkable degree, the 50% increase in the DoD baseline (since 9-11-01) has gone to funding the program of record on September 11, 2001 (i.e. the weapons that were already in the pipeline on 9-11-2001)." After September 11, 2001, the defense budget was increased dramatically to pay for the wars in Iraq and Afghanistan and to fund America's homeland security; but there was not a significant shift away from cold war weapons. The transformation that Secretary Rumsfeld asked for and that seemed to be needed did not take place because there was no resource constraint placed on the planning process. Money was simply added as it was required, and if the basic budget did not cover the expense, then supplemental budgets were added.

From an industry perspective, the changes were also add-ons. All of the major defense firms recognized the importance of the information technology that was developed in the post–cold war decade and added a focus on systems integration to their operations. In addition, recognizing the shift taking place toward buying services to support the ongoing conflict, they also added capability in the professional-service area (in both cases, largely through acquisitions). Finally, because each of the military services had faced significant personnel cutbacks in the post–cold war era, the fastest way to build up again was through the use of contractors. By early 2009, 266,688 contractors were in the combat area of the Middle East[65] (outnumbering the military and government personnel in the region), and almost all of these contractors were supplying services (including food, housing, equipment maintenance, and logistics support). In fact, the overall Department of Defense procurements shifted to 60 percent services. In just three years, the number of service-contract actions grew from about 325,000 in 2001 to over 600,000 by 2004,[66] and over that same time period, the number of federal professional service contractors grew from 45,000 to 83,000.[67] Although a large number of the service contractors were small firms (since the barriers to entry are smaller in the services area than in the hardware area), several major nontraditional defense firms increased the amount of defense work they were doing. Traditional defense contractors such as Lockheed Martin, Northrop Grumman, and Boeing were listed in the top five of professional contractors in 2004, and they were joined by Halliburton and Bechtel. These new entries were brought about by the changed nature of the support required for military operations in the twenty-first century.

Exploding Defense Dollars

After September 11, 2001, there were unprecedented sustained increases in the defense budget (the war in Iraq and Afghanistan lasted longer than World War II) (figure 2.8). Not only were there annual increases in the defense budget, but there also were annual supplemental budget items that by fiscal year 2008 reached $189.3 billion (the total of that year's two supplementals).

Nonetheless, the Pentagon continued to request increased basic budget dollars plus growing supplementals, and not only did the president present those requests to Congress, but Congress often added to them. By 2008, there was a budget request of $625 billion (which was over twice the 2000 budget). The problem was that if the supplementals had to be folded back into the annual budget requests, they would appear to be far too large, and the DoD would have to face the difficult choice of dropping some cold war weapons to pay for the needed expenditures for twenty-first-century scenarios. Most of the army's maintenance dollars for equipment being used in Iraq and Afghanistan were contained within the supplementals, as were the procurements of ground robots (for land-mine removals) and other critical equipment for these operations. If these dollars were put back into the budget, then either the budget itself would have to be increased or some traditional equipment purchases or manpower costs would have to be reduced.

The budget problem was compounded by the fact that the military was suffering from the procurement holiday of the post–cold war decade and badly needed to replace aging equipment from the Reagan buildup in the 1980s. So the defense

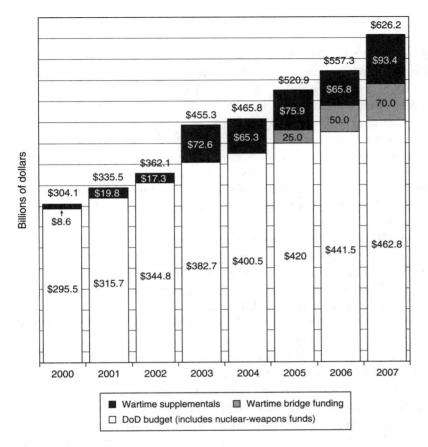

Figure 2.8
Defense appropriations, 2000 to 2007. *Source:* Office of Management and Budget, research reported in *Defense News*, February 12, 2007.

budget simply kept expanding, even in the presence of large administration-ordered and congressionally approved tax cuts. The administration, the Congress, the DoD, the defense industry, and even the public seemed far less concerned about broader economic considerations. The country's economic condition was declining because of tax cuts, huge increases in security expenditures (including the Defense Department and the Homeland Security Department), the supplementals, mandatory increases in entitlements (such as Medicare and social security), and the growing interest on the national debt. The country faced an enormous and growing deficit, a significant decline in the value of the dollar, and an extremely large trade unbalance, and these were compounded by the huge bailouts and stimulus packages that the government used to counter a widespread economic meltdown in 2008 and 2009.

During this post-9/11 buildup, the Department of Defense was living in a rich man's world since it could afford to buy the kinds of things that it bought in the twentieth century as well as the things that it needed for twenty-first-century conflicts. As the Wall Street Journal stated in 2006, "The U.S. Defense machine is still churning out weapons made for old-style, conventional conflicts, even as it needs new tools to battle terrorists and insurgence."[68] Worst still, the estimated lifetime costs of the Pentagon's five biggest weapons systems (in 2006) was 89 percent more than these programs were projected to cost in 2001,[69] and this rising cost trend continued. The GAO noted in 2008 that the planned commitment for weapons' programs in 2000, $790 billion, had grown to $1.6 trillion by 2007.[70] But everybody seemed happy to live in this Alice in Wonderland world, and no one chose to look behind the mirror. The services continued to do their planning based on the assumption that the budget would continue to go up. As the House Armed Services Committee commented about the navy's plan in the 2007 authorizations process, "According to the Navy's estimates, execution of this plan requires a significant increase in ship-building funds, from $8.7 billion in Fiscal Year 2006 to $17.2 billion in Fiscal Year 2011."[71] Surely a doubling of the ship-building budget in a period when the total dollars for defense were anticipated to decline means that something else will have to give. Yet in the president's request for defense spending in 2008, according to the Wall Street Journal, "just about every major weapon system is set to get more funding than in the current year."[72] The DoD acknowledged (in its Quadrennial Defense Review) that additional ground troops are required to handle scenarios such as Iraq and Afghanistan, but rising manpower costs make this unaffordable unless the budget continues to grow significantly. With money pouring into the defense industry, the Standard and Poor Aerospace and Defense 500 Index outperformed the broad market averages from 2001 through 2007.[73]

One issue that repeatedly came up during the large increases in the defense budget after 9/11 was the question "If the world has changed so much, what should we be buying instead of the old ships, planes, and tanks?" In spite of the huge increase in available dollars, there was a growing separation between the items requested in the defense budget and the items needed for twenty-first-century conflicts. If the budgets were to flatten out or decline, then there was bound to be a looming DoD fiscal crisis.

New Perspectives and New Organizations

One obvious lesson that could be learned from the events of September 11, 2001, was that national security for the United States requires a multinational perspective. No single nation can battle global terrorism alone. As Defense Secretary Gates stated in 2008, our "ultimate success or failure will increasingly depend more on shaping the behavior of others—friends and adversaries, and most importantly the people in between."[74] He went on to say that crafting a military design for more complex wars among civilian populations demands that all the services critically examine their cultures and discard those parts that are barriers to change. Gates also has quoted from Mark Perry's book *Partners in Command: George Marshall and Dwight Eisenhower in War and Peace* that "Eisenhower was a commander who believed that building and maintaining an international coalition of democracies was not a political nicety . . . but a matter of national survival."[75]

On the domestic side, many organizations—including border protection, harbors, airports, and police—interfaced with homeland security, but these each operated independently. It was decided that the government should establish a single agency that would be responsible for homeland security. It would cover natural disasters (such as hurricanes, tornadoes, earthquakes, and nationwide epidemics such as SARS) and security actions (including domestic acts of terrorism and external attacks on the country). The twenty-one agencies that previously were involved in these issues (including the Coast Guard and the Federal Emergency Management Agency) would be integrated into one single organization called the Department of Homeland Security.

A second major organizational change that followed the terrorist acts of 9/11 involved recognizing that having some intelligence agencies focus on domestic issues and others on international issues led to a lack of sharing of information among these organizations. It was decided to integrate the seventeen agencies responsible for collection and analysis of intelligence. This involved roughly 100,000 people in the U.S. intelligence community and an annual budget of around $42 billion.[76] The objective of the new director of national intelligence was to integrate these seventeen intelligence agencies and to encourage them to share their data and analyses (something difficult to achieve with organizations that had prided themselves on their ability to keep secrets). The attempts to integrate the nation's Central Intelligence Agency, the National Security Agency, and other defense-oriented agencies with the intelligence branches of many of the domestic agencies (such as the FBI and the Border Patrol) encountered many of the problems that had been faced in creating the Department of Defense from the old War Department (the army) and Navy Department. The challenge was to ensure that these individual organizations continued doing outstanding jobs in their own areas as they moved to more of a joint operation (in the way that the military did when technology required the integration of air, land, and sea in military operations). The Department of Homeland Security and the Office of the Director of National Intelligence would have to create new, integrated cultures for these organizations. One way that integration for these new organizations will be achieved is through the industry that commonly serves them. The types of problems and technologies that the Defense Department faces in the twenty-first century are similar to those that are faced by the Department of Homeland Security and the intelligence community. All are heavily information-based. Thus, the industry that supports them will undoubtedly be a national security industry that consists primarily of firms that have grown up in the defense industry. This integration on the supply side may help to achieve the desired integration on the demand side—not only within each of the three organizations (defense, homeland security, and intelligence) but between those organizations as well.

One last major structural change was highlighted by the events of 9/11 and the conflicts that followed it: security can no longer be seen exclusively in military terms. The United States will need to have close alliances with friends and allies around the world (which involves the State Department), and most of the nation's regional efforts will include both geopolitical and military aspects. Additionally, the activities will involve not just warfighting but also national stability and reconstruction. The State Department's Agency for International Development (AID) has been very much involved in Iraq and is likely to be so for some time. There is now a need for far greater interagency working relationships and coordination than existed in the past. The twenty-first century will need to have many agencies (the Departments of Defense, State, Homeland Security, Commerce, Energy, and Treasury; the Office of the Director of National Intelligence; the National Institutes of Health) all involved in an integrated approach to the nation's twenty-first-century security. This will undoubtedly require structural and institutional arrangements that do not currently exist.

In this new integrated and globalized world, those who are responsible for America's security will need to understand other cultures and languages—those of both its adversaries and its allies. This area has needed increased attention, and incentives have had to be created for its effectiveness. Early in the post-9/11 period, the Department of Defense directed that no future officers in the military could rise to the rank of general or admiral unless they spoke a second language and understood a second culture. Officers were encouraged to speak and learn about cultures such as Arabic, Chinese, and Farsi (rather than languages commonly taught in U.S. schools, such as Spanish, French, and German). Understanding the cultural behavior of our adversaries and our allies will be critical in the twenty-first century and is an area for the DoD to focus on for the nation's future security.

Cultural understanding will have significant value in establishing international agreements that help to control dangerous pathogens and the proliferation of nuclear weapons. These technologies are increasingly spread around the world, so the only way to keep the genie in the bottle is with multinational agreements that are achieved through multiagency activities, including within each nation.

Personnel Shortages

Even with over $600 billion per year of defense appropriations during the Iraq and Afghanistan conflicts, the U.S. active-duty military manpower (numbering around 1.4 million) has been stretched thin, and repeated call-ups of many reservists have been needed to sustain operations in Iraq.[77] Military tours of duty in Iraq and Afghanistan have been extended, and repeat tours have been required without the typical time back at home with families or for training for the next assignment. By 2008, there had been over 4,000 military deaths in the Iraq and Afghanistan conflicts and a much higher number of serious injuries (improved protective armor actually has led to an increase in the ratio of injuries to deaths). These circumstances have made it increasingly difficult to find qualified people to volunteer to fight (in a desert or in the mountains) against insurrectionists in a war that is increasingly unpopular with the general public. Large reenlistment bonuses and added incentives (such as increased GI Bill benefits) increased recruiting costs, and minimum acceptable standards for new recruits began to be implemented.

The second of the serious personnel shortages during this period was caused by the rapid buildup in the procurement area of the defense budget. When the procurement account plummeted during the post–cold war period, the services chose to take significant personnel cuts in their acquisition workforce (military and civilian) to maintain their fighting force. They needed a smaller acquisition workforce anyway because lower procurement budgets meant that less contracting and managing were needed.

Then as the government continued to cut back on its acquisition workforce and procurements increased, noninherently governmental services work began to be outsourced. As Deputy Secretary of Defense John White stated in 1996, "Let DoD do what it does best; and let contractors do what they do best."[78] That same year, DoD published a report entitled "Improving the Combat Edge through Outsourcing." This was the direction in which the commercial world was moving. IBM used to make every part of its computers, but Intel now makes IBM's chips, Microsoft makes its software, and other firms make its modems, hard drives, and monitors. IBM even outsources its call centers. Outsourcing sometimes confuses workforce statistics. When General Motors began outsourcing its employee cafeteria functions to Marriott, some of its workforce transferred from General Motors to Marriott. This appears in labor statistics as lost manufacturing jobs, but in reality the service portion of the industry was previously mischaracterized.[79] By 2005, the Department of Defense was outsourcing $4.6 billion per year, and its five-year plan was to increase this to $6.7 billion by 2010.[80] This resulted in high performance at significantly lower costs, but it required more DoD contracting and management personnel—which did not exist.

One final personnel deficiency that was recognized during this period was the growing shortage of U.S. scientists and engineers, particularly in aerospace and defense (both in industry and in government). This deficiency was highlighted in a study undertaken by the National Academies, titled: *Rising above the Gathering Storm: Energizing and Employing America for a Brighter Economic Future.*[81] A clear shift was taking place during the post-9/11 period as the emphasis was placed on the immediate problems of the conflicts in Iraq and Afghanistan. Essentially, the U.S. defense establishment was choosing to eat the seed corn and give up an historic, long-term defense strategy of technological superiority. In fact, the research budget that the army submitted in 2006 was 21 percent below the 2005 level.

Short-Term Focus
During his Defense Department confirmation hearings, Robert Gates was asked to name the areas that he would emphasize during his tenure as secretary of defense. He responded that he had three priorities: "Iraq, Iraq, and Iraq." Such a perspective is understandable during war, particularly one that had lasted longer than World War II and was consuming a large share of the overall security budget of the United States. However, this response also reflects directly on the trade-off that had to be made between long-term security concerns and immediate needs. Even with a large annual defense budget, the services were saying that they were each over $20 billion a year short, and yet something had to be cut. The Defense Research budget was one area where dramatic cuts were being taken, even though technology—in areas such as information technology, nanotechnology, and biotechnology—was leaping forward rapidly. The United States could ill afford either economically or politically to fall behind in technology areas that were expanding exponentially annually. (The life cycle for new technology in the information arena is down to approximately eighteen months, for example.) As Charles Darwin observed, "It is not the strongest of the species that survives, nor the most intelligent, but the one most responsive to change."[82]

During this period, two significant changes were taking place in the commercial-technology arena. First, technology and corporate research were rapidly spreading globally. Many nations were accelerating their competitiveness by investing heavily in research parks and in the development of science and engineering in universities and industrial research laboratories. In addition, U.S. firms were establishing research centers in many other countries, particularly throughout Asia (in India, China, Singapore, and so on). Traditionally, the U.S. defense industry did not look to foreign sources for new ideas (taking an autarkic perspective). Second, because the commercial world was moving rapidly in many high-tech areas (such as information technology and biotechnology), it actually moved ahead of the defense world in some areas (a trend that reversed what was typical during most of the twentieth century). Again, defense traditionally viewed itself as different and therefore tended not to look to the commercial world for its technological advances. By the end of the first decade of the twenty-first century, more and more people were urging the DoD to search out and apply technologies from both the commercial world and the global market.[83]

Increased Protectionism

In 2004, the U.S. House of Representatives passed a new version of the Buy American Act that would have required "every part, in every U.S. weapons system, to be made in America, and on U.S. machine tools." It would have lowered the performance of U.S. weapons systems (since every system contains high-performance foreign parts) and at least doubled the cost of each weapon. Special lines would have been needed to produce the parts that came from high-volume production offshore and to provide the machine tools on which they could be built—since there was no U.S. machine tool industry of any significance at that time. Fortunately, the U.S. Senate did not pass this bill, but it is indicative of that period's protectionist environment.

In addition, significant restrictions were being placed on foreign students and foreign scholars who were at U.S. universities and were working on government-funded, fundamental research.

As James Woolsey (former secretary of the Navy and former CIA director) once pointed out, "nothing is more dangerous to civil liberties than an enraged democracy." But the U.S. public and its representatives in the Congress were sufficiently enraged by the events of September 11, 2001, that restrictions on non-U.S. citizens and on exports of U.S. technology became much more extensive. In fact, the U.S. defense industry began to suffer significantly (compared to its foreign competitors) in the sale of equipment to be exported—even to our allies. Because of these export restrictions, commercial firms became increasingly cautious about allowing their products to be incorporated into defense products and therefore restricted from the worldwide marketplace—without extensive export-control paperwork and pleading.

Given that there was an increased need for international cooperation in areas like terrorism and that increased U.S. protectionist measures would reduce the likelihood for that cooperation, the United States was hurting its own long-term security posture through the extensive protectionist actions taken in the decade following the terrorist acts of 9/11.

Increased Government Control and Regulation

Finally, government procurement regulations increased significantly in the post-9/11 period. Because the Department of Defense did not have adequate control over the enormous budget increases that occurred during this period, a large number of fraud cases were uncovered. In addition, corruption scandals occurred within domestic contracting. An assistant secretary of the air force (Darleen Druyun) and a Boeing vice president and chief financial officer (Michael M. Sears) were jailed after she helped Boeing on a large competition in exchange for future employment. A lobbyist (Jack Abramoff) and a congressman (Randall Cunningham) were each jailed for improper actions in assisting small defense contractors to receive contracts. Congress decided that it would fix the problem by adding extensive procurement restrictions and new process regulations, which significantly slowed down the defense acquisition process. They also significantly reduced and discouraged risk taking by procurement officials—even when such risks could result in significant advances but represented a nontraditional procurement approach (such as using commercial practices to acquire commercial items rapidly for DoD use).

Unfortunately, this increase in government procurement regulations was happening at a time when the worldwide commercial market was offering many advanced technologies that could be easily acquired and used by insurrectionists. The DoD was barred from access to this commercial technology by the increased regulations.

Those outside of the Congress worried that the controls that were introduced to combat corruption would undo two decades' worth of improvements in defense weapons and services acquisition. As retired Air Force Lieutenant General Ronald Kadish stated in congressional testimony in 2009, "efforts to improve the acquisition system [by Congress and the Executive Branch] have added unnecessary rules and processes and created unmanageable expectations. In an effort to improve the system, we have made it almost unintelligibly complex."[84]

Several concerns were raised about these regulations. First, they would lead to large cost increases in weapons systems and services procurements. Second, they would create high entry barriers for commercial firms (especially the smaller ones in the lower tiers of the defense supplier base). Third, they would slow down the time it takes to provide goods and services to the fighting forces. These three outcomes have been shown to result from increased regulation and isolation from best commercial practices. Fourth, world-class commercial suppliers would be discouraged from entering the defense market, and their future potential (through the use of flexible manufacturing) would be removed. Finally, integrated civil and military production lines—which offer great cost savings as well as crisis-surge potential (through rapidly shifting work from civil to military)—would be diminished. All of this is clearly contrary to the DoD's future need for low-cost, high-performance technology and for rapid and flexible industrial responsiveness.

The post-9/11 period can best be described as an era of dramatic change in national security. Table 2.7 summarizes some of the driving forces of change.

Table 2.7
Changes that are driving defense transformations

Domestic economics: debt, Medicare, social security, supplementals, trade balance	*Technological changes:* information, bio, nano, robotics, high-energy lasers
	Industrial changes: horizontal and vertical integration, commercial high-tech advances
Threat changes: asymmetric warfare (bio, cyber, IEDs), worldwide terrorism, pandemics, weapons proliferation, rogue nuclear states	*Globalization:* rapid spread of technology, multinational firms, foreign sourcing
New missions: homeland defense, missile defense, counterinsurgency, stability, reconstruction	*Government workforce:* aging, wrong skill mix, judgment versus rules, managers versus doers
	Corruption scandals: Druyun, Cunningham, Abramoff, Iraq frauds
Warfighting changes: integrated data, open sources, language and culture understanding	*Isolationist moves:* Buy American, discourage foreign scholars, energy independence
China: future adversary, economic competitor, large military sales market, or strategic partner	*Defense budget shifts:* from equipment to personnel, operation and maintenance, Homeland Security

The Effects of Globalization

The shifts that have occurred as a result of globalization are perhaps the most dramatic structural changes in the international economy. As defined by the International Monetary Fund, *globalization* is "the growing economic interdependence of countries worldwide, through the increasing volume and variety of cross-border transactions in goods, services, and international capital flows; as well as through the more rapid and widespread diffusion of technology."[85] As related to the defense industry, this includes the globalization of capital (finance), production, trade, technology, and labor plus the changes in global governance that structure the forces of globalization.[86]

Globalization itself is nothing new. Government policies have long affected trade for economic development (for example, sixteenth- to late eighteenth-century mercantilism). The twentieth century saw a great expansion of multinational corporations and globalized outsourcing (including manufacturing, supplies, and services). In the early twenty-first century, many new forms of international business activities were made possible by the globalization of the Internet.[87]

Globalization was building up quite significantly in the industrial world during the twentieth century, but after the end of the cold war, the bipolar international system that it represented also collapsed. According to a 2005 report by the World

Trade Organization, world merchandise exports doubled from $1.8 trillion in 1983 to $3.7 trillion in 1993, doubled again to $7.4 trillion in 2003, and rose to $10.2 trillion in 2004.[88]

There are valid concerns about the negative potential effects of globalization, but this trend is here to stay and is growing. As the world continues to shrink—in terms of international knowledge flow, communications, capital flow, and transportation—all countries need to take advantage of globalization rather than try to fight it. The full breadth of government policy—technological advances, skilled labor development, and national security—is needed to deal with it explicitly in all acquisition and industrial base considerations.

Broad Industrial Trends

These broad industrial globalization trends are directly related to the defense industry. Consider the Boeing 787 Dreamliner. Its wings are made by Mitsubishi, Kawasaki, and Fuji Heavy Industries, all of Japan. Italian companies are building part of the fuselage. Boeing has contracted with its former Wichita operation, now owned by Spirit Aerosystems (a Canadian firm), to make other parts of the fuselage. Parts of the subassemblies will be integrated at subcontractor Vought Aircraft Industries in South Carolina, and the final assembly will be done in Boeing's Everett, Washington, assembly plant. Although Boeing engineers still create the integrated concept for the new aircraft and perform the overall integration of the systems with the fuselage and engines, on the 787 they are outsourcing more than 70 percent of the airframe. Most important, they are giving all the aircraft suppliers the responsibility for doing the detailed engineering designs—outsourcing both manufacturing and detailed engineering.[89] The 787 is a combination of offshoring and domestic outsourcing.[90] Boeing is not unique in this worldwide-distribution supply chain. In fact, to counteract Boeing's activities in China, Airbus (the aircraft manufacturing subsidiary of a French, German, and Spanish company—European Aeronautics Defense and Space Company) is planning to build an assembly plant in Tianjin (in response to China's announced $10 billion deal to buy 150 Airbus A320s). The battle for the large Chinese market continues. By 2006, Boeing had $600 million in supply contracts in China, and major Chinese-made parts could be found in roughly 34 percent of the 12,000 Boeing planes in service around the world. China's objective is to build its own large aircraft industry, along with taking an increasing piece of the competition between Boeing and Airbus.[91]

The reason for such activities varies widely. Boeing has simply tried to capture the largest of the world's growing commercial airline markets—China. The buyer, the Chinese government, is interested in having work done in its country for a variety of reasons—high-skilled labor employment in design, manufacturing, support and technology transfer from the United States (in order to aid the buildup of its domestic aircraft industry).

Because the United States is overwhelmingly the largest of the world's defense markets, foreign defense firms want to be in the U.S. market. They find that they are more welcome if they set up their facilities in America rather than try to sell their products from abroad (for the same reasons that Boeing and Airbus are going to China). In addition, in many high-technology areas, the United States is no longer the leader in the next generation of products. The Defense Department frequently buys a foreign product because it is the best available, and it does this to maintain its overall military technological leadership posture. (The fact that the foreign product often has the lowest cost is simply an added bonus.)

But getting close to the buyer's market is not the only reason for U.S. firms to go overseas or for foreign firms to come to the United States. This strategy also allows them to get behind any legislative trade barriers or perceived trade barriers (to address the U.S. preference to buy American). Additionally, the high production volume that some of the foreign producers are able to achieve with their high-performance products often also means higher-quality products. For example, the U.S.-based *Consumer Reports* identifies only one traditional U.S. brand in its top dozen automobiles as ranked by reliability.[92] It therefore is not surprising that every single U.S. weapon system made today contains some foreign parts.

Another reason for using foreign sources is the availability of a skilled workforce, often at a lower cost. Firms have gone to India for software and to Russia for aerospace engineers (both Boeing and Airbus have aerodynamics design centers in Moscow).[93] Evidence of U.S. industry's move to capture the high-skilled labor force offshore can be found in the results of a survey of R&D sites planned for construction between 2007 and 2010. The survey revealed that 77 percent were planned to be built in China or India (often using U.S. corporate financing).[94] China also has supplanted the United States as the world's number one high-tech knowledge exporter.[95]

Finally, the U.S. benefits significantly when foreign-owed firms set up operations in America. In 2004, U.S. affiliates of foreign (majority-owned, nonbank) companies employed 5.1 million Americans, contributed $515 billion to U.S. GDP, and accounted for 19 percent of U.S. exports and 26 percent of U.S. imports.[96]

Concerns about Globalization

As globalization trends continue, politicians and labor leaders have decried the loss of jobs to globalization. Over the last decade, millions of jobs have moved offshore in areas in which the United States is no longer competitive (in terms of either higher performance or lower costs with comparable performance). But millions of jobs have been created or saved by foreign companies that have invested in the United

States. More than 5 million people (4 percent of the American private-sector work-force) are employed in the United States by companies that are headquartered overseas, primarily in Europe or Asia. According to data from the Department of Commerce and the Organization of International Investment, roughly one-third of those U.S.-based jobs are in manufacturing, an area in which the United States is frequently believed to have lost its edge. Perhaps another surprise is that foreign-owned factories that are based in the United States do more than cater to the huge American market. These businesses also export nearly $170 billion worth of goods made in this country. That is nearly a fifth of all U.S. exports. Additionally, foreign direct investment in the United States continues to grow (jumping 88 percent between 2005 and 2007 to a level of $204 billion). Perhaps a perverse benefit of the weak dollar is that it brings greater foreign investment into the United States.[97] Globalization creates a shift in employment from one sector to another and from one region to another. The net benefits appear to be positive. Not only does the labor tend to balance out, but the result (from increased competition) is higher performance at lower costs. The consumers of any of these products tend to benefit. This includes the U.S. Defense Department when it takes part in a globalization effort. For example, when the U.S. Air Force decided to buy a new tanker fleet, it had the choice of going sole-source to Boeing (with a U.S. design but with lots of foreign parts and subsystems) or going to open competition between Boeing and Airbus (with Airbus choosing to team with Northrop Grumman and build its U.S. Air Force tanker in Alabama with many American subsystems). The net effect appeared to be that both suppliers would end up with approximately 4,800 direct and indirect jobs nationwide, but as a result of the competition, the air force would obtain a higher-performance and overall lower-cost fleet of tankers. The issue of foreign competition is both politically charged and highly emotional, but the ability of the DoD to gain the best the world has to offer is critically important to the nation's security.[98]

Nonetheless, for the family of the worker whose job was moved offshore or for the city whose plant was closed down, there is definitely a displacement effect that must be considered (in terms of federal actions associated with retraining and other efforts).

In addition to concerns about loss of specific jobs, there is the issue of lowering U.S. wages to be competitive with foreign, low-cost labor. To overcome this valid concern, the United States will have to increase productivity significantly (thus increasing the output per unit of labor while maintaining a high unit labor cost). This means using robots, computers, and other productivity-enhancing techniques. But it also requires a skilled manufacturing workforce that is capable of using advanced automation tools, which is a challenge for America's education system.

In addition to the economic competitiveness and employment issues that global-ization raises, there are direct security concerns. For example, will the exporting of weapon systems or their embedded technologies fall into the hands of terrorists or other potential future adversaries? Or could foreign parts, software, or systems purchased from offshore contain Trojan horses that can adversely affect future U.S. military capability? Or will the exporting of weapon systems around the world (by the United States and others) cause a proliferation that can later be used by adver-saries to enhance their performance and eliminate a U.S. advantage through a countermeasure? Finally, does the increased world trade associated with globaliza-tion result in widespread illicit trafficking in arms or weapons of mass destruction? Such critically important issues must be dealt with explicitly.

Defining *U.S. Company*

Increases in world trade have led to uncertainty about the definition of *U.S. company*. Is the company's nationality determined by the percentage of U.S. ownership? Loca-tion of its corporate headquarters? The nationality of the majority of its workforce? Brand name?

The Department of Defense has addressed this problem in the *Code of Federal Regulations*, where it added a rule that says (1) the definition will be based on the location of the production of the item[99] (not on the location of the company's head-quarters, the owners, or the stockholders) and (2) if more than 51 percent of the company's stock is owned by a non-U.S. person or entity that chooses to do classi-fied work, then the U.S. operation must have a U.S.-majority board of directors, approved by the DoD.

The final issue in this area is the nationality of the workers, even if the work is performed in the United States. There is a concern that non-U.S. citizens who work on defense products could be terrorists or foreign spies who seek information about technology for security or economic-competitiveness reasons[100] (even though histori-cally most spies in this country have been U.S. citizens). In spite of the fact that the U.S. military allows non-U.S. citizens to become active-duty military personnel (3 percent of the current force are non-U.S. citizens),[101] they cannot work on national security projects, even if the project is not classified but is considered sensitive.[102] In 2006, one-fourth of all college-educated workers in science and engineering occupations in the United States were foreign-born. This figure rises to 40 percent for doctorate degree holders in these occupations and even higher in some fields, like computer science (57 percent), electrical engineering (57 percent), and mechanical engineering (52 percent).[103]

To take advantage of foreign scholars and students, particularly in the area of fundamental research (either directly or as collaborators), President Reagan issued National Security Decision Directive (NSDD) 189, which stated that fundamental research should be free to be entered into by anyone and also should be free to be published. This directive was reconfirmed during the George W. Bush administration by the national security adviser (Condoleezza Rice) and put into the *Federal Acquisition Regulation* as FAR 27.404(g)(2). Even so, the Department of Defense, the Department of Homeland Security, the Department of Energy, and the defense industry (in its pass-through contracts to universities) have restricted such fundamental research to U.S. citizens. The Department of Defense's inspector general and the Department of Commerce's inspector general issued reports that recommended significant restrictions on the use of certain types of fundamental research equipment. The DoD's inspector general even suggested that non-U.S. citizens should be badged on U.S. campuses. Fortunately, many of these proposals were resisted and not implemented.[104] In July 2008, with the approval of Defense Secretary Gates, Undersecretary of Defense John Young signed a directive that required all Defense Department employees to implement NSDD 189, thus ensuring that the United States could take advantage of foreign scholars and students to advance fundamental research in the nation's security and economic-competitiveness interests.

Despite the potentially significant contributions that foreign scholars and foreign students could make to U.S. economic competitiveness and national security, current immigration policy limits the number of high-skilled H1-D visas that can be issued to foreign residents. These visas allow them to come to the United States and become permanent residents. Applications for this category are greatly oversubscribed and experience extremely long processing delays of up to seven years.[105] Applicants who are on a terrorist watch list or who raise concerns in any State Department interview are understandably denied visas, but if the United States is to maintain its economic competitiveness and leadership in national security technology, then the overall benefit-to-risk ratio seems to warrant fewer restrictions—especially given the current shortages of scientists and engineers in the United States.

Military Necessity

For geopolitical reasons (more than military reasons), U.S. involvement in any future military operations is virtually certain to be as part of a coalition of allies. This is true at all levels of military operations, including arms control; regional conflicts; operations against terrorism, insurgency, rogue nations, and peer competitors; and reconstruction and maintenance of security (peacekeeping). All of these activities require international cooperation, particularly in the deterrence phase but also through the conflict and post conflict periods. For maximum overall force effectiveness, America's coalition partners need the best equipment available, and their forces need to be totally interoperable with U.S. forces.

As U.S. and allied forces move increasingly toward netcentric warfare, interoperability and technology sharing become even more critical for military effectiveness. To achieve the required interoperability, two things are necessary. First, the United States must agree to share technology with its allies (those who have agreed to third-party controls). Second, U.S. training and exercises have to include its allies. It is counterproductive in an interdependent environment for the United States to take a protectionist perspective regarding its technology and its defense industry—particularly where, in many cases, the country will be dependent on foreign technology. Instead, the U.S. defense industrial strategy must maximize the benefits of globalization, protect a few highly critical and sensitive technologies, and keep U.S. weapons technology and products competitive on battlefields and in global markets. The goals are for our military to have the best possible equipment, for our allies to provide the best possible support in integrated military operations, and for our defense industry to remain on the leading edge of technology and be both effective and profitable. In this new, globalized model of industrial support, integrated military operations will present major security considerations, and each must be addressed to ensure maximum force effectiveness while simultaneously protecting the nation's security.

Globalized Industries

The most obvious way in which globalization benefits can be realized in the defense arena is through multinational programs. Prices of both development and production can be reduced significantly through the sharing of technologies, R&D efforts, and shared production (particularly if this is done on a common production line). Perhaps the best known of these joint development and production programs is the F-35 fighter plane (formerly known as the Joint Strike Fighter). In this U.S.-initiated program, nine partner nations have agreed to provide significant development money, to share common equipment, and to base each partner's contribution on only its world-class equipment (rather than simply on what it would like to have in exchange for its contribution). As a result, the high volume of common equipment, supplied by all of the participating nations, achieves the lowest cost and the best equipment for all of the participants. In the program, Australia, Canada, Denmark, Italy, the Netherlands, Norway, Turkey, the United Kingdom, and the United States are all committed to buying certain production quantities. Additional production slots are being made available for Singapore and Israel to join in, and others (such as Spain and Japan) are also considering joining the program (this will become the largest defense program in history).[106] This program is not unique. Some international programs focus on a common, single-nation's design, which is sold around the world. For example, the United States' advanced medium-range air-to-air missile (AMRAM) is procured by over twenty nations and is manufactured using fourteen foreign subcontractors. The U.S. transport aircraft C-130J is 20 percent owned by the United Kingdom, and the content of the C-130J is provided using the labor of over 2,500 U.K. employees.[107] This trend toward increased multinational programs is expected to increase. Such multinational teaming arrangements initiate from a variety of causes. Governments can decide to work together, or manufacturers can propose joint efforts to governments. Either way, the arrangements require considerable government negotiations, are complex to manage, and require significant educational efforts. The barriers (of resistance) are high and vary widely— different budget cycles, languages, exchange rates, and approaches to program management.

One important characteristic to be considered in any international program is the way in which competition can be created to get the best ideas at the lowest cost. Consolidation in U.S. and European defense industries has considerably reduced the number of firms available. Nonetheless, there are still enough suppliers to allow competition in each of the critical platform areas—military aircraft, helicopters, missiles, satellites and launch vehicles, and combat vehicles (figure 2.9).

Often this competition can be structured by the industry. For example, a U.S. firm and a European firm might form team A, and different multinational firms might form team B. For the U.S. light cargo aircraft (LCA), a U.S. firm (L-3) teamed up with an Italian supplier, while Raytheon teamed up with a Spanish supplier.

Because many nations (including the United States) have a strong preference for producing military equipment in their own country, it is not uncommon for a U.S. firm to search out a European partner in the competitions and to propose a European design that would be built in the United States. In the presidential helicopter competition, for example, both U.S. potential suppliers offered European designs. (Figure 2.9 shows the prominence of European helicopter suppliers, so such an approach is not surprising.) The teaming arrangements are not limited to the United States and Europe. Other countries are gaining strong leadership positions in various military technologies as these teaming arrangements branch out. For example, in 2007, because of Israel's leadership position in small satellites, Northrop Grumman Corporation formed a partnership with Israel Aerospace Industries, Ltd. to propose lighter, more flexible spy satellites to the U.S. military and intelligence agencies.[108] Sometimes, a U.S. firm teams with a foreign firm and proposes that a foreign design be built in the United States. In this type of scenario, politics plays a significant role. Members of Congress sometimes proclaim that we must buy American,[109] even though the production is planned for the United States. The key point here is that no nation (even the United States) can afford a position of autarchy in the twenty-first century. Cooperation is needed for military reasons (described above), but no nation is able to lead in every technology area, and competition brings both innovations and economic cost savings. There must be multinational

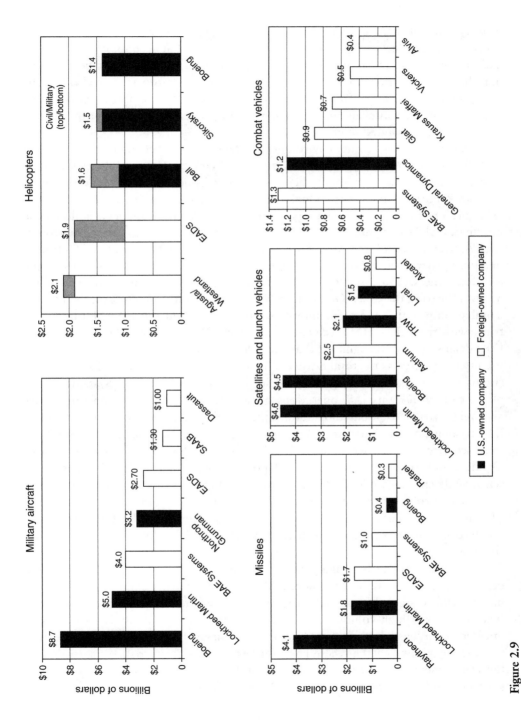

Figure 2.9
Existing U.S. and European suppliers: Platform level. *Source: Government Executive,* August 15, 2007.

security agreements, however. All parties to technology transfer must agree to control any leakage to third parties (who might use that technology against the nations involved), and any violation of these transfer controls must be seriously punished. Finally, these controls must apply not just to hardware but also to software, which is becoming increasingly globalized as well. In 2007, *Business Week* ranked the world's information-technology companies, and only one of the top ten was based in the United States.[110]

In this twenty-first-century environment, defense firms are changing their business models. At one time, they focused on domestic markets, and then they looked for foreign military sales to maintain their dwindling production lines. Today, they look to both domestic and international markets when planning their products. For example, Lockheed Martin (the largest of the U.S. defense suppliers) is doing the multinational F-35 fighter with eight partner nations, the presidential helicopter with Agusta Westland, the Atlas 5 with the Russian RD180 engine, the T50 trainer in a joint program with South Korea, the MEADS antimissile system with Germany and Italy, the C-130J with the United Kingdom, the F-2 fighter with Mitsubishi heavy industries, the Coast Guard deep-water aircraft with EADS-Casa, the Littoral Combat Ship with 21 percent international content, and the U.S. Marine Corps truck with the U.K.'s HMT vehicles.[111] Similarly, BAE Systems (the largest of the U.K. defense firms), recognizing that the U.S. defense procurement market is more than twice as large as the total European market, has chosen the mergers and acquisitions route to gain a strong foothold in the United States. BAE Systems' stated objective is to have its U.S. operations be as large as its European operations. As all foreign-owned, U.S.-based operations that involve classified programs have done, BAE Systems, North America set up a majority-U.S. board of directors and follows strict security controls (according to U.S. law). It was allowed to purchase U.S. firms (Sanders and Traycor) that design and produce some of the United States' most sensitive defense technologies (such as those used in electronic warfare) because its security controls were considered equal to or even better than those of U.S. firms. Military and economic benefits—with both the nations involved and the firms involved—must be constantly weighted against potential vulnerability and security concerns.

Perhaps the most challenging of the globalization issues associated with the defense industry is at the parts level. Many of these items come from the commercial world, since commercial parts tend to be advanced, reliable, and low cost (because of the high-volume sales in the commercial world). It is in America's interest to purchase these parts to have state-of-the-art military equipment. Because of concerns about whether these parts represented a security risk, Congress asked the Department of Defense (in 2001) to conduct a study on the effects of foreign sourcing, and on its own initiative (in 2004), DoD repeated this study, contacting

800 prime contractors and a large number of first- and second-tier subcontractors to collect data and evaluate twelve example major weapon-system programs.[112] These representative systems had seventy-three foreign suppliers. In one case, the dollar value of these suppliers represented 12.5 percent of the system, but in all other cases it was between 0.1 percent and 6.2 percent of the total value (for an average of 4.3 percent). The DoD found that "the use of foreign sources has not negatively impacted long-term readiness or national security."[113] In fact, it stated that the use of non-U.S. suppliers (1) permits the DoD to access state-of-the-art technologies and industrial capabilities, (2) promotes consistency and fairness in dealing with U.S. allies, (3) encourages development of interoperable weapon systems, (4) encourages development of mutually beneficial industrial linkages that enhance U.S. industry's access to global markets, and (5) exposes U.S. industry to international competition, helping to ensure that U.S. firms remain innovative and efficient. This Department of Defense study went on to state that "the identified foreign sources do not constitute a foreign vulnerability that poses a risk to national security," that "utilization of these foreign sources does not impact the economic viability of the national technology and industrial base," that "in some cases, the national technology and industrial base is being enhanced as domestic capabilities are being established for several key items now procured from foreign sources," and that out of the seventy-two foreign sources "the Department identified only four instances where domestic sources were not available to compete for items subcontracted to foreign suppliers."[114] These four will be tracked carefully to ensure that there are not any future vulnerabilities in these areas.

In spite of such data, the U.S. Congress has become significantly more protectionist, and these feelings are not limited to the United States. For many years, each European country wanted to be totally self-sufficient, but those countries have been moving toward a more integrated European defense industrial base. This situation raises the question of whether there will be cooperation or competition between the United States and its European partners in the North Atlantic Treaty Organization (NATO). The roles of NATO and the European Union (EU) (for example, NATO standards and procurements) must be addressed.

One last observation about a recent U.S. trend in globalization is the move to Mexico of dozens of aerospace companies that have been lured by low labor costs and proximity to the United States. Baja California has more than 12,000 aerospace workers (including 1,400 at Rockwell Collins, 1,000 Gulfstream, and 850 each at Honeywell Aerospace and Hutchinson Seal). Typical of these is the Eaton Corporation's Tijuana facility, which turns out aircraft components (such as electronic switches, hydraulic and fuel tubes, and air ducts) for Rolls-Royce engines. Some of these parts are destined for military aircraft, including the F-35 Joint Strike Fighter and the C-17.[115] As with much of the aerospace industry, there are both commercial and military applications of much of the work performed in Mexico. This work is not limited to U.S. firms. For example, the Labinal Division of Safran, a French company, is doing more than a third of its annual business in North America and has, for the first time, named a U.S. citizen as chair and chief executive officer of Labinal. It has some 1,700 employees in Mexico who work at labor-intensive activities (such as the wiring harnesses that go into the Boeing 787 as well as some defense systems).[116]

Such actions have raised considerable political opposition—not only because jobs are moving from the United States to Mexico but also because a skilled welder earns about $3 an hour in Tijuana and up to about $24 an hour in the United States.[117] It is difficult for the DoD not to take advantage of such a large difference in labor costs for its labor-intensive activities. In the long run, this work can be returned to the United States through greatly improved productivity enhancements (such as automation) to make the work far less labor intensive. To take advantage of this, the workforce must be trained in the use of the automated equipment. Future broad U.S. economic policy emphasis will be required if the nation is to remain competitive in such areas.

Foreign Military Sales

For a variety of political, military, and economic reasons, many nations (both developed and underdeveloped) buy and sell weapons. Historically, the United States has been the world leader in foreign military sales (FMSs), with annual sales in the range of $10 billion to $40 billion. (The end of the first Gulf War set off a $42 billion peak demand for U.S. weapon systems, particularly in the oil-rich Middle East.)[118]

These transactions have many benefits:

- *They strengthen the industrial base.* Traditionally, foreign military sales have been highly profitable. Since the buyer is usually responding to either military or political demands, these transactions tend not to be very price-sensitive. Particularly in periods when the U.S. defense budget is declining, such foreign sales can make the difference between keeping a production line open or not. As a result, defense firms aggressively pursue such sales.

- *They provide political support to allies.* In the post-9/11 period, the Bush administration acknowledged using foreign arms sales as a way to reward allies and cement international relationships.[119] Ironically, foreign arms sales have sometimes been used as a way of achieving stability and even peace in a region. For example, as part of the peace agreement between Israel and Egypt, it was agreed that the United States would supply tens of billions of dollars of arms to both sides (for their self-protection). As one would expect, allowing sales to other countries depends on the political situation at the time. For example, India, Pakistan, and

Indonesia were once barred from buying American weapons, but the Bush administration lifted that ban, and its removal has resulted in significant sales.

• *They provide aid to allies.* Closely related to the political-support argument is the importance of military sales that strengthen our allies. Many countries cannot afford the research and development or the production of many of the complex and sophisticated state-of-the-art weapon systems. Because we want our allies to be capable of self-defense and to support us in times of coalition operations, this rationale is often used as the basis for allowing foreign arms sales. In 2005, for example, the United States announced sales of the GBU-12 (Paveway II) laser-guided bomb (with an inertial navigation systems aided by a global positioning system) as the first commercial sale of a U.S. weapon system to the army of the Czech Republic.[120]

• *They provide support for our military.* It is in the U.S. military's interest to ensure that its coalition partners have the best equipment to complement U.S. forces. And to achieve maximum total-force effectiveness, their forces must be interoperable with those of the United States.

• *They balance military capability in a region.* The best way to avoid an arms escalation in a region is to keep arms out of the region (through arms-control agreements and other similar means). Unfortunately, as countries begin to afford to buy arms, they feel that it is necessary to do so to strengthen their own military position in the region. It is not uncommon to find an arms race developing.

Both sides of a potential conflict can adopt this kind of rationale. The French, for example, began supplying submarines to Pakistan in 1970, and the Russians and Germans began selling them to India in 1974. But when the French became interested in strengthening their relations with India, they agreed to sell six submarines of an advanced type to India (which had been increasing its purchases of other weapon systems from France). To balance the French sales to India, Pakistan then asked France for additional submarines,[121] which India was unhappy about.

• *They prevent countries from aligning with others.* As countries begin to buy their weapons from countries such as Russia or China, their military and later their political leaders might become far more aligned with the seller as a result of the sharing of these weapons systems. Therefore, as Russian and Chinese sales begin to build and the buyers and sellers begin to have military-to-military training and exercises with these new weapons, the United States may feel the need to pursue military sales activities with these countries to ensure their continued neutrality in any potential future conflicts (for example, because of their oil and other natural resources). The United States has attempted not to start arms races in historically neutral areas, but today's realities may push it into doing so.

• *They help with the balance of trade.* By 2005, America's trade deficit in goods and services hit a record $68.9 billion (with China accounting for over $20 billion of that).[122] With tens of billions of dollars of potential arms sales and a large number of potential U.S. manufacturing jobs at stake, balance-of-trade issues become significant in Congress's consideration of potential foreign military sales. Often, these arguments are sufficient to override hesitancy (from the State Department or Defense Department) about a particular arms sale.

• *They incur Defense Department fees.* Sales of military equipment can be accomplished through two routes—either directly (as commercial sales by a firm) or through the U.S. government (as foreign military sales). The latter is frequently preferred by foreign government buyers, since the U.S. government would then stand behind the sales (in terms of their deliveries, their quality, and so on). To do this, the government must manage the programs, and the DoD places an administrative surcharge on foreign military sales (in 2006, this fee was raised from 2.5 percent to 3.8 percent).[123] With tens of billions of dollars of sales annually, even a small percent change results in hundreds of millions of dollars back to the Department of Defense.

In spite of the many apparent benefits of foreign military sales, they raise some significant concerns:

• *Weapons may later be used against the United States.* There is no guarantee that a country that is currently an ally of the United States will not become an adversary in the future. Thus, the state-of-the-art equipment supplied by the United States could end up being used against U.S. forces. This is clearest at the small-arms level because the United States is the world's largest supplier of small arms and light weapons.[124] In 2007, it was discovered that, as a result of the arms transferred to the Iraqis, 190,000 arms (110,000 AK47s and 80,000 pistols) were missing.[125] Many of these could have fallen into the hands of the insurgents who were fighting against U.S. and coalition forces in Iraq.

Further up on the sophistication scale, the United States supplied American-made Stinger anti-aircraft missiles to the Mujahedeen fighting the Soviet army in Afghanistan, and those missiles were later used against U.S. forces. Before the Iranian revolution, the United States sold sophisticated fighter aircraft to Iran. Fighter planes, ships, and other equipment might be sold as part of an FMS package to a country that is aligned with the United States, but in the future that country may no longer be an ally. The U.S. military is concerned about this and often resists political pressures from other parts of the U.S. government to sell advanced-technology equipment.

• *Third-country transfers can occur.* Although third-country transfers are prohibited under foreign-arm-sales agreements, recipient countries can choose (legally or illegally) or involuntarily be forced to transfer equipment to a third country (which may become an adversary of the United States). Third-country transfers of both equipment and advanced technology can adversely affect both military success and commercial uses for future economic competition with U.S. firms.

• *They support politically less desirable nations.* Congress and political activist groups raise concerns about selling arms to countries that are undemocratic, have a poor human-rights record, are unreliable in the battle against terrorists, have been unsupportive of the United States in its regional conflicts, and are politically unstable. In this area, there are strong differences of opinion between those defending the economic and military benefits of such a sale and those criticizing the recipient country's current or future political conditions.

• *U.S. sales contribute to the growing proliferation of arms sales.* There is concern that other countries will feel, "If the United States sells to everyone, then we should do so, too." Many counter this argument by saying, "They will do it anyhow," but when the United States refrains from making sales to certain countries or certain regions, it establishes a significant deterrent. However, as the capability of many countries (including those that formerly were not in the arms-sales business) begins to build up, concerns about arms proliferation become very real. When countries such as North Korea and Pakistan begin exporting nuclear weapons, this is of great concern.

• *They contribute to arms races in third-world countries or regions.* Examples of these concerns are noted above in connection with arms races in the Middle East. More recently, the Chinese have been active in Africa, and in 2007, the Russians exported two advanced Fulcrum fighter planes to Algeria.[126] The United States has not been the leader in these third-world sales. Russia is first in the developing world's global arms bazaar, which by 2005 had reached $30.2 billion.[127] Of this, Russia captured $7 billion, and France took $6.3 billion.[128]

One particular area of recent concern is South America. Since the Monroe Doctrine, South America has been an area of U.S. military interest, and the country has had strong military-to-military relations with countries such as Argentina, Brazil, and Chile. The Venezuelan president, Hugo Chavez, has been fanning anti-American feelings within the country, however, and in 2006, he agreed to a $3 billion deal to buy jets and helicopters from Russia.[129] Also in 2006, Russia agreed to sell Venezuela equipment to build a plant to produce AK-101 and AK-104 Kalashnikov guns.[130] In that year, Russia also was negotiating arms sales to Argentina with the idea of trading Argentine beef (of which Russia is the largest importer) for military helicopters and armor-plated patrol boats.[131] Such sales offsets are common in foreign military sales agreements.

Foreign Ownership

Many countries have strict rules and controls associated with the foreign ownership of defense firms, especially if the firms deal with classified or sensitive information. In the United States, the Departments of Commerce, Defense, and State all are involved in these purchases, and Congress (either for political reasons or to protect a firm in a Congressman's district or state from added competition) frequently becomes heavily involved. If the foreign-owned company wants to deal with U.S. classified material, it must have a U.S-dominated board of directors. These controls are effective because the foreign owners recognize that they have to be purer than Caesar's wife and have been found to have extremely good controls.

Nonetheless, significant changes have occurred in the world since September 11, 2001, and countries such as China and India have experienced dramatic growth. Foreign purchases of U.S. firms are controlled by the Committee on Foreign Investment in the United States (CFIUS), and the CFIUS review process is likely to be revised again due to congressional pressures. This is being driven by the growing sovereign wealth funds that various foreign governments (as contrasted to the private sector) have been building up. For example, the Chinese have a fund of $200 billion, the Russians have a large oil investment fund, and the oil-rich countries of the Persian Gulf have a $1 trillion fund.[132]

Technology Transfer

In many cases, the issue of concern is not a product but rather the technology that is embedded in the product. The first concern is military, but a second concern is that the technology may have a dual-use potential and also be used for commercial competitiveness. For this reason, the United States has set up long lists that are controlled by the State Department and the Commerce Department, with DoD having strong input. One list includes items that are considered critical for either direct military application or for dual-use (commercial and military) technology. Another list shows countries that are acceptable for initial technology transfer (with tight controls on those countries' ability to pass them on to third countries). Unfortunately, these lists tend to be considerably out of date relative to the global spread of technology, so they are overly restrictive and require an enormous amount of bureaucratic data processing to get approval before a drawing, report, presentation, or piece of equipment can be exported. Although there are over 70,000 annual license requests for technical assistance authority (TAA)—which are extremely complex and time-consuming and must be individually processed—99.5 percent of all export licenses have eventually passed through the system without denial.[133]

To try to address these bureaucratic barriers with trusted allies, in 2008, the United States began a series of treaty discussions and subsequent signatures—first, between the United States and the United Kingdom (over 19,000 of those license requests are related to the United Kingdom) and then a similar treaty with Australia. The objective of these treaties was to bring these countries under security controls that are similar to those that the United States has had for many years with Canada. The goal is to create a security circle that includes these countries. The hope is that this can then be extended to other trusted allies in the future. Nevertheless, after the treaties were signed by the U.S. president and the prime ministers of two trusted allies, they remained unapproved by the Congress until late in 2010.

As technology becomes more global and as systems become more sophisticated, the United States needs to move to a simplified process with trusted allies. Each engineering drawing in each report on a given program need not be individually approved. Instead, this could be done on a blanket release for that program and with that country. Such a process (the Defense Trade and Security Initiative) was approved by both the Defense Department and the State Department at the end of the Clinton administration,[134] but it did not become law. In fact, things tightened up after September 11, 2001.

Security Assistance

As with most U.S. weapon systems, the major share of the dollars is not for the equipment itself but for the lifecycle costs of operations, maintenance, training, and support. These services have become a major portion of the DoD acquisition budget, and for DoD assistance to foreign countries it is similarly significant. Thus, when a foreign country purchases a piece of U.S. equipment, it normally also purchases the training, spare parts, upgrades, and even (in some cases) the maintenance associated with this equipment. Normally, this is done through the Defense Security Cooperation Agency (DSCA), whose function is to supply foreign assistance to the nation's allies. It has over 900 security assistance personnel located in 102 countries, and it also supervises over 14,000 international military students annually and spends $50 million a year in humanitarian aid. Finally, the agency handles section 1206 funds, which are responsible for global training and equipment programs that are designed to "build the capacity of partner nations supporting the global war on terrorism." In 2008, the funding for this was approximately $300 million, and the program had spread to cover coalition partners in Iraq as well as assistance to Algeria, Chad, the Dominican Republic, Indonesia, Lebanon, Morocco, Nicaragua, Pakistan, Panama, Senegal, Sri Lanka, Thailand, Yemen, Sao Tome, and Principe. Additionally, section 1207 funds provide $200 million in Defense Department equipment or funds for stability assistance and reconstruction (which is to be shared with the State Department).[135] Of particular importance is the International Military Education and Training (IMET) program, which provides military training to select foreign military and defense-associated personnel on a grant basis. In this case, individuals are selected to attend military schools in the

United States, or subject-matter experts travel from the United States to teach groups of individuals on a regional or bilateral basis. Decisions about level of funding and the programs are made by the DoD and administered by DSCA and the military representatives in the U.S. embassies abroad. Strong associations are developed in this way on a military-to-military basis, and they last long after the formal educational process is completed. This has proven to be valuable when multinational cooperation is required on security activities. Finally, a significant portion of these funds ($200 million in 2006) is spent to train and equip foreign countries for counterterrorists' operations[136]—something of clear value both to the country concerned and to the United States.

Government Policy
Globalization can result in significant benefits to the United States' national security posture, but it also raises significant concerns. The challenge for government policy is to maximize the benefits (economic and security) while minimizing the risk (such as vulnerability).

A nationwide poll that asked the question "Do you believe that globalization, especially the increasing connections of our economy with others around the world, is mostly good or mostly bad for the country?" found that 60 percent responded that globalization is "mostly good" and only 35 percent responded "mostly bad."[137] The latter's principal concerns were about protecting the environment and protecting jobs, not about security. Although jobs may be the principal reason, security is frequently cited (particularly by the U.S. Congress) as the reason for passing legislation that requires purchasing in the United States rather than offshore.

In today's world of globalized technology and globalized industry, the United States is no longer the leader in every technology and in every piece of equipment. The challenge is to take advantage of foreign technology and equipment without being vulnerable, losing jobs, or weakening the U.S. defense industry.

With regard to the vulnerability question, William Greenwalt, the deputy undersecretary of defense for industrial policy (and previously a member of the Senate Armed Services Committee staff) stated in 2006 that so far "we haven't had any problem with any foreign suppliers."[138] He also said that "I've heard of no reliability issue [with foreign parts] with regard to any weapon system or any foreign contractor." In fact, he stated, "during the Korean War, the Vietnam War, [and events since,] the Russians never cut off anything to us. Neither did anybody else." At that same meeting, Jonathan Etherton (also a former staff member of the Senate Armed Services Committee) stated that "the GAO actually did a study in the early 1990s and reached the same conclusion, that they could find no examples where there was any interruption of supply or even any question of it."

Ultimately, America's choice comes down to either building a fortress America or taking advantage of globalization (while addressing potential vulnerability). A typical example of gaining the benefits of globalization is the situation that arose from the attacks of roadside bombs on the unarmored U.S. vehicles in Iraq. It was decided that the United States must urgently build a mine-resistant, ambush-protected (MRAP) vehicle. It selected a V-shaped hull that was originally developed and refined in South Africa, armor that was designed in Israel, robust axles that were developed in Europe, and electronic devices that were manufactured in Asia. DoD would not have been able to field the MRAP as quickly as it did had it not leveraged innovative technologies and products from the global marketplace. In this case, it was decided to do final assembly of the units in the United States in multiple factories but to obtain much critical engineering and many parts from offshore.

With increased recognition of the globalization changes taking place in the world, there is a growing need for the United States to reassess its historic import-control policies (most of which were written in an environment in which the United States was the technological leader in most areas critical to defense). There is enormous political resistance to such changes. In fact, most of these rules were written more for political reasons than for security reasons. For example, a "critical" provision added to the Buy American Act (1933) is the so-called Berry Amendment, which was written in 1941. It was proposed as a "way to insure members of the military were clothed and fed with U.S.-produced items." The Berry Amendment requires 100 percent of the goods in three categories (food, textiles, and tools) to be domestically produced, manufactured, or home grown (the intent was primarily to ensure that U.S. troops in World War II wore military uniforms and ate food produced in the United States).

Over time, Congress has incrementally expanded the list, and in the early 1970s it included "specialty metals."[139] The specialty metals portion of this list was the most troublesome because it applied to a wide range of items—including the stainless-steel flatware that the troops eat with, the solder used in electronic components, and the smelting of the metals used in jet engines. As electronics and jet engines became globalized and were used in both commercial and military applications (with the commercial being the largest volume by far), this became a major problem for the Department of Defense. The Berry Amendment required an electronics manufacturer to set up a special line for the small quantities of an item produced for the Department of Defense to ensure that all of the item's basic materials satisfied the amendment (since commercial firms do not track each part in the bin to determine its country of origin). Similarly, it required a special line for any jet engines to be produced for the DoD, which would be separated from the commercial production for the same reason. Thus, the cost of these small quantities of production items for defense applications rose astronomically. For example, in the case of electronics, the DoD is less than a 1 percent consumer, so the cost of an item would go up by more than an order of magnitude.[140] Similarly, in the case of jet engines, the government was required (by the Berry Amendment) to check down to the level of a "13-cent part on a subassembly." In one situation, the government contracting officer questioned whether $1.30 worth of a $4 million aircraft engine satisfied the Berry Amendment.[141]

No one said that those eating utensils, boots, and anchor chains on the Berry Amendment list were more critical for national security than the allowable specialized glass that was used in reconnaissance systems and missile guidance systems (and that was coming from Germany, Korea, and Japan) or than the allowable semiconductors that were being used throughout all of the electronic equipment in the Department of Defense's weapons systems (and that were coming from Thailand, Japan, Korea, and China). When soldiers were being killed or maimed by roadside bombs in Iraq while driving in unarmored vehicles, the troops tried to add metal plate (which they could obtain at a local store in Iraq) to their vehicles. They were told by their contracting officers that their purchases were violations of the Berry Amendment and that they would have to get the materials from the United States.[142]

The Berry Amendment list also was proposed to be added to all purchases by the Department of Homeland Security in a 2006 amendment by Representative Robin Hayes (R-NC).[143] Again, the national-security rationale was used (that is, the nation's security would be at risk) "unless the items are grown, reprocessed, re-used, or produced in the United States."

In the Defense Authorization Bill for fiscal year 2007, Senator John Warner (R-VA) introduced an amendment to address the need for a change in the Berry Amendment to address a "specialty metal problem associated with electronic components."[144] As stated by the Information Technology Association of America's executive vice president, Olga Grkavac, "The Berry Amendment's restriction on sourcing of specialty metals is no longer viable in the global market that controls the information technology arena, and the electronic components we use. Most hardware used in IT goods and services are not, and will not, be compliant with these outdated restrictions."[145] (Fortunately, the 2007 Defense Authorization Act did exclude commercial electronic components from the Berry Amendment.)[146] Yet over sixty-five years after the Berry Amendment was written, people are still trying to apply autarchic laws. Others recognize the changes that have taken place in the world in this time period and are attempting to overcome the politics of the issue in the interests of true national security and U.S. economic competitiveness.

Finally, a severe penalty is associated with noncompliance to the Berry Amendment. In 2005, the Justice Department announced three major settlements with office-supply companies that had reportedly purchased supplies from China and

Taiwan and then sold them to government agencies through contracts with the General Services Administration. Staples, Office Depot, and OfficeMax paid $7.4 million, $4.75 million, and $9.8 million, respectively—all for violation of the "domestic-sourcing" requirements' clauses of the Berry Amendment.[147]

The Berry Amendment is not the sole piece of legislation in this category. For example, the 1920 Jones Act (named after Senator Wesley Jones from the state of Washington) limits the amount of repair and construction on U.S.-flagged ships that can be done overseas and regulates maritime commerce. Today, this law largely protects U.S. defense industry shipbuilders and DoD ship maintenance yards—since the U.S. shipbuilding industry is basically noncompetitive, on a global basis, to build large commercial ships. Thus, if an allied nation's navy is using a ship that would be advantageous and immediately available to the United States, the technology has to be transferred to the United States and built here—at significantly higher cost and with long delays. There are areas in which the United States is a technological leader (such as aircraft carriers, nuclear submarines, and shipboard fire-control systems), and these sectors will remain domestic. Additionally, there are other areas where the shipbuilding industry has modernized and is increasingly competitive. The question is whether the U.S. Department of Defense benefits most from subsidizing an industry or from being able to afford the quantity and quality of weapon systems that it needs. This is a difficult choice, but it needs to be addressed as the world is changing and as the DoD can take greater advantage of these changes—especially, in a resource-constrained environment.

Besides the many restrictions on U.S. purchases from offshore, extensive controls are placed on the export of goods, technology, and services to our allies. In many cases, these are cumbersome and outdated relative to the spread of technology elsewhere and its availability to our adversaries—while we withhold it from our allies and friends.

Since the terrorist attacks of September 11, 2001, the controls on export of technology have become much more restrictive for fear that they may fall into the hands of terrorists and be used against the United States.

Because of these export restrictions, it is often difficult for our allies to have equipment that is interoperable with U.S. equipment—when we go to war together. And it becomes difficult for them to have state-of-the-art equipment when the United States is ahead. It is even worse when the allies have technology that is more advanced than ours and we agree to purchase it from them. When we try to send it back for repairs or for upgrading, we have to complete detailed paperwork and experience time-consuming delays to get an export license from the United States to send the equipment back to the people who supplied it to us. A few technology areas are extremely sensitive and are not available elsewhere, and under those conditions, it makes sense to have restrictions. Even in those cases, it also makes sense for us to share it with some of our trusted allies, as long as we are assured that it will not be passed on to third parties. Most of our allies also have restrictions on third-party exports, and they work with us to ensure that we have the ability to confirm their controls (should there be any questions).

This is more than just a military issue. It is also an economic one for the United States, and it is harmful to both defense firms and commercial producers. For the defense firms, it removes the world market from them and opens it to foreign producers of similar products. This happened in infrared, and the French captured the world market. For many commercial firms, it discourages them from doing defense business. For example, if a commercial firm sells a part to the Department of Defense and that part goes into a weapon system, from that point on that commercial part becomes an item that has to be covered by the export-control provisions for technology transfer. Since the DoD is a small customer compared to the commercial world (for most equipment), this is a significant deterrent for commercial firms—which now would have to face the delays and paperwork associated with dealing with the export-control provisions for all of their foreign commercial sales. In fact, by 1999 (again prior to the tighter restrictions put on to the export-control regime after 9/11), the large German defense contractor Dasa sent a memo to all its program managers discouraging them from using American suppliers. The delays and uncertainties in receiving export licenses for U.S. components were believed to be holding up Dasa's programs. According to the memo, "because of this uncertain export-license situation, the use of U.S. goods, especially U.S. defense goods, should be avoided at all costs. Whenever U.S. goods are being used, they should be substituted as quickly as possible with non-U.S goods."[148]

The penalty for violating these export controls can be severe. The Boeing Company was fined $15 million for including a commercial two-ounce, one-inch-diameter chip embedded in the flight box of a $60 million commercial aircraft because this commercial chip was also used in a weapons system and therefore was covered under the export-control provisions. Boeing had sold nineteen of these commercial jets to China, and the export of listed defense items is prohibited to China.[149]

As is discussed later in this book, there are many barriers for U.S. commercial suppliers to do defense business—even when they represent the highest performance, reliability, and availability and the lowest cost. And these export-control provisions are simply one of those barriers (which must be removed for both future national-security and U.S. economic competitiveness). As a result of the restrictions on U.S. exports of these commercial items, foreign suppliers can dominate the worldwide commercial market, and these items then become available to America's adversaries, even though they cannot be purchased from the United States. Today, the State Department processes approximately 60,000 export licenses a year, and few are rejected (the largest share of these were items for the United Kingdom, and in 2005 and 2006, only six of these were refused).[150] But the process, the risk, and certainly the delays greatly discourage U.S. commercial suppliers from becoming part of that system. These control provisions extend equally to defense services, technologies, and products.

In fact, public law states that defense services include (1) the furnishing of assistance (including training) to foreign persons (whether in the United States or abroad) in the design, development, engineering, manufacture, production, assembly, testing, repair, maintenance, modification, operation, demilitarization, destruction, processing, or use of defense articles and (2) the furnishing to foreign persons of any technical data controlled under this subchapter, whether in the United States or abroad.[151] At today's American universities, over 50 percent of the graduate students, especially in science and technology, are non-U.S. citizens and many of the faculty also are not U.S. citizens. If they are shown or use things that are on the export-control lists (such as a supercomputer or a biotech processing facility), then the university must get an export license for each incident of foreign student or faculty involvement—even if it occurs on the U.S. university's campus. The law states that when a foreign person uses or is exposed to the technology for any item on the export-control list (even if it takes place in the United States), this encounter is considered to be a "deemed export" and thus must be controlled (approved). Because this was causing a problem in fundamental research, President Bush set up a special commission to make recommendations on "deemed export," but it remains to be seen how this policy will be implemented in practice.

The United States Government Accountability Office summarizes the need for changes in the policies and practices of the U.S. government in an age of globalization: "government programs established decades ago to protect critical technologies are ill-equipped to weigh competing U.S. interests, as the security environment and technological innovation continue to evolve in the twenty-first century. Accordingly, we are designating the effective identification and protection of critical technologies as a government-wide high-risk area that warrants a strategic reexamination of existing programs to identify needed changes and insure the advancement of U.S. interests."[152]

3

National Security in the Twenty-First Century

The Changing Nature of Potential Threats

With the official end of the cold war in 1991, as Alvin and Heidi Toffler state in their 1993 book *War and Anti-War: Survival at the Dawn of the Twenty-First Century*,[1] the industrial wars of the nineteenth and twentieth centuries (which were marked by huge armies, mass production of modern weapons, and mass destruction) could be said to have ended. Industrial-age warfare was being replaced in the twenty-first century by information-age warfare. But in the post–cold war period, large standing armies continued to exist in the United States and elsewhere, and the organizations, doctrines, policies, and equipment of the cold war era continued to be emphasized. The focus of U.S. military planning in the last decade of the twentieth century was on being able to fight two concurrent regional conflicts (major-theater wars)—one on the Korean peninsula and one in the Middle East. The model was still a bipolar, relatively stable, conventional-warfare environment. Large national forces would oppose each other in traditional industrial-war scenarios—tank on tank, aircraft versus aircraft.

As Gary Hart has stated, the terrorist attacks of September 11, 2001, "fundamentally altered the nature of national security and how to achieve it. . . . It demonstrated America's vulnerability to a kind of savagery never seen in our country's history."[2]

Perhaps America should have seen this coming. In his 1993 book, *Out of Control: Global Turmoil on the Eve of the Twenty-First Century*, Zbigniew Brzezinski (national security adviser under President Jimmy Carter) warned that in the greater Middle East an impoverished, shapeless Islamic cluster was permeated with anger at the West but lacked sufficient cohesion either to lift itself into modernity or to strike forcefully at the West. The result, he predicted, would be a vast region of chronic instability that is caught between the competing impulses of traditionalism and modernism.[3] Similarly, Henry Kissinger (secretary of state under Presidents Richard M. Nixon and Gerald R. Ford) in his 1994 book *Diplomacy* said that the twenty-first century would move from the bipolar confrontations and universalists' ideologies of the twentieth century to a world of great pluralism, change, and uncertainty, which would make it hard for all countries to steer their foreign policies in sensible directions and might make them unable to preserve peace if their interests and identities collided.[4] But changing from one paradigm to another is difficult[5] without a true crisis (such as the one that was brought on by the terrorists' attacks of September 11, 2001). Not until after that event did people begin to realize how the world had been changing significantly in the national security arena. And after that, America was at war in Iraq and Afghanistan.

The environment changed between the cold war era and the post–cold war era, and this gradually became widely recognized.[6] Perhaps the final recognition of this changed national security environment was given in a set of speeches that Secretary of Defense Robert Gates made to the military. In an April 21, 2008, speech to cadets at West Point, he stated that the military must better prepare to fight "brutal and adaptive insurgencies and terrorists" in "long, messy, *unconventional* conflict."[7] Against such enemies, he said, traditional measures of military might (such as the amount of fire power that can be directed at a target) will be less important than other elements of national power, such as economic and diplomatic might. He went on to urge the military services to stop spending money on costly weapon systems that are designed to fight big, conventional wars and to focus instead on training and preparing to fight irregular wars and to battle terrorist networks. In April 2009, he proposed significant budget shifts (such as stopping production of the F-22 fighter aircraft, which was not used in Iraq or Afghanistan) and increasing funding for ground robots and unmanned intelligence aircraft (which have proved valuable in twenty-first-century scenarios). Recognition of this changed environment for military operations was made official when the Chairman of the Joint Chiefs declared (on January 15, 2009), that "the future operating environment will be characterized by *uncertainty, complexity, rapid change,* and *persistent conflict.*"[8]

In this new environment, the changed requirements for national security are affected by globalization not only on the supply side (the defense industrial base) but also on the demand side. The interconnectedness of the "flat earth"[9] has come about through the globalization of industry and technology, an explosion in international trade and investment, increases in international travel (facilitated by intercontinental jet aircraft), the worldwide communications capability presented by communication satellites, the widespread use of the Internet, and worldwide television coverage (such as by CNN and BBC). These have shrunk the world so that oceans and continents no longer represented the barriers that they were in the past. And these were accompanied, in the military arena, by such things as intercontinental ballistic missiles that are armed with nuclear warheads. A person in one part of the world can activate these missiles by pushing a button and thereby launching enormous destructive power against cities on the other side of the globe. In the same regime of weapons of mass destruction, biological, chemical, and radiological weapons can give small groups of people enormous power without requiring the large level of financing that nation-states once needed to achieve this level of destructiveness. This interconnectedness and interdependency of society also has made nations more vulnerable to acts of terror—both physical and psychological.

In addition, many in the world have not benefitted from globalization. In fact, the gap between poor and rich was actually widening during this period (by 2007, 75 percent of the world's population had only 25 percent of its wealth).[10] And this disparity between rich and poor continues to widen (on a per capita basis) due to the rapid population growth in the poorer countries. Because America is viewed as the wealthy superpower and therefore in control of the world, it receives the focus of the frustration and wrath of these unemployed, poor people in the urban areas of the underdeveloped world.[11]

In summary, we have moved from a relatively stable and predictable bipolar world to a world with many players (often not at the national level) who have great frustration, hatred, unemployment, and poverty and yet who are capable of possessing weapons that can cause great harm to many people around the world—including those in the United States. In the twenty-first century, the United States is facing ten areas of potential threats: (1) terrorism at home and abroad, (2) the proliferation of weapons of mass destruction (nuclear, chemical, biological, and radiological), (3) cyberwarfare and cyberterrorism (against military and civilian infrastructures and the economy), (4) violent Islamic fundamentalism, (5) international narcocriminals, (6) regional conflicts (that pull in the United States), (7) failed states (that cause great instability and harm in a local region and bring in the United States), (8) struggles for scarce resources (such as oil, gas, water, food, minerals), (9) global pandemics and natural disasters, and (10) potential future peer competitors. Each of these ten potential future threats will affect the military demand for equipment—from the restructured twenty-first-century national security industrial base of the United States and from the rest of the world.

1. Terrorism at Home and Abroad Based on recent terrorist incidences—the 2001 attacks in the United States, the 2000 attacks on the U.S.S. *Cole* in Yemen, and the 1983 bombings at the marine barracks in Beirut—the military are likely to get involved whether attacks are on the civilian population or on the military. In the twenty-first century, terrorism may well be linked to other, more traditional conflicts. (Many people, including the author, were surprised that, when the United States attacked Iraq, terrorist actions did not take place within the United States as part of the Iraqi military response.) Such terrorist actions can be initiated—at the national level and at the small-scale, individual level—with significant effects, particularly with weapons of mass destruction. In many cases, it may be difficult to trace the actions back to their origin. This was the case with the anthrax attacks in the Post Office of the Congress of the United States.

Terrorists cannot be defeated by traditional military means. As Secretary Gates stated, the risk is that "smaller, irregular forces—insurgents, guerrillas, terrorists—will find ways, as they always have, to frustrate and neutralize the advantages of larger, regular militaries."[12] It is impossible to prevent all acts of terrorism. Nonetheless, their effects must be minimized—whether in terms of homeland defense or in terms of actions abroad (against our military, our citizens, or our allies); and we cannot continue to treat the activities of the Department of Defense and of the Department of Homeland Security as separate issues since they are intimately interrelated.

2. The Proliferation of Weapons of Mass Destruction (WMDs)   Weapons of mass destruction (WMDs) include a range of potential threats, including, in order of priority, biological, nuclear, radiological, and chemical. These can easily have as much of an effect in a disruptive fashion as they can in terms of their destructive capability since the psychological aspects associated with these weapons can be significant.

A well-thought-out biological attack has the potential to be, by far, the most destructive form of attack in terms of casualties and adverse economic and financial effects. An attack conducted with a contagious agent, such as smallpox or plague, could kill tens of millions worldwide and effectively shut down global trade for a significant period of time. Such an attack could involve the near-simultaneous release of an agent or volunteers infected with the agent in major population centers worldwide. Under such a scenario, the use of a contagious agent, combined with the high mobility of today's society, would ensure the spread of the disease over most of the globe before the symptoms were identified.[13] Documents captured in 2003 revealed that al-Qaeda was close to producing anthrax bacteria in labs in Afghanistan.[14] In fact, the best defense in this case is mitigation (for example, through a stockpile of vaccines that can counter the attack). The increasing use of bioengineered techniques to create totally new pathogens makes it difficult to mitigate the effect of such an attack, however. Thus, this area of defense against bioterrorism is receiving greatly increased funding at the National Institutes of Health, the Department of Defense, and the Department of Homeland Security. Researchers are developing vaccines and drugs to mitigate the effects of whatever pathogen is utilized.

The next most dangerous type of WMD attack is a nuclear one in a heavily populated urban area. This could result in hundreds of thousands of casualties, the displacement of hundreds of thousands of people, and billions of dollars of economic loss (including the high cost of the medical coverage for those exposed but not killed). The cost of building such a nuclear device is high and would, most likely, be sponsored by a country. However, there has been a large proliferation of nuclear weapons capability in recent years (for example, from Pakistan), and many countries around the world now either have or are likely to acquire nuclear weapons capability. Some of these (such as North Korea and Iran) might not be as susceptible to deterrence through mutual assured destruction as the Soviet Union was. In addition, because there are large numbers of nuclear weapons in Russia and elsewhere, a weapon purchased or stolen from those stockpiles could easily achieve the same objective. For that reason, the United States has been emphasizing the desirability of helping (through funding) the protection or destruction of those weapons and their delivery vehicles. But many countries are also developing the capability for missile, aircraft, or even ship-based delivery of such weapons. Graham Allison, in *Nuclear Terrorism: The Ultimate Preventable Catastrophe*, has documented the case of weapons of mass destruction or weapons-usable material in Russia that could be stolen and sold to terrorists or to hostile nation states and used against American troops abroad or citizens at home.[15]

The third category of WMD threats is radiological weapons. The yield is significantly lower than with nuclear weapons, but it is much easier to gain access to the material needed to combine a conventional, high-energy explosive with radiological material to make a dirty bomb. The materials can be stolen (for example, from a hospital) and then set off in a concentrated, urban area. In this case, the primary damage effects (beyond the initial destruction to structures and people) are primarily psychological concerns about having been irradiated and the lingering effects of the long-term radiation in the area involved. Nonetheless, a few such explosive dirty bombs set off in a number of cities around the country could certainly cause significant panic for millions of people in the local areas.

The final category in this WMD area is chemical weapons. Here the potential physical damage (from high explosives alone) has been shown to be significant, and the chemical damage (for example, from the spreading of mustard gas) can be widespread and extremely dangerous. When an initial attack occurs, it is important to know whether it is a chemical or a biological attack. In the case of a biological attack, people need to stay in the area so that they don't spread it. In the case of a chemical attack, people need to get out of the area as quickly as possible so that they are not infected. Because the form of attack must be detected, sensors need to be located in most major urban areas.

3. Cyberwarfare and Cyberterrorism Perhaps the newest of the twenty-first-century threats is the result of the technologically wired society in which we now live. Military systems are increasingly being designed to be protected (as much as possible) against cyberattacks, but the most vulnerable areas are the civil infrastructures, where attacks can be enormously destructive. These vulnerable systems include the central banking systems, hospital computers (interchanging blood types), and central power systems (causing massive blackouts). This form of twenty-first-century threat is the most common. It is seen in attacks on personal computers by hackers and others who disrupt or flood our systems. But some nations and special-interest groups are working to put together significant attacks, and the number of these against the Pentagon, other countries, and the U.S. infrastructure increase daily. Because the Internet was designed for trusted users (originally for communication among university researchers), adding security into the system is a recent innovation. Most software system suppliers are adding protection (as they introduce new versions of their software), and many software security firms are taking advantage of this growing problem. This situation is not unique to the United States. The port of Singapore is totally computer-controlled and is the hub of most transit shipping in the greater Asian region. In 2007, the country of Estonia was found to be under a cyberattack that was believed to originate in Russia. And before Russia rolled into Georgia with tanks in 2008,[16] it first took out the Georgian government's national communications and information systems with an extensive cyberattack. Future security operations will combine both cyberattacks and kinetic attacks against both military and nonmilitary targets.

4. Violent Islamic Fundamentalism   To Islamic fundamentalists, the United States is a morally corrupt society that embraces materialism and sexual licentiousness at the expense of religious piety. They believe that the country is guilty of the worst possible heresy—the separation of church and state and the maintenance of a secular society. It is considered the "great Satan," not because it threatens military aggression with a new colonialism but because it is capable of being a great seducer and destroyer of Islam's moral purity. Finally, they hate the United States because of its support of Israel, which is viewed as an alien infidel regime and a Middle East outpost of the Western crusade against Islam. This allows the Islamic fundamentalists to fan hatred of the United States to mobilize the Arab masses in support of their political agenda in the Middle East—to expel the United States, to extinguish Israel, and to restore the entire Middle East to Islamic purity.[17]

Unfortunately, modern technology (the Internet, global television, mass communication) empowers the modern terrorist, who is already intoxicated with religious hatred, to encourage others to become violent in their actions. Deterrence is of little value in inhibiting these religious extremists because they believe that they enter paradise if they are killed while attacking their enemy. They would use weapons of mass destruction even if it meant retaliation of any form (conventional or even nuclear). This belief in divine approval presents a major barrier to any inhibition that might otherwise come from the deterrence associated with U.S. military strength. Unfortunately for the world, radical Islam not only employs terrorism and other acts of violence but strongly opposes what the Middle East needs to cure its ills—modernization, economic prosperity, and democratization. As Secretary Gates has stated,[18] even after a withdrawal of forces from Iraq, American troops "will continue to battle violent Jihadist networks" in other countries. He then went on to say, "To paraphrase Bolshevik Leon Trotsky, we may not be interested in the long war, but the long war is interested in us." For this reason, violent Islamic fundamentalism is of much concern for future U.S. national security.

5. International Narcocriminals   In the mid-1990s, when the Defense Department budget was around $350 billion a year, it was estimated that the worldwide narcotics kingpins had an annual budget that was comparable. And illicit drug trafficking and smuggling have been steadily growing due to growth in both demand and supply (in opium, cocaine, heroin, and other drugs). In his 2005 book, *Illicit: How Smugglers, Traffickers, and Copycats Are High Jacking the Global Economy,*[19] Moisés Naím observes that international organized crime, empowered by technology, has risen dramatically in recent years to a point where it has led to the criminalization of politics in several countries and threatens the stability of international politics in many others. He observes that illicit trafficking—in human beings, weapons, drugs, commercial manufactured products, biological organs, intellectual property rights, art, and money—has soared in the past decade. And there are huge profits to be made in these activities. He further observes that globalization has made illicit trafficking far easier because it has opened national economies, knocked down trade barriers, integrated global markets, and facilitated currency exchange and international financing. Also, given the enormous financial power of these international crime bosses, governments in many countries are powerless to deal with them. Since the end of the cold war, many superfluous military arsenals are available for sale on the world market; and middlemen are buying arms cheaply (in places such as Eastern Europe) and airlifting them to Africa and the Middle East at high profits. So there has been a global proliferation of large quantities of rifles, machine guns, grenades, mortars, missiles and rocket launchers, and man-portable missile systems that are capable of downing aircraft.[20] What is of increasing concern to America's national security community (particularly those involved with Latin America and Africa) is the growing linkage between the terrorist community and the illicit trafficking trade. Historically, this has not been a traditional military arena, but in recent years the military has been increasingly involved (for example, in stopping the drug trade from South America into the southern United States). With extensive modern technology (such as small, diesel-fueled, drug-carrying submarines), modern sensors, secure communications, and advanced weapons available to these illegal operators, their links to the terrorists is of increasing importance as a growing threat to U.S. security.

6. Regional Conflicts   U.S. planning scenarios for the post–cold war period were based on trying to fight two conventional regional conflicts simultaneously, and the emphasis was on conventional—massed forces, fighting tank battles, and air-to-air conflicts. But twenty-first-century regional conflicts are expected to be very different. Continued instability in the Middle East and Africa is likely to exacerbate the conditions that cause insurgencies, civil war, and ethnic strife, and such conflicts are likely to end up involving the United States. Many of these chronically insecure regions are also venues for genocidal violence (as witnessed in Rwanda and more recently in Darfur), and many call for U.S. intervention to prevent further violence. The Kosovo conflict, for example, might be noted as a nontraditional war since it was waged by air power alone and ended without a single battlefield fatality among U.S. troops (both facts being highly nontraditional for modern warfare). The United States has been reluctant to go into another country to stop genocide (respecting the other country's natural sovereignty), but as this practice has been spreading, there is increasing pressure for the United States to enter and bring peace. Ethnic and religious violence has been increasingly present (for example, in Rwanda, Somalia, and Sudan).

In addition to these less traditional cases, there are still the more common cases of potential regional conflicts—between North and South Korea, China and Taiwan, India and Pakistan, Russia and its neighbors, Palestinians (with perhaps help from its neighbors) and Israel, and aggression from countries like Iran and Syria. Any and all of these conflicts could easily involve the United States.

7. Failed States   As with regional conflicts, as states fall apart, there is a strong likelihood that the United States will be drawn in—to introduce stability, for humanitarian reasons, to assist a threatened neighbor, or for a wide variety of other reasons. Robert D. Kaplan, in his 2000 book, *The Coming Anarchy: Shattering the Dreams of the Post–Cold War*,[21] uses the ethnic violence in the Balkans (based on centuries-old struggles among the Orthodox, Christian, and Muslim religions) to describe conditions of failed states as both producers of and victims of overpopulation, poverty, urbanized ghettos, social stresses, environmental decay, crime, tribal violence, and incompetent governments. All of these left ungovernable masses in settings of chaos and anarchy where national borders have little meaning.[22] Zbigniew Brzezinski gave a similar description of what he called the "Eurasian Balkans," which stretch from the caucuses (Georgia, Armenia, and Azerbaijan) to central Asia (including Kazakhstan, Uzbekistan, Turkmenistan,

Tajikistan, Kyrgyzstan, and Afghanistan). He described this as a region that is marked by unstable governments, Islamic fundamentalism, poverty, and instability and yet that contains considerable riches in oil and natural gas. The region therefore is of considerable interest to neighboring states and to those around the world that need gas and oil.

Such instability is not unique to the areas of Eurasia and the Balkans but is also frequently found in portions of Africa, the Middle East, Southeast Asia, and even Latin America. Thus, civil wars, racial strife, incompetent and even criminal governments, poverty, and widespread unemployment lead not only to failed governments but to long-term instability and insurrections. It is difficult for outside organizations (even multinational ones like NATO) to come in and introduce peace, solve all of the problems of the nation, and get out quickly.

8. Struggles for Scarce Resources   Many Americans remember the long lines at gas stations in 1973 and 1974, when the Organization of the Petroleum-Exporting Countries (OPEC) put an embargo on Middle Eastern oil. Gas prices escalated, U.S. inflation went up significantly, and the overall U.S. economy suffered. It reminded many older Americans of the gas rationing and coupon books of the World War II era. In 2008, gas prices again skyrocketed, and it became a topic of concern. America is a rich country with its own oil and gas and a strategic reserve; however, when this scenario is projected onto a wealthy country such as Japan, which has no natural resources, the effect is far greater. And with many of the world's poor countries (the vast majority of nations around the world), scarce resources (such as dwindling food supplies and water reserves during a period of drought) are even more urgent. These shortages often cause mass migrations, further increasing the instability in the world. This is not a new problem (Israel and Jordan have argued for centuries over the rights to the water in the Jordan River). But as large lakes dry up in south-central Eurasia and as China and India (with their large populations) experience dramatic economic growth, fuel demands will increase, and struggles for scarce resources will lead to future instabilities. All modernizing economies will need access to energy supplies (especially oil and natural gas), and with limited supplies and increasing costs associated with accessing those supplies, the likelihood of future struggles significantly increases. Unfortunately, many nations tend to view their security in national terms and not in terms of multilateral cooperation; so conflict in this area is highly likely.

9. Pandemics and Natural Disasters   As the world becomes more and more interdependent, a natural-occurring event in one part of the world is immediately communicated to all other nations and often becomes of immediate concern to them. For example, people got into planes and flew around the world, spreading the SARS pandemic and transmitting social and economic costs to many regions. Hurricanes, earthquakes, and tidal waves cause massive deaths and destruction to one region, but their effects pass, both economically and societally, to many other parts of the world. The first instance is not a military issue, but the military usually is called in both for help and for control. The military also usually has the resources necessary to be able to take action (with transportation, communications, and supplies). Understandably, many countries are suspicious when U.S. troops come to help them, and their politicians tend to see U.S. aid (especially if there is already a strong anti-American feeling among the population) as an excellent way to divert attention from the humanitarian crisis. So U.S. help can easily lead to a deterioration of relations between the countries rather than having the desired positive effect. In the case of a spreading disease, the refusal of America to accept any travelers from countries that have it can similarly cause strong political reactions and subsequent anti-American feeling among their population. In the same way, if a country markets a questionable product, there can be strong anti-American feelings if the United States embargos the product. In general, although this category of threat may be the least direct cause of concern to America's security, in the long term the indirect effects may be significant.

10. Potential Future Peer Competitors   As one set of authors has observed, "no peer military power, or power block, will emerge to either challenge U.S. supremacy or relieve it of its global security burden before 2020."[23] Nonetheless, to ignore the long-term possibility (with countries such as a resurgent Russia, China, or even India) would be imprudent. As China emerges as a huge nation-state anchored in a dominant culture and acquires great strategic and military power,[24] China's culture of collective rather than individual values and of authoritarian political leadership makes it unlikely to become a liberal democracy, even as it embraces capitalism (of a sort). But a more powerful China is likely to seek dominance in Asia—not militarily so much as politically and economically by creating a web of relationships that draws other Asian countries into its orbit.[25] Many believe that China will not focus on the use of force to achieve its objectives (but will have the potential military capability, should it be necessary to use it) and instead will focus more on the soft use of power (backed by military strength) to achieve its objectives. Nonetheless, for the United States, the wise strategy with regard to China, Russia, and India (and any other possible future peer competitors) is to pursue political and economic dialog toward mutually beneficial agreements. China has a problem with its terrorist group in the northwest, and it has major environmental and energy problems. These are areas of mutual concern that the United States can work on with these countries (without confrontational tactics). Nonetheless, the United States cannot afford to ignore any possible future peer competitor, as that would guarantee weakness in future geopolitical negotiations with other nations possessing strong, global military power.

In summary, the above discussion makes it is clear that the twenty-first century represents a period of great challenges in the national security arena. As Admiral Michael Mullen, chairman of the Joint Chiefs of Staff, stated in 2008, "We live in an extraordinary time, a time of change and a time of great challenge; and a time of great uncertainty. But in a time of change and uncertainty, I believe there is also great opportunity."[26] This opportunity is fleeting, however, and if we don't pursue this path of negotiations for mutually beneficial solutions, the world could descend into a new dark age of anarchy and violence and a new cold war between the United States and China.[27]

In addressing these ten threats to future national security, the nation must balance its investments in its security strategy—between maintaining its quantitative and qualitative superiority in high-intensity, conventional conflicts against potential peer competitors, and its need to address far less defined and less traditional needs of the military in irregular future conflicts. This balance is essential. The irregular conflicts cannot be viewed as simply lesser cases of the peer-competitor war, and none of the future security threats can be viewed only in a military context. Rather, they must be viewed in a political, economic, and military context. As we make the necessary choices, we must recognize the significant transformation of military operations that will be required in the twenty-first century.

The Transformation of Military Operations

To address all ten of the twenty-first-century threats described above affordably and effectively requires rethinking military operations. The only one of these that might be considered traditional is the potential peer competitor, where the focus needs to be on avoiding the conflict by shaping the potential adversary's actions in a way that results in cooperative threat reductions. For all of the ten areas of concern, the nation needs to think in terms of political-military activities, not simply military operations. Gradually, the importance of such interagency activities is being recognized. For example, the new Africa Command (AFRICOM) has a deputy commander from the State Department, and the Southern Command (SOUTHCOM) also has been restructured to have a State Department deputy commander and to focus on war and peace rather than simply on war.

As Carl von Clausewitz said in the early nineteenth century, "the first, the grandest, and the most decisive act of judgment which the statesman and the general exercise is rightly to understand the war in which he engages; not to take it for something, or to wish to make of it something, which by the nature of its relations is impossible for it to be. This is, therefore, the first, and the most comprehensive of all strategical questions."[28] Unfortunately, since the end of the cold war, many in the Department of Defense, the Congress, and the defense industry have resisted recognizing the reality of the new model of military operations.

Many now believe that the new paradigm for the twenty-first century will be "war amongst the people"[29] and that it has the following characteristics:

- The ends for which we fight are changing from the hard objectives of interstate industrial war to more malleable objectives that have to do with individuals and with societies that are not states.

- We fight among the people, not on the battlefield, and media are constantly present and projecting the war into America's living rooms.

- Our conflicts tend to be timeless and may take years or decades.

- We fight to preserve the force rather than risking all to gain an objective.

- On each occasion, we find new uses for old weapons and organizations, the enemy finds new uses for globally available technologies and products, and all of these are applied in unexpected ways.

- The sides are mostly nonstate, comprising some form of multinational grouping against some nonstate party or parties.

The Iraq and Afghanistan conflicts represent an example of this war among the people. The contrast between these conflicts and those of the past is not incremental. Rather, this is "a period of tectonic shift in the nature of warfare . . . the enemy has changed the Clausewitzian 'ends, ways and means' of warfare."[30] In this new environment, perhaps one of the most critical aspects is to understand the human terrain—the culture and language of the enemy.

When we look at the conflicts in Iraq and Afghanistan, we see that they are carried out at the individual and small-unit levels and against adversaries that are usually hidden (often in plain sight), disguised, and difficult to identify. The United States is involved in a conflict over control of a country that we are not interested in controlling. Rather, we are interested in having a cooperative ally in the area. Finally, the adversaries are using tactics (including detonating suicide bombs, hiding behind women and children, and tolerating large numbers of collateral deaths, even among their own people) that are foreign to Western cultures and therefore are unexpected.

Increasingly, the term *irregular warfare* is being used to describe the likely twenty-first-century warfare environment. In 2006, the deputy secretary of defense, Gordon England, signed off on a working definition that described irregular warfare as a "form of warfare that has as its objective the credibility and/or legitimacy of the relevant political authority, with the goal of undermining or supporting that authority." This means that the United States is fighting to support or replace an existing foreign government by using "the full range of military and other capabilities to seek asymmetric approaches, in order to erode an adversary's power, influence, and will."[31]

The other terminology frequently used (for example, in the DoD's *Quadrennial Defense Review* of 2006, which is an overall strategic statement published every four years) is focused on the challenge of fighting the *long war*—such as the diverse and lengthy military actions taking place in Iraq, Afghanistan, and other places where U.S. forces are in extended conflicts with terrorists and other adversaries, many of which are not the regular military forces of nation-states. Additionally, some have suggested that since much of this long war will be fought with other than traditionally military means, the term *long struggle* might better describe the nature of this conflict.[32]

A characteristic of this irregular warfare is that it tends to require a relatively large, multipurpose ground force that is capable of operating among civilian populations, exercising strong self-protection, and causing minimal harm to friendly civilians. It also requires better U.S. civilian agency capabilities (such as the State Department and the U.S. Agency for International Development), considerable interagency coordination, and significant international cooperation and burden sharing.[33]

Besides the imbalance in personnel and objectives, the other principal characteristic of this asymmetric type of warfare is the difference between the equipment used by the adversary and traditional U.S. equipment. Roadside bombs, commonly referred to as improvised explosive devices (IEDs), have been responsible for almost 50 percent of the casualties (both mortal and injured) sustained in Iraq and nearly 30 percent in Afghanistan. They increased significantly after the secession of major (more traditional) combat operations in 2003. In 2003, there were fifty fatalities in Iraq from IEDs, and by 2006, there had been a total of 452.[34] In Afghanistan, the number of roadside bomb attacks increased from twenty-two in 2002, to 2,615 in 2007, and to 8,159 in 2009.[35]

In this new form of war among the people, many traditional weapon systems are inapplicable. For example, Israel found that many of its advanced standoff weapons were not used in the 2006 Lebanon war because of the need to target specific individuals and minimize collateral damage to others.[36] By contrast, the Hezbollah terrorists had no qualms about using highly inaccurate rockets to terrorize the Israeli population. The Israelis also found, as have the Americans in Iraq and Afghanistan, that these small groups of adversaries in asymmetric conflicts tend to learn and adapt to circumstances rapidly and to develop new abilities to thwart the opposing (more traditional) forces. For example, when the United States began to jam the cell phone and radio links that were being used to set off roadside bombs, the adversaries switched techniques and used hard-wired connections to remote receivers. Increasingly, adversaries are using modern communication techniques and other modern, globally available technologies from the commercial world to adapt to and outfox the slowly reacting and bureaucratically anchored U.S. forces.

The ability to respond rapidly to surprise is critical. Early in the conflict in Iraq, for example, snipers and suicide bombers began to kill soldiers, and the army immediately ordered as many bullet-proof vests as could be produced. It took the army forty-seven days from when General Richard Cody (who was in charge of equipping the soldiers) issued his order for bullet-proof vests to allocate the money needed before contracts could be awarded. Overall, it took the Defense Department five and a half months to start delivering bullet-proof vests to soldiers in Iraq, and it took weeks and months for thousands of other soldiers to receive them— as American casualties continued to mount.[37] This response was far from effective, and yet this equipment was critical for soldier protection in twenty-first-century combat environments.

Another important area of change is that advanced technology used to be used to win decisive victories (for example, a better airplane or a better tank to fight against other airplanes or tanks) whereas technology today influences intentions and the minds of combatants. Today, threats (defined in the prior section) are not to seize our territories or our nation but primarily are to the security of our people and of our way of life.[38] In Iraq and Afghanistan, we share an objective with our adversaries, and that is to influence the will of the people. And the best technology for doing that is modern communications. Here, insurgents have been quick to exploit powerful communication tools like the cell phone and the Internet for recruiting, training, communications, educating, and controlling new members. They have shifted from mass mobilization to targeted, individual mobilizations.[39] Essentially, insurgent campaigns are based on strategic communications campaigns, are supported by guerilla and terrorist operations, and attempt to attack the minds of decision makers.[40]

For the United States to win the hearts and minds of the populations within which the insurgents are operating (for example, in Iraq and Afghanistan), the country needs experienced personnel who are trained to communicate with foreign audiences and are knowledgeable in both their language and their culture. In the commercial arena, the United States has a whole industry (advertising) that leads the world in getting people to buy things through a variety of advertising techniques (thus influencing their hearts and minds). But in the political-military arena, small groups of adversaries seem to be doing a much better job than the United States is doing. As more and more people around the world go online (through the Internet or other communication media), this area of psychological operations will be critical for twenty-first-century political-military operations.

The Effects of Information Technology

The Department of Defense has adopted a strategy that leverages the capabilities of information technology, known as "netcentric warfare," consisting of a large number of distributed sensors and shooters that are linked together by a common command, control, communication, and intelligence network. The focus here is on the data itself and the information that it contains, and the force multiplier comes from the network (through combining all the various data sources into a fused set of information). In this model, every soldier or marine on the ground is potentially a sensor or collector (as well as a shooter). The actual system was first known as Land Warrior (later changed to Land Soldier System). It required each individual on the battlefield to be equipped with a personal global positioning system (GPS) receiver (for positioning data), a radio (for transmitting and receiving data), a small computer and chest-mounted mouse (run on Microsoft software), a gun-mounted infrared and TV camera, and a helmet-mounted prism eyepiece—for a full-color display of all the available intelligence on the network. As commercial information technology has driven down the size and costs of these technologies, enormous numbers of army and marine users are making this twenty-first-century capability into a practical and affordable reality. With this system, every combatant knows where each comrade is and (through the intelligence gathering) where each enemy is. All of these data are available to higher-level commanders as well. The important thing is not to flood each combatant with all possible data but to allow the user to take what he or she needs when it is needed: "This will create a flat network that is unencumbered by echelons; and, unlike current databases, which are compartmentalized and isolated from each other, this will provide a single source of data."[41] The emphasis in this system is to focus not on greater bandwidth, but on the use of the information. One problem is that all of these digital systems on the battlefield must be integrated to be effective. When the United States went to Iraq, it had seven different "blue [friendly] force trackers" that didn't talk to one another. Similarly, when NATO went to Afghanistan, there were thirty-nine different, friendly-force trackers.[42] In the absence of an enforceable data strategy (requiring people to operate in a common domain), the potential benefits of shared information cannot be realized. The United States is now building a set of blue-force tracking devices with an expectation that over a quarter of a million combatants will be online (which can be handled with advanced information technology) and that the common operating picture is where the large benefits occur. The payoff from this extends across the full spectrum of military operations—greatly enhanced warfighting capability, decision making at the soldier level, and rapid response for medical attention to individual combatants. In the future, this system of systems—an integrated digital battlefield that connects people, sensors, weapons, and command operations—will operate on a single (multiservice) common set of data.

It is a complex, software-management challenge. In fact, by March 2008, the system had grown to 95 million lines of code.[43]

This integrated digital battlefield concept is not limited to ground forces. War-fighting for aviators has also fundamentally changed.[44] The focus of aerial activity has shifted from the flight line and cockpit to the Combined Air Operations Center (CAOC), where the data from multiple aircraft are fused and analyzed as they come in. In Iraq and Afghanistan, the air missions have been focused primarily on intelligence gathering (surveillance and reconnaissance) to analyze enemy locations and actions with the data from F-15Es and F-16s (with high-resolution, day and night optical sensor pods), from RC135 Rivet Joint signals-intelligence aircraft, and from a large number of unmanned Global Hawks and lower-altitude, unmanned Predator vehicles. Systems onboard each of these vehicles notify the command center about their locations, and other aircraft (such as JSTARS aircraft) do airborne searches (along with the above-noted aircraft). All of this information is being sent back for a common display of an integrated air picture, which then is combined with the integrated land picture to give a total battlefield picture of the air and land battle. Although the importance and technical feasibility of the integrated digital battlefield are beyond question, the challenge is overcoming the cultural resistance to sharing such data and the fear that it will be compromised. Trust and maximum information security become key elements of such a system. To implement such a system-of-systems effectively and efficiently, significant organizational, doctrinal, and even cultural changes are required.

One of these changes is in the process of acquiring a weapon system. In the past, the stovepipes of individual platforms could be developed from the component level on up through the subsystems, with the platform integrator (prime contractor) delivering a vertically integrated platform. However, with the new model, the various subsystems (such as sensors and communication equipment) need to be part of an overall network and an architecture to achieve full system-of-systems integration. When these subsystems are put on various platforms, the platforms themselves need to be viewed as nodes in the overall system of systems and optimized not on the basis of the individual platforms but on the basis of the overall, integrated system of systems. This is very different from the traditional weapons' acquisition process.

New and Retained Missions

A particular challenge for the Department of Defense in the twenty-first century is balancing the demands (for resources, equipment, organization, and personnel) of traditional military missions and new missions. Of the latter, nine stand out.

1. Missile Defense Today, large and powerful nations (such as Russia and China) have or are getting long-range or intercontinental ballistic missiles, but the widespread proliferation of these missiles has allowed many other nations to acquire them. Therefore, the United States and its allies are increasingly required to develop, acquire, and deploy missile defense systems—to help prevent their populations from being held hostage to a few long-range missiles or even threatened by an inadvertent launch of one or two missiles. Today, the United States is spending over $11 billion a year on the development and deployment of such missile defense systems to protect the country against future potential peer competitors and also against potential threats from so-called rogue nations (such as Iran and North Korea).

2. Biodefense The September 18, 2001, anthrax attack on Capitol Hill (which left five dead and seventeen seriously infected) was a domestic example of what will be faced in the United States and also by our troops and allies abroad. Unfortunately, creating a deadly pathogen is relatively inexpensive (this one was estimated to cost $25,000)[45] and relatively easy, and instructions are increasingly widespread.[46] The United States has begun biodefense "exercises" in which the Department of Defense, Department of Homeland Security, and the U.S. medical infrastructure will be required to take part.[47] Since our troops in the field will be vulnerable to this form of attack, they must be fully prepared for it. Similarly, although chemical weapons do not have the mass propagation effects of biological weapons, there is a long history of their use in warfare. The nation must also be prepared for their use by terrorists.

3. Countering Terrorism Terrorism is basically a means of coercion that cannot be defeated by traditional military means. Many questioned the terminology that President George W. Bush used in referring to a "war on terrorism" since it is different from traditional military conflict. Yet this war involves the military in its activities—whether domestically or internationally.

Terrorism is not a new phenomenon, but because of modern telecommunications and other forms of information technology, even small groups can have a worldwide influence. Similarly, modern weapons of mass destruction (particularly biological and nuclear) allow a small group to be very destructive. Finally, terrorists and criminals (often drug-related) are increasingly linked throughout the world— a linkage frequently referred to as *narcoterrorism*.

Countering terrorism is one of the most difficult military activities since it is unpredictable in time, location, and method. It can be used against U.S. citizens, U.S. industry, or U.S. military anywhere in the world. The capabilities for countering it include enhanced human intelligence, persistent surveillance, special operations forces (SOF), cultural awareness and understanding, prompt strike capabilities to attack fleeting targets on a global scale, rapid countering of enemy propaganda,[48] identity management, credentialing, biometrics, and many other evolving techniques.

4. Cyberwarfare   In the twenty-first century, the information technology network needs to be thought of as a weapon system. Cybersecurity (or information assurance) involves a wide variety of techniques. On the detection and prevention side, these include overcoming denial of service, authentification, validity, integrity of data, confidentiality, and nonrepudiation. On the offensive side, they include response. Cyberwarfare can occur when a nation attacks another nation, when cyberterrorists attack infrastructure (commercial and military), and when cybercriminals attack industry, individuals, and financial institutions (an estimated $60 billion to $500 billion is lost annually to cybercriminal actions). Each of these elements has grown increasingly sophisticated in the early twenty-first century. Terrorist groups probably will begin to use cyberattacks in a highly offensive fashion, as well (for example, attacking U.S. networks and computer-based infrastructures, both military and civilian). Russia did this against Estonia, and in 2008, the first large-scale example of combining cyberwarfare with kinetic warfare occurred when Russia attacked Georgia's government information systems and then brought in tanks.

Both U.S. industry and the U.S. government have reacted strongly to this new form of warfare. In 2002, Congress passed the Federal Information Security Management Act (FISMA), which set information-security certification requirements for federal agencies and is also being applied widely to the agencies' industrial suppliers. By 2004, the federal government was spending over $4 billion annually on cybersecurity, and by 2009, this had grown by 73 percent to $7.3 billion, of which over $4 billion (approximately 55 percent) was being spent by the Department of Defense). This increase was stimulated by the January 8, 2008, presidential signing of National Security Presidential Directive 54 and Homeland Security Presidential Directive 23, which established a $17 billion dollar program (over five years) to stop hostile penetration of U.S. information networks.[49] Nonetheless, penetrations of DoD and U.S. Government Web sites have been growing exponentially. The head of U.S. Cyber Command, General Keith Alexander noted that in 2010, attacks on DoD sites reached 250,000 times an hour (or 6 million times a day).[50] As the Department of Defense moved toward more netcentric operations, protecting its computer and network system became a higher priority (by December 2006 it was the "number four priority" in the U.S. Navy).[51] Cyberwarfare is the Achilles heel of twenty-first-century netcentric warfare, and as other countries move to follow the U.S. emphasis on netcentricity in its military operations, this area becomes more central (defensively and offensively) to both military and commercial operations, and its difficulty is compounded as netcentricity is applied on a multinational and multiagency basis.

Cyberwarfare is not going to be only a military security issue. Many U.S. infrastructure areas (including banks, investment firms, utilities, and telecommunications) are also frequently under cyberattacks—all of which represent significant national security concerns. As Mike McConnell, the former director of national intelligence, stated in discussing the seriousness of cyberattacks on nonmilitary targets, "the ability to threaten the U.S. money supply is the equivalent of today's nuclear weapon."[52]

5. Countering the Proliferation of Weapons of Mass Destruction (WMDs)   Because a small group with biological or nuclear weapons can have an enormous destructive effect on a large nation, knowledge of these weapons and their delivery mechanisms must (at a minimum) be controlled and, if possible, eliminated. Unfortunately, this problem is compounded by widely available instructions and the relative ease with which biological weapons and even radiological weapons can be made. The only way that counterproliferation efforts can succeed is through multinational agreements accompanied by supervised, mutually agreeable verifications. This was done during the cold war with arms-control agreements and limits on nuclear weapons and their delivery vehicles, and such agreement regimes need to be greatly expanded on a multinational basis in the nuclear and biological arenas.

Incentives also must be provided for nations, groups, and even individuals to forgo the development and proliferation of these weapons. What makes this particularly difficult is the close proximity between the research being done (particularly in the biological area) for medical cures and the research that is required for potential offensive-weapon technology. In many cases, the necessary controls and prohibitions on publication and dissemination have to be placed at the level of the individual researcher. Monitoring and control often rest first at the institutional level and then go up to the governmental level.

The high costs of covering the full spectrum of potential military needs and the destructive power of just a few of these weapons of mass destruction make it clear that the United States should invest a significant share of its resources in counterproliferation and deterrence of use.

6. Maintaining the Nuclear Deterrence   Although nonproliferation of weapons of mass destruction is critical, preventing their use (especially large-scale nuclear use) or even the threat of their use is a necessity. The United States must maintain a responsible and credible nuclear deterrent force. It must be secure, safe, and (for economic reasons) not excessive, and potential adversaries must believe that it will be used and that it will work—or it loses its deterrent value. With more and more nations gaining nuclear capability, the United States cannot afford to neglect its nuclear deterrent—hoping and expecting never to use it but preventing others from either using theirs or even threatening to use theirs to hold the United States hostage.

7. Maintaining a Conventional Capability Overmatch   The United States must shift its resources (including people, equipment, budgets, planning organization, doctrine, and training) to focus on the new areas of twenty-first-century threats (such as terrorism, insurgency, and cyber- and psychological operations). But the country still needs to balance this shift with an ability to join with our allies and use traditional weapon systems to overmatch any potential regional adversaries or potential future peer competitors. Because of the costs associated with the overall expanded domain of potential threats, efficiency and effectiveness become critical, and excessive overkill is not affordable. This means that the United States must focus on performing continuous net-assessments; staying ahead technologically; designing lower-cost equipment; stressing verifiable arms-control agreements (strategic and tactical); working closely with our allies (from planning through exercises); emphasizing intelligence gathering, warning, and analyzing "what ifs" (red teaming to avoid surprises); and developing agility for fast responses (in policy and actions and in doctrine, tactics, equipment development, and fielding).

8. Postconflict Security, Stability, and Recovery   The United States learned a bitter lesson in the war in Iraq—that a great military victory (the rush to Baghdad, in which the U.S. military overwhelmed Iraqi forces) is only a first step in the world of the unstable twenty-first century. A listing of the states of instability now is done annually,[53] and in every instance, the U.S. military force is orders-of-magnitude superior to these countries' forces. But if the United States involves itself in these nations (and they are increasingly being drawn into their conflicts), then the challenge is to maintain security, stability, and economic recovery after the major conflict has ended. This is likely to be for an extended period of peacekeeping. For example, although the Bosnia conflict ended in 1995, 30,000 NATO peacekeepers were deployed to enforce the treaty, and in 2008 the United States still had troops in Bosnia. In fact, President George W. Bush referred to these operations of stability, reconstruction, and peacekeeping as "the long war" (including not only operations against terrorists but also insurrectionists and others who are simply fighting—often among themselves—for various religious and political reasons). A major role for the military in these operations is working with local national forces and police forces to help achieve security, stability, and even reconstruction (often this reconstruction is being done in an environment of considerable insecurity). In such cases, a major function of the U.S. military is to train and build up the military establishments in these countries. For example, in Africa, the goal is to make the military establishment capable of maintaining order and quelling terrorism, and in Colombia, the goal is to make the military capable of countering drug production, terrorism, and violence within the national borders.[54] The training of foreign troops has become a major item in U.S. military planning, and it is only one element associated with the military's role in this overall regime.

9. Homeland Security   Until September 11, 2001, the basic assumption was that the oceans and the nuclear deterrent would largely protect America's territory from military operations. There was some concern after the 1995 bombing of the federal building in Oklahoma City by domestic terrorists, but the events of 9/11 were a dramatic reminder of the need for homeland defense. Missile defense systems are one form of homeland defense (against intercontinental missiles), but there are also shorter-range concerns about missiles launched from ships offshore (from submarines or even commercial vessels) and the growing likelihood that there will be foreign terrorists' attacks, either by individuals or in connection with military operations elsewhere. The Department of Homeland Security (DHS) has primary responsibility for America's homeland defense. But even with the many formerly independent agencies that have been placed under DHS, the department is allocated a small fraction (more than an order of magnitude smaller) of the resources allocated to the Department of Defense, so the DoD needs to play a significant role in homeland security. For this reason, the DoD created a U.S. Northern Command and has begun working with other federal agencies to prepare for various contingencies, such as biological attacks, other weapons of mass destruction, and cyberattacks on the U.S. infrastructure (power systems, banking systems, and so on). As the DHS budget increases, traditional defense firms have emphasized this growing market. Increasingly, national security is being seen in a more holistic perspective (by both government and industry) that includes worldwide military operations in the traditional security area and also domestic protection operations.

Future Transformations of Military Operations
The transformation of military operations in the twenty-first century will involve operations that span a wide spectrum—diplomacy, information operations, traditional military operations, and economic and societal, cultural, and development activities. The United States will be involved in irregular warfare—in terms of the type of equipment used and the adversaries themselves (often small groups of nonnation players but organizationally globalized through information networks). There will be a heavy emphasis on cooperative security—multinational operations and multination agreements on controls. All of these operations—counterterrorism, the countering of the proliferation of weapons of mass destruction, imposing controls on cyberwarfare, achieving stability and security in unstable countries around the world—require international cooperation, and these partnerships need to be built and planned prior to the events, not after they have begun. Early preventative measures should be taken to stop local problems from escalating and

to enhance the flexibility and freedom that the combined forces will have. These activities also will require multiagency involvement within the U.S. executive branch, including the State Department, Homeland Security Department, and Treasury Department. These interagency operations require a smooth and well planned response before the need for joint action arrives. This is the purpose for restructuring combatant commands in both the Africa Command (AFRICOM) and the Southern Command (SOUTHCOM). In both cases, the State Department will supply the deputy commander, and the necessary military and political activities will be planned well in advance of being needed (including interagency integration, multinational representation, strategic communication, and public and private partnering).[55]

We also need to recognize that many of the critical networks involved are social, not electronic. We must learn to work with our allies, native forces (military and police), and local political leaders. This requires an understanding of language and culture. Again, this is a multiagency activity.[56]

In addition to being multinational and involving numerous nonmilitary agencies, future operations will be expeditionary. They will likely last a long time, and they will involve large numbers of contractors intermixed with the forces. There also will be heavy dependence on special forces operations—because the special forces have special warrior skills and are responsible for the psychological operations that will play a big part in future military activities.

Finally, we should expect to see significant shifts in resources—both personnel and budgets. This shift in resources is a response to both the changed nature of the threats and the geopolitical changes in the world and also dramatic changes in the technologies related to warfare.

The Effects of Technological Changes

Many books have been written about how technologies—including the long bow, the rifle, airplanes, radar, and precision guided missiles—have affected warfare (and the industry that supports it). So it is no surprise that twenty-first-century technology will also significantly affect the nature of warfare and the industry supporting it. But large institutions resist change and tend to be slow to adapt. For example, even after Israel successfully demonstrated the effectiveness of remotely piloted vehicles in the Bakka Valley, it took two decades for the U.S. military to respond by integrating remotely piloted vehicles into U.S. operations.

The latter part of the twentieth century was known as the information age, and the commercial world took full advantage of information. Federal Express and United Parcel Service, for example, transformed themselves from transportation companies to information companies. But small terrorist groups have also been able to shift rapidly to new technologies and use them to their advantage. For example, the Internet became a worldwide information technology only in the final decade of the twentieth century, but by 2007, Abdul-Rahman Al-Hadlaq, the supervisor of the Saudi Arabian Interior Ministry's Good Counsel Committee, observed that the Internet is responsible for 80 percent of the recruitment of youth for the jihad.[57]

Perhaps the greatest near-term effect of technology on U.S. military operations is the shift taking place from a platform-centric perspective to a network-centric perspective. There are three potential issues associated with the DoD's move in this direction. First, there is still a tendency to try to optimize each individual node (each platform, manned or unmanned) of this complex system rather than optimizing the overall integrated system of systems. When the system is not viewed as an integrated system of systems, each node becomes extremely expensive and, in a sense, suboptimized. The overall system is not viewed as a system of systems but as the connection of a lot of independent and expensive systems. The second issue is the complexity and vulnerability of the software and communication system. A significant effort needs to be made in the software area to ensure its invulnerability to cyberwarfare and its fail-safe operation in the event of any problems. Finally, the third major issue is the need for an independent organization to establish the architecture for the system-of-systems and to select the various elements that make up that system. This became particularly important when the defense industry dramatically consolidated in the post–cold war period. Thus, if a single firm is given the responsibility for doing the architecture for the system of systems and for supplying many of the elements in that system of systems, a conflict can develop between selecting the best elements for any of the nodes of the system and putting the prime contractor's own equipment at each of the nodes. By 2008, Congress began to legislate that the large-scale integrator (that was responsible for the integration role for the system of systems) should not be able to supply the equipment for any elements of the system of systems. But most of the previously independent firms that existed during the cold war period and were willing to take the required hardware-and-software-exclusion contract clauses no longer existed and would have to be recreated to satisfy this need.

The first step (toward the needed architectural flexibility) being taken for software is to require modular open systems architecture (MOSA), which uses standard interfaces. For hardware, continuous upgrading of the systems (via spiral development) while using the best technology available (as it is proven) is the preferred alternative. If this can be done using commercial interface standards, then the DoD is free to draw on the best in class, on a worldwide basis, of commercial and military technologies (always keeping in mind the importance of security). An additional technique in the software area is that of open-source software.[58] Everyone has access to open-source software, and perhaps counterintuitively, it is believed to be extremely secure because it is constantly being tested by everyone (so the likelihood that someone could insert malicious code into the program and have that malicious code go unnoticed or unchallenged by anyone is highly improbable).

The effects of information technology on twenty-first-century warfare are already clear, but many other technologies are currently proliferating and also can dramatically affect future military and industrial activities. Biotechnology is one of these, as a weapon of mass destruction and as a subject of research for developing biodefense capabilities). Closely related to this is the increased use of biometrics for tagging and tracking individuals at border crossings and elsewhere. (For example, it has become common in Iraq and Afghanistan to use biometrics to monitor insurgents.)

A more recent biotechnology threat and one of increasing concern is synthetic biology—man-made bugs. Biohackers are the practitioners of malicious applications of this dangerous technology. As nations focus on biodefense against the known pathogens, the threat of newly invented ones becomes even harder to address (requiring, for example, as yet unrealized vaccines). This is an area (like information security) where the continuous challenge of measure, countermeasure, and counter-countermeasure must remain a continuous and vigilant chase.

Another major technology that will be used widely is robotics. A significant amount of equipment (airborne, ground, and sea-based) will be robotic. All ground-based soldiers and marines will probably have a small robot in their backpacks that they can send into a cave or down an urban canyon for initial reconnaissance and for a search for potential traps. They also will carry a small unmanned air vehicle to see what is on the other side of a hill and to send the information back. These robotic vehicles are becoming increasingly sophisticated and in many cases will also be armed.

Two weapons that will be widely used in the twenty-first century are high-energy lasers (for killing) and high-powered microwave devices (for nonlethal use). Both of these nontraditional weapons have received considerable resistance from those within the DoD and limited support in their development. Nonetheless, they will receive increasing attention. The nonlethal weapons are particularly attractive in operations with insurgents that take place among civilians (as in Iraq) and in homeland security for protecting nuclear power plants and even stopping suspicious ships in American waterways.[59]

When the Soviet Union's *Sputnik* introduced the age of satellites in 1957, the worlds of communication, navigation, intelligence, and weapons changed dramatically. Fortunately, the use of weapons in space has been largely controlled by treaty, but it is a continuing concern. In all other areas, satellites have dramatically affected military operations. Today, the United States depends on its space systems—its system-of-systems communications and command and control—for many of its weapons guidance systems (such as GPS), for much of its intelligence gathering (including radio and telephone intercepts as well as photographic and radar target intelligence), and for missile-launch warnings and tracking. This dependence makes the United States vulnerable to antisatellite technology—through kill by direct interception (as both the Chinese and the United States demonstrated in 2008), through jamming, and through attacks by high-energy lasers. The commercial world and many nations have put significant assets in space (in the areas of communication, navigation, and intelligence), which potential adversaries (nations, terrorists, or insurgents) can use or purchase on the commercial market. Thus, the United States is required to keep its own developments on space systems continuously evolving (with higher performance and lower costs). It also needs to address the growing antisatellite capabilities of potential adversaries and the use of commercial and military space systems against the U.S. military and against the commercial infrastructure of both the United States and its allies. (For example, the atomic clocks in the GPS satellites control the international banking system.)

Another technology that could significantly affect the future of warfare and the defense industry is nanotechnology—the science of creating and working with materials that are about 1 nanometer wide (one-billionth of a meter). As a point of reference, a human hair is about 80,000 nanometers across. One early application of this in the military has been to develop advanced body armor for ground warriors. This would take advantage of the fact that when normal carbon atoms are fixed into a tubelike shape (called *nanotubes*), they are 100 times stronger than steel and only one-sixth of its weight. Another application of such technology being researched by the Defense Advanced Research Projects Agency (DARPA) is a 1.5-inch, 0.32-ounce reconnaissance nano air vehicle with a single rotating wing and a range of 3,300 feet. The rocket-powered, rotating-wing vehicle flies like a maple seed, is remotely controlled, and transmits stable video images.[60] Many commercial companies are working in the nanotechnology field on a wide range of applications (including many combinations of bio- and nanotechnologies) that will have widespread application in the commercial and military worlds.

A critical technology for future use in expeditionary environments is the ability to have two-way, automated-translation capability. Without this, an expensive translator must be sent with each soldier to deal with insurgents among the people. The average annual pay for a U.S. citizen working as a translator in Iraq in 2007 was $176,000 (one company, Titan Corporation, had about 6,900 translators—U.S. and foreign—on its payroll in the war zone).[61] Language itself is not sufficient. Cultural understanding is essential, and many training tools need to be developed to enable soldiers to work in the dramatically different cultures in which they will be immersed. An important lesson learned from the sustained operations in Iraq and Afghanistan is that the war is won not simply with bullets but also with words.

Finally, quantum computing is a technology that is rapidly advancing to realization, and it could significantly affect military operations. Computing speed and capability are important, but cryptography—making code breaking almost impossible—helps the United States with information security. It also greatly disadvantages the country's ability to read other people's mail (in all communications forms). This is not an area in which the United States is the sole world leader. Other countries have also been investing in quantum computing; and eventually it will be globally available (for commercial and military use). It is a research area in which the United States (particularly the intelligence community) must be actively engaged.

In considering the implications of technology for America's economic and military competitiveness, it must be recognized that in the twenty-first century, the U.S. military is no longer the sole leader in all critical military technologies. In many areas (such as quantum computing), the United States is equal to or behind both commercial and foreign military technologies. Globalization has achieved a great deal of technological leveling, and technology is increasingly the differentiator among commercial firms. The advances in commercial technology and the widespread distribution of this technology have made it necessary for the Department of Defense to search out foreign military and dual-use commercial technologies that might be applicable.

Perhaps the single greatest distinction between commercial and military applications of technology is that commercial business tends to use technology to improve performance and lower costs, while the military has focused primarily on performance improvements. The distinction here is between the best performance at the lowest cost versus the best for our boys, at any cost.

Addressing Affordability and Effectiveness

Year after year, the cost of defense weapons systems has continued to skyrocket to the point where one aircraft carrier now costs over $12 billion (and that is without the airplanes), a destroyer costs over $3.6 billion,[62] and a new nuclear submarine over $7 billion. Similar prices exist for other high-cost equipment (such as a B-2 bomber at $1.2 billion each and an F-22 fighter at $143 million each). At these high prices, the quantities that are affordable are extremely small, even for the U.S. Department of Defense's large budget. For wide-ranging security, training, and maintenance requirements, numbers are critical, but at these high prices, the needed quantities are simply unaffordable. These high costs are being driven by the complexity of the weapons and the increasing materials and subsystems costs that go into them. The cost of nickel, for example, rose from $13,000 a ton in 2005 to $35,000 a ton in 2006, which caused the cost of batteries to skyrocket. But mostly, these high costs are driven by the fact that because only a few are affordable, the high overhead associated with the industrial infrastructure (driven by the government-unique procurement requirements) has to be absorbed by just a few systems. Because there are not adequate quantities for production learning, the government is simply paying for the high cost of the first few systems. To make matters worse, these systems often are fuel guzzlers, and the basic designs make few accommodations for minimizing fuel use. In fact, even the cost of fuel is charged off as though it were being bought by the gallon at a pump rather than being charged with the full cost of the airborne tankers, the fuel-supply ships, and the refueling vehicles that are required to go along with aircraft, ships, and tanks to support them. Delivery dramatically increases the actual full cost of fuel. A Defense Science Board study in 2000 estimated this cost to be around $400 per gallon. Finally, not only is the DoD building fewer and fewer of each weapons system because of their high cost, but it can afford fewer and fewer different weapons programs in each decade. For example, as shown in table 3.1, fewer and fewer different aircraft programs are being started in each decade.

As Secretary Gates has stressed, "The perennial procurement cycle—going back many decades—of added layer upon layer of cost and complexity on to fewer and fewer platforms, that take longer and longer to build, must be ended. . . . Without a fundamental change in this dynamic, it will be difficult to sustain support for these kinds of weapons programs in the future."[63]

There appears to be only one solution to this affordability issue. If the military is going to be able to buy the type and quantity of equipment that it needs, then it must make lower cost a design requirement. The commercial world starts out by setting certain requirements for a new device—certain performance capabilities and a market price that is affordable. Similarly, the military must have the price that it pays for its weapon systems be part of its firm requirements process—to be able to afford the quantity of systems that it requires. Until cost becomes an engineering design requirement (not an accountant's issue), the current trends are likely to continue, and the DoD will be able to afford fewer and fewer of the increasingly expensive systems that it needs for the nation's future security. This concept is not a new one. It had been urged on the DoD before.[64] For example, a 2000 DoD directive (signed by the vice chair of the Joint Chiefs and the undersecretary of defense for acquisition, technology, and logistics) stated that cost should be a military requirement. Yet only a few systems have actually done that. The JDAM missile was specified (by the chief of staff of the air force) to work reliably, hit the target, and not exceed $40,000 each. Since cost was a strong design requirement, the directive was followed, and the current missile costs around $17,000, was produced in sufficient quantities to meet the military need, is reliable, and hits the target. A few other systems—such as the Global Hawk unmanned aircraft and even the Joint Strike Fighter aircraft (now known as the F-35)—started out with cost as a firm

Table 3.1
Military aircraft program starts

1950s		1960s	1970s	1980s	1990s	2000s
XFY	XP5Y	A6	F14	F117	F22	JSF EMD
F8U	A2D	B52	S8	F20	EMD	UCAV
U2	XC120	SR71	YA9	X29	YF22	
SY3	F4D	SC4A	A10	T46	YF23	
F105	F3H	X21	F15	T45	JSF C36	
X13	B52	X19	F18	B2	JSF X37	
C133	A3D	C141	YF-17	V22	C17	
F107	X3	B70	B1			
F5D	S2F	XC142	YC15			
X14	X2	F111	YC14			
C140	F10F	A7	AV8b			
T2	F2Y	OV10	F/A18			
F4	F100	X22	F-16			
A5	B57	X26B				
T39	F102	X5A				
T38	R3Y1	X24				
AQ1	F104					
X15	A4D					
F5A	B66					
X1B	F11F					
F101	C130					
T37						

Source: Mark Lorell, "The U.S. Combat Aircraft Industry: 1909–2000: Structure, Competition, Innovation," RAND Corp., Santa Monica, CA, 2003.

requirement. However, these two were allowed to grow in cost to satisfy increasing performance requirements (at the expense of increased costs), so their quantities had to be reduced. For example, the Global Hawk was originally specified to cost $10 million each, and by 2009, when fully equipped, it cost $200 million each. Since designing things to a given cost is the commercial norm, engineers familiar with that discipline could be valuable in implementing that approach within the military environment. It is also an argument for the DoD to use more commercial equipment since it has been designed to have lower costs. However, as it starts to modify commercial equipment, the military must be aware that costs should still be a major consideration in the modified design. It should not simply assume that because the original product was low cost, the modified commercial item will remain low cost—unless it had low cost as a design consideration. Only if cost is a major design consideration for future military systems will the DoD be able to afford the quantities and types of weapons that it needs for the full spectrum of twenty-first-century warfare.

Finally, a lesson learned from the Iraq and Afghanistan wars that must be (and was not) planned for is that contractors will play a major role in the conflict areas in twenty-first-century scenarios.

Contractors in the Combat Zone

As the data in table 3.2 show, having contractors on the battlefield is nothing new.

In fact, during America's Revolutionary War, General George Washington had contractors drive his wagons and supply food and clothing to his troops. But as table 3.2 shows, by early 2008, there were approximately the same numbers of contractors and military personnel in the Iraq theater. Although a similar 50 percent ratio existed in the Balkans, the magnitude of both the personnel and the funding were dramatically different. In the Balkans, from fiscal year 1996 to 2000, the total

Table 3.2
The presence of contractor personnel during U.S. military operations

Conflict	Estimated personnel (thousands)		Estimated ratio of contractor personnel
	Contractor	Military	
Revolutionary War	2	9	1 to 6
War of 1812	Not available	38	Not available
Mexican-American War	6	33	1 to 6
Civil War	200	1,000	1 to 5
Spanish-American War	Not available	35	Not available
World War I	85	2,000	1 to 24
World War II	734	5,400	1 to 7
Korea	156	393	1 to 2.5
Vietnam	70	359	1 to 5
Gulf War	9	500	1 to 55
Balkans	20	20	1 to 1
Iraq theater (as of early 2008)	190	200	1 to 1

Sources: Congressional Budget Office, based on data from William W. Epley, "Civilian Support of Field Armies," *Army Logistics* 22 (November–December 1990): 30–35; Steven J. Zamparelli, "Contractors on the Battlefield: What Have We Signed Up For?," *Air Force Journal of Logistics* 23 (Fall 1999): 10–19; Department of Defense, "Report on DoD Program for Planning, Managing, and Accounting for Contractor Services and Contractor Personnel during Contingency Operations," October 2007, 12.

contract dollars were \$2.168 billion,[65] while in Iraq, from 2003 through 2007, total contracts dollars were \$85 billion.[66] The data in table 3.2 does not include contractors in Afghanistan or contractors working for the Iraqi government, other governments, or companies that were not funded by the Department of Defense. The actual number of contractors in the war zone was significantly higher than that shown in the table for Iraq alone. In Afghanistan (for 2006 and 2007), 65 percent of the total force were contractors,[67] and by 2009, that ratio increased to 75 percent.

As can also be seen from the data in table 3.2, more contractors were present in the American Civil War and World War II. But the ratio of contractors to military personnel was significantly different in those wars, and those contractors were placed in significantly different environments. The prior conflicts were closer to warfare in its traditional sense (head-to-head force-on-force fighting), and the contractors were behind the line of battle. Although in the Iraq and Afghanistan situations the primary function of the extended operations was to introduce stability and reconstruction into the country, continuous violence from insurgents operating within the population placed contractors in continuous danger.

The question that this raises is how we got into a situation where there are more contractors than military personnel in the war zone. First, and most critical, in the post–cold war period, the military drew down its active force from 2.1 million to less than 1.4 million by the year 2000. The remaining forces were focused in the combat units, so major shares of the personnel reductions came in the support units. In addition, during the peacetime period, weapons systems became increasingly more complicated, so there was a growing dependence on contractors for the maintenance and support of that high-tech equipment. Thus, when the Iraq and Afghanistan operations began, the military was heavily dependent on contractors for support functions across the board. As Lieutenant General David McKiernan (Third Army commander) stated in 2003, "a lot of what we have done, in terms of reducing the size of active and reserve component force structure, means there's a greater reliance on contractors. And there's a lot of technology that requires contractor support."[68]

The problem was that these changes—in the environment in which contractors operated, in their large numbers, and in the military's heavy dependence on them— was not recognized or addressed by the DoD. This fact was highlighted by a 2003 GAO report entitled "Military Operations: Contractors Provide Vital Services to Deployed Forces But Are Not Adequately Addressed in DoD Plans."[69] This report stated that "as the defense industry boosts its staff overseas, companies are increasingly concerned about their workers' safety. The government's responsibility to contractors, in the event of hostilities, is not clear; causing confusion and complicating management of the civilians. . . .The Joint Chiefs of Staff says it is a contractor's responsibility to provide security, while the Army puts the responsibility on the local military commander."[70] Even by the time the Iraq operation had been underway for five years, Jack Bell, the deputy undersecretary of defense for logistics and material readiness, stated at a hearing: "Frankly, we're not adequately prepared to address . . . this unprecedented scale of our dependence on contractors."[71] At that same hearing, Stuart Bowen (the special inspector general for Iraq reconstruction) and William Solis (the Government Accountability Office's director of defense capabilities and management) indicated that the military does not have enough trained personnel to oversee the contractors in Iraq and Afghanistan. Finally, David Maddox (retired army general and member of the Commission on Army Acquisition and Program Management Expeditionary Operations) reiterated one of the Commission's findings—that the army does not yet recognize the full effects of contracting and contractors on expeditionary operations and on the mission's success.[72] In essence, the DoD did not recognize these contractors in its training activities, military exercises, doctrine or operations planning, staffing, personnel policies, contracting, or financial plans. Thus, an across-the-board set of changes was required. But there was considerable institutional resistance to recognizing that the types of activities being undertaken in Iraq and Afghanistan were likely to be the events of the future and that the structure, culture, and practices of the military were geared toward much more traditional operations. Finally, in 2008, the army rolled out the first revision of its operations manual since the terrorists' attacks of September 11, 2001, officially putting stability operations (or nation building) on a par with combat. At the time, army officials stated that this revision reflected a focus on fighting terrorism and a full recognition that such activities could well be a part of their uncertain future.[73] As Secretary Gates stated, "the U.S. needs a military whose ability to kick down the door is matched by its ability to clean up the mess and even rebuild the house afterward."[74]

In the Iraq theater, the 190,000 contractors identified in table 3.2 and defined in table 3.3 are composed of a combination of U.S. citizens, local nationals (about 20 percent), and third-country nationals. Most U.S. citizens listed in table 3.3 are retired military who have volunteered for these high-risk positions because of the high salaries (approximately two and a half times what they would get in equivalent jobs in the United States). They are employed primarily in high-skilled jobs (such as driving logistics vehicles and maintaining high-tech military equipment).[75] A large share of the workforce is made up of local nationals, and this is desirable in terms of the objectives of stability and reconstruction within the country (under the assumption that an employed Iraqi is far less likely to be an insurrectionist than an unemployed one). Finally, third-country nationals comprise the bulk of general support personnel. They perform a wide range of functions (many work in dining facilities) and come from a variety of different countries (including Sri Lanka, the Philippines, and Bangladesh). They are managed by a small group of U.S. supervisors and perform their jobs less expensively than the U.S. military would.

Table 3.3
Number of contractor personnel working in the Iraq theater, by department agency awarding the contract, 2008

	Location	U.S. citizens	Local nationals	Third-country nationals	Total
Department of Defense	Iraq	29,400	62,800	57,300	149,400
	Elsewhere in the Iraq theater	6,700	3,500	20,100	30,300
Department of State	Iraq	2,300	1,300	3,100	6,700
U.S. Agency for International Development	Iraq	200	2,900	300	3,500
Other agencies	Iraq	200	100	200	500
Total	Iraq theater	38,700	70,500	81,000	190,200

Source: Congressional Budget Office, based on data from U.S. Central Command, "Second Quarter Contract Census Report," Department of State, U.S. Agency for International Development, April 30, 2008.

The data in table 3.3 also show that the Iraq theater operations are made up of multiagency participants. Operations that aim to achieve stability and reconstruction require both hard and soft efforts (often in nondefense roles). The environment is very different from Europe after World War II, which was rebuilt via the Marshall Plan, but it still combines military with humanitarian objectives. As Theodore Roosevelt put it: "Our chief usefulness to humanity rests on our combining power with high purpose."[76] The table does not include the subcontractors working for the State Department or for the U.S. Agency for International Development, but it does include under "Other agencies" contractors supporting the Departments of Agriculture, Commerce, Health and Human Services, Interior, Justice, Transportation, and Treasury as well as the General Services Administration. As an example of what these people do, in Bosnia and Kosovo in fiscal year 1999, 100 percent of the maintenance, food service, laundry, sewage, hazardous material, mail, water, fuel, and heavy equipment transportation and over 70 percent of construction were supplied by support contractors.[77]

A more inclusive listing of contractors in the overall Central Command operations (including Iraq and Afghanistan) and subcontractors working for USAID is shown in table 3.4.

Here, the total rises to 265,000 contractors, and again, U.S. nationals, Iraqis, and third-country nationals are shown. This table presents them by function as well.

Table 3.4
Contractors and functional areas in central command operations, 2007 to 2008

	Agency and numbers	Composition
Reconstruction	Department of Defense, 25,000	Mostly Iraqis
	State Department (USAID), 79,100	
Logistics and base support	DoD, 139,000	U.S. 24%, third-country nationals (TCNs) 49%, Iraqis 27%
	State, 1,300	
Interpreters	DoD, 6,600	Mix of U.S., TCNs, Iraqis
	State, 100	
Advisers and other	DoD, 2,000	U.S. and some TCNs
	State, 2,200	
Security (excluding bodyguards)	DoD, 6,300	Mostly TCNs and some Iraqis
	State, 1,500	
Bodyguards	DoD, 700	U.S. and U.K.
	State, 1,300	
Totals	DoD, 181,600	U.S. 15%, TCNs 30%, Iraqis 55%
	State, 85,500	
	Total, 267,100	

Sources: Data from Congressional Budget Office, *Contractors' Support of U.S. Operations in Iraq* (Washington, DC: Congressional Budget Office, August 2008); Jennifer K. Elsea, Moshe Schwartz, and Kennon H. Nakamura, *Private Security Contractors in Iraq: Background, Legal Status, and Other Issues* (Washington, DC: Congressional Research Service, July 11, 2007); Jack Bell, deputy undersecretary of defense for logistics and materiel readiness, Testimony before the U.S. Senate Committee on Homeland Security and Governmental Affairs, February 27, 2008; John J. Young, undersecretary of defense for acquisition, technology, and logistics, Testimony before the House Appropriations Subcommittee on Defense, March 4, 2008; Department of Defense, "Report on DoD-Funded Service Contracts in Forward Areas," July 2007; T. Christian Miller, "Contractors Outnumber Troops in Iraq," *Los Angeles Times*, July 4, 2007. Figures include subcontractors for the U.S. Agency for International Development but exclude contractors working for the intelligence community. Figures also exclude informal tribal arrangements such as Sons of Iraq local security forces.

As shown in table 3.4, a major share of contracting activity has to do with logistics and base operations support. To get a feeling for the magnitude of this work, consider the following: "A year after entering the theater, KBR [the contractor] had 24,000 employees and subcontracted personnel working in Iraq and Kuwait. In one six-month period, they delivered and installed 34,000 living-container units [tents or barracks], 10,000 toilets and 10,000 showers to accommodate 80,000 soldiers. In less than a year, it opened 64 dining facilities and served 40 million meals. It annually processed a million bundles of laundry, disposed of 1.5 million cubit meters of trash, transported and delivered 13 million pounds of mail, moved 1 million equipment and supply containers from Kuwait to Iraq, and transported 1.8 billion liters of fuel. In order to accomplish its transportation function, they had to hire, mobilize, and train 1,500 certified heavy truck drivers."[78]

On the reconstruction side, twenty-nine Iraqi state-owned enterprises restarted their production operations by the end of February 2008, and forty-eight projects were in process to restart the Iraq industrial base in preparation for private investments. Over 3,900 private Iraqi businesses were registered in all industrial sectors, and three major private investments in large, state-owned industries were approved by the Iraqi government (for cement plants in Kirkuk, Muthanna, and Al Qain). Foreign investment teams were working on proposals for hotels, office construction, food processing, food services, and new industrial construction.[79]

Looking at the data in table 3.4, fewer than 10,000 of the 265,000 contractors are involved in security, and a small percentage (20 percent) of those 10,000 are involved in personal protection (the bodyguards who protect senior government officials when they go out into the field). The rest of the security functions are at fixed government installations. They carry guns but are limited to self-defense roles. This small group of contractors has received the most publicity and visibility. Many other security people are there as subcontractors to protect contractors doing reconstruction and to provide base support in an area where they are highly vulnerable. This work is not done by military personnel because military personnel are needed to fight the insurgency. The need for contractors to perform these functions was partially recognized by the Congress in the 2003 Defense Authorization Act, which allows contractors to be used in guarding military bases.[80]

Another listing of the functions that are performed by contractors, including examples of the contractors doing that work, is shown in table 3.5.

This table includes two significant functions that have not previously been observed. First, the training function involves working with the police and military of the countries in which the United States is involved. The goal is to introduce a highly desired stability. This function is increasingly important and usually is performed by retired military and police with the assistance of translators, where required. Second, the intelligence function involves contractors not as spies but as

Table 3.5
Types of support provided by U.S. contractors in Iraq, 2006

Type of support	Examples
Support to military forces	Food preparation (Kellogg Brown and Root), laundry, equipment maintenance
Restoration of services	Water, sewer, power, transportation, bridges, railways, airfields (Bechtel, Fluor)
Construction and reconstruction	Major facilities, hospitals, schools, oil refineries (Bechtel, Halliburton)
Civil affairs	Food distribution, training, election support, media (Fluor, DynCorp, Northrop Grumman)
Intelligence	Analysis of improvised explosive devise attacks, attacks on officials, primary danger areas (Kroll)
Security	Protection of officials, construction sites, housing areas, convoys, other contractors (Blackwater, Kroll)
Miscellaneous	Interrogation, interpretation, judicial training, legal support (L-3, Global Linguistics, CACI, Systex)

Source: Marion Bowman, "Privatizing While Transforming," *Defense Horizons* (July 2007): 3.

analysts. In insurgency operations, analysis in support of the intelligence data being received from multiple sensors around the country (both airborne and ground-based) is critical. This highly skilled and sensitive work requires security clearances and is a compliment to the work being done by the military and government-civilian security analysts. Because this is a sensitive area, these people are not included in the contractors listed in table 3.4. They are estimated to add 20,000 to 30,000 contractors to the totals in table 3.4.[81]

In general, having contractors in the combat zone supports the mission of the combatant commander. To do this, three forms of contracts are available—external support contracts, systems support contracts, and theater support contracts. Each of these has been given official DoD definitions.[82] Systems support involves the operation or maintenance of weapons, surveillance, targeting, or intelligence systems that are involved in deployed contingency operations. Most contractors in this category are associated with the major weapon systems being used in the expeditionary operations. These people tend to do work similar to what they do back in the United States, although the environment is significantly different. For example, the Lockheed Martin maintenance people in Iraq found that they were under mortar fire for 180 consecutive days.[83] The external support contracts began when the army in the mid-1980s recognized that as forces were being drawn down, there was a need for contractor support in contingency operations to surge as required. A policy was initiated that called for army components to plan and contract for logistics and engineering services for worldwide contingency operations.[84] In 1985, the official contract for implementing this was the Logistics Civil Augmentation Program (LOGCAP), and its first use was in 1989 in the Balkans. In the 1990s, the navy and the air force followed the army's lead and entered into worldwide blanket contracts to provide certain types of support for contingency operations as well. These were known as Air Force Contract Augmentation Program (AFCAP) and Contingency Construction Capabilities (CONCAP), respectively.[85] Finally, theater support contracts may provide many of the same supplies and services as external support contracts but are under the direct control of the theater commander (unlike the external support contracts, which are usually run through contracts issued in the United States). All three types of contracts are considered to be contingency contracting, and under certain wartime conditions, expeditious treatment is required to respond rapidly to an urgent need. Under certain circumstances, the typical terms and conditions of the Federal Acquisition Regulations can be waived to meet these rapid-response needs.

The largest of these contingency contracts is the Army's LOGCAP. Although it is periodically recompeted, it is an ongoing contract "for the use of civilian contractors to perform selected services, in wartime, to augment Army forces" and to "release military units for other missions or [to] fill shortfalls." The original concept was simple.[86] The contractor would keep a list of willing and qualified personnel and would have the ability to recruit these individuals rapidly. In peacetime, there would essentially be no cost to the government, not even the training and personnel costs associated with reserve units. When a conflict occurred and the military needed augmentation, the contractor would provide personnel with specified skills at the required locations. Because the contract was already in place, this augmentation could happen quickly. Since the army is the executive agent in Iraq and Afghanistan, the LOGCAP contract is the one that has become most familiar. From 2003 to 2007, the LOGCAP contract received obligations for logistics support, construction, petroleum products, and food totaling $22 billion.[87] In general, this contract has been found to be of great value (as testified to by the army, for the results from both Bosnia and from Iraq and Afghanistan).[88] For Bosnia alone (which was significantly smaller than the Iraq and Afghanistan activities), the contractor, Brown and Root (which later became a part of KBR), hired about 6,700 workers to perform tasks that would have required 8,500 troops, and the army is estimated to have saved $140 million. The LOGCAP contract explicitly covers only support functions and no functions "that would jeopardize [the contractor's] role as a noncombatant." Thus, the intent of this contract is not to replace army soldiers in their combatant roles or government civilians or military in any functions that are inherently governmental. Nonetheless, it is extremely dangerous work. In fact, in

June 2006, KBR stated that ninety-five of their employees and subcontractors had been killed in Iraq, Kuwait, and Afghanistan, and an additional 430 workers and subcontractors were injured from hostile actions. Nonetheless, that year they had 165,000 perspective employees contact them about job opportunities in Iraq, Kuwait, and Afghanistan, and they stated that at that time they had over half a million resumes on file.[89] These were not the most dangerous jobs, since in many cases, they were done on protected bases (yet within the combat zone). The L-3 Services Group, which provided translators and interpreters for the army (who were frequently out in the open in the combat zone itself), suffered the worst casualties in Iraq, with 261 workers killed by the end of 2006 (including thirty-two in the last three months of that year). Many of these victims were Iraqis who were known to be working with Americans as translators and interpreters, and they were frequently assassinated in off-duty hours.[90]

Another highly dangerous function in Iraq has been truck driving.[91] A typical truck driver who made $30,000 a year in the United States could make more than $80,000 in Iraq, and if the driver stayed more than 330 days, he or she could also get a sizeable tax break. Again, most of the people who signed up for this were former military and were used to a wartime environment. Nonetheless, vehicles delivered supplies on a two-day trip across 425 miles of roadway, carrying fuel and other general supplies (such as weapons, uniforms, ammunition, and body armor) from Kuwait to a depot outside of Baghdad. They were subject to attack by insurgents at virtually any point along the way. In 2006, there were over 7,000 convoys of this sort, and over 600 of them were attacked (with roadside bombs, small arms fire, or mortars). These convoys were protected by convoy security teams. One contractor that supplied such support, ArmorGroup, in 2006 ran 1,184 convoys in Iraq and reported 450 hostile actions. It also noted that on the dangerous roads north of Baghdad, "you generally attract at least one incident every mission."[92]

Although it is difficult to get an overall account of the number of contractors killed in Iraq during this period, a tracking of some of the newspaper releases gives a feeling for the degree of danger in the area. For example, a *Washington Post* article on October 23, 2005,[93] stated that the number of non-Iraqi civilian contractors killed since the start of the war in April 2003 was 320, while a *Washington Post* article in December 2006 stated that "about 650 contractors had died in Iraq since 2003, according to Labor Department statistics" (and noted that these figures do not include subcontractors, which would substantially increase the figure).[94] A May 19, 2007, *New York Times* article noted that during the first quarter of 2007, 146 contract workers were killed in Iraq and that Labor Department statistics show that an additional 3,430 contractors filed claims for wounds or injuries occurring in Iraq in that same quarter.[95] On August 20, 2007, the *Washington Post* reported that Labor Department figures show 1,001 civilian contractors had died in Iraq as of

June 30, 2007.[96] Finally, an independent analysis by Steven Schooner stated that "as of June 2008 more than 1,350 civilian contractor personnel had died in Iraq and Afghanistan supporting [U.S.] efforts. And about 29,000 contractors had been injured, more than 8,300 seriously."[97] The risks of contractor death are high (perhaps approximately 25 percent of the deaths for military in actual combat operations), and the chances of significant injury are dramatically higher (perhaps twenty times as large). The number of U.S. citizens' deaths are approximately proportional to the ratio of U.S. citizens to Iraqi and third-party nationals covered by the support contracts—about 20 to 30 percent of the total.

Finally, most U.S. citizen contractors who are preparing to go into the war zone (if they are to spend thirty days or more there) receive a brief indoctrination at Fort Benning, Georgia, that includes medical exams, seminars on the region, and a thorough check on all needed documents. Nonetheless, in comparison with the detailed training that the military receive before going into the war zone, the training seems insufficient.[98]

Contractor Issues to Be Addressed

When a contractor population that is essentially equal to or greater than that of the military forces operates in a combat zone like Iraq or Afghanistan, a significant number of issues are raised that must be addressed for future such operations.

Expeditionary Contracting   The first government procurement people who were involved in the expeditionary operations in Iraq and Afghanistan were trained according to the standard Federal Acquisition Regulations (FAR) and detailed federal procurement practices—as they are implemented in the United States. When the combatant commander asked them to do something "immediately," the procurement people responded by saying, "Yes, sir, but we will have to first spend a few months getting agreement on the details of the request for proposal. Then the contractors need a few months for their response, and the detailed source selection procedures need a few months. At that point, we need to conduct final negotiations with the winning contractor." Needless to say, this lengthy process caused significant problems. Similarly, there were a multitude of FAR requirements to satisfy—such as the Buy American Act, the small and minority business requirements (as well as requirements about women-owned businesses, which rarely exist in that part of the world), the specialized cost-accounting requirements, the "instant" audit requirements, the security issues, the occupational safety requirements, and the export control compliance rules. In addition, there were the problems of dealing with the cash economy and the extremely high life and medical insurance costs for people operating in a war zone. Perhaps most important, the contracts, in most cases, were being administered back in the United States, while the people writing the requirements and those doing the work were in the war zone. Finally, in 2008, a manual on expeditionary contracting was issued that incorporated all of the special clauses in the FAR that allowed for exceptions under wartime conditions. At that point, the contracting people who were going to go to the war zone needed to be trained in these clauses.

Who Is in Charge?   According to military principles of war, unity of command is critical. However, in normal contract operations, any task that is added to a contract has to be done through a modification of the contract by the contracting officer. In most of the expeditionary contracts (for example, in the case of the LOGCAP contract), the contracting officer resides in the United States, and army policy clearly states (in "Contractors Accompanying the Force," Army Regulation 715-9) that "contractor employees are not under the direct supervision of military personnel in the chain of command." There is an opportunity here for considerable ambiguity.[99] For example, at the Abu Ghraib prison,[100] contractor employees assisted the military in interrogation of prisoners; and soldiers, including officers, thought that contractors were in the chain of command. The same belief was held by a U.S. Army spokesperson in Washington, who stated that civilian contractors at Abu Ghraib and elsewhere "fall in line with the current command structure" and are treated just like regular army personnel.[101] A spokesperson for the contractor involved made a somewhat similar statement: "all CACI employees work under the monitoring of the U.S. military chain of command in Iraq."[102] Under extreme circumstances, such as war, it is difficult to get contract modifications approved in the United States (which is also on a different time zone) when something is needed immediately. Thus, chain-of-command issues must be clarified in the future.

Military Responsibility for the Contractors   Related to the above-noted point is the question of the responsibility of the military for the contractors. For example, is the military responsible, in any way, for personnel protection of the nonmilitary personnel? Is it responsible for tracking nonmilitary personnel (which, if not, may make the latter vulnerable to "friendly kills")? Is it responsible for planning and training contractors in their stability and reconstruction operations? Is it responsible for recovering civilians who are wounded while in the war zone? (And contractors tend to be more vulnerable than military because they have fewer restrictions on their travel than the military do.)[103]

Will Contractors Simply Walk Away?   Military personnel can be court-martialed for leaving the battlefield, and initially, it was believed that contractor personnel might "run if under fire" since the worst that could happen is that they would not be paid for breaking the contract. Perhaps because many of these personnel were former military, there were almost no reported incidences in which contractors did not perform their assigned duties, either at the individual employee level or at the company level. In one case, a corporation decided not to renew its contract because of the environment. Bechtel said that when it was awarded its original contract in 2003, it was "assured the company would have a safe environment for its workers." But after three years, fifty-two of its people had been killed, and much of its work had been sabotaged as Iraq dissolved into insurgency and sectarian violence. Some employees and subcontractors had been kidnapped, others dragged from their offices and shot, and a significant number had been wounded. Bechtel therefore chose not to renew its contract.[104] It had received $2.3 billion for its work over that three-year period (for work on roads, power plants, waterworks, and other construction activities)—which was the typical business that the company does worldwide—so it was not easy to walk away from a follow-on contract of this sort, even though the company felt that working conditions warranted it. Other contractors would step in to do that work on the next contract, however, because it was lucrative. From 2003 to 2007, the United States awarded $85 billion in contracts for reconstruction operations in Iraq.[105]

Compensation for Government Civilian Volunteers   In the contracting area, most army contracting people are government civilians. Only 3 percent of the contracting personnel are regular army. So when contracting is required in the combat zone, civilians are asked to "volunteer" to go. For Iraq and Afghanistan, they actually have been discouraged by their bosses from going since their allotted slots would not be back-filled. The managers in the United States were experiencing a significant increase in contracts during the buildup and were reluctant to let their employees volunteer to go overseas. In addition, the volunteers would not have their personal life insurance covered in the event of death from war (since most civilian policies have a war exclusion clause). They would not receive long-term medical coverage (as the military did), and their total compensation would be limited by Congress (even though they were expected to work seven-day weeks, twenty-four hours a day). All of this work is done under extremely hazardous conditions. Those people who do volunteer to serve under such dangerous conditions are dedicated and very competent, but many required positions cannot be filled. This is another area that needs to receive congressional attention for the future. Proper procedures would be to have a set of prevolunteered personnel who would go to the battlefield when needed—in a sense, like the ready reserve (and many of them could come from the reserves). Pay and benefits provisions would be previously worked out and available on a stand-by basis, and these people would be trained to do expeditionary contracting.

Contractors Doing Inherently Governmental Work   According to the Joint Chiefs of Staff's "Operational Contract Support" document, "There are some functions considered inherently governmental functions that should not be contracted, or it should be contracted with great caution. Most combat support and sustainment functions can be partially or fully contracted. Some specific functions are deemed inherently governmental. These include combat operations, contract awards, and supervision of military members and DoD civilians. Importantly, contractors are prohibited from taking a direct or active part in hostilities."[106] This does not prohibit contractors from supporting functions that are inherently governmental. For example, because there was a shortage of government contracting personnel, government employees would be the final party to sign the contract, but they could be assisted by contractors as long as they had no conflicts of interests (personal or corporate) with the contractor that was going to do the work. Nonetheless, in view of the large number of different contractors and subcontractors involved in the operation and the urgency under which many activities took place, government personnel supervising these activities had to ensure that no conflicts of interests were present and that contractors were not doing inherently governmental work. As with the chain-of-command issues described above, it can be hard to distinguish which functions are inherently governmental and which can be done by the contractors—especially under emergency conditions.

Rights of Contractors under the 1949 Geneva Convention   Under the Geneva Convention, "Persons who accompany the Armed Forces, without actually being members thereof, such as . . . contractors, who fall into the hands of the enemy, and whom the latter think fit to detain, shall be entitled to be treated as prisoners of war, provided they have received authority from the Armed Forces which they accompany, who shall provide them for that purpose with an identity card." The rules are clear, but whether insurgents would honor them is uncertain. Similarly, there was confusion about whether contractors were exempt from Iraqi law. In theory, authorities exist for applying U.S. law under the Military Extra-Territorial Jurisdiction Act (MEJA) or the Uniform Code of Military Justice (UCMJ), but these authorities had not been exercised before the Iraq and Afghanistan wars, and mechanisms for applying them did not exist. The only remedy seemed to be to fire the individuals involved and ship them out of theater if they violated any laws.[107] To clarify this, Congress amended the UCMJ to cover civilians in support of military operations, and the Department of Defense issued the necessary implementation guidelines. Legal action against contractors can now be taken—by either the Department of Justice under MEJA or by DoD under the UCMJ. The first such court-martial occurred in June 2008.[108]

Can Contractors Carry Guns?   The issue of contractors and guns is an area of great ambiguity. If contractors with guns are captured, are they taking part in combat? Who is allowed to carry a gun for self-defense? What are the rules of engagement? These issues apply to contractors who perform security in bodyguard functions and also to the far larger number of contractors who are in harm's way (when they drive through dangerous areas to perform logistics functions, accompany troops for translation, or participate in reconstruction in dangerous areas). In October 2005, the Department of Defense attempted to clarify some of these questions by issuing instructions that essentially said that the military commander is to decide whether contractors can wear military clothing and carry government-issued or privately owned weapons.[109] Thus, even for self-protection, contractors must have the express permission of a combatant commander to be armed.[110] The decision by the combatant commander is to be based on whether the DoD contractor employees are at risk of physical harm and whether military forces can adequately protect the contractor employee (on an individual basis). If not, then the contractors can be armed to provide for their safety in dangerous situations. One condition for arming contractors is that they are eligible to possess weapons under U.S. law or under the laws of their home nation (for example, they need to have proper training in the use of the weapons and have no prior felony convictions). With the exception of contractor personnel performing certain security functions, the policy limits contractor employees to carrying only a pistol. (As of February 28, 2008, 638 contractor employees in Iraq and Afghanistan and about 200 DoD civilians were armed for self-defense).[111] Even contractors who perform private security functions, however, are subject to rules of the use of force that are more restrictive than the rules of engagement governing military forces. They are not allowed to engage in any offensive military operations. As of April 2008, 5,613 of DoD's security contractor personnel in Iraq were authorized to be armed with small arms similar to those used by infantry soldiers.

Funding Flexibility   A major problem that occurred in the large LOGCAP contract during these expeditionary and expedited operations was that contractors often were asked to do work for which they were not yet funded and for which funds were flowing slowly into the war zone from the United States. To be responsive to the combatant commander's requests, contractors often were asked to put up large amounts of their own money to get the tasks done on time while waiting for the government to modify the contract and release the funds. In one year, there were 141 modifications to the LOGCAP contract simply for funding releases. This problem was recognized during the Balkans operation, and Congress approved an "overseas contingency operation transfer fund" that allowed flexibility in the field for using funds in a variety of ways. For example, dollars could be shifted from "procurement" to "operations and maintenance" as long as there was immediate follow-up reporting to the DoD and to Congress on the actual use of the funds after the fact. Such flexibility did not exist in the large LOGCAP contract or other similar contracts in Iraq and Afghanistan, and stand-by waivers did not initially exist on such things as Buy American. So there were both legal and financial barriers to operating effectively and efficiently under these wartime conditions, and this must be corrected in future operations. Such flexibility does exist for USAID, but it has not existed for the much larger DoD funds associated with wartime operations.[112]

Multiagency Operations   In the war zones of Iraq and Afghanistan, there are multiple U.S. military services (in joint operations among the army, navy, air force, and marines), multinational militaries (with a subsequent need for coordinated multinational military efforts), and various U.S. agencies (the Department of Defense and the State Department, including USAID). At one point, DoD and State were paying different salaries to local workers and competing for their services. But more critical was the need for coordinated efforts on contracting and on stability and reconstruction efforts. In fact, the poor coordination of efforts to restart the Iraq economy and increase employment opportunities ultimately "sowed the seeds of economic malaise, and fueled insurgency sympathies."[113] Most critical was the need for coordination of the private security contractors that each agency was using. Finally, in May 2007, a "Memorandum of Agreement" was signed between the Department of Defense and the Department of State, and it outlined how U.S. government private security contractors were to be controlled in the war zone so that the rules would be common for all those involved.[114] There is still a long way to go in coordinating between the State Department and DoD for future expeditionary political and military operations. If these are to be successful, they must be planned and exercised in a coordinated fashion beforehand. Initial steps in the right direction are being taken by the new Command for Africa and by the Southern Command, which have asked that State Department deputies be assigned and that all planning and exercising that is required for an efficient operation under emergency conditions be done in advance. To do this, the State Department will undoubtedly require additional resources, and Congress will need to provide these (in both dollars and personnel). In testimony before the Senate's Homeland Security Subcommittee and Government Affairs Subcommittee, Stuart Bowen Jr., special inspector general for Iraq reconstruction, stated that "the contracting process in Iraq suffered from a tapestry of regulations applied by diverse agencies, which caused inconsistencies and inefficiencies that inhibited management and oversight."[115]

Three Major Personnel Issues: Contracting Personnel, Security Personnel, and Government and Contractor Cost Comparisons

Contracting Personnel   By late 2007, over ninety accusations of fraud and other illegal actions had been made against contractors in the Iraq and Afghanistan theater. Nonetheless, the special inspector general for Iraq reconstruction observed that the number of examples involved a relatively small percentage of the overall reconstruction investments and relatively few individuals.[116] There also were examples of equipment unaccountability and examples of potential inappropriate action on private security contracts. Special taskforces were set up to address these three issues. The Department of Defense established a special commission to look into "how to prevent such obvious contracting problems in the future" (by making institutional changes). The Commission on Army Acquisition and Program Management in Expeditionary Operations[117] found that the contracting people in Iraq and Afghanistan were unprepared for expeditionary operations, for large numbers of contracts and contractors, for expedited conditions, and for very dangerous conditions. Over a hundred interviews were conducted, and interviewees made comments such as these: "I can't get certified Army personnel (civilian or military) to fill my contracting needs." "Only 38 percent of those in contracting positions, in theater, are certified for the positions they hold." "In theater, we had lots of people in Washington telling us the rules but little sense of urgency." "We're not trained as we fight." "In theater, we had no ability to do pricing or contract closeouts." "We need to have a section in every leadership course [for combatant commanders] on contracting and contractors." "Next time I go overseas, I don't want it to be *ad hoc*." "Contracting for expeditionary services requires far greater sophistication." "We are deploying government civilians to the theater based on personnel rules established thirty to forty years ago."

The commission found that the army's contracting workload during this buildup period grew by a factor of seven but that the workforce itself was dramatically down as a result of post–cold war choices that were made between combat forces and support (civilian and military) forces. For example, from 2001 to 2006, the Army Material Command's contracting actions (the AMC is responsible for the army's buying activities) grew by 653 percent, the dollars it spent grew by 331 percent, but contracting personnel were down by 53 percent. The problem was not auditors (there were more auditors than contracting personnel in theater). The problem was too few people, too little training for this special environment, and too little value placed on the importance of the contracting function by senior army personnel (even though 50 percent of the total force was contractors). As a result of the overall force drawdown in the post–cold war period, many upper-level positions—all five general officer positions in the army that required contract background, the four general officer positions in the Defense Contract Management

Agency, and half of the general officer and senior positions in the navy and air force—were eliminated. These eliminations showed the low priority that was given to this area. One particular concern was the postaward period, where the government's contract management had to ensure that the work was being done on time, for the cost bid, and with the required quality. Here, military personnel were being asked to perform that function as a secondary duty with no training. In addition, the Defense Contract Management Agency, which performed that function for weapons buying in the United States, was not responsible for this function in the war zone and had itself been drawn down from 25,000 people to 10,000.

Changes were required for military operations, both in Iraq and Afghanistan and in future activities of a similar nature. Fortunately, both the army and Congress recognized the need for change and began to take actions consistent with those recommended by the commission. Particularly critical among these recommendations was the need for the expeditionary organizations to have senior military officers who had contracting backgrounds (and experience in planning, training, and operations). Since these are wartime conditions and under military command, people in uniform have a significant role to play. Additionally, these senior positions need to exist before junior people will choose to follow career paths in this direction.

Security Personnel   Contractor security personnel are the most controversial of over 265,000 contractor positions. According to table 3.4, they number around 10,000 personnel, but other estimates place them at closer to 20,000.[118] Only about two-thirds are armed, and most are non-Iraqi, uniformed, and often indistinguishable from military personnel.[119] Nonetheless, a few incidences have caught the media's attention. For example, in Baghdad, on September 16, 2007, security guards, in an effort to escape from a car-bomb threat, were alleged to have fired on innocent civilians, killing and injuring dozens.

There is a great deal of misunderstanding about the function of these security personnel. About three-fourths of them protect fixed facilities inside major bases and never venture outside the wire. This function received a significant increase when, in 2005, there was a suicide bombing at a dining facility in Mosul, which highlighted the need to screen personnel who enter heavily populated facilities. Although some of these internal security personnel are military, the majority are contractors—generally, third-country nationals. For example, Salvadorians guard the U.S. Agency for International Development Compound in the Green Zone, while Ugandans guard facilities for the Marine Corps. Their main function is to screen personnel entering facilities, which is done by checking identity cards. Most people in this group have never fired a shot in anger, and they are similar to the security guards who work guarding U.S. banks and shopping malls at home.

However, the bodyguards (or personal security details) have generated the greatest controversy. As noted in table 3.4, there are about two thousand of these in the combat area (considerably less than 1 percent of all the contractors). Yet they are responsible for virtually all of the violent incidences that are reported in the media. These personal security contractors come from a group of over sixty multinational firms,[120] including Triple Canopy, Dyn-Corp, International, Aegis Security, and the now-famous Blackwater USA.[121] The security workers are frequently referred to as private-sector soldiers or even rogue mercenaries (as *Fortune* magazine called them in its May 2004 edition).[122] They are highly professional, highly trained, and almost always former military. Nonetheless, their work is controversial. Most of them work for the State Department and, until the agreement between DoD and the State Department (noted above), have been outside of any military control (see table 3.4).

Historically, the State Department has had three layers of security for its personnel. The first is through the host nation (which is responsible for the protection of all diplomats and diplomatic facilities in its territory). The second is the marine detachment that normally guards the core of the fixed facility. Contrary to many beliefs, the marine embassy detachment does not provide bodyguards for diplomats. It guards the facilities and U.S. citizens and property within embassies. The third layer is that of the contract guards who, within Iraq, have had to expand considerably because diplomats require protection whenever they leave the diplomatic facilities. The 2004 ambush of Blackwater guards in Fallujah, where four guards were killed and their bodies hung from a bridge, occurred, in part, because Blackwater had not coordinated with local military authorities. The guards' job is to protect "the principle" [the guarded employee] at all costs, and this means against the insurgency efforts. Blackwater, for example, prides itself on never having lost "a principle." For bodyguards, this is the only measure of effectiveness. Unfortunately, the lack of coordination with the DoD and the so-called bodyguard mindset led to the shooting incident of September 16, 2007, in which a number of Iraqi citizens were killed and wounded. This led the State Department to issue new guidelines that brought contractors under military control, required State Department security officials to accompany every embassy convoy, and issued rules on the use of force by bodyguards. In an environment in which State Department personnel are exposed to rioting crowds and insurrectionists, body guards have a particularly difficult job maintaining adequate control and doing their job. The sooner the desired level of stability can be achieved in any country and in any future operation, the better these issues can be resolved. Although few civilian deaths by contractors have occurred, they receive heightened attention from the press and the Congress, and they need to be minimized.

Government and Contractor Cost Comparisons   The Congressional Budget Office compared costs between government personnel and contractor security personnel and stated that "the cost of a private security contract is comparable to those of a U.S. military unit performing similar functions. During peacetime, however, the private security contract would not have to be renewed, whereas the military unit would remain in the force structure."[123] Some people assume that because the hourly rate for military personnel is much lower than the rate for private contractors, that it would be much cheaper to use military personnel for these functions. However, the cost of the contractor includes all overhead costs and equipment costs, and they are hired only for the time period of the effort—with their retirement contributions, medical insurance coverage, and so on included. On the other hand, military personnel hourly rates do not include all of the "tail" that goes along with them (in terms of medical coverage, retirement, hostile-fire pay, life insurance, family separation allowances, administrative support in theater, postservice veterans benefits, in-service education, midtour or home leave, and training leave). Military rates also do not include the equipment to support military personnel or the overhead associated with their management. Most important, military personnel operate on a rotation basis. At any given time, a second person will be in training to replace the current service member, and in many cases, a third person will be on rotation leave. So for each soldier deployed, between 1.2 and 2.0 additional soldiers at home need to be charged against that position (which is not the case for the contractors). As is noted in table 3.3, most security personnel (excluding the bodyguards) are third-country nationals, who are generally paid much less than U.S. personnel (civilian or military). The Congressional Budget Office analysis concluded that the cost of having military units replace contractors over the long term would cost 90 percent more than using contractors and would have high up-front costs associated with equipping the new units.[124] The big advantage in using contractors is that when they are no longer needed, the costs terminate. Military personnel remain in service, and their costs continue (usually for twenty years)—whether or not there is war.

Summary of Contractors in the Combat Zone

As Defense Secretary Gates notes in his 2009 article in *Foreign Affairs*,[125] the environment that the United States has experienced in the Iraq and Afghanistan wars is likely to be similar to the environment in which future military operations will be conducted (although traditional force-on-force, nation-versus-nation conflict could also occur in the future). The country needs to recognize that this type of scenario is realistic for the future and that perhaps 50 percent of the total force will be contractors (for the reasons described above). This was recognized by the Department of Defense in its *Quadrennial Defense Review of 2006*, where it stated that "the Department's total force—its active and reserve military components, its civil servants, and its contractors—constitutes its war-fighting capability and capacity."[126] The culture—its organization, doctrine, planning, and exercises—must change to make such activities the norm, and the "culture change" literature shows that two things are required.[127] First, there must be a recognition of the need for change (which the Iraq and Afghanistan experiences have demonstrated), and second, leadership needs to have a vision, strategy, and set of actions that can make the change happen. Defense Secretary Gates, the services, and the Congress have initiated such efforts. In January 2008, Secretary of the Army Pete Geren ordered the establishment of the U.S. Army Contracting Command "to provide a more effective structure through which to execute expeditionary contracting efforts."[128] The Congress passed the National Defense Authorization Act for Fiscal Year 2008, which in section 849 (on contingency contracts and training for personnel outside the acquisition workforce and evaluations of army commission recommendations) directs implementation of many of the commission's recommendations. Additionally, in a 2007 editorial, Senator Richard Lugar and then-Secretary of State Condoleezza Rice asked for a civilian "reconstruction reserve" to be established. It would be similar to the military reserve but could be called up (as President Bush stated in his 2007 state of the union address) to "ease the burden of the Armed Forces by allowing us to hire civilians with critical skills to serve on missions abroad when America needs them."[129] This initiative is supported by both the DoD and the State Department. In many ways, this is similar to the "sponsored reserve" that the United Kingdom has. Under this sponsored-reserve concept, services that contractors normally provide in peacetime are provided for expeditionary operations by members of the contractor's workforce who are also reservist members of the armed forces.[130] The contractor maintains a workforce of people who have volunteered to become members of a reserve force. In a number of ways, this addresses some of the key issues described above, since these employees are prevolunteered and become part of the military chain of command after they are called up. Although the United States should not limit itself to the United Kingdom's model of sponsored reserves or to Lugar and Rice's suggestions, some steps need to be taken in this direction so that the United States will be able to function efficiently and effectively in future operations.

Key Elements of Future U.S. Security Leadership

U.S. security leadership in the twenty-first century has eight key objectives:

1. Maintain a strong U.S. economy. Without it, national security struggles in a competition for federal dollars.

2. Plan and implement effective interagency operations and training.

3. Build international partnerships focused on common interests. All twenty-first-century security issues require multinational solutions.

4. Shift focus and resources to twenty-first-century threats, conflicts, and post-conflicts. This shift is needed to correct the strategy and resources mismatch.

5. Maintain technological leadership. This leadership is critical for both long-term economic competitiveness and for national security, and it requires agility and rapid responsiveness.

6. Prepare for and expect to deal with uncertainty. Uncertainty is a principal characteristic of twenty-first-century security.

7. Take full advantage of commercial and foreign-military globalized technology.

8. Focus on people. Military and civilian security leaders are critical to the nation's future security, and government and contractor personnel on the battlefield must be trained and rewarded for the jobs they do.

Implementing these eight key requirements effectively and affordably will not be easy and will take time. But they are essential if the nation is to maintain its security leadership throughout the twenty-first century.

4

Characteristics of the Defense Industry in the Early Twenty-First Century

The Structure of the Defense Industry

Because government and commercial markets are different in terms of regulation, political involvement, unique contracting, specialized cost accounting, and buyer concentration, firms that operate in both sectors tend to separate their government and commercial operations into separate divisions and profit centers. Of interest here is the government sector, particularly the federal portion of it. But in the twenty-first century, there is growing interest in breaking down the legislative and regulatory barriers that have artificially forced separated defense and commercial operations and, instead to encourage dual-use industrial operations.

In 2007, federal procurement in the United States was more than $400 billion dollars a year and involved over 169,000 different contractors.[1] However, only a few government contractors hold an overwhelming share of the dollars awarded, and the great majority of the firms supplying goods and services to the federal government are small businesses. For example, in the services business (almost 69,000 firms in 2005),[2] over 70 percent of the firms are small businesses (as defined by the U.S. government).[3] In spite of the large number of firms involved in the federal marketplace, the concentration of firms is high, particularly in the defense sector (which is by far the largest of the federal sectors). In 2005, the share of defense dollars going to the top twenty-five firms was 85 percent of research and development, 70 percent of services, and 74 percent of hardware procurement dollars.[4] As shown in table 4.1 (for fiscal year 2006), the top ten firms captured 36 percent of all Department of Defense contracts and approximately 30 percent of all of the federal government contracts. There is a high correlation between the ranking of the firms in the total federal marketplace and their position in the DoD marketplace—because of the dominance of the DoD in the total federal marketplace.[5]

The overall structure of the defense industrial base tends to be separated into product markets, such as aerospace, ships, and armaments (see figure 2.2) Although some firms function in multiple sectors, their operations tend to be separated due

Table 4.1
Top ten government contractors, fiscal year 2006 (billions U.S. dollars)

Government rank	Firm	Total	DoD	Civilian government	DoD rank
1	Lockheed Martin	$33.5	$27.3	$6.2	1
2	Boeing	$22.8	$20.9	$1.9	2
3	Northrop Grumman	$18.6	$16.8	$1.8	3
4	General Dynamics	$12.4	$11.5	$.88	4
5	Raytheon	$10.9	$10.4	$.51	5
6	KBR	$6	$6	$.02	6
7	L-3	$5.7	$5	$.62	7
8	SAIC	$5.3	$3.4	$1.9	10
9	United Technologies	$5.1	$4.6	$.56	8
10	BAE Systems	$4.7	$4.5	$.19	9
Total, top ten		$124.8	$110.3	$14.5	
Percent of total (top ten)		29%	36%	12%	

Source: Government Executive, August 15, 2007.

to major differences in their tasks (building a ship, for example, is very different from building an airplane). As a result, different products have different customers (one branch of the navy buys ships, for example, while another branch of the navy or air force buys aircraft). Thus, corporate executives tend to associate themselves with a specific product sector or even subsector of their business. For example, the aircraft carrier business for the navy has an industrial base coalition that represents that industry, and the industry itself consists of over two thousand companies in forty-six states that provide design, material, construction, maintenance, and services for aircraft carriers.[6] Yet at the prime contractor level, only one shipyard—Northrop Grumman's shipyard in Newport News, Virginia—is capable of building an aircraft carrier. This example illustrates the concentration at the prime contractor level (where there is one firm) and the wide diversity of firms as business moves down to the lower tiers. A single aircraft carrier costs more than $13 billion[7] (an amount that excludes the costs of the aircraft that go onto it), so there is plenty of money to go around.

In recent decades, the most dramatic structural change in the national security industry occurred during the enormous consolidation that took place in the post–cold war era as the Defense Department's budget plummeted (particularly in the procurement account). This period transformed the U.S. defense industry. When horizontal consolidation finally stopped, the handful of remaining large defense prime contractors shifted (with equal vengeance) to vertical integration (and even these began to attract the interest of antitrust regulators, who imposed a broad range of consent decrees restrictions) (see chapter 2).

After September 11, 2001, the U.S. defense budget grew rapidly, and foreign companies (particularly from Europe) began making significant investments and acquisitions in the U.S. market. The U.S. defense firms shifted, with the DoD demands, into supplying services (of a wide variety of types), systems-of-systems integration, and equipment support (as major business areas).

Perhaps the best way to see the overall structure of the current defense industry is to review it layer by layer, beginning at the top.

Prime Contractors

The top five defense firms (which were also the same top five for total federal government awards)—Lockheed Martin, Boeing, Northrop Grumman, General Dynamics, and Raytheon (see table 4.1)—had sales to the DoD of approximately $87 billion in 2006 (and an additional $11 billion from other federal agencies), which represented a growth for these five firms alone of over 40 percent in the decade from 1996 to 2006. But perhaps even more surprising is that, in that same decade, their volume of services income grew by 180 percent, and their research, development, testing, and evaluation (RDT&E) income grew by approximately 200 percent (the latter ensuring their future control over DoD dollars).[8] A part of this growth came through acquisitions, but the major share of the growth was stimulated by the significant increases in the Defense Department's budget in the post-9/11 period. Additionally, a significant cause of the growth among these few firms was attributable to the fact that there were only a few new major defense programs in development. Because they were captured by one of these five firms, the share of the total DoD business continues to be heavily concentrated.

As shown in table 4.2, a few large programs (such as the Joint Strike Fighter for the air force, navy, and marines, and the future combat system for the army) cause a great deal of concentration in the industry, especially since the aerospace and defense firms tend to outsource 50 percent less of their major assemblies and testing operations than the equivalent commercial-sector firms.[9]

The challenge for the Department of Defense is to maintain two or three firms in each major sector as the number of weapons' programs is significantly reduced. With only one firm in each sector, the potential for competition is eliminated. The government needs to address this potential danger continuously, and it has various techniques for doing so. For example, when there is only one firm in production in a given product area, a second firm can be awarded a next-generation program in that area to maintain the potential for future competition. The market also can be opened to include foreign firms. In addition, contracts can be awarded to both of

Table 4.2
Cost of the Defense Department's top five programs, fiscal years 2001 and 2006 (billions 2006 U.S. dollars)

2001		2006	
Program	Cost	Program	Cost
F/A-22 Raptor aircraft	$65.0	Joint Strike Fighter	$206.3
DDG-51 class destroyer	$64.4	Future combat system	$127.5
Virginia class submarine	$62.1	Virginia class submarine	$80.4
C-17 Globemaster airlifter	$51.1	DDG-51 class destroyer ship	$70.4
F/A-18E/F Super Hornet	$48.2	F/A-22 Raptor aircraft	$65.4
Total	$290.8	Total	$550.0

Source: Department of Defense data, 2007; GAO analysis and presentation, 2007.

the two remaining firms so that they can continuously compete—rather than going to a sole source after an initial down-select competition (see chapter 7 for a discussion of the benefits of continuous competition).

Unfortunately, although maintaining two sources in each critical area has many benefits (in terms of innovation, higher performance, and lower cost), the practice is not widely accepted. People continue to hope that "this time it will be different" and that the monopoly supplier will continuously strive to improve its performance while lowering its costs (in spite of the overwhelming empirical data to the contrary). Another way to maintain two or more sources is by using the higher volume of commercial-military integrated operations (in engineering, manufacturing, and support). However, in many product areas (such as missiles, fighter aircraft, large navy warships, and tanks), there is little commonality at the final assembly level.

Subcontractors and Parts Suppliers

Subcontractors and parts suppliers are often referred to as the "critical lower tiers" of the defense industrial base. When a warship is built, only 12 to 18 percent of the ship's cost goes to the shipbuilder (the prime contractor).[10] The big cost drivers (high-risk, high-technology, state-of-the-art elements) are subsystems, such as the command-and-control systems, the advanced radars, and the propulsion plants. Similarly, 70 to 80 percent of the costs and the high-risk elements in a missile system are not in the prime contractor's missile final assembly but in the electronics, sensors, and propulsion. Even in the production of advanced fighter aircraft, only about 20 percent of the cost goes directly to the aircraft producer. The big costs and high-risk items are usually in the subsystems, such as the avionics, sensors, and engines.

This lower-tier area also includes the basic parts and material suppliers. A critical issue is often the timely ability to obtain adequate quantities of parts and materials, especially when there is a surge in demand (a demand for a rapid increase in any given area). In the first Persian Gulf War, a large number of rockets were launched against Saudi Arabia and U.S. troops, and the U.S. response was to attempt to build more of the antimissile system Patriot II. Although the prime contractor (Raytheon) had ample production capability at its plant, the company did not have a sufficient quantity of semiconductor chips on hand to build the missile guidance systems, and there was an eighteen-month lead time for these critical parts. In the Iraq war, roadside bombs were planted by insurgents, which led to a U.S. decision to build armored, mine-resistant, ambush-protected (MRAP) vehicles. The lack of armor material—and not the limitation of the production capacity at the prime contractor level—contributed to years of delay in delivery of the vehicles.[11]

Part of the problem at the raw-materials level is that the defense industry often competes with the commercial economy for critical materials. Since the DoD's surges in demand are highly unpredictable, the DoD tends to be a far less predictable and dependable customer than commercial customers. Because of its high strength and light weight, titanium is increasingly being used in the aerospace and defense industry and for commercial aircraft. But there are a limited number of sources of the raw material (the principal source is Russia). In the case of nickel (imported from China for use in batteries), prices are rapidly rising, and the dependability of the sources may be a problem (even when the Defense Department has the legal right to exercise a priority (over commercial needs) on the materials if they are needed for national security reasons).

Congress recognized the importance of the nation's strategic dependence on foreign raw materials after World War II when it passed the Strategic and Critical Materials Stockpiling Act of 1946, with the intent of allowing the United States to stockpile critical and strategic materials for use in times of national emergency. By 1975, about $8 billion worth of materials was stockpiled, including chrome, titanium, , and castor oil.[12] These stockpiles are intended to be based on specific war scenarios. For the "short war" (which was the primary basis for U.S. planning in the late twentieth century), there was no need for investments in the critical materials stockpiles, but for longer scenarios, these investments have value. However, the dollars for material sales from these stockpiles go to the general (national) treasury, not to the DoD (and therefore sales from the stockpile could easily be used as a budget-balancing technique rather than being held for potential Defense Department needs).[13] Additionally, DoD requests for increases in the stockpiles require separate congressional action (and are therefore subject to political manipulation—since representatives and senators may participate in stockpile buying to support a firm within their district or state by stimulating demand for its products). In more recent times, Congress has used the strategic stockpile to obtain fuel, and the stockpile has been used more often for economic reasons than for military considerations. Finally, because of the great unpredictability of likely wartime scenarios in the twenty-first century (discussed above), it is also difficult to determine which materials should be stockpiled. This makes it more difficult to justify diverting billions of dollars to this insurance policy (at the raw-materials level) versus investing it in completed weapons systems that could be readily available for wartime crisis. The result has been a primary focus on final weapon systems rather than on stockpiling of parts and materials for increased demand or restricted supply in long-war scenarios.

At the government level and even at the prime-contractor level, there is often poor visibility regarding the availability of critical parts and materials. In 1983, the DoD officially stopped tracking critical parts that were awarded through various subcontracts and subsubcontracts. This fact was brought to light in 2007, when a proposed amendment to the Federal Acquisition Regulations required contractors to report (on a publicly available Web site) on any subcontracts that were awarded with federally appropriated funds.[14] But even this requirement was only for large subcontracts (over $1 million) and would not provide visibility at the parts and materials levels. As more and more parts and materials are dual-use and are used in both the commercial and military worlds, the DoD gains the advantage of the high volumes for commercial use, which lowers costs and increases reliability (since bugs can be worked out during the high-volume production process). This is particularly true in electronics and software, which are becoming a greater share of weapon systems' capability and costs. The DoD's semiconductors and software programs are being produced by the same companies that build microprocessors for personal computers, amplifiers for cell phones, and high-tech elements for cars and smart appliances. Defense benefits significantly from the lower costs and higher performance of such dual-use equipment. Thus, Congress has increasingly mandated greater use of commercial items. For example, sections 2377 and 2501 of title 10 of the United States Code, respectively, call for a "preference for acquisition of commercial items" and state that for "National Security objectives concerning national technology and industrial base: a Civil-Military integration policy (1) relying, to the maximum extent practicable, upon the commercial national technology and industrial base and (2) reducing the reliance of the DoD on technology and industrial base sectors that are economically dependent on DoD business and (3) reducing Federal government barriers to the use of commercial products, processors, and standards are highly desirable." Unfortunately, actual DoD practices have not been following this mandate. If they had done so, parts and materials would be readily available for DoD surge requirements, which could be satisfied by simply shifting commercial parts and materials from the commercial marketplace to the military marketplace. (The DoD has legal authority to do this by exercising its priority when parts and materials are required for urgent military needs.) Unfortunately, the government has created barriers to this desired commercial-military integration, such as highly specialized cost-accounting requirements. Another barrier is having the defense prime contractors pass on all defense-unique contractual and regulatory requirements to the lower tiers—so that the primes take on no added risk themselves (as they believe they might by allowing their subcontractors and suppliers greater flexibility). One final benefit that the DoD can realize through civil-military common use is that as lower-tier industrial dual-use and commercial suppliers make more profits, they will invest in more capital equipment and research and development and will not be as dependent as prime contractors and defense-unique lower-tier suppliers on the government to supply equipment and research investments. In 2006, lower-tier firms with a balanced DoD and commercial marketplace had a median return on sales of 12.6 percent—which is significantly higher than the profit for the large defense firms, so they could afford the investments.[15]

Small-Business Considerations

Innovation is critical for maintaining U.S. technological leadership. Innovation also helps to maintain the economic competitiveness of the nation and stimulates growth in the economy, allowing significant investment in the national security area. Studies have shown the many innovations made by small businesses.[16] These contributions have been significant in recent times, with the increase in consolidations at the large-firm level. It has been found that "in recent decades, 60–80% of all newly created jobs have been in small to medium sized companies (with fewer than 500 employees)."[17]

Because far greater innovation, per R&D dollar invested, has been seen coming from small firms, Congress established the Small Business Innovative Research (SBIR) program[18] in 1982. Before this date, a large share of the overall federal government's R&D budget had been going to the prime contractors and had not been passed on to the small businesses. The SBIR program mandated that 2.5 percent of all government, externally funded research and development must go to small businesses. Although many in the government community object to this mandate (claiming that it should be a voluntary allocation and even calling it a "tax" on their R&D program), the fact that it was mandated made it realizable. A similar program in the United Kingdom is voluntary and largely has not been realized.

The U.S. SBIR program has been extremely successful. It is a highly competitive program that begins when each government agency lists those areas where innovation is required to meet mission needs. Large numbers of proposals are received from small businesses, evaluated, and awarded in multiphased efforts—which increase in dollar value as their feasibility and effectiveness are demonstrated. (The program was described in detail in a series of National Academies Studies in 2007.)[19] Venture-capital firms note which small businesses are awarded SBIR contracts, since it demonstrates government interest and a potential market for these firms' products—thus encouraging further private-sector investment in them. All of these actions lead to the early realization of innovations (as commercial and government products), as intended by the legislation. The government also tries to find "homes for these innovations in future mission equipment" (such as in weapons systems for the Department of Defense), and similar efforts were made to encourage the success of a mentor and protégé program[20] in which the experience of larger firms (in managing innovation through its development and deployment phases) can assist small firms in realizing the commercialization benefits of their innovations.

Because most regions of the country have many small businesses, Congress's efforts to stimulate government funding to small businesses are attractive politically (and therefore equally subject to potential political abuses). Congress has mandated a 23 percent goal for small business contracting by the federal government, and by each agency. This is mandated at the direct government-contract level only, so subcontracts to small businesses do not count in these totals. Typically, the federal government has been meeting this goal. For example, in 2005 it achieved 25.4 percent,[21] in 2006 the total was 22.8 percent, and in 2007 it was 22 percent. The dollars awarded during this period (especially by the DoD) were rising rapidly and going primarily to the big prime contractors for equipment in the Iraq conflict. The actual dollars allocated to small businesses were rising, but their percentage was slightly declining. (Since the law establishes the percentage as a goal, there is no penalty for not achieving the legislative objective by any given agency or by the federal government.)[22]

Because small business set-asides are attractive politically, Congress continuously tries to raise the amount of the set-aside. In 2007, the House of Representatives passed the Small Business Fairness in Contracting Act (H.R. 1873) by a vote of 409 to 13. This attempted to increase the goal from 23 percent to 30 percent. Congress also has established numerous other such goals—a "small disadvantaged business" goal of 5 percent, a "minority-owned business" goal of 5 percent, a "woman-owned business" goal of 5 percent, and a "businesses located in historically underutilized areas" goal of 3 percent. These goals amount to very large dollar figures since they apply to the entire federal government. For example, in 2005, $79.6 billion was allocated to small businesses. Minority-owned small businesses received $10.5 billion in direct, government-contract awards; businesses in "historically underutilized areas" received $6.1 billion; women-owned small businesses received $10.5 billion; and service-disabled, veteran-owned businesses received $1.9 billion.[23]

One interesting example of special privileges can be found in the Small Business Administration's 8(a) program. The Alaska Native Corporations (ANCs) are exempt from the $3 million limit on sole-source contracts that is applied to other 8(a) businesses, and yet they count toward giving credit to an agency's small business goals.[24] This legislative flexibility allows many ANC firms to subcontract much of the work out to large non-Alaskan firms. In one case, the Energy Department gave an ANC firm an $80 million contract, and the firm planned to give most of the work to a large incumbent contractor, although the work could be sole-sourced to the ANC firm.[25] Since the law relates only to ownership and not to location of work, only 21 percent of the dollars awarded to ANC firms for fiscal years 2000 through 2008 was spent in Alaska.[26] In fiscal year 2008, this amounted to $3.9 billion. As a result of growing ANC abuses, more and more of the small-business set-aside dollars were going to the ANCs. In fiscal year 2008, obligations to ANC firms represented 26 percent of all 8(a) dollars, even though ANCs constituted just 2 percent of companies in the 8(a) program.[27] Congress went on to expand such privileges to native Hawaiian organizations and then to Indian tribes.[28]

Lower-Tier Concerns

Politically motivated legislation allows for considerable abuse through the use of "front" companies. These appear in various small business or special-interest categories. Large or medium-size firms are almost forced to be subcontractors to the small and special-interest firms to gain access to 25 to 30 percent of the total federal acquisition budget. An obvious corrective action would be to change the rules for counting awards to small business to include subcontracts to the small and historically disadvantaged businesses, thereby allowing subcontracts to be counted (perhaps even allowing for a larger percentage of the total business to be set as a goal, such as from 23 percent to 30 percent). In this way, Congress might also be able to use prime contractors to achieve the goal of small business set-asides, without abusing the intent (as now happens when a large subcontract to a major defense firm is made under a small business "front").

A second significant concern at the lower tiers of the defense industry has been increased vertical integration.[29] As noted above, the large defense firms have shifted to an acquisition strategy of vertical integration by acquiring firms at the lower tiers. One concern is that there is a reduced level of competition at the lower tiers, as the prime contractor chooses its own divisions for subcontracts. Another concern is that after a large firm acquires a small firm, there is reduced innovation. This is partly because the innovators from the small firm leave after the acquisition and partly because the large firm shows institutional resistance to new and sometimes disruptive innovations that are proposed by the former small business. The solution is to require the spinning off or deintegration of the innovative smaller divisions from the prime contractors, which could be encouraged by government procurement practices. Such actions can be stimulated through greater government oversight of the openness of the subcontractor selection process by the prime contractor (that is, the decision to make or buy). This government transparency should be explicitly specified in future source-selection criteria.[30]

Another growing concern at the lower tiers of the defense industry is the limitation on competition as one or two large corporations (and their preferred suppliers) win two or three contracts in a row, thus creating a diminishing-sources problem. This eliminates future competition and results in significant bottlenecks at the supplier base due to the limited capacity in the one or two remaining firms. For example, in a March 2008 analysis by the Department of Defense,[31] it was noted that such bottlenecks are appearing in nickel-hydrogen space batteries, K-band traveling wave tubes, and high-output solar cells.

When the U.S. Government Accountability Office (GAO) looked at the problem of diminishing sources in 2008, it found two significant issues. The government was often down to only a single supplier of a critical item, and in many cases, critical parts were no longer available for replacement because the government kept the systems for too long. In fact, of the twenty weapon-system programs that GAO reviewed, fifteen had critical items that were now available only from a single source. Eleven of the twenty programs had critical parts that were now obsolete and could not be obtained from any sources. In these cases, one would have to go back to the original development and recreate an obsolete part or completely redesign the system to be able to take new parts.[32] The DoD will need to have far greater visibility into its lower-tier supplier base to address these issues.

Foreign Sourcing

One way to address the diminishing sources of U.S. lower-tier defense suppliers and to gain the benefits of innovation taking place around the world is to search for potential foreign sources, which are often more advanced than U.S. sources. This would involve removing the barriers to the acquisition of items from these sources and also addressing any potential vulnerabilities that might result from these sources (through high visibility and monitoring of areas of foreign dependency in both hardware and software). Because most of these parts are dual-use, foreign espionage (even in U.S. plants)[33] needs to be addressed (even though the benefits of using foreign scientists and engineers in U.S. industry far outweigh the small risk associated with such concerns).

All U.S. weapon systems have foreign parts in them. A detailed study of this by the Office of the Secretary of Defense[34] examined twenty-one important U.S. weapons systems and identified seventy-three lower-tier foreign suppliers. The percentage of prime contract value varied. They ranged from one at 0.1 percent, to one at 12.5 percent. The average was 4.3 percent of the prime contract value. This DoD study found the following:

- "utilization of these foreign sources for the programs studied does not impact long-term readiness."
- "the identified foreign sources do not constitute a foreign vulnerability that poses a risk to national security."
- "at no time did the foreign suppliers restrict the provision or sale of these components to the Department because of U.S. military operations."
- "utilization of these foreign sources does not impact the economic viability of the national technology and industrial base."
- "in all but four instances domestic suppliers are available for the parts, components, and materials provided by the foreign sources."
- "the foreign subcontractors [were selected because] they offered the best combination of price, performance, and delivery."

Researchers also found that this study was consistent with prior studies. In October 2001, for example, a "Study on the Impact of Foreign Sourcing of Systems" found that subcontracts to foreign sources represented less than 2 percent of the value of all subcontracts for the programs. The report also noted that most foreign purchases were for subsistence, fuel, construction services, and other miscellaneous items. These results are also consistent with a 1999 Defense Science Board report on globalization and security, which stated that "globalization offers tremendous benefits to U.S. security that, if embraced by the Department of Defense, could counter the associated risks."[35] In 2005, the Heritage Foundation (a conservative think tank) published a report on "The Military Industrial Base in an Age of Globalization" that stated "not participating in the global defense marketplace will increase, not decrease, the risk to the U.S. . . . in providing the best systems, U.S. acquirers will look routinely beyond U.S. sources. This practice encourages innovation and provides better products at reduced costs. The question is not whether a given commodity, system or material is available from a U.S. company on U.S. soil, but whether these products are competitively available through the global marketplace."[36]

Nonetheless, the United States needs to have visibility into any dependency that it may have on foreign sources, though achieving this is becoming increasingly difficult as more of the lower tier elements are dual-use. Trey Hodgekins, the director of defense programs for the Information Technology Association of America, stated that "it's become very difficult to create an information technology product that is 51% American-sourced, simply because of the global marketplace of the industry."[37] A 2005 report from the Homeland Security Department's inspector general revealed that neither the department's contract database nor the federal procurement data system was able to track data about the origin of purchased products. A 2002 Defense Department inspector general audit of military purchases found that 67 percent lacked the required domestic sourcing requirement clauses.[38] For many subcontracted parts (from countries of trusted allies), changes in international conditions are going to require changes in the provisions associated with foreign purchases to avoid harming U.S. national security through legislative prohibitions on offshore purchases. Yet potential vulnerabilities can be introduced through such purchases, and specific steps must be taken to minimize them:[39]

- Sensitive data do not need to move offshore. The development and testing can be done offshore using dummy or scrambled data.
- Network elements on sensitive projects can be physically or virtually separate from the service providers' networks.
- Computer floppy drives, share drives, and USB connectors can be separated across the organization.
- Offshore projects may be conducted within physically enclosed areas that are accessible only to approved personnel (on whom detailed background checks have been performed).

Such offshore policies depend on five key concepts—personnel security, data security, network security, physical security, and policies and procedures.[40]

A Mix of Defense and Commercial

As the commercial world becomes increasingly high-technology oriented and dependent on information technology, commercial and military industrial structures would be expected to integrate. However, although the engineering and manufacturing may be similar, major (government-imposed) barriers strongly discourage the integration of commercial and military industrial operations. In fact, the barriers are so high that companies usually are forced to separate their military and commercial divisions. These barriers include the following:

- *Specialized cost-accounting requirements* As one CEO of an electronics company said, "I separate my two factories because the DoD wants to keep track of every single dollar expenditure against each part; while, in the commercial world, our objective is to reduce the cost of every part we produce." In other words, the DoD (through its legislative mandates) is concerned about accounting for the costs embedded into every item produced, while commercial businesses are concerned about the final price that they pay. Because the DoD focuses on trust and the commercial world tries to minimize what items cost to produce, the Department of Defense pays significantly more for parts to be sure that it has total visibility into all costs. This results in extensive increased overhead for these specialized cost-accounting rules and tracking systems. The cost of compliance with the regulations is estimated to add around 15 percent added costs.

• *Disclosure of accurate, complete, and current cost data in price negotiations*   This requirement comes from a legislative mandate—the Truth In Negotiation Act (TINA). It is again based on the government's desire for full visibility at the cost level rather than total prices paid, and commercial firms are reluctant to provide such proprietary cost information. They also are often unable to calculate this information because their pricing basis is on a broad allocation of costs, whereas the government's regulatory requirement is to identify each dollar of cost with each individual product.

• *Risks of losing intellectual property*   The government demands the rights to all data for government use so that it can set up a second source to compete with the original source if it believes it necessary. Commercial firms resist this and make great efforts to protect their intellectual property.

• *Export-control provisions*   When a commercial item is embedded in a military system, it becomes subject to export controls, and foreign sales of that commercial item can be delayed or even postponed. In some cases (as described above), this has significantly limited commercial sales of a product.

• *Budget uncertainties*   In the commercial world, the market is determined by buyers, but the defense market can easily be influenced by Congress as it annually debates how much money to put into a given product. Such uncertainty causes a great deal of turmoil in planning for efficient operations and for labor-force requirements. Although multiyear contracting greatly reduces this uncertainty, Congress has been reluctant to make such multiyear commitments.

• *Logistics support differences*   Commercial businesses tend to improve products continuously and can have many different versions of a product in the field. For information-based systems, this upgrade typically occurs on an eighteen-month cycle. By contrast, the DoD tends to lock in a design and require that all systems in the field be identical. One typical example of this difference occurred in the development of jet engines. The commercial world was continuously improving its engines, but the DoD insisted on keeping the older models. Jet engine suppliers were forced to set up two separate production lines—one to build the old design for the DoD and another to build the modern, improved design for the commercial world. The DoD suffered in both performance and cost.

• *The requirements process*   Commercial buyers constantly make trade-offs between the performance that they would like to have and the costs that are associated with that performance. Essentially, they are buying "best value." In contrast, the DoD requirements process tends to be much more rigid and offers far less flexibility in trades between the desired performance and the cost and time necessary to achieve that performance. This yields a far longer defense development cycle and a much more expensive item, which would not capture a commercial market.

• *Profit policy*   Regulations in the defense world tend to focus on minimizing profit (versus minimizing total price paid). In the commercial world, the focus is on minimizing total cost and recovering as much profit as possible—to allow a return to the investor and further investments in research and development and capital equipment. This difference in approach can lead DoD products to have very high costs and small profits (particularly in the high-tech industry). In the commercial world, there is a focus on lowering the cost (to raise the profit) while maintaining a minimal total price as paid by the customer. Microsoft products might be inexpensive for the DoD to buy as a software item, but their high profit margin might still make headlines in a congressional hearing (which does not consider that this profit has been reinvested in subsequent new innovations and further price reductions).

For all of these reasons, doing business with the government is very different from doing business with the commercial market, which leads corporations that are involved in both sectors to separate their businesses into different divisions and different locations. The result is actually detrimental to the nation's security because it is paying more for its products as a result of this forced separation. Boeing used to build its commercial and military transport aircraft (which have similar characteristics) in the same facility in Wichita, Kansas. The government was gaining the benefits of the economies of scale that resulted from the higher volume of the combined production. However, the government's unique cost-accounting system required that the independent research and development that Boeing was doing on its military aircraft had to be divided, as a function of the percentage of sales in that overall plant, between the commercial and military. This forced the commercial systems to incur higher costs (and be less competitive). Boeing chose to move its commercial transport business out of that facility, which significantly raised the cost of the military transports purchased by the DoD.

Such civil and military separation has expanded to nonmanufacturing businesses, where even the service sectors tend to be separated. Booz Allen Hamilton is one of the government's largest contractors, with more than $1.2 billion annually coming from the Department of Defense. In December 2007, chairman and chief executive officer Ralph Shrader stated, "Our global commercial consulting practice and our U.S. government business have very different needs for operating [in terms of] people models, regulatory requirements, and capital funding. . . . the long-term success of each operation could be enhanced by focusing on its individual market."[41] So it split up the two.

A significant number of firms—such as Boeing (with its large commercial aircraft) and General Electric (with its wide variety of commercial products and military jet engines)—operate in both the commercial and military sectors. But the firms view these markets as separate and find it easier to diversify into other product areas within their respective markets than to diversify across the military-commercial divide. During the dramatic dropoff in defense expenditures in the post–cold war period, many defense firms (and divisions) tried to diversify into the commercial market but found that their familiarity with the DoD market created barriers to entering such a totally new market. In fact, the defense conversion experience of most firms was extremely unfavorable.[42] These attempts at defense conversion were largely abandoned with the return of large Defense Department budgets after September 11, 2001. However, while the DoD budgets were declining, corporations that had strong commercial sales tended to sell off their defense business and concentrate on the commercial market. IBM, for example, sold off its federal government operations. As the DoD budgets rose again, many information-based companies (such as EDS, CSC, and Accenture), which had focused heavily on the commercial world, also began to increase their emphasis on government business. IBM refocused on the government market, and in 2007, its federal contracts amounted to over $1.3 billion, but in separate operations.

Although there was increasing movement toward operation in both the military and commercial sectors, integration was being achieved primarily at the corporate accounting level rather than at the operations level. This deprived the government of some major benefits that could be achieved through integrated operations. As the commercial world continued to move rapidly into leadership positions in high-tech sectors (often those applicable to national security), it became clear that both the executive and legislative branches needed to address the removal of many existing barriers to the integration of commercial and military operations.

The Public Industrial Sector

For almost exclusively political and historic reasons (rather than military or economic reasons), a large portion of the defense industrial base has been maintained in the public sector. Table 2.3 shows estimated totals for government civilians and contract personnel (precise data are not generated in this area).[43] The dollars shown are associated with the directly funded operations and maintenance, but they exclude the portion that is funded with the working capital funds. In the aviation depots, for example, these are of equal or larger levels than the billions of dollars shown on the table. The dollars shown also exclude costs for military personnel, depreciation on plant and equipment, and approximately one hundred government-owned and operated laboratories and engineering centers. Despite its large size, the public sector of the U.S. defense industry is not viewed as part of an integrated public and private industrial base that could be optimized for efficiency and effectiveness. Rather, it is controlled by legislated mandates. For example, the largest caucus on Capitol Hill—the depot caucus—has over 135 members that actively pursue work for their home-states' maintenance depots. They helped pass legislation requiring that 50 percent of all military equipment maintenance work be done in government facilities by government workers. Thus, a large share of DoD maintenance work is done in a noncompetitive fashion (with few incentives for increased efficiency). There is also potential for considerable excess capacity through the artificial maintenance of government operations (in case they are needed for a potential future surge requirement). For example, the navy is procuring only three or four new ships at any given time and needs to have repair work done on existing ones, but there are six, large, privately owned shipyards[44] (now concentrated in two firms, Northrop Grumman and General Dynamics) and four, major, government-owned shipyards (doing only maintenance work), so there is ample capacity for the limited work that needs to be done. However, when Secretary of the Navy John Lehman attempted to spur competition (for ship maintenance work) between the public and private-sector yards,[45] political opposition to continuing this approach was too great. During wartime, the excess capacity in the government shipyards, air logistics centers, and maintenance depots is used to repair equipment. However, in peacetime, this considerable excess capacity (in both facilities and labor) has to be spread over the remaining repair and upgrade work—raising costs significantly (and leaving the private facilities without work).

One recent trend aimed at increasing efficiency and effectiveness within these large, government-owned operations is the formation of partnerships between the public and private sectors. This can work in either direction: the government facility can outsource some of its work to the private sector (over the objections of both government unions and Congress), and the private sector can subcontract to the public sector to take advantage of the government's experience and political leverage. When done in a competitive fashion, both of these arrangements have significant potential benefits and should be encouraged. When done on a sole-source basis, however, these arrangements are essentially a monopoly—with little incentive for either efficiency or maximum performance. Nonetheless, the political leverage provided by these facilities has attracted significant interest from the private sector, which either has employees work directly in the government facilities or builds facilities nearby. For example, BAE Systems acquired United Defense Industries (which was in the armored-vehicle business). In 2005, BAE had a significant share of its business on Bradley vehicles at Red River Army Depot in Texas, and it built a $13 million factory to overhaul other armored vehicles at the Anniston Army Depot. In 2006, the Congress approved $17.1 billion to repair, upgrade, and replace army vehicles. This was $4 billion more than the administration's budget request for fiscal 2007 and a significant increase over the depot workload for fiscal 2006 (and was justified as a result of the activities in Iraq and Afghanistan).[46] When the DoD chooses to put the work that is currently being done in the public sector up for competition between the public and private sectors, it encourages partnerships to be established in a cost-effective fashion. This practice should be encouraged, but Congress has been resisting such competitive sourcing.

Insourcing

One of the Obama administration's major initiatives was insourcing—bringing work in from the private sector to the government. This was originally motivated by the loss of many experienced government acquisition positions in the post–cold war period (especially in contracting). However, many interpreted this initiative as an opportunity to build up the overall government workforce. The air force wanted to bring more aircraft maintenance work into the government depots, and the army moved vehicle maintenance in-house. Although the historic data showed that significant performance and cost benefits could be gained by competitively sourcing this work, its political appeal resulted in a shift from the private sector to the public sector.

A Growing International Industrial Base

Globalization is blurring the distinction between U.S. defense firms and foreign defense firms. For example, BAE Systems' headquarters is located in London, but by 2000, it had sold more to the American government than to the British,[47] and depending on the stock trading on any given day, the majority of its stock could easily be owned by Americans. Most of BAE's sales in the United States are built by U.S. workers under a U.S. subsidiary that has a board of directors comprised primarily of U.S. citizens and that performs highly classified work for the U.S. government. BAE is not unique. The Italian firm Finmeccanica, the French firm Thales, the Israeli firm IAI, and the French-German firm EADS all have U.S.-based subsidiaries actively involved in national security business. Additionally, most of the large U.S.-headquartered defense firms have European-based subsidiaries that have been gained through either acquisition or greenfield investment (investing in an area where no previous facilities exist). This all is driven by globalization—of technology, of industry, of the high-technology workforce, of finance, and, most important, for national security—because of the geopolitical and military coalitions necessary for countering the full spectrum of security issues (terrorism, regional conflicts, and stability and reconstruction).

In the twenty-first century, industries and governments are faced with a dilemma regarding their national security industrial structure. Should they create trade barriers that keep their markets closed and protect their industries? Or do they strengthen their overall national security by realizing the full economic, technological, and military benefits of globalization?[48] This is a decision for all countries that want to have a strong security posture at an affordable price. The risks of third-party technology-transfers to potential adversaries must be addressed, but the benefits of taking advantage of globalization appear to be far greater than the potential risks. In spite of the politically appealing protectionist perspectives of many elected officials in the U.S. Congress (and in the legislature of many other countries), the trends seem to be overwhelmingly in the direction of an international industrial base.[49] Perhaps best known among the programs in this area is the F-35 (previously known as the Joint Strike Fighter). America has taken the lead in the development of this advanced, stealthy fighter aircraft; but other countries have put in significant amounts of money in the development phase, and eleven countries (Australia, Canada, Denmark, Israel, Italy, the Netherlands, Norway, Singapore, Spain, Turkey, and the United Kingdom) have committed to buying this system.[50] This aircraft consists of the best-in-class items being supplied by the participating countries, and all nations will use the same systems to gain production efficiencies from the economies of scale. Many believe that future (multinational) programs should be structured to follow this model—allowing participating nations to benefit from higher performance and lower costs, and to agree to third-party controls of the transfer of technology beyond the consortium. There will still be alternative aircraft on the market (e.g., the Euro Fighter, Gripen, and Rafale), which will ensure that programs such as this remain competitive on an international basis.[51] This program is not unique. The antimissile Patriot PAC-3 production is shared between Lockheed Martin in the United States and EADS in France, Germany, and Spain. The Rolling Airframe Missile is shared between Raytheon in the United States and BGT in Germany. The Meteor missile is being shared between Matra in France and the United Kingdom, Alenia Marconi in Italy, EADS in France, Germany, and Spain, SAAB in Sweden, and Boeing in the United States. There is a strategic alliance for medium-caliber ammunition between Primex in the United States and NAMMO in Norway; there is a joint venture on tactical transport aircraft between Lockheed Martin in the United States and Alenia in Italy; the Gripen aircraft involves Volvo in Sweden and Honeywell, Lockheed Martin, and Sunstrand in the United States.

These joint efforts are initiated on a government-to-government basis or through industrial teaming (on proposals to a variety of nations). Their advantages for government partners are lower costs, best technologies, and a solution to the political (labor) problem through some form of local production and support.

Perhaps the most significant steps toward a globalized national security industrial base are the result of transatlantic mergers and acquisitions (in both directions). As noted, BAE Systems has been the most active, making over $7 billion worth of investments in America between 1999 and 2006. It became the seventh largest domestically-located supplier to the Department of Defense in fiscal year 2005, and the only one among the top ten not headquartered in the United States.[52] But BAE was not unique. The French firm Alcatel bought the U.S. telecommunications firm Lucent for $13.4 billion in 2006 (gaining what was the old Bell Laboratories in the process); and in 2008, Finmeccanica of Italy purchased the U.S. defense firm DRS Technology, spurring many more such U.S. investments by European firms. This trend was not unique to defense. Many foreign firms moved some of their significant operations to the United States (perhaps most noteworthy being the auto industry). In fact, by 2004, U.S. affiliates of foreign (majority-owned, nonbank) companies employed 5.1 million Americans, contributed $515 billion to the U.S. gross domestic product, and accounted for 19 percent of all U.S. exports.[53]

Direct foreign investments have had a significant positive effect on the U.S. economy, and the benefits of these investments have been realized in America's national security posture. Similar acquisitions by U.S. firms in Europe have also been taking place. For example, the American firm United Defense bought Bofors; General Dynamics bought the Spanish armored vehicle company Santa Barbara: and General Electric bought the U.K.-headquartered Smiths Aerospace.[54]

These foreign investments in national security areas have received resistance from the U.S. Congress and from many foreign governments. For example, the German government proposed legislation to limit foreign investments in German defense companies to 25 percent after its conventional-submarine maker, Howaldtswerke Deutsche Werft, was purchased by the Chicago-based venture-capital firm One Equity Partners. Even in Great Britain (which was long seen as the most open market for U.S. defense companies), there was a political uproar over Carlyle's purchase of an effective controlling stake in QinetiQ (which had been the administrator of the U.K. Defense Advanced Research Laboratories until they were privatized in 2002).[55]

Benefits and Concerns Regarding a Globalized Industrial Base

By 2006, almost a hundred foreign-owned firms operating in the United States had agreements with the Pentagon allowing them access to classified government programs.[56] This represents almost a doubling from a decade earlier. Eighteen countries are represented on the list (as supplied by the Defense Security Service), and all but four (Australia, Bermuda, Israel, and Singapore) are European. These foreign-owned or -controlled companies work with classified DoD information and are subject to a specialized set of rules. They must set up U.S. subsidiaries with separate boards of directors that include members approved by the DoD, they must have their own email systems and network servers, and they must fully document all communications with employees of the parent (foreign) company. Despite adding to complexity and cost, these rules address some of the main concerns associated with such operations. The companies must use U.S. labor (with appropriate security clearances), provide transparency for both the technical and economic operations of the U.S. subsidiary (to ensure that U.S. interests are adequately protected), place controls on the export of both information and equipment (for protection against third-party transfers), and reduce the vulnerability of the United States to the use of foreign technologies (for example, through U.S. domestic production).

Both political and substantive concerns have been raised about the globalization of the U.S. national security industrial base. As long as these concerns are addressed (as they are with the procedures noted above), the potential benefits of such a globalized industrial base far exceed any potential risks. These benefits include the following:

- *Enhanced military capability* Through this international industrial base, the U.S. military gains the technology offered by other countries, which, in many cases, may be more advanced than U.S. technology. It also encourages interoperability between the U.S. forces and its allies, so that when they go to war, all the forces have maximum capability and can operate effectively together (which greatly enhances the combined, overall force effectiveness). Since it is inconceivable that the United States will be involved in any future military operations without coalition allies (for geopolitical more than military reasons), this integrated, overall force effectiveness is particularly important.

- *Economic benefits* By setting up joint production operations, the United States can take advantage of investments in research and development by allied nations. It also can benefit from joint developments in which multiple countries share development costs. In either case, the United States gains the benefit of the economies of scale that come from the high volume associated with joint production programs. In addition, foreign-owned, U.S.-based operations make significant capital investments in the United States when they set up their facilities, thereby greatly strengthening the overall U.S. industrial base. Finally, these foreign-owned, U.S.-based operations supply equipment to the United States and also (subject to U.S. export controls) contribute to the overall positive export to import trade balance of the defense firms (which for the aerospace industry alone was $38 billion in 2005).[57] This creates significant additional opportunities for employment in the United States.

- *Providing enhanced competition* Besides bringing in advanced technology from other countries, this globalization of the industrial base also provides significant competition when there is only one U.S. producer in a given field. This encourages the U.S. source to continue to innovate, giving rise to higher performance at a lower cost. For example, when the U.S. Air Force needed to replace its tanker fleet, the only domestic source was Boeing, but Northrop Grumman teamed with the European firm EADS and proposed an Airbus variant to be built in Alabama. The air force benefited significantly from this competition—in terms of both performance and costs. When the army needed to buy a light transport aircraft, the U.S. firm L-3 Communications set up a joint venture with an Italian firm, Alenia, and Raytheon set up a competing joint venture with EADS Casa (a Spanish firm).[58] The benefit of having a foreign option is also seen in the case of the United States' recent underinvestment in helicopters. The U.S. Army needed a next-generation, light utility helicopter; and the award went to American Euro Copter, a joint subsidiary of EADS North America and Euro Copter. American Euro Copter planned to establish a large facility in Columbus, Mississippi, where the production of the helicopter would be transferred from Germany for both full assembly and subsequent U.S. manufacture of major subsystems.[59] And the BAE Systems North American operations won a competition against Lockheed Martin to supply the U.S. Army's next generation of laser-guided missiles for its combat helicopters.[60]

In addition to introducing competition for contracts for major weapon systems, globalization of the industrial base also has significant potential benefits at the major subsystem level. When the DoD wanted to develop a set of next-generation radios at extremely large quantities (over 200,000 were to be produced), competitive contracts were awarded to a French firm, Thales, and a U.S. firm, Harris. This ensured continuous competition and improved performance (of these digital radios) at lower costs.[61] It is also assured interoperability of U.S. and European forces. In the jet engine area, for the F-35 Joint Strike Fighter (the largest weapons program in history), the original Pratt and Whitney engine had competition from an engine that was owned by several partners—50 percent General Electric, 40 percent Rolls-Royce, and 10 percent other international partners.[62] Finally, in aircraft landing gear, the sole U.S. producer (B. F. Goodrich) is in constant competition with the Canadian operation of Messier-Dowty.

In each case, the presence of foreign competition enhanced overall U.S. weapon-systems performance—a benefit that would not have existed without a globalized industrial base. The challenge is to overcome the political barriers that are created by Congress, including the export and import trade barriers (such as the International Traffic in Arms Regulation and the Berry amendment) and emotional concerns about buying a foreign product.

Foreign Military Sales (FMS)

In both good and bad times (but particularly when there is a downturn in U.S. Defense Department procurements), the defense industry has been aided by sales to the world market. These sales can be made either through direct sales (from the firm directly to the foreign government but with the approval of the U.S. government) or through foreign military sales (FMSs), which are conducted through the U.S. government on a government-to-government basis. Foreign governments usually prefer the latter approach, since they then get both financial and management support from the U.S. government. The Defense Security Cooperation Agency (DSCA)—an entire organization within the Department of Defense—has 900 security assistance personnel in 102 countries, supervises 14,000 international military students annually, and is spending around $50 million annually in humanitarian aid. It also handles so-called section 1206 funds, which are intended to provide global training and equipping programs to "build the capacity of partner nations supporting the global war on terrorism." In 2008, funding was at $500 million to cover coalition partners in Algeria, Chad, the Dominican Republic, Indonesia, Iraq, Lebanon, Morocco, Nigeria, Pakistan, Panama, Principe, Sao Tome, Senegal, Sri Lanka, Thailand, and Yemen plus an additional $200 million in Defense Department equipment funds for "stability assistance and reconstruction, to be shared with the State Department."[63] For providing these services and to cover DoD expenses, the DSCA receives a 3.8 percent administrative surcharge on all foreign military sales.[64]

Over the years, the principal sources of foreign military sales have been the United States and Russia (formerly the Soviet Union) (see table 4.3).

However, this is an extremely competitive market, and large swings can take place in annual sales as a result of a single, large purchase by an individual country. For example, American defense contractors doubled armed sales from $10.6 billion to $21 billion from September 2005 to September 2006 as a result of a large sale in the Middle East.[65] For individual U.S. companies, large orders can boost the

Table 4.3
Foreign military sales: Major suppliers, 1981 to 2005 (millions of 1999 U.S. dollars)

	1981	1986	1991	1996	2001	2005
United States	$11,797	$10,229	$11,641	$10,377	$5,516	$7,101
Russia	16,814	14,378	5,221	3,589	5,548	5,771
France	3,622	2,629	902	1,651	1,133	2,399
Germany	1,673	1,302	2,372	1,618	640	1,855
United Kingdom	1,919	1,733	1,394	1,526	1,070	791
Netherlands	697	342	423	381	190	840
Italy	1,549	334	506	414	185	827
Sweden	172	275	184	118	459	592
China	825	2,143	1,100	707	408	129
Ukraine	n/a	n/a	n/a	236	702	188
World total	$41,997	$37,241	$25,928	$22,079	$17,332	$21,961
U.S. percent of total	28.1%	27.5%	44.9%	47.0%	31.8%	32.3%

company's annual sales. For example, General Dynamic's 2008 overseas sales outpaced its U.S. bookings for the first time.[66]

Historically, such foreign sales were focused primarily on the United States' European allies and were primarily sales of military equipment. Recently, however, there has been a great increase in training, support, spare parts, and upgrades for worldwide allied nations and a considerable increase in the funds for the training and equipping of foreign countries (in an effort to counter worldwide terrorism). Most dramatic has been the increase in purchases by the Middle East and Asian markets.

The oil-rich Middle Eastern countries have become a significant market for foreign military sales, which is not surprising, given their growing wealth and the considerable instability in that region. From a U.S. perspective, these sales are as much political as military in their initiatives. Although the focus historically was on Israel and Egypt, which both received significant amounts of financial support to maintain peace and stability in the region, the war in Iraq and growing concerns about Iran have shifted the focus of international security to include the many other countries in the Middle Eastern region. Their oil wealth has meant that the focus is primarily on sales rather than aid—but with a recognition of the importance of Middle Eastern oil (on which the U.S. economy is dependent). Iran and Syria also have been buying large quantities of weapons from Russia (and passing some of them on to Hezbollah and Hamas to use against Israel), and there is a growing concern that other weapon exporters (such as China) might become aggressive in this region to gain both sales and political leverage toward the oil resources.[67]

The stakes are high in the competition for sales in this region. In 2007, the United States announced the sale of an arms package of around $20 billion for Saudi Arabia and a similar amount for the other five members of the Gulf Cooperation Council—Bahrain, Kuwait, Oman, Qatar, and the United Arab Emirates.[68] There is congressional resistance to some of these sales. For example, members of Congress have objected to large sales to Saudi Arabia on the basis that the Saudis have been unhelpful to the United States in the war in Iraq and not as supportive as they could be in the fight against terrorism.[69]

Although past sales (with congressional approval) of military equipment were based primarily on the foreign purchase of equipment used in the U.S. inventory, recently the trend has been toward oil-rich countries paying for further advances in U.S. equipment for themselves (and for the United States) to use. The United Arab Emirates made a major investment in the development of the next-generation F-16 fighter plane with an enhanced new radar, which the United States will use as well. This means that the United States will benefit from an advanced system (whose research and development has been paid for by the UAE) and will gain the economy-of-scale benefits of the volume of units (which will be shared between the two countries, as well as any potential future foreign sales to other countries).

Finally, the last of the large and growing foreign markets is Asia. The big arms bazaars used to be held at the Paris air show or the London air show (in alternate years). Today, however, the Singapore air show has become an equally important sales arena for worldwide defense firms. The 2006 Singapore air show included representatives from 940 international companies, and 35,000 people from the aerospace business from eighty-nine countries (including, for the first time, China) attended the six-day air show.[70] Close U.S. allies (such as Japan, Singapore, and Australia) have always been allowed to purchase some of the most advanced U.S. weapons, but more recently, the market has expanded to include India, Thailand, and Taiwan. As in the Middle East, this is a highly competitive and increasingly significant market. For example, India needs to replace its aging fleet of Soviet-era Mig-21 jets, which it purchased in the early 1990s. India's increased wealth, location in a critical part of the world, and modern tendency toward an open market have inspired the United States to expand its focus from a Europe-centered world to include Asia as well. China is banned from the U.S. export list for military equipment, but is still a significant market for Russian equipment.

Summary of the Changing Defense Industrial Base
Several characteristics of the structure of the U.S. national security industrial base have been changing:

- *Consolidation* Defense-industry consolidation has been occurring both horizontally and vertically, and the government has tried to maintain sufficient competition to stimulate innovation and lower costs.

- *Technological shifts* The industry has experienced a growing dependence on information technology—more integrated systems of systems, more information that comes from intelligence systems of all types and is widely available to all users, more unmanned systems (for their lower cost and their benefits in saving human lives), and greater sensitivity to information security (in networks and computers).

- *Greater emphasis on services* Over 60 percent of DoD purchases are on services, including engineering, maintenance, and training. Even historically equipment-oriented firms have added service divisions (often through acquisitions).

- *Civil and military integration* As technology has expanded in the commercial world and as leadership in advanced technology has frequently come from the commercial world, more integration is taking place between the commercial and military industrial structure. There is an increasing need to remove many of the barriers to integration that have existed historically in this area.

• *Globalization*   Both in structure (horizontally and vertically) and in markets, the security area has been dramatically moving toward a globalized perspective. This follows the trend set by the commercial world and recognizes the strong interdependence of security and economics in the twenty-first century.

The Conduct of Defense Business by Government and Industry

The process by which industry and the government supply goods and services for America's national security has been both successful and unsuccessful. This process has built the best weapon systems in the world, but it is expensive, time consuming, and often does not achieve the desired results. As David Walker, the former comptroller general of the United States and head of the U.S. Government Accountability Office (GAO), stated: "DoD is number one in the world in fighting and winning armed conflicts—it's an A+. But, in my opinion, DoD is a D (rated on a curve and given the benefit of the doubt) on economy, efficiency, transparency, and accountability."[71]

The cost growth in weapon systems receives the most attention. A GAO report noted that between 2001 and 2006, the planned Pentagon investments in new weapon systems doubled from about $700 billion to nearly $1.4 trillion,[72] and individual weapons had similar results. Additionally, the army's Future Combat System went from an estimated $82.6 billion to $127.5 billion (even before it was built), and the air force's F-22 advanced fighter aircraft program went from $81.1 billion for 648 aircraft to $64.4 billion for only 181 aircraft (a cost increase per airplane of 188 percent).[73] Both of these results were a significant basis for the programs termination (by Secretary Gates) in 2009.

The causes of these weapon-acquisition problems are well known:

• DoD initiates more programs than it can afford. Essentially, it attempts to "buy in" at optimistically low dollar levels to start a larger number of programs within the likely available budgets (and hoping for later DoD budget growths).

• DoD starts programs before it is sure that the capabilities it is pursuing can be achieved using existing state-of-the-art technology and within available resources and time constraints. The GAO found that programs using mature technologies grew only 4.8 percent while those using immature technologies grew 34.9 percent in their development costs alone.

• DoD has allowed many new requirements to be added during the acquisition phases of programs (thus adding complexity, time, and cost after the program is initiated).

• DoD has tried to satisfy a large array of weapons' requirements with a single weapon, thus using fewer but larger, more complex, and more expensive individual weapons.[74]

The schedules, costs, and performance problems of defense weapon systems are not new phenomena. For over fifty years, the defense acquisition system has been called "terribly broken" and "unresponsive, cumbersome and terribly bureaucratic."[75] Hundreds of studies have suggested ways to reform the defense acquisition system. One analysis looked at the time period from 1986 to 2005 and noted that seventy major studies[76] had been done by the GAO, the Defense Science Board, some congressional commissions, and the DoD. All acknowledged the extreme complexity of the process itself. Additionally, incentives and fixes in the system have often had adverse effects relative to the desired objectives of maximum performance at low cost and with rapid deployment.

There are two major misconceptions about this complex process—that these processes can't be done efficiently and effectively, and that poor performance is caused by intentional abuse and illegal actions. Fortunately, there are examples of high-performance weapons that have been developed at low cost, similar to the commercial market's experiences with the decreasing costs and increasing performance of computers. As previously noted, the joint direct attack munitions (JDAM) missile achieved the desired reliability and high accuracy, and its cost was reduced from the target of $40,000 each to a realized cost of $17,000 each. As another example, industry was incentivized to provide performance-based logistics availability and rapid response for the navy's F/18 stores management system. Availability of the system was increased from 65 percent to 98 percent, and its response time for critical parts replacement went from 42.6 days (on average) to two days domestically and seven days worldwide. Many other success stories illustrate this point, but they do not happen often and are not widely known. This book provides greater visibility into techniques that can improve the acquisition of national security goods and services.

The second of the major misconceptions about the acquisition process is the widespread perception of illegal actions. Out of millions of annual procurement actions by the DoD, there have been a few cases of fraud. But the public perception is shaped by the press, which, particularly in periods of rapid expansion of the defense budget, uncovers and prominently heralds examples of abuse. In 1985, overpriced toilet seats, hammers, and coffee pots received widespread publicity during the rapid expansion of the Defense Department's budget during the Reagan buildup. To respond to this abuse, President Reagan created the Blue Ribbon Panel on Defense Management (referred to as the Packard Commission after its chair). This panel made major structural changes to the system (later implemented in the Goldwater-Nichols bill), but Congress then legislated the maximum price of a toilet seat ("not to exceed $660") and added 5,000 auditors (which did not improve the contracting process). Another example was the huge increase in Defense Department expenditures in 2007, including hundreds of billions for wartime supplemental budgets. After uncovering numerous cases of fraud in contracting in Iraq, Army Secretary Geren established the Commission on Army Acquisition and Program Management in Expeditionary Operations (known as the Gansler Commission after its chair, the author of this book). This commission noted that DoD had significantly reduced its emphasis on its acquisition workforce and the need for corrective actions; which the DoD began with the creation of the Army Contracting Command, in 2009.

These two examples highlight the fact that it often takes a crisis to bring about dramatic change to defense programs. But both of these commissions emphasized and directed their corrective actions toward broad structural issues. They did not focus on the relatively small effects of illegal actions but instead highlighted the waste and inefficiency associated with the process itself. The abuses are often caused by the process, not the players. For example, some of the most highly publicized purchases—the $435 hammer, the $640 toilet seat, the $91 screw, the $2,917 wrench, and the $7,000 coffee pot—were a result of unique government accounting rules that required allocation of overhead charges by transactions rather than in proportion to the cost of the individual items. In this case, no illegal actions took place. A poor management system did not allow for visibility into the costs themselves, Additionally, a set of military requirements often drove the costs for individual items to far higher levels than are sensible (such as a requirement that a coffee pot survive after an aircraft crash).

There is enormous waste in the current acquisition process, but this waste is not due to lack of oversight. Each agency has inspector generals who find problems and distribute appropriate punishments. There is also an entire organization (the Defense Contract Audit Agency) that ensures that proper accounting practices are being used by DoD suppliers. Many laws and regulations provide checks and controls in the oversight of government procurements. They are not geared toward achieving increased efficiency or effectiveness, however, but rather toward ensuring total compliance—that all rules are followed and that there are no illegal actions. They effectively minimize illegal actions and ensure high ethical behavior by industry and by the government itself. Daniel Terris, director of Brandeis University's International Center for Ethics, Justice, and Public Life, maintains that "in America the Defense industry has the most developed set of ethics programs of any business sector."[77] He investigated the Lockheed Martin Corporation (the largest defense contractor) and observed that the company spends millions of dollars each year on ethics initiatives, employs sixty-five ethics officers, and requires all employees (more than 130,000) to consider ethical issues for at least one hour each year. Thus, the focus of the acquisition reforms must be on broad structural changes in the process, not on adding additional laws and regulations that actually impede the effective and efficient operation of the process. But reform needs to recognize the differences between the government's acquisition process and that of the commercial marketplace.

Uniqueness of the Defense Market[78]
Perhaps one of the most interesting aspects of the defense acquisition process is the relationship between buyer and seller, which distinguishes it from the other sectors of the U.S. economy. Here, the DoD is a single (monopsony) buyer that can make purchases from only a few, select suppliers in each critical sector of the economy (including fighter planes, navy ships, jet engines, and radars); and the market operates in an extremely regulated and transparent environment. Both of these characteristics are unlike anything in the commercial world, where many buyers and many suppliers operate in a largely free market. The noted economist Walter Adams has called this unique defense environment "a closed system of buyer and seller, interrelated for common interests" that "defies analysis by conventional economic tools."[79] James McKee has said that it is a relationship in which "the large buyer has a direct influence on the policies and decisions of the large seller" and that "what we observe is a kind of behavior that is not adequately described by any of the commonly employed 'models' of market relationships in economics."[80]

Although there is a close and acknowledged commonality of interests at the national security level, on individual defense programs the actual situation is closer to an adversarial relationship than a mutually beneficial joint effort. This is because buyers in the commercial world have a choice of sellers. To negotiate the desired price and quality in the commercial world, the buyer can go to other sellers, and the seller can seek other buyers. In the defense world, most of the contract is negotiated directly between a single buyer and a single supplier for an individual program.[81] This delicate relationship is sometimes referred to as porcupines making love or Sumo wrestlers battling within a confined space. During the negotiation process, the government negotiator worries that he or she might be taken advantage of by the large defense contractor, and the contractor attempts to maximize its sales on what might be one of its few major program opportunities. Because of the high public visibility of negotiators on both sides of this type of relationship, there is rarely a case of collusion between the government and industry in this environment.[82]

Similarly, because only a few firms are involved in a competition for a large program award, there is often concern that two or three firms might get together and collude. However, no serious studies of the defense industry[83] have yielded any data to show any form of conspiracy among large defense suppliers (again, this can be attributed to the extreme transparency associated with such activities). Large orders are rare and often are received in lumps, so there is little opportunity for two or three firms to conspire to divide up a market. In fact, if a conspiracy did exist, there would be a huge incentive for one firm to break out of the alliance and bid low to win the large contract.

Two highly interrelated areas distinguish the defense market from the commercial market—public accountability and regulation. All of the government's decision making and all of the industry's records are subject to detailed review by Congress, the public, the press, and authorized examiners. In the DoD alone, over nine thousand military and civilian personnel audited and investigated the DoD in 1978,[84] and by 2008 this number had increased to thirty thousand.[85] In 2007, there were more auditors than government contracting people in the Iraq and Afghanistan war zone.[86] Although a law requires full and open competition for defense procurements, a large series of policy substitutes—ranging from regulation to management controls—have developed to replace or correct for the lack of a free market. The government is intimately involved in the operation of the defense market. It controls almost all research and development, provides most of the money for progress payments, and provides much of the critical plant and equipment. In the day-to-day operating details of the firms, the government's involvement is so great that the defense market becomes totally unique and ceases to be a market in any traditional sense.

The legal basis for this involvement comes from congressional legislation that led to the Federal Acquisition Regulations (FARs) and the subsequent Department of Defense Acquisition Regulations (DARs), which contain over sixteen thousand pages of text and hundreds of pages of appendices.[87] These regulations provide detailed information on exactly how defense business is to be conducted. They require firms doing business with the Department of Defense to have special accounting systems, special quality-control procedures, special drawings, special soldering techniques, and so on. Firms that are in both commercial and military business must separate their operations so that the heavy burden of defense regulation costs are not added to their commercial business.

Many of the regulations are the result of congressional investigations into the activities of the defense industry. When there is evidence of, or potential for, an abuse, another regulation is added—to be applied universally to the entire industry. For the single case that spurred the new regulation, the corrective action may or not have been the right solution; however, the cumulative effect of these actions on most other cases that did not need further regulation is rarely considered. The cumulative costs on defense weapons systems are often unintended—but are significant.

The defense industry is never listed as a regulated industry (even though it clearly is) because the way in which it is controlled is unique. The regulator and the buyer are the same, unlike typical regulated industries in which an external regulator acts in the public's interest. Since government decision makers and regulators tend to focus on individual programs and specific, detailed regulations, they tend not to consider the overall structure of the industry when they implement policy or regulatory decisions. As Larry Ellsworth points out, "the Department of Defense determines, by its procurement decisions, whether there will be more or less concentration,"[88] yet no regulations cover the allowable degree of concentration or even establish a broad policy about the desired structure of the defense industry. By making individual programmatic decisions that select one of the two or three suppliers in a major business sector, the government controls the structure of the industry. They can, as Walter Adams noted, "create more monopoly in one day than the anti-trust division can undo in a year."[89]

To show how this can happen (and the role that politics and lobbying can play in this process), this chapter reviews the step-by-step process of acquiring weapon systems. But before doing so, it is necessary to dispel two widespread beliefs. First, decision makers in the DoD are thought to decide "whose turn it is to receive the next contract"[90] and thereby allow firms to maintain their position in the business and the DoD to maintain its industrial base. In fact, detailed proposals and source-selection activities preclude such a simplistic process, but because of the oligopoly rivalry that takes place, the final result may be the same as if turns had been taken because the winning firm is so badly in need of business that it makes a very attractive bid. The second false belief is that the defense industry closely resembles a normal free market (as required by procurement legislation) and that the selection of the supplier of the next weapon system is, in fact, based on the lowest cost. The award is more frequently based on the maximum performance promised because the DoD is striving to achieve technological superiority. Unlike in the typical commercial market, where prices of comparable items on a shelf can be compared, the costs and performance of the complex and differentiated items sold in the defense market are difficult to compare. It is not simply a matter of opening the envelope and picking the lowest bidder.

The Weapons-Acquisition Process

Weapons acquisition is not a single process but a set of multiple, interrelated processes—a budget process, a requirements process, a procurement process, a congressional process, and an overarching acquisition process (which includes many of the above, as well as the research and development process, the production process, the test and evaluation process, the logistics process, and the many services and support processes). Whole books have been written on each of these processes and their intersections, and they affect the structure, conduct, and performance of the industry that supplies goods and services to the national security community.

The budget process determines where the dollars are spent. In theory, the budget process is a top-down process in which the president establishes priorities (for example, a greater emphasis on education, transportation, or security) for the coming five-year period. That information is given to the Office of Management and Budget for the overall allocations (within the total budget top line) to the various executive branch agencies. These are then compared with the bottom-up requests from the agencies, which are usually accompanied by extensive rationale about why last year's budget was inadequate and why they need an increase. The constraint of the overall process is the top line, in which revenue is compared with expenditures, inflation projections are made, and the desired macroeconomics for the coming period are set.

Then each agency secretary—in this case the secretary of defense—provides guidance to the military services for their five-year plans, based on the secretary's priority items. For example, in fiscal year 2008–2009, the secretary of defense had five priority items for the upcoming budget cycle[91]—to prevail in the current war on terrorism, to increase ground capabilities, to improve force readiness, to develop future combat capabilities, and to improve the quality of life for military personnel. Such general guidance is intended to shift the resources of the military services. However, the services usually try to negotiate for increased resources because their prior efforts to achieve their priorities often came up short—with" inadequate" resources cited as the cause. The Office of the Secretary of Defense then has to balance these service requests to achieve an integrated DoD budget.

The overall budget is divided in two ways—among the various funding categories (research and development, production, support, personnel, facilities, and so on, with separate congressional subcommittees providing oversight in each category) and then by individual program elements within each funding category (so that each missile, vehicle, and so on is separately itemized and funded). Throughout the years, attempts have been made to group these various categories and program line items to obtain a clearer picture of their general purpose. In the 1970s, the "mission-area summaries" gave an indication, by the various categories of defense missions, of how many resources (dollars, weapons, and people) were applied to each mission. Thirty-five years later, arguments were made for similar types of groupings by "joint capabilities areas". Although grouping as a technique for budgeting does provide analytic understanding of various priorities and capabilities, it has been strongly resisted by both Congress and the individual services. Since the congressional budget process uses different committees and subcommittees to review each detailed line item, these committees are lobbied by contractors for individual line items on a program-by-program basis during the congressional budget cycle. In the Lyndon Johnson era, Secretary of Defense Robert McNamara introduced a five-year planning, programming, and budgeting system (PPBS) so that large capital equipment (such as ships, which take five years to build) could be assigned a fiscal plan that has the stability required for efficient operations on the industrial side. In spite of this logic being exactly correct, the system is highly unstable; largely because of the effects of external events and the politics of who builds what and where.

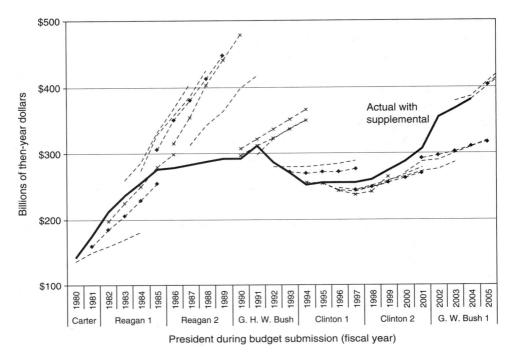

Figure 4.1
The president's budget projections and actual defense budgets, fiscal years 1980 to 2005. *Source:* Stan Szemborski, principal deputy director, Office of the Secretary of Defense of Program Analysis and Evaluation, Paper presented before the Defense Science Board Taskforce on Defense Industrial Structure, January 4, 2007.

The planned expenditures over a five-year period have rarely been realized. Figure 4.1 compares five presidents' projected five-year fiscal plans in dotted lines and the actual realized dollars in solid lines. As can be seen, the difference between planned and realized dollars could be over $100 billion in any given year. The introduction of supplemental budgets during the war in Iraq has led to even greater deviations. Such significant year-to-year unpredictability in the budget for individual programs causes great inefficiency because industrial operations managers cannot adequately plan for their labor and material needs in the coming period. Ordering long-lead parts often takes eighteen months for delivery, and hiring personnel similarly takes a considerable period of time. From the viewpoint of the Defense Department, not much can be done about it because Congress allows reprogramming authority at only an extremely limited $5 million to $10 million level, which is not enough to run these large programs efficiently. Additionally, every year has its share of unexpected events. To pay for a dramatic increase in fuel costs, the DoD might have to stretch out other programs, causing them to increase in cost, thus creating a compounding effect.

Further complicating this budget process is the requirement for a three-year projection of each of the annual budgets. When the new president took office in January 2009, he inherited nine months of the current year budget for fiscal year 2009 (the fiscal year begins October 1). The fiscal budget for 2010 has to be submitted to Congress just weeks after the inauguration, so the new president had very little effect on that year as well. Finally, in February 2009, the budget preparation for fiscal year 2011 began (literally weeks after he took office), and with very little preparation time, he was already budgeting for the third year of his administration (and there may well be surprises during the first two years that require significant changes in the third year's budget). Finally, the complexity and unpredictability of this budget process have led some to attempt to beat the system. For example, because it takes five years to build a ship, the navy has tried to allocate 20 percent of the costs per year against its annual budget, over a five-year period. This would commit the Congress to the four out-years because it would not stop the funding in the middle of construction. To prevent this, Congress passed legislation with a "full-funding" provision that requires that the full cost of any item be fully funded in its first year.

The British use an approach called private finance initiatives (PFIs) to move items off budget. Instead of spending tens of billions of dollars to purchase aerial refueling tankers (to supply fuel to jet fighters and bombers on their way to the front line), they simply lease the tankers when they need them (similar to renting a car rather than buying one). The British have also used this approach for large contract awards related to training functions (including fighter pilots).[92] In the United States, a similar approach has been used to pay for privatized housing when the DoD could not cover the cost of upgrading military housing to acceptable standards (estimated by Secretary William Perry to cost approximately $20 billion) since it would have interfered with the procurement of major weapons systems. Other than for housing, however, this PFI concept has been strongly resisted by the congressional appropriations committees because it reduces their control of the budgets.

Perhaps the most unrealistic of all defense budget-planning forecasts is that used by some in the defense industry who believe that there is a Defense Department budget macrocycle. In fact, approximately every eighteen years, there has been a large buildup in the Defense Department budget, which is followed by a dramatic decline (figure 4.2).

Although these drastic shifts were clearly driven by external events (such as the end of the cold war and the terrorist attacks of September 11, 2001), some think that they are a natural phenomenon based on equipment wearout and they feel that cyclical shifts will continue in the future, they base their forecasts on them. This

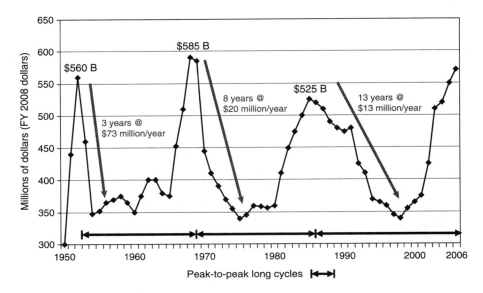

Figure 4.2
Defense budget cycle, 1950 to 2006. *Source:* National defense budget estimates for the fiscal year 2008 budget (*Green Book*), briefing by C. J Bowie and K. Rogers of Northrop Grumman, December 18, 2007.

belief becomes particularly evident when the Defense Department budget cycle is in a downturn and those in the industry look for a rationale to assume that it will shift upward.

Two critical decisions must be made in the acquisition process. The DoD must ensure (1) that it is buying the right things, and (2) that it is buying them right. These two issues, of what we buy and how we buy, are interrelated, but the current process tends to separate the two by saying that the requirements process is the role of the military. Issues of unit cost, delivery schedule, and technical feasibility tend not to play as major a role here as they should. There is still controversy over what part of the military should drive the requirements process. By law (title 10 of the United States Code), the services are responsible for training and equipping the forces, but should they solely manage these processes? The combatant commanders are responsible for the forces needed for fighting the wars. In the current system, the services put together the budgets and decide what and how many to buy. The combatant commanders simply use what the services provide. In the old days, when battles were fought separately in the air, on land, and at sea, separate requirements could be written for each of the services. But by the mid-1980s, most conflicts were joint—that is, integrated among the services. It was therefore desirable to write requirements in a joint fashion (and interoperability of equipment became a major requirement). In a joint system-of- systems, it is necessary, for example, for a sensor in the air to talk to a shooter on the ground. To address the need for integration in the requirements process, the Goldwater-Nichols bill (1987) established the Joint Requirements Oversight Council (JROC) under the vice-chairman of the Joint Chiefs of Staff. The objective was to ensure that all requirements considered joint warfighting. Because the membership of the JROC was composed of the vice chiefs of staff of each of the services, however, the requirements process remained slanted much more toward the suppliers (the services) than the warfighters (the combatant commanders). A strong recommendation for future changes would be to have combatant commanders represented on the JROC.[93] This recommendation was proposed by the Senate Armed Services Committee in 2009.

Another significant shortcoming in the requirements process is that the budget process is driven by individual weapon line items. Thus, the requirements process considers individual weapons first and establishes requirements for next-generation weapons (which leads to an almost automatic evolution from one aircraft to the next). As modern communication systems have evolved to play a major role in netcentric warfare, however, the requirements process needs to optimize an overall system –of-systems rather than the individual platforms within a system. To do this, extensive work on systems engineering and systems architecture needs to be done early in the evolution of the requirements process.[94] The systems engineering also needs to include the costs and technical feasibility associated with each element of the system-of-systems. A close working relationship is required between the people writing the requirements and the people responsible for developing the systems.

There is a secondary reason for considering the unit cost of individual systems as part of the requirements process. If a department is resource-constrained (that is, it has a certain amount of money set aside for buying either platforms or systems-of-systems), then the requirement must be resource-constrained as well. There is a direct correlation between the number of systems that can be purchased with those dollars and the unit costs of the individual elements. Since numbers matter in terms of warfighting effectiveness and are a military requirement, there must be a military requirement for the unit costs of weapon systems that is specified at the initiation of the program—and not discovered later during the bill-paying phase. Trade-offs in cost versus performance—within the likely total mission dollars available, the overall desired number of systems, and the existing technological capabilities—must be addressed early in the requirements process.

With the rapid changes in technology, warfighting, regional environments, and adversary capabilities, the requirements process needs to be flexible to avoid developing systems that are obsolete by the time they become available. This problem is not unique to defense weapon systems. It also is typical in commercial software, electronics, and other areas. A solution that has evolved in the commercial world

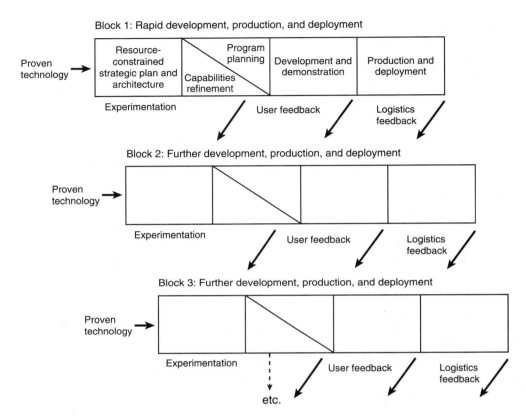

Figure 4.3
Spiral development of systems

is spiral development. Using existing (proven) technology, the first block of the system is rapidly developed, produced, and deployed, while the next block is being further developed (figure 4.3).

This approach can be contrasted to an approach that develops one major weapon system over a twelve- to twenty-year cycle—the so-called "big bang" process. Spiral development allows capabilities to be fielded much earlier and at far lower risk in terms of technical performance, schedule, and cost. It also greatly reduces technological obsolescence and allows for a more robust and competitive industrial structure. If a selected company does not continue to improve performance at increasingly lower costs, then competition can be introduced at any milestone on the next block (at either the prime-contractor or subsystem level). Even in the automotive industry, this process has been found to reduce costs by about 30 percent and to provide continuous performance inputs and redesigns based on early field availability and user and maintainer feedback.

Spiral development and deployment dramatically affect each element of the overall acquisition process. Because the requirements process is no longer fixed but continuously changes with each block, the test and evaluation process determines whether the next block has a significant added military value. This is unlike the "big-bang" approach, where there is a test and evaluation pass/fail exam on whether a fixed, long-term, desired performance has been achieved (here the tests determine the system's capabilities and limitations for that block, and this provides valuable inputs for the R&D on the next blocks). Similarly, the budget process is no longer a linear process from research through development, production, and support. Now, these activities are performed in parallel on subsequent blocks. Also, the logistics system needs to be configured so that multiple blocks can be in the field simultaneously, which often requires contractor support (perhaps with warranties).

Spiral development also has other advantages for the requirements process in addition to its ability to adapt to a changing environment and incorporate continuous feedback from equipment users. If properly done, it avoids the current problem of analyzing requirements in a worst-case scenario, which generates requirements for things that "might be needed," resulting in a system that is unnecessarily expensive and limited in flexibility. For example, in response to insurgents' use of roadside bombs in Iraq and Afghanistan, a heavily armored mine-resistant, ambush-protected (MRAP) vehicle was developed that weighs 60,000 to 80,000 pounds. Its weight presents significant logistics difficulties, not just in Iraq and Afghanistan but in almost any other war zone. According to Brigadier General Ronald Johnson, the assistant deputy commander for plans, policies, and operations of the U.S. Marines, "72% of the world's bridges cannot hold the MRAP. . . . [In addition,] These vehicles cannot fit aboard the pre-positioning amphibious ships that carry Marine equipment and supplies."[95] At over $1.5 million each, they also are expensive.

Another major problem with the requirements process is that although commercial equipment can potentially satisfy the needs of the requirement writer, is readily available, and costs less than new technologies, it might not satisfy all the desires of the requirement writers. It might be an 80 percent solution. If the trade-off cannot be made, then people will continue to demand higher performance—at any cost.[96] There are many examples of this problem—when the marines wanted to buy an existing helicopter for use as the presidential helicopter, when the navy tried to buy existing ships for use as the littoral combat ship, and when the air force tried to buy a modified, commercial aircraft for its tanker requirements. (For the tanker, the requirements document listed over 800 different requirements,[97] with thirty-seven called "critical.") In each case, the extreme "requirements" demanded major redesigns; causing high risks, high costs, and great schedule delays.

A major (and valid) criticism of the requirements process is that it is impossible to specify the need for a revolutionary new capability before the details of how it could be achieved are known. As John Chambers, editor of the *Oxford Companion to American Military History,* has written: "None of the most important weapons transforming warfare in the 20th century—the airplane, tank, radar, jet engine, helicopter, electronic computer, not even the atomic bomb—owned its initial development to a doctrinal 'requirement' or request of the military."[98]

Finally, in areas in which technology is changing rapidly (such as electronics), there is a tendency to keep modifying the requirements as the technology evolves. For example, the army's chief information officer, Lieutenant General Jeffrey Sorrenson, has observed that from 2004 to 2007, the army "generated more than 5,000 'requirements' documents for the purchase of information technology systems."[99]

The problem of loading excess requirements onto a new weapon system is widely recognized. In introducing the Defense Acquisition Reform Act of 2007, Senator John McCain stated that "All too often costly requirements, many of which are unrelated to what the Unified Command say they need, are piled onto these programs [in the requirements process] irresponsibly—without regard to the bottom line."[100] He noted that at one point, the navy was issuing seventy-five change orders a week while the littoral combat ships were under construction.[101] These added requirements increase weapon-system costs and reduce the quantities that are bought.

An acquisition strategy needs to be developed for any given purchase of goods or services. A critical consideration is generating incentives in planning the acquisition strategy so that both contractors and the government are motivated to achieving the highest performance at the lowest cost (not simply one or the other). The most effective incentive is to have an initial competition and to maintain the option of some form of competition throughout the program. This does not mean that every phase needs to be accompanied by competition between contractors, but if there is a readily available alternative, then the existing contractor may be continuously motivated to improve performance at increasingly lower costs (or be faced with credible competition and lose the bid). In some cases, this is impractical since the government may be committed to buying a type of a ship or a type of a high-cost aircraft for which the maintenance of an alternative would be prohibitively expensive. In those cases, other forms of incentives must be planned. For example, the DoD might vary the award fee on the contract, or promise to purchase more systems if the cost is decreased. This price elasticity is essentially what happens in the commercial world when prices fall and demand subsequently increases. This use of price elasticity is also an incentive for the DoD to encourage lower prices, as any savings normally would go back to the treasury (a disincentive to both the government program manager and the industrial supplier). In the proposed situation, the

DoD gets to keep the money and gets more of the equipment (assuming that it is needed).

Today, over 40 percent of contract awards are given as follow-ons to the existing contractor on a sole-source basis, which takes away a large percentage of total dollars without competition. For these cases, the DoD must either structure a way to stimulate competition or build significant incentives into the contract structure, paying attention to the original proposal "promises" as the basis for the award fee (rather than allowing significant revisions to the contract and then setting the award). Many other acquisition approaches have been implemented. In recent years, there has been a large shift toward indefinite delivery, indefinite quantity (IDIQ), a form of contracting that is valuable for the many service contracts that are issued (for more than half of the DoD awards). In the service area, it is often difficult to define the contract needs in advance and to determine exactly how much of the service will be required in the future. The current approach has been to award IDIQ contracts to multiple competitors. As each new task arises from the needs of the buyer and is defined into specifications, two or three winners could then bid on performing that task with an assumption that the initial two or three winners (of the overall IDIQ) are selected because they have the capability in each of the task areas. Unfortunately, the attractiveness of this approach has led to incorrectly applying it. The government has been known to award initial contracts to twenty or more "winners" (of the right to bid on the subsequent tasks) and then initiate competition for each task among the large pool of "winners". This has disadvantages in terms of the high cost of the proposal effort itself and discourages the winners, which have a low probability of winning any individual task. One extreme example of this occurred when the army made an award—in the highly sophisticated simulation and training area—to 142 winners.[102] An even more extreme case is the Navy's "seaport" contract in which 1,800 "winners" have the right to bid on tasks in over 20 business areas. The concept of competition needs to be applied more efficiently and effectively.

An initial analysis of the acquisition strategy for a given program must consider all possible benefits. For example, perhaps the product or service might be used to stimulate small businesses, taking advantage of the innovation they offer and satisfying the congressional mandate for a significant share of the business to go to small businesses.

When the government buys commodities, it can shift to a more efficient and effective practice, such as using inverse auctions or purchasing from the General Services Administration (GSA) schedule for the items (the schedule lists items for which the GSA has negotiated significant volume discounts). Additionally, using government purchase cards has brought about significant cost savings.

Alternatively, government franchising allows one government agency to procure a particular item or service with a volume discount for multiple agencies. This technique is effective only with well-defined, common commodities. When a product or service is unique to a particular agency, this technique has not been successful, and the agency is usually better off procuring the item on its own.

Finally, "other transactions authorities (OTAs)" are used when products or services can come from firms that are commercially oriented and have commercial products or services meeting DoD needs. OTAs allow the government to use best commercial practices for its procurements with nontraditional defense suppliers as long as the practices are within the law, rather than being required to follow unique federal regulations and practices normally used in government procurements. This satisfies urgent DoD needs and attracts nontraditional suppliers to DoD. Thus, the supplier base is broadened to commercial firms that normally avoid the complex and bureaucratic processes associated with government transactions. As the commercial world becomes increasingly high-tech in many critical technology areas that are essential to national security, OTAs in the government's acquisitions becomes increasingly attractive. However, in order to take full advantage of OTAs, since many of the commercial items fit best at the lower tiers of a weapon system, it is necessary for the prime contractor to utilize OTAs in their purchases, and they have been reluctant to do this. A change here is desired, and will (in some cases) require some legislative changes.

Teaming

Mergers in the defense industry have reduced the numbers of suppliers in a given area to only two or three firms. In these situations, sometimes the volume of sales is too small to support more than one supplier. Rather than allowing one of the two or three to go out of business as a result of an all-out competition, the Defense Department has increasingly encouraged the limited suppliers to team together. This practice forms a monopoly but keeps both suppliers in business for potential competition in the future. The down side for the government is that it loses the benefits of the competition on the current program and pays higher prices as a result. For example, when the two nuclear submarine suppliers (General Dynamics and Newport News) formed a team to build advanced submarines, they both remained in business, but costs were estimated to increase by $500 million per submarine. Similarly, when the two rocket suppliers for medium and heavy launch services (Boeing and Lockheed Martin) created the United Launch Alliance, the DoD stated that this was the only way that it could keep both suppliers in business. But the Federal Trade Commission (FTC) analyzed the structure of the proposed merger and stated that "the proposed joint venture is likely to have a substantial adverse affect on competition in the market for U.S. government intermediate and heavy launch services. The anticipated result of this anti-competitive consolidation would be to reduce the rate of innovation and other non-priced benefits and increase the prices that the government, including the Air Force, NASA and other government agencies, would pay for these services. . . . the proposed transaction also raises vertical issues. Boeing and Lockheed are two of only three competitors—the third being Northrop Grumman—in the government satellite market. Today, competition between Boeing and Lockheed for launch services may positively impact the company's willingness to cooperate with Northrop. After Boeing and Lockheed merged their launch vehicle businesses, there may be no competitive incentive to optimize their launch of vehicles for use with Northrop's satellites. Further, as vertically-integrated suppliers, Boeing and Lockheed likely would have incentives to share confidential Northrop information (obtained as a launch vehicle services supplier, with respect to their satellite businesses), thereby adversely affecting the government satellite market."[103]

In addition to the monopoly concerns that are associated with these trends in teaming and joint ventures, questions have been raised about whether this is an efficient and effective management structure. Referring to the above-noted rocket joint venture, the *Wall Street Journal* asked, "Can Boeing and Lockheed Work Together?"[104] The concern is that these two defense industry giants will be in an awkward joint venture in one area while continuously competing in many other areas of defense business. A similar concern was raised by NASA in selecting Lockheed Martin as the prime contractor for the $8 billion Orion crew exploration vehicle. It stated that there was confusion over how the losing team (Northrop Grumman and Boeing) would actually work since the two aerospace giants had agreed to switch off taking the lead in different competitions. NASA was "concerned that two very large companies, integrating and interacting as prime and sub, will be a recurring management challenge."[105]

The teaming partners typically note that there is insufficient volume to support both companies, and the government desires to keep two firms in the general area of business so that they can be subsequently split up and compete in future competitions. These are valid considerations. Two alternatives (to teaming) also can be considered to maintain competition in the future. One is to use the savings that come from the competition between two suppliers (versus the monopoly pricing of the team) to fund an R&D contract with the loser of the competition. This allows the losing firm to stay in the business (admittedly at a much lower level), ensures that the engineering and manufacturing talent (to build a prototype) is available for subsequent future competitions,stimulates innovation through next-generation system funding, and keeps pressure on the winner (regarding both cost and performance). The second alternative is to allow foreign competition in the business area for future activities, which would then keep the remaining U.S.

supplier in a constant-competition mode. But the United States would have to allow a serious competition with the foreign source and would have to pay for an R&D program with the American company if it loses, so that it can stay in the business.

Lead Systems Integrator (LSI)

As the government moves more toward netcentric systems-of-systems that combine distributed sensors and shooters on various platforms (air, land, and sea) and that are integrated with complex communications and command and control systems, the question of how to manage such activities arises. Historically, complex systems were managed by establishing a strong government program office with experienced program managers, systems engineers, and program control people. Admiral "Red" Raborn ran the Polaris program (a combination of submarines and long-range ballistic missiles), and Admiral Hyman Rickover ran many complex naval nuclear power systems this way.

But in 2002, when the Coast Guard decided to modernize and integrate its 91 ships, 49 aviation drones, 124 small boats, and 195 new or upgraded helicopters and connect them with a new communications system, it turned over responsibility for this massive Deepwater program (a twenty-five-year $24 billion effort) to a consortium created by Lockheed Martin and Northrop Grumman called Integrated Coast Guard Systems. The rationale was that the Coast Guard lacked the personnel to manage a program of this size and complexity. The Department of Defense faced a similar shortage because its acquisition workforce had been cut by over 50 percent at the end of the cold war and was not built back up in the post-9/11 period (since all increased dollars were going to the warfighters in the Iraq and Afghanistan conflicts). When the army decided to modernize its forces for the twenty-first century with a program known as the Future Combat System (FCS), it chose a joint effort by Boeing and SAIC to manage a major modernization of all army vehicles, missiles, robots, command and control, and communications systems.

In these LSI efforts, the prime contractor (which, in these two examples, each used a team) would perform the overall architecture and systems engineering and would select all of the subcontractors that would make up the elements of these complex systems-of-systems (the platforms, sensors, and communications system). For example, in the Deepwater program, the prime contractor (the team of Lockheed Martin and Northrop Grumman) would decide which ships and which aircraft were needed and which subcontractors would design and build the subsystems in them.

Two major concerns about this LSI concept grew among the Congress and the DoD. The first was the question of adequate government visibility into and control of the program structure, content, and performance. A report issued by the Department of Homeland Security's inspector general found that Coast Guard officials had limited influence over contractor decisions.[106] This lack of government insight and control exacerbated the second of the major concerns about the LSI concept—the potential for significant conflicts of interest on the part of the prime contractor. Since the prime contractors were selecting each platform and major subcontractor in this system-of-systems, they were gaining a profit from that effort and could configure the system in their inherent favor by selecting their own divisions as the suppliers of the various elements of the system-of-systems. Thus, the overall configuration (regarding overall performance and costs) could be optimized in favor of the prime contractor rather than the government's needs. The many elements in that system-of-systems could be selected on the basis of either their own suppliers or ones that they prefer versus having a free and open competition for the best in class for each element of the system-of-systems (which again would not be in the government's interests but in the interests of the prime contractor).

In spite of these concerns and primarily because of the shortage of qualified government people to do these jobs, the LSI concept continued to be expanded.[107] For example, Boeing was selected as the lead systems integrator on the national missile defense program, and the Homeland Security Department selected them to manage SBI net (a $2 billion effort to create a virtual fence along the U.S. border with Mexico that combined sensors, cameras, and other equipment). Some of these programs encountered problems. The first of the Deepwater ships was a rebuilt patrol boat that formed cracks in the decks and hulls and experienced a series of mechanical problems. The Coast Guard pulled the renovated ships from service and permanently retired them because the repairs would cost another $50 million on top of the $100 million already spent on the renovations.[108] Headlines in *U.S. News and World Report* announced "Deep Trouble for Deep Water."[109] With considerable pressure from Congress, the Coast Guard reclaimed the management of the program and relieved Lockheed Martin and Northrop Grumman of their lead systems integrator role.[110]

As problems with the lead systems integrator programs continued to grow and with mounting concerns about lack of government control and conflicts of interest,[111] Congress (in the Defense Authorization Act for fiscal year 2007) placed limitations on contractors acting as lead systems integrators: "no entity performing Lead Systems Integrator functions in the acquisition of a major system by the Department of Defense may have any direct financial interests in the development or construction of any individual system or element of any system-of-systems."[112] The Department of Defense made this limitation applicable to all contracts entered into after December 31, 2006, which removed programs such as the Future Combat System from being covered by this bill but ensured that all future systems would be included. Congress allowed two exceptions to this rule. The Secretary of Defense could certify that a contractor is the best of industry's suppliers of that particular element or that it was chosen only after the Defense Department conducted a formal competition to which the selected contractor was the only respondent.

Because of the government's personnel shortages and inability to manage large and complex systems-of-systems, it sometimes hires an independent company as the systems architect and systems engineering firm. This firm must be willing to take a hardware and software exclusion in its contract. But since most of the firms that historically were independent have been absorbed in the vertical integration that took place during the defense-consolidation period, this requirement has meant either that a large firm takes a hardware and software exclusion on a given program (something that is undesirable for them) or that new firms are created or spun off from the large firms to fill this gap. (In 2009, the National Reconnaissance Office forced Northrop Grumman to sell off their TASC Division since they were doing systems engineering for the government's Program Office while other Divisions were building satellites for them). In essence, the independent firm works for the government to support the government's program office that is in charge of the integration, and it gets its staff from the independent firm. Then the selection of the various elements within the system-of-system is the responsibility of the government (with advice from the independent firm). This solution addresses both major problems that are faced by the LSI approach: the government has full visibility and is in charge, and the prime contractor has no conflicts of interest since the systems integrator has taken a hardware and software exclusion in their contract.

Procurement[113]

Because hundreds of billions of dollars of taxpayer money are involved, the government's procurement system must be perceived as being equitable, efficient, effective, and transparent. Every time an incident occurs that does not have those results, there is likely to be a new piece of legislation or regulation written to make sure that it never happens again. As a result, the government procurement system is extensively (and many say, excessively) detailed, regulated, stretched out, and expensive; with extensive checks and balances as well as oversight. The added costs of this government-unique regulation and oversight (compared to regular commercial practices) have been estimated at between 10 and 50 percent.[114] A detailed study by the auditing firm of Coopers and Lybrand placed the added cost at 18 percent.[115] The government incurs a significant cost by operating in this unique, highly specialized market.

Particularly noteworthy is the size of the DoD procurement system. In fiscal year 2006, there were 3,681,301 procurement actions for a total of $284,965,796,000. Although 25 percent of the actions were for awards of under $25,000, over 98 percent of the dollars went to awards over $25,000, and of the latter, more than 80 percent went to a few very large firms.[116]

Because the government makes millions of awards of very small purchases annually (which, if done by the normal, extensive procurement process, would tie up an enormous number of people), it has moved to a purchase-card program known as GSA-SmartPay. In 2006, this program handled $23 billion in overall federal government purchases and was believed to have saved the government over a billion dollars in federal acquisition processing costs.[117]

Franchising

To be more efficient in its acquisitions and to compensate for the significant post–cold war cutbacks in contracting personnel, the DoD tried to use contracting organizations from other government agencies. Frequently, however, the people who were issuing the contracts were not familiar with Defense Department procedures or mission needs. When the Department of Defense used two Interior Department procurement operations, the DoD inspector general found that they "routinely violated rules designed to protect U.S. government interests." In forty-nine contracts evaluated, 61 percent had evidence of "illegal contracts, ill-advised contracts, and various failings of contract administration procedures," and 96 percent lacked sufficient monitoring.[118] When the DoD made purchases through Fed Source, the Department of the Treasury's contracting entity, the DoD inspector general found that fifty-eight of sixty-one task orders had "inadequate contract surveillance plans" and had many other contracting deficiencies.[119] Newspaper headlines in the press announced that Interior Department officials bought armor to reinforce army vehicles from a software maker and bought furniture for the Defense Department from a company that had not previously been in the furniture business.[120] Since these other government agencies charged a fee for doing contracting work (whose effectiveness was questionable), the practice was largely discontinued.

Request for a Proposal

To give everyone a fair chance to bid on what the DoD is interested in buying, an extensive process defines what will be requested from the various industrial bidders. This process is often preceded by a request for information from industry that helps companies determine how they would solve a problem that the government has and what goods or services they might currently have available to satisfy the government's need. Essentially, this is a market survey. The request for information is followed by a request for proposal (RFP), which is an extensive effort to have government purchasers describe, in detail, exactly what they want. If the item to be procured is essentially a commodity that is readily available and undifferentiated among producers, then a request for quotation (RFQ) can be sent, and purchasers can simply open the envelope, and the low bidder wins. But this is an increasingly rare situation because of the complexity and sophistication of the goods and services being procured. In fact, since 60 percent of the total procurements are now services[121] and since services are hard to describe and compare, the use of RFQs is rarely used today.

In 1907, the U.S. Army issued Signal Corps Specification No. 486 for a "heavier-than-air flying machine." It was, in effect, a one-page request for a prototype aircraft that could "be quickly and easily taken apart and packed for transportation in army wagons," be "capable of being assembled and put in operating condition in about one hour," and "be designed to have a speed of at least 40 miles an hour in still air" followed by a discussion of how it would be tested to demonstrate that it satisfied the requirements.[122] After reviewing the responses for one month, the army awarded Wilbur and Orville Wright a two-page, fixed-price contract for a total cost of $25,000 "to be paid as soon as practicable after the acceptance of completion of the contract." Over the hundred-plus years since then, the Congress and the executive branch have greatly complicated this process. The RFQ may now be hundreds of pages, the time period for response and evaluation is greatly expanded, and the contract itself is far more complex. But some places are attempting to do something very similar to what this Wright brothers' case intended and achieved. For example, the Defense Advance Research Projects Agency issues a broad area announcement (BAA), which states that the government is looking for ideas to solve a problem in a broadly defined area. It usually limits the page numbers in the response so that it can move quickly to make multiple awards and get the investigations under way. But this is not the norm. The typical RFP issued today for a new weapon system or even for sophisticated services is an extensive document that has been widely coordinated among all interested government parties and that often takes months to prepare. This is usually followed by a bidders briefing, which provides an opportunity for potential bidders to ask clarifying questions and for answers to be provided for all. Bidders are typically given six months to respond (and are given data about the performance desired).

Proposals

In general, companies tend to put their best people on proposals since winning them is often an "all or nothing" situation. The government would prefer to have these people working on the contracts, but from the industry's perspective, winning in the proposal competition is the main priority. On the large programs, only a few companies are capable of responding (for example, to build a new fighter aircraft), and the result is a "fierce rivalry."[123]

Many of the dollars awarded by the Defense Department do not have a competition, for three primary reasons. First, sometimes only one firm is capable of responding to the request. For example, only one qualified company (Newport News Shipbuilding) has adequate facilities to build a nuclear aircraft carrier. Second, if a company is clearly going to win the competition and it is extremely expensive for others to bid against that company, then the government will often either get a single bid or will make a sole-source justification (for example, for a follow-on production order for a complex weapon system where only one company currently is in production on it). Finally, when there is a critical time urgency for the product or service, the government might select, on a sole-source basis, a company that it feels is most qualified and can satisfy the urgent need. In fiscal year 2004, one-third of the government's procurement dollars were awarded noncompetitively; and even when competitions were held (in 2005), 20 percent of the requests received only one offer.[124] The primary reason that a significant percentage of dollars are awarded on a sole-source basis is simply that prior competitions were won by that remaining producer. For example, on a major aircraft program, there would be fierce competition for the initial award. But after a company is in production, rarely is that program recompeted for future production quantities. The maintenance of that aircraft is also unlikely to be competed and, instead, will be done either by the government or the original contractor on a sole-source basis.

Because of the all-or-nothing aspects of these rivalries for multibillion-dollar, multiyear awards, companies spend millions (even hundreds of millions) to win these competitions. They assemble large proposal-writing teams, often bring in consultants to help, and sometimes even build hardware to demonstrate their capability. Since the dollars available to the government for these large programs are already known (through the budget process) and published, the industry knows them. This sets an upper limit on the costs that can be proposed. However, history has demonstrated that, as the program evolves, hundreds and even thousands of changes will be introduced into the program, and since they occur after the award, they can be quoted by the winning contractor on a sole-source basis. Thus, there is an enormous temptation to bid low ("buy in") to win the competition and assume that the program will grow significantly through the changes. The contracts allow the government to make unilateral changes to the contract through the changes clause and allow the contractor to prove to the government what that change will cost when implemented. As the program evolves (often in terms of quantities and performance modifications), these changes in the requirements of the government are a principal cause of the cost growth in a defense weapons program between the initial low bid and the final cost of the program. Other causes include government budget changes and technical problems.

The bargaining power between the government and the industry changes dramatically during this process. In the competitive preaward phase, the government is the sole buyer and has all the power as a few industrial firms bid for these large programs. After the award, the winning contractor (making a unique product that the government badly needs or providing an in-place service that the government badly needs) is in a strong position in any negotiation on government-desired changes. In an ideal situation (from the government's perspective), every effort is made to minimize the changes to a contract after the award has been made. However, as technology is improved, the government tends to want the better performance offered, and as the world environment changes, the government's needs change, so a statement of "no changes" (which the government frequently makes at the beginning of a program) is hard to implement as the program evolves.

As an extreme example, on the F-111 aircraft program there were over 492,000 total changes (many on the electronics). Even though this was a "fixed price" contract, the costs rose dramatically as each change was quoted on a sole source basis.

Source Selection

The source-selection decision determines which company will get a multiyear, multibillion-dollar award to build a critically needed weapon system for the Department of Defense. Because of the importance of this decision and of the need to appear to be totally fair to the bidders (who have spent many months and many millions of dollars putting together their detailed proposals), the government forms source-selection teams to evaluate the performance and cost data received from each contractor. These proposals offer very different solutions to the government's stated need, so there are two ways in which this evaluation can be done. The first is to weigh various aspects of cost, performance, and schedule by each bidder. The weighting factors are announced in the RFP and include detailed weighting factors within each of those three parameters. The one with the best overall score wins. The alternative method is to say that each bidder is either technically acceptable or not and, among those that are "technically acceptable," to pick the low bidder as the winner. This method is far less desirable than the best-value alternative (combining cost, performance, and schedule) because performance and schedule do matter. At times, paying a little more to get much more performance is valuable to military capability. If that is the case, then best-value alternatives are far more attractive. This is the way that commercial buying is usually done.

To do a best-value evaluation, the previously separated source-selection teams associated with cost and performance must be combined. But a second consideration with regard to cost is the cost realism of the bidder. To determine the realism of the bid, the government must perform an independent cost analysis (ICA). Each of the military services and the Office of the Secretary of Defense are able to perform an ICA on a given proposal, and this should be used to determine the realism of a given bid. Although it is attractive for the government to accept a low price from a large corporation, history has shown that the government is safer using its independent cost-analysis estimates as the basis of its awards. If it accepts an unrealistically low bid, the winning bidder is likely to take advantage of the changes clause and bid those changes on a sole-source basis. This will lead the program to have a large cost overrun, and (in order to stay within the total DoD budget) either the overall program will be cut back or other programs have to be cut back—both of which are undesirable results.

One final source-selection criterion that was introduced in the 1990s is "past performance." In the commercial world, if a firm does not do a good job in providing a service or provides a faulty product, then consumers will buy from someone else the next time. They have used past performance in their selection process. By introducing past performance as an important selection consideration, contractors are motivated to perform well on products or services in their current contracts so that by succeeding with cost, schedule, and performance goals they will win in the future. Past performance is difficult to measure when companies are delivering sophisticated products and services that have many variables (as subsets of cost, performance, and schedule). Moreover, the government will probably change the program frequently during its duration, which makes the evaluation of past performance even more difficult. A number of suggestions have been made about how a company's past-performance score card can be improved. Some of these include looking at comparable products and services, separating out the cause of any bad performance (government versus contractor), allowing contractors to review the evaluations and discuss them with the government, and including both the contractor's and the government's comments on the score card.[125] This area requires further government attention since it is an excellent incentive to encourage companies to do a good job, and it will result in quality providers being used for their goods and services.

Contract Types

The government has a wide variety of options in awarding contracts. These include the following:

- *Firm fixed price (FFP)*   Firm fixed price is the traditional way in which commercial business is usually done. It is highly appropriate when the products are well defined and the technology has been fully demonstrated, so that there is low risk of not performing the function for the dollars quoted. The firm fixed price contract form also works for a best-efforts activity where the results are not guaranteed but the contractor will make its best effort to achieve the results within the dollars bid. Despite some people's desires,[126] it is not an appropriate vehicle for a high-risk R&D program, which can be bid in only two ways. The contractor can (1) put in a high contingency to cover the risk, which means that the government will pay much more than might otherwise be the case for that R&D effort, or (2) bid low to win the contract and then maximize the many expected changes that the government will impose and that will be bid in a sole-source environment. This idea (of fixed-price developments on high-technology defense products) has been tried in the past (for example, on the F-111 fighter aircraft, (see above) the C-5 transport aircraft, and numerous others), always with the same results—extremely large cost growths (exceeding those found with cost-based development contracts). There is always the hope that "this time will be different" and that the government will manage the program without any changes in the budgets, quantities, technologies, or mission needs. On the other hand, this fixed-price form of contract is appropriate to be used for large production programs after the product has been demonstrated but not for major, high-risk development efforts. The advantage of this form of contract for the government is that the costs are known (as long as there are no further changes) and for industry is that firms can make a larger profit if they can improve their productivity. For the appropriate programs, this is a highly desirable form of contract.

• *Cost plus fixed fee (CPFF)*   A cost-based contract is appropriate for programs for which the requirements cannot be specified or the technical capability that might be realized is unknown (that is, where there is a high risk). Under these conditions, the contractor is not likely to undertake the project on a fixed-price basis (because the risk is too high) but will do so on a cost-based effort. When the fee is fixed, the contractor does not receive any added fee if the cost grows (as long as the scope stays the same), and there is no reward (that is, no added fee) for reducing the program costs.

• *Cost plus award fee (CPAF)*   The government can use a cost plus award fee to motivate a contractor to improve performance, cost, or schedule). A preset awards schedule varies the fee as a function of the contractor's performance. Another form of this is cost plus incentive fee (CPIF), where the objective is the same. In both cases, the amount of fee awarded is a function of the performance achieved on the contract. In theory, this form of contract makes a lot of sense. If the contractor comes in under cost or exceeds the specified performance, it is rewarded with a higher profit. But it has generated a great deal of criticism because the award fees often are given without the desired award-based results. A 2006 GAO report found "that the DoD has paid out an estimated $8 billion in award fees regardless of whether acquisition outcomes fell short of, or met, or exceeded DoD's expectations,"[127] and a 2009 GAO report found that this failure had not significantly improved.[128]

• *Cost plus award term (CPAT)*   With this form of cost-plus contract, the contractor has a large incentive to perform well against preset targets because if it does, it will be awarded the next phase of the effort (whether for additional services, additional quantities of equipment, or continued development of the product). This is not a common technique, but it is attractive to the government because it gives a significant incentive to the contractor, and it is attractive to the contractor because it gets a significant follow-on effort if it does well.

• *Urgent wartime need* In a wartime environment (where lives are being lost or the mission cannot be performed), a crisis sometimes requires a rapid response. There is no time to go through the full contract process—request for a proposal, source selection, detailed design, technology demonstration—to make a fixed-price bid, but the product or service is needed immediately. In this situation, many standard procedures must be waived, and awards are made on a cost-based arrangement (with or without competition). Special legislative provisions exist for this set of conditions.

• *Time and materials (T&M)* In this common commercial form of contract for services, the contractor is reimbursed (with a small fee, since the risk is low) for all of their labor and materials costs. In the competitive phase of this effort, contractors tend to minimize their bid by bidding very low-cost labor and low-cost overheads. In the implementation phase, they attempt to maximize the amount of high-cost labor to maximize their revenue. When the scope is poorly defined, this is a convenient contract vehicle to use since the government can control the scope as the contract moves along. However, it is an input-based vehicle, and the results achieved (not how much labor or materials were put into the program) matter. In addition, the contractor has the perverse incentive to maximize costs—since each dollar of labor or material carries a fee with it (even though it is a small percentage fee).

• *Indefinite delivery, indefinite quantity (IDIQ)* In this form of contract, the scope and quantity of goods or services to be delivered are not yet available in detail. This form of contract is used in a broad area of work by awarding multiple contracts to two or more suppliers and, as tasks come up, competitively selecting between the suppliers for each individual task. In this way, the government has the flexibility of maintaining competition while defining each task as the work is needed. This type of contract was particularly attractive for small service efforts, and by 1996,[129] the concept of multiple awards for IDIQ contracts began to catch on. Unfortunately, some people in the government felt that they got better competition through having many contractors on a given IDIQ contract,[130] and they also found that they could eliminate any bidder from protesting the award by simply awarding it to many of them. The concept became perverted by allowing large numbers of winners for the basic contract and then holding large competitions for each individual task (which, as previously noted, is grossly inefficient).

• *Other transactions authority (OTA)*   This form of contract is allowed by law but is not defined in the law. It basically takes advantage of the way in which the law was written to cover contracts, grants, and other transactions authorities. Rick Dunn, DARPA general counsel, took advantage of this lack of definition. He provided a vehicle that Congress would allow to be flexible in order to expedite the development and fielding of new military capabilities by using commercial practices and to bring in commercial firms (and their products) for technological advancement that they would never have bid on if they had to go through the full government legislative and regulatory environment.[131] Congress first authorized the use of OTAs for the Defense Advanced Research Projects Agency in 1989. In 1991, OTAs were made permanent and expanded to the military departments. The original authority (United States Code, title 10, section 2371) was directed at research, but its flexibility and its success in bringing in nontraditional contractors led Congress to expand this authority in 1994 (Public Law 103-160, section 845) to a prototype authority. Finally, since a company that built a prototype under the OTA agreements would not be willing to have standard (DoD unique) contract clauses suddenly applied when it went into production, the Congress allowed programs that had been started under OTA to go into production on that same basis. Unfortunately, some very large programs (one for a navy ship and one for a whole next-generation army system-of-systems) attempted to use the OTA approach at the prime-contract level, which Congress felt was going too far; so the concept was temporarily set back. Its main advantages—offering flexibility and bringing in nontraditional suppliers—are valuable, and it should be used wherever applicable. As noted above, one area that it should be expanded to is subcontracting, where the tendency of the prime contractors has been to pass on (to all of their subcontractors) all of the terms and conditions that the government puts into the prime contract. This greatly discourages commercial suppliers, even though in many cases, the commercial suppliers at the lower tiers have the most to offer. Efforts must be made to find ways to encourage the prime contractors to use OTA subcontracts wherever applicable to bring in the best possible suppliers from either the traditional defense world or the commercial world (where the latter are now largely excluded).

• *Grants*   For universities and other organizations that do not satisfy specialized defense requirements (such as specialized cost-accounting systems), a fixed-price grant for research efforts or similar activities is appropriate and commonly used for these situations (usually for relatively small contracts).

• *Cooperative research and development agreement (CRADA)*   At times (particularly in research activities), where it makes sense for the government to work cooperatively with an industry or a university in a joint activity. In this case, the government pays for its share, and partially or fully funds its "partner." A new vehicle was required, and the CRADA fills this need.

Profit Policy

The defense industry needs to make a profit on its business in order to invest in future research and development, to purchase capital equipment, and to offer a return on stockholder investments. But, because significant public funds are involved in DoD contracting, profit tends to be treated in much the same way as it is in a regulated industry (such as public utilities), and the perception is that it is in the public's interest to keep the profits relatively low. In fact, a 1977 survey performed by the DoD's director of procurement found that government procurement workers felt that their primary objective was to minimize profit (as contrasted to the expected response, which should have been to minimize total costs, since profit is a relatively small percentage of total cost).[132] Although watch-dog groups and politicians tend to think that defense contractors are making huge profits, their profits are significantly less than those in the regulated industries. In 2008 (a record year for defense contractors due to huge increases in the DoD budget and the large supplementals added to it), a survey of a cross-section of more than one hundred government contractors found that 42 percent of the surveyed government contractors had either no profit or profit rates between 1 percent and 5 percent of revenue, and 12 percent had profit rates from their government contracts of over 15 percent (and many of these were at the lower tiers of the industry and operated on fixed-price contracts).[133] About 40 percent of the revenue from federal contracts in this survey came from cost-reimbursable contracts (yielding results contrary to the general perception that these contracts resulted in excessively high profits). The reality is that these cost-reimbursable contracts received high visibility through detailed government auditing, and one area that is looked at closely is profit margin. Most people were surprised when it was revealed that the base profit on the contract for the multibillion-dollar logistics-support effort in Iraq and Afghanistan (the LOGCAP contract) was negotiated at a base profit of only 1 percent of revenue (with some potential for a small increase for an award fee).

Corrective action with regard to profit needs to be taken on the award fees on contracts. There has been much public coverage of contractors that significantly exceed anticipated costs, are behind on scheduled deliveries, and are not achieving the desired performance but are still receiving well over 80 percent of the incentive award fee (which was intended to reward firms that meet costs, schedule, and performance). Many of the criteria for the award fees were found to be based more on process-oriented milestones (such as reports delivered on time) rather than on the actual overall program cost, schedule, and performance. For example, the GAO reported that the Comanche helicopter was 41.2 percent over its budget (by $3.5 billion) and nearly three years behind schedule, and yet the team of Boeing and Sikorsky aircraft received an 85 percent award fee of $202.5 million.[134] It found that the F/A-22 Raptor fighter plane was 47.3 percent over budget (by $10.2 billion) and more than two years behind schedule, and yet Lockheed received an award fee of 91 percent for $848.7 million. It also found that the Joint Strike Fighter was 30.1 percent over budget (at $10.1 billion) and eleven months late, and yet Lockheed received an award fee of 100 percent for $494 million.

Examples such as these on large programs run by major defense contractors give the impression of major profit abuses in the defense industry. In many cases, however, the cost increases and schedule delays were brought about by government changes in requirements. So it becomes difficult to determine whether the government or the contractor was responsible for the overruns and the schedule delays on any given program. The reality usually is a combination of the two. Nonetheless, this area needs to be worked on since the intent of the award fees is to create an incentive for completing programs within budgeted costs and on time. It is critical that both the government and industry focus on cost and schedule as much as they traditionally focus on performance achievements.

One final point relative to profit is that it should be related to the risk that the company is taking on a given program. Although the regulatory guidelines state that this should be a major consideration, in many cases it does not receive sufficient attention. The defense industry's relatively low profits depend on the government often assuming much of the risk (essentially, becoming a self-insurer). For example, in the commercial world, a high-risk consideration is the customer's termination of a contract after the firm has made significant investments in long-lead parts or capital equipment or commitments to the labor force for termination costs. With defense contracts, termination liability is covered by the government. If a program is terminated, then the contractor submits a termination-cost bill to the government for all labor and capital costs. In 2006, a troubled spy-satellite contract with the Boeing Company was terminated, and Boeing expected to receive between $400 and $500 million to cover the costs of shutting down part of the program. In 2005, the Pentagon was going to terminate the Lockheed Martin C-130J transport plane but decided to keep the program alive partly because the termination costs were estimated at up to $1.6 billion.[135]

Multiyear Contracting

If a company operates from year to year on a DoD production contract, then it normally has to wait for the next year's contract before placing orders for next year's parts, and even to increase or reduce its labor force. Both Congress and the Department of Defense comptrollers prefer the annual contract because it gives them great flexibility in shifting resources from one program to another and in ordering more or less of a given item, depending on the top line of the total DoD budget. But this is a grossly inefficient way to run a business, particularly at the lower tiers. If prime contractors have multiyear contracts, then parts can be ordered in advance (they typically take eighteen months to be delivered) and therefore will be ready when the next year's order comes in, and they will cost much less, since they will be built in larger quantities and gain the benefits of the economies of scale. The firms (primes and subs) also can plan their labor force with far greater stability, which makes a big difference in cost. Long-range planning for high-priority major weapons programs could contribute enormously to the efficiency of the effort. The navy's Polaris, Poseidon, and Trident programs always had a clear picture of how much money they would have in the next few years and therefore were among the best-managed programs in independent assessments made of Defense Department management. Typical savings from multiyear contracting are in the range of 10 to 15 percent. The air force and Lockheed estimated that a multiyear contract on the F-22 Raptor would provide $225 million in savings over a three-year period.[136] Boeing estimated that a four-year, multiyear contract for the navy's Super Hornet fighter jets could save the navy 10 percent (over purchasing the aircraft on an annual basis).[137] Finally, Bell and Boeing were awarded a $10.4 billion, five-year contract to produce the Osprey tilt rotor aircraft for the marines and air force special operations command, and the vice president of the Bell and Boeing program office stated that the multiyear procurement contract "allows the industry team to stabilize our production plans, create savings for the taxpayer, and increases the number of aircraft being produced for the war fighter."[138] One problem that has been highlighted by the GAO[139] is that the DoD does not track multiyear results against original expectations and makes little effort to validate actual savings. This information would help DoD justify future multiyear awards to the Congress. The problem here is the same as it was for tracking the award-fee basis: during the multiple years of the contract, the government changes the program requirements, which makes it difficult to determine what the effects of the multiyear contract are and whether the projected initial savings were actually realized. Nonetheless, it would be worth the effort to establish the approximate savings realized since it should be clear that the benefits are inherent in the concept and tracking them would be important in justifying future multiyear contracts.

Protests

If a firm bidding on a particular procurement believes that the government did not follow the proper procedures in arriving at its decision, it has the right to protest either to the GAO or to the Court of Federal Claims. It has the right to protest the process that was used to arrive at the award decision but not the award decision itself. The normal procedure is to go to the GAO first, since that method is free and relatively fast. The GAO is required to have a finding within one hundred days, but there is no time limit on the court decision, which could take another six months. The protestors are not limited in the number of times that they can come back on a protest (if they believe they have found a cause), and again, they can go first to the GAO and then to the court. The finding of the GAO is simply a recommendation that the DoD is not bound to take, although it usually does. If the GAO finds that the DoD did not treat the bidders equally in the process (perhaps supplying more information to one than to others) or stated in the RFP that it was going to weight certain parameters in a defined fashion and then changed the relative weighting, then the GAO would likely recommend that the competition (the full process of the request for a proposal and the source selection) be redone.

Recently, the DoD has been increasing the size of individual procurements and reducing the number of these large programs, so each award becomes a do-or-die event for the contractors. There is an increasing tendency for large defense firms to hire lawyers and protest whenever they lose. The number of protests has risen significantly. Between 2002 and 2006, annual contractors' protests with the GAO increased by 10 percent (to 1,327 protests), and the number of firms taking their cases to court rose 50 percent.[140] In the post-9/11 period, however, the rate of increase in protests has been less than the rate of increase of defense procurements. Congress has passed legislation to encourage protests arguing that it is only fair to the losers if the process has been improper. But the growing number of protests has caused concern in the Congress and executive branch. In May 2008, the House Armed Services Committee raised the possibility of fining companies that submit frivolous or improper protests to the GAO. It wanted to discourage contractors from logging protests as a "stalling or punitive tactic."[141] The problem is that it is difficult to determine which protests are frivolous or vindictive and which are legitimate. In general, the GAO tends to side with the government in finding that the protest had no merit. In 2007, only one-quarter of the total of 1,318 protests were found to have merit and required an official decision. That is a slight increase from five years previous (when only 20 percent of the protests were found to have merit). The increased protests appear to be triggered by a combination of large programs with a winner-take-all award and the loser's desire to delay the award (either because it is the incumbent or because it does not want to give the advantage to their competitor as the winner). There also have been an increasing number of multiple bid protests. The losing contractors keep going through the protest cycle with the GAO almost as a fishing expedition, hoping that they might be able to get their protest sustained but at least knowing that the award will be delayed by months or, in some cases, by years. The multiple protests on the air force's combat, search, and rescue helicopter (CSAR-X) replacement program held up the award for over two years.[142] By going to court after the GAO has ruled, the delay can be much more significant and probably explains why firms are taking their case to court far more frequently.

Another reason that protests have increased is because the probability of sustainment (success in the protests) on very large, complex procurements after they were found to have merit has increased significantly. These very large, very complex procurements receive a lot of press coverage, as did the sustained protest against the award of the multibillion dollar air force tanker procurement in 2008. (So that even though replacement of the aging air force tankers was its highest priority program in 2005, it was still not even awarded by 2010—and then they had to be built!)

This increasing failure of the government to follow the procedures set up for the source-selection process has been attributed to a variety of causes. First, after the war on terrorism was initiated, Defense Department budgets increased greatly, and large budget supplementals were granted, but the number of contracting personnel in the DoD declined dramatically in the post–cold war cutbacks, and these people were not replaced in the post-9/11 era. This meant that there were inadequate numbers and seniority of people handling the contracting functions in the DoD. In addition, communications between government and industry declined dramatically in this period. Some say that there was fear of improper communications, but the reality was that an open channel of discussion had broken down. This lack of communication often resulted in an improper understanding of what the government was looking for and how it was preparing and implementing the source-selection process.

Additionally, the number of contractors in the program offices and involved in the source-selection teams has increased (again, because of the reduction in government contracting people), and protests have been made claiming that some of these contractors have conflicts of interest. A GAO report found that contractors account for up to 88 percent of the acquisition workforce at fifteen Department of Defense offices, where they are involved in critical areas of the awards process. The GAO noted that of all the laws related to personal conflicts of interest in government, contractor employees are covered only by the prohibition against bribery and kickbacks.[143]

Finally, with more multiple winners in the IDIQ contracts, losers can protest each new task, thus increasing the number of opportunities, even if they are all on the same contract vehicle. (One ruling by the Court of Claims observed that there were twenty-eight winners and many more losers, that the losers all had a basis for protests because they were not included in the winners, and that they had a basis against one or two of those that were selected on a procedural error.[144] A similar case arose when the GAO sustained a protest filed by four large defense firms against the Pentagon's Defense Information Systems Agency (DISA) after it awarded a computer services contract (valued at $12 billion) to five other companies. In that case, the

GAO concluded that DISA had meaningful discussions with the winning companies but not with some of the losers.[145]

The protest process in the government is somewhat like the professional football coach's challenge and request to game officials for an instant replay. If the challenge is sustained, then the decision is reversed, and there is no penalty to the challenger. However, if the challenge is not sustained, then there is a penalty to the challenger, who loses one of a limited number of timeouts. Perhaps the government will need to impose a penalty on the protesting firm if a protest is not sustained (such as paying the winner's and the government's legal fees) and a penalty on the government for improper procedures (such as paying the protester their costs) when the protest is sustained. Given the high costs to the government and the firms for the large number of protests found in recent years, this area would be fruitful for further investigation.

Oversight

Since the Department of Defense spends hundreds of billions of dollars of public funds annually on purchasing goods and services from the defense industry, considerable oversight of these expenditures is required. Transparency is achieved through a variety of regulations and organizations that oversee such activity. The process begins with the requirement that all major defense contractors use the approved cost-accounting standards, which are established by a Cost Accounting Standards Board of appointed experts in government accounting. This bookkeeping is overseen by the Defense Contract Audit Agency (DCAA), which has regional offices around the country and often assigns specific individuals to major contracts and individual corporate plants.

After contracts are signed, the Defense Contract Management Agency (DCMA) monitors all major contracts, and plant representatives remain resident in the major contracting facilities. While there, they check progress, quality, and item-by-item delivery of the contracted items.

There are various inspectors general—one for the Department of Defense and others for each of the separate agencies and departments within the DoD. Altogether, there are 1,737 people within the Office of the Inspector General.

Contracting specialists are assigned throughout the DoD to monitor each contract (and modifications thereto). There are over thirty thousand contract specialists within the Defense Department.

Finally, over 300,000 auditors work within the Department of Defense.[146] In 2006, a DoD-chartered acquisition performance assessment project found that there was extreme (and almost unanimous) frustration with the current state of acquisition oversight. The project's report stated that "existing oversight relies upon overlapping layers of reviews and reviewers at the expense of quality and focus. . . .

programs advance in spite of the oversight process, rather than because of it."[147] Similarly, a 2007 secretarial commission examined the problems associated with the 190,000 contractors in the battle area of Iraq and Afghanistan and found that "there were more auditors in the area than there were government contract specialists."[148] Nonetheless, in a March 31, 2008, report to the House and Senate Armed Services Committees, the Department of Defense inspector general stated that his office was "greatly understaffed" and that he "needed a 33% increase in staffing."[149]

In addition to this internal oversight and auditing, the press and independent, nonprofit organizations try to uncover waste, fraud, and abuse within the Department of Defense. One such organization is the Program on Government Oversight (POGO). Many of these organizations have preconceived biases and seem to believe that "good news is no news."

Finally, congressional committees and subcommittees have authorization and appropriations functions but also have an oversight function. In particular, the House and Senate Committees on Government Oversight are interested in turning up headline-making cases of waste, fraud, and abuse as well as in writing legislation to prevent it from ever happening again.

With all of the internal and external oversight within DoD operations, many authors have noted that far more oversight is provided for this public expenditure of funds than for private-sector operations. This is demonstrated when a large, private-sector scandal (such as Enron or Madoff) hits the headlines.

Additionally, it is often pointed out that fixing defense acquisition will require changing the process, not adding more auditors to monitor the results of a poor process. It is analogous to having more checkers at the end of an auto assembly line versus correcting the problems while the cars are being built.

Congress

The single greatest contributor to the conduct of the defense industry is the U.S. Congress, and it plays three major roles. First, through various authorization committees and subcommittees, it establishes what is to be bought and how these items are to be bought. It establishes the types of ships, planes, and tanks that will be procured each year and in what quantity. It also specifies the rules (laws) under which all of these items will be procured. Second, various budget and appropriations committees and subcommittees establish how much will be spent for the items that are authorized. At the top line, the budget committees establish the levels of total dollars to be given to the DoD out of the total U.S. government's budget. Within that top line, appropriators decide how much money goes to each program annually. In theory, each committee (the authorizers and the appropriators) is responding to the proposals received annually from the executive branch (that is, the Department of Defense). The DoD asks for the equipment and services that it believes it will need to achieve its mission and money to cover these needs. But the Congress is not required to fulfill the executive branch's requests in these matters. Finally, in addition to the authorization and appropriations role, Congress is an instrument of oversight, addressing the question of how well the executive branch implemented the laws and budgets that the Congress authorized and appropriated each year.

In 1974, when the United States was in a hot war in Vietnam and a cold war against the Soviet Union, the defense authorization bill was less than one hundred pages long. By 2001, the defense authorization bill was nearly a thousand pages long. Congress has gone into far greater detail in addressing defense needs. During this time, congressional staffs were growing dramatically while the number of representatives and senators remained the same, and the number of congressional office buildings has tripled from one location each for the House and the Senate to three each to accommodate these large staffs.

Some of the details in the thousand-page authorization bills are requests for studies (these usually come from defense firms through their local representative). These are actually unfunded mandates, which require the DoD to spend its own money. They are not funded by the Congress. Many unfunded mandates appear in each year's bill. After they are added to the bill, they become part of the law and must be performed. Many are actually funded out to industry to perform the studies, and although they often result in little change, legislators can show that they responded to their constituents by requiring the study. The bill also contains a large number of acquisition policy and process changes. The National Defense Authorization Act for fiscal year 2007 included sixty-one acquisition policy and practice changes and reports on them due to the Congress.[150]

As the Congress elaborates—in minute detail—on executive branch operations, it decreases the DoD's management flexibility to efficiently and effectively operate at minimum cost. When a problem is found in an individual case on an individual program, the Congress is tempted to write a new law that will prevent its recurrence. These new restrictions are applied to all other programs and all other acquisitions. This slows down and complicates all other cases—all to prevent one mistake from being repeated, without doing an analysis of the costs and benefits of such a change.

Congress's lawmaking process also tends to highly resist change—even as the world changes dramatically in terms of technological progress, warfighting requirements, business practices, and globalization. Sixty Senate votes are needed to take up important legislation, let alone pass it. As Steven Pearlstein wrote in the *Washington Post*, "Immigration reform, a major energy bill, global warming legislation, the housing bill, overhaul of the aviation system and fixes for the alternative minimum tax have all been bottled up in the Senate, thanks to those quaint rules."[151]

The world of defense has been globalized. The DoD gets advanced technology from offshore, U.S. defense firms sell U.S. equipment offshore, and the defense industry has multinational interests. However, the Congress continues to take a highly protectionist position in terms of both imports and exports. Restrictions enacted in the 2007 Defense Authorization Bill stalled delivery of more than 1,000 new trucks to the U.S. Army because the trucks contained metals from foreign suppliers. The presence of foreign metal was thought to violate Buy American provisions, which require that all specialty metals in U.S. defense hardware be sourced domestically.[152] In another example, when the air force selected an Airbus design for its new in-air-refueling tanker, Congress complained loudly about U.S. jobs that would be lost and threatened to cancel the program—despite the fact that the tanker was to be built in Alabama.[153]

Unfortunately, many laws that are written for valid reasons to address special cases have unintended consequences in a broader context. The export-control provisions and the Buy American Act have not been updated to reflect the globalization of technology that has taken place. Although these laws were written to protect U.S. industry, they limit the Department of Defense in obtaining the higher-performance and lower-cost systems and components from offshore. They ultimately have a negative impact on U.S. national security. Similarly, in the mid-1990s, the Congress legislated a 25 percent cut in the DoD acquisition workforce to cut back on overhead. As a result, the inadequate workforce was incapable of handling the large number of acquisition actions and the dollars expended in the first part of the twenty-first century as the dollars built up dramatically after 9/11.

It is not surprising that members of the House and the Senate want to send dollars to their districts and states in the appropriation of funds. At election time, major points will be made by elected officials who have sent home large amounts of money. Besides attempting to garner votes with these budget appropriations, members of Congress are also influenced by contributions to their campaigns. Lobbyists walk the halls of Congress and remind their delegates of the jobs in their districts and states, the contributions from their firms, and the importance of their company's programs. In 2007, lobbying expenditures reached $2.79 billion, with significant portions coming from major defense firms. Northrop Grumman, Boeing, and Lockheed spent over $10 million each on lobbying.[154]

Key members of the authorization and appropriation committees and subcommittees that deal with defense received significant contributions from defense PACs for their reelection campaigns. In 2006, when Senator Jim Talent (R-MO) was chair of the Senate Armed Services Sea Power Committee, he accepted large sums from political action committees. Boeing contributed $52,400, and General Dynamics, Lockheed Martin, Northrop Grumman, and Raytheon contributed over $10,000 each. His challenger received a total of $250 from the defense sector.[155]

These lobbying efforts and PAC contributions were intended to achieve two objectives—to maximize dollars for a company's programs and to increase congressional "earmarks" for them. Naturally, lobbyists sought to maximize the number of dollars placed into the appropriations bills for their company's programs. However, since the top line was somewhat limited (although appropriators often exceed the guidelines from the budget committees), an increase in some areas resulted in a reduction in others. When the House Armed Services Committee composed its budget for fiscal year 2008, it added three more ships and a host of additional aircraft, ultimately exceeding the amounts that the military had sought. However, the committee took out $1.6 billion from the requested funds for missile defense and the army's future development plans.[156] Additionally, when the chief of naval operations urged Congress not to add the additional DDG-51 destroyers to the budget because it would be moving back to 1980s technology, Representative Gene Taylor (D-MS), the chair of the House Armed Services Sea Power Committee at that time, added them anyway. Taylor's district is home to the Northrop Grumman Ingalls Shipyard, which was facing the prospect of shutting down its DDG-51 production line. Ultimately, the chair of the House Appropriations Defense Subcommittee, John Murtha (D-PA), refused to approve the DDG-51 purchase but wanted to add five other ships, specifying that one of these would be an additional Virginia-class nuclear attack submarine.[157] As these examples demonstrate, there is not always agreement between the authorizers and appropriators. Budgetary questions often become a power struggle with the one who controls the money holding the power. One must keep in mind the high costs involved in these actions—in this case, billions of dollars for just one submarine. Later, seven House members inserted a $2.42 billion addition into the defense appropriations bill for fiscal year 2008 for Boeing to build new C-17 transports for the air force. These were not included in the Pentagon's budget request, and, in fact, the Air Force had set aside money to halt production of the program.

As the Congress raises and lowers hundreds of individual budget items, it introduces a great deal of unpredictability and instability into the industrial planning for each year's labor force, regardless of whether it adds or subtracts dollars. The result is considerable inefficiency in industrial operations. In addition to these inefficiencies, uncertainties are associated with the rise and fall of quantities of equipment that will be authorized and appropriated. Long-lead parts cannot be ordered in advance, numbers of capital equipment for a given production quantity may be inadequate, and labor forces cannot be hired or have to be laid off in anticipation of the changed need.

The military services are not totally innocent of these actions either. The Office of the Secretary of Defense may decide not to fund a program in an attempt to balance the overall DoD budget, even though the relevant service wants it to continue. In response, the services will often indirectly let it be known on Capitol Hill that they would really like that particular program to be inserted by Congress, and they will certainly get strong support from their industrial partner (and their industrial partner's lobbyists and their labor union's representative).

The second and perhaps best-known effects of lobbying and congressional contributions are congressional "earmarks." With 34,785 registered Washington lobbyists, many inserts are added to either authorization or appropriations bills by a congressman or senator in the interests of a local constituent. In fiscal year 2007, there were 15,500 earmarks, worth $64 billion (according to the Congressional Research Service).[158] The significance of this figure depends on what is categorized as an earmark. For example, does the addition of a few ships to be built in a congressman's district for a few billion dollars count as an earmark, or should only small additions be counted, like money added for a local university's library? Nonetheless, the dollars earmarked for defense are enormous. In 2008, the House defense authorization bill had $9.9 billion in earmarks, and the Senate bill contained an additional $5.4 billion (amounting to a total of $15.3 billion).[159] *Government Executive* examined the earmarks in the fiscal year 2008 defense appropriation bill and found that thirteen of the twenty largest defense contractors received eighty earmarks (that includes large orders for ships, planes, and tanks and major equipment add-ons). Only House rules require sponsors of earmarks and their intended recipients to be publicly identified. Senate rules require sponsors to certify that the earmarks will not result in personal gain (approximately 40 percent of the legislations' earmarks—comprising $5.3 billion—were inserted by senators on behalf of unknown recipients).[160] Needless to say, these earmarks can be highly disruptive to an efficient operation planned by either the DoD or the industry.

When the president receives a defense bill, he can veto the whole bill or approve it. He does not have the option of vetoing individual line items within the bill. He might strongly object to the addition of these billions of dollars worth of earmarks, but he can do nothing about it unless he vetoes the whole bill—which would stop the operation of the government. After signing the fiscal year 2008 appropriations bill, George W. Bush maintained the following about the 9,800 earmarks totaling more than $10 billion: "These projects are not funded through a merit-based process and provide a vehicle for wasteful government spending."[161]

The biggest effect of congressional micromanagement—continuous changes in budget line items and insertion of earmarks—is inefficiency and reduction in national security effectiveness. It also should be noted that senior executives in the Department of Defense and in other government agencies must spend significant amounts of time preparing and presenting testimony before congressional hearings that the multiple authorization and appropriation committees and subcommittees require. An extreme example of this process can be found in the Department of Homeland Security, where eighty-eight congressional committees and subcommittees have jurisdiction over some aspect of homeland security.[162]

In addition to the regular hearings on authorization and appropriations, there are also many hearings in connection with Congress's role of oversight. Cynics claim the objective is not to improve the system but rather to catch someone and make headlines in the process. When a problem is discovered—whether a cost overrun on a program, a violation of one of the congressional dictates in the law, or an inappropriate application of the government-unique cost accounting rules—hearings will be held, and new rules will be proposed. As noted above, these rules may prevent such an event from ever happening again, but when applied to all other programs, they usually have the adverse effect of slowing down operations and making them less efficient or effective. The transparency provided by such hearings (and usually amplified by the press) serves a valuable function in ensuring legal behavior, but despite the large funds being awarded by the Congress and the large dollars being provided to members for their reelection campaigns, there are actually very few examples of illegal actions. Although a Republican Congressman, Randy "Duke" Cunningham, was convicted in 2006 of taking millions of dollars in cash and gifts in exchange for earmarks benefiting a military contractor, it was considered a rare incident. Its visibility in the public media serves as the equivalent of a public hanging that discourages such behavior on the part of other public figures.

Waste, Fraud, and Abuse

Newspaper articles have proclaimed scandals in Defense Department procurements for centuries. There were questions about the prices that George Washington's troops paid for food and clothing at Valley Forge. In the mid-1930s, the famous "merchants of death" hearings were led by Senator Gerald Nye,[163] and in the early 1940s, the "war profits hearings" were led by Senator Harry Truman. But actual scandals regarding illegal actions are not responsible for billions or even hundreds of millions of dollars worth of cost overruns or ineffective weapons systems. Rather, they are relatively low-cost incidents. In many cases of such incidents, a common item could be purchased from a local store at a much lower price. In the "spare-parts scandal" of the mid-1980s, the government was found to have paid $9,609 for a wrench.[164] In this case, the government offered a rational explanation that involved the way in which overhead costs for the overall manufacturing facility were allocated. The difference between the price at a hardware store and the price that the government was paying covered the costs associated with the defense factory's overhead and was not profit that the company was realizing. But the public's perception was that most of this exorbitant price was going into the company's pocket as profits. In fact, a survey conducted at the time found that Americans considered waste and fraud in Defense Department spending a large and serious national problem.[165] On average, Americans believed that almost half of the DoD budget is lost to waste and fraud, that fraud accounts for the loss of as many dollars as waste, and that anyone involved in defense procurement—especially a contractor—is likely to commit fraudulent and dishonest acts. Their assumption was that defense contractors must be making enormous illegal profits on everything from hammers to major weapons systems.

To determine how much of the approximately $450 billion a year in Defense Department contracts (as of 2008) is actually consumed by illegal actions, one must first define waste, fraud, and abuse (although largely due to media presentations, the public tends to view these three terms as interchangeable). Fraud is the performance of illegal actions, waste is the inefficient and ineffective use of government money through poor management, and abuse is an unintelligent, wrong, but not strictly illegal action. Examples of waste include the following:[166]

- Unreasonable, unrealistic, inadequate, or frequently changing Department of Defense requirements,
- Failure to use competitive bidding in appropriate circumstances,
- Failure to engage in selected precontracting activities for contingent events (such as hurricanes or military conflicts), and
- Congressional directions (such as earmarks) and agencies' spending actions that violate an objective value-and-risk-assessment in considering available resources.

In 1985, the Grace Commission defined 104 categories of alleged waste in the Department of Defense.[167] The three largest in number (by far) were high overhead charges by defense contractors (due to the absence of incentives for cost reduction in the management of weapons systems), instability in the budgeting and procurement process (which leads to uneconomical production rates), and a lack of cost consciousness in the designing of weapons (and correspondingly in the requirements process). Thus, to save billions of dollars of waste, the focus should be on the broad structural issues of the weapons-acquisition process.

Another major source of waste (and a significant cause of the high overhead noted above) is the regulatory process, which is estimated to add from 15 percent to 20 percent to the total cost.[168] The regulatory process includes excessive paperwork, socioeconomic programs, specialized cost-accounting procedures, and other regulatory barriers to the integration of commercial practices and products into the Defense Department. Other examples of waste include turning production lines on and off, requiring custom-made items, and buying in excessively low quantities.

Some of these categories can run into very big dollars—particularly when related to a weapon system and the poor management of that program. Even if these wasteful dollars run into the billions, however, these negligent acts are not illegal but simply ineffective or inefficient use of public funds. The examples of waste that tend to get the biggest attention are actually not the most costly. In 1998, a DoD inspector general found that a buyer had significantly overpaid for some small electronic spare parts for an aircraft. The Pentagon received a number of letters from Capitol Hill asking "who was fired over the incident." Defense Secretary William Cohen responded in a broadcast to the entire Defense Department that he resisted such requests, was committed to figuring out what went wrong and why, and wanted people to "think more about innovation than about being punished for making honest mistakes." The investigation showed that the buyer had incorrectly paid for the immediate delivery of a small supply of parts when the actual order called for a large quantity to be put on the shelf for subsequent use as spare parts. When told about the error, the buyer corrected the mistake and received a significant price reduction for a large-volume discount. The action was not illegal but simply an honest mistake. In this case, the buyer had creatively tried to buy from a catalog rather than negotiating in detail for the parts, so the corrective action was not firing this individual but issuing a training manual on buying from catalogs, which should be encouraged whenever applicable.

In the abuse category, contractors often take advantage of existing laws without committing any illegal action. Because the law requires a large amount of total DoD business to be set aside for small and minority companies, for example, large companies often use a small company as a "front" to manipulate such regulations. Although such subcontracts from small firms to large firms are not illegal, they are not the intent of the small business set-aside laws.

All cases of waste and abuse are undesirable, but only cases of fraud are illegal. Again, these tend to comprise a very small dollar value of all DoD business. Even in the case of the spare-parts scandal and other abuses during the Reagan buildup, the DoD's inspector general (whose job is to uncover as many improper actions as possible) stated that "for every dollar wasted at DoD . . . only two cents are stolen; the rest is lost because of mismanagement."[169]

The most dangerous type of fraud occurs when a supplier intentionally provides inferior parts. This damages equipment effectiveness and can result in loss of life. Thus, maximum effort is made to minimize all instances of compromised quality. Nonetheless, it occasionally does happen. Because government policies require free and open competition (as opposed to limiting competition to proven suppliers), there have been cases as drastic as a supplier who operated out of her cellar, bought parts from China, recategorized them, and sold them to the Defense Department with a significant markup but still at the lowest price available from an American supplier.[170] In another case, a Sioux manufacturing firm in North Dakota did not meet military specifications in the weaving of its Kevlar threading for the helmet armor for troops in Iraq and Afghanistan. The firm was fined $2 million but subsequently received a $74 million contract from the Defense Department to make more helmet armor. In this instance, there may have been a quality-control procedure that was corrected.[171] As a third example of fraudulent actions by small business suppliers to the DoD, a now-defunct metals company in Florida was found guilty of altering test certificates for metal parts that it was selling to NASA and the DoD.[172]

Another type of fraudulent action is overcharging for parts or services. In one well-publicized case, a small South Carolina parts supplier billed the army hundreds of thousands of dollars to ship items worth no more than a few dollars to Iraq and Florida. Because these were priority items, they usually were paid automatically by the DoD purchasing system. In this case, the supplier took advantage of a weakness in the DoD purchasing system.[173] Another example of this occurred in the services area, when KBR was accused (and found guilty) of inflating prices for various goods during the construction of Camp Stobendsteel in Kosovo under a contract to the army for logistics support during the Balkans operations in 1999 and 2000.[174] As these examples illustrate, the urgency of the time frame of some situations causes significant waste and occasionally allows some fraudulent behavior to go unnoticed—although it is often caught later. The most common illegal charging activity is labor mischarging, in which a worker charges time against a cost-reimbursement contract when the charges should have been part of a fixed-price contract. The government ends up paying for costs that should have been profit losses against the fixed-price contract.[175] One GAO study showed that this represented over 30 percent of the fraud cases found.[176] Again, detailed auditing usually catches these abuses, and the presence of such auditing greatly discourages it, but it still occasionally happens.

One last example of illegal actions is the exporting of U.S. military technology to countries or organizations that are not approved for such exports by the U.S. government. The most common technique is to request the equipment under the guise of a "front" company in an approved country for subsequent shipment into the unapproved areas. For example, during the reign of the shah, Iran purchased U.S. military equipment, including F-4, F-5, and F-14 warplanes, as well as Cobra, Chinook, and Sikorsky helicopters. However, after the Iranian revolution, an embargo was imposed. To keep these aircraft flying, Iran had to be able to acquire spare parts, and some arms traders unwittingly shipped this equipment to Dubai and South Africa, and it was subsequently forwarded to Iran.[177] Although small in dollar value, such actions must be stopped because they are important in terms of U.S. security policy. The detailed auditing required to locate these few cases of abuse or illegal action is expensive due to the large number of cases that have to be reviewed to find the few improper ones. As one air force officer observed, when involved in the spare-parts scandal, every analysis done has shown that "the cost of finding these cases was much more than the result in savings."[178]

The government takes significant actions to counter fraud cases as they are discovered. In the 1980s, one of the first actions was to amend the False Claims Act (an 1863 statute aimed at Civil War profiteering) by strengthening the government's investigative powers and increasing the likelihood of civil cases against contractors for fraudulent claims.[179] The amendment provided for subpoena power, investigation, prosecution, and the conduct of trials outside the federal judiciary. The last of these provisions is an acknowledgment that the Justice Department could not thoroughly pursue many of the fraud cases developed by other federal agencies. As Associate Attorney General Steven Trotts stated: "The Defense Procurement System is one of the most complicated processes with which we have ever been confronted."[180] Finally, the government used *qui tam*, a legal concept of paying individuals who bring to justice those who are defrauding the government. This provided additional incentives for rightful and wrongful "whistle blowing". Unfortunately, it also encouraged individuals to make frivolous and even vindictive accusations with the hope that the government would go fishing and find something and give the accuser a large financial reward.[181] Along with these actions, the government considerably increased the number of government auditors. One estimate was that five thousand additional auditors were added in the 1980s.[182] Many of these auditors were physically located in the contractor's plants. Similar actions were taken during the Iraq buildup. For example, in approving the fiscal year 2008 defense appropriations bill, the House increased funding by $12 million for the Defense Contract Audit Agency, $17 million for the Defense Contract Management Agency, $24 million for the Office of the Inspector General, and $21 million to temporarily assign six hundred contract specialists from the General Services Administration to the Department of Defense to assist with contract oversight.[183] Finally, because of the significant increase in defense-industry globalization in the twenty-first century, U.S. defense firms have been working with European defense firms in creating a common code of ethics, standardizing principles for use with common weapons programs.[184]

Money flows more freely during periods of rapid DoD buildups (such as during the Reagan buildup in the 1980s) and particularly when contracting is being done in a battlefield environment (such as during the Iraq and Afghanistan buildup in the post-9/11 period). Examples of waste, fraud, and abuse are more prevalent during these times. Besides the overpriced spare parts during the Reagan buildup, there was also the ill-wind scandal, in which a former employee of Boeing provided the company with illegal help while employed as an assistant secretary of the navy. In the buildup of the 2000s, much attention was given to the Druyun Affair, in which a deputy assistant secretary of the air force provided illegal help to Boeing in pursuit of contract awards while seeking employment with the firm (actions for which both she and Boeing's chief financial officer went to jail). The large amounts of money being spent in Iraq and Afghanistan and insufficient government contract management personnel have led to investigations into over ninety cases of potential fraud. These incidents included an Iraqi subcontractor that paid $133,000 in kickbacks to a procurement official at Kellogg, Brown, and Root Services,[185] a local firm that gave money and other items of value to a military contracting officer in Iraq in exchange for steering hundreds of thousands of dollars of contracts to that local firm,[186] and a series of $30,000 bribes that were given to a group of military personnel for construction contracts in Afghanistan.[187] The Special Inspector General for Iraq Reconstruction (SIGIR), Stuart Bowen, noted that corruption is widespread in the Iraqi government but that "the incidents of corruption within the U.S. Reconstruction program—judging from most cases that we have uncovered thus far—appear to constitute a relatively small component of the overall American financial contribution to Iraq's reconstruction."[188] He found that of the 47,321 reconstruction projects, only 112 were terminated for default on the part of the contractor (a 0.2 percent default rate).[189] He also found numerous examples of waste, such as $4.2 million in unauthorized construction (including an Olympic-sized swimming pool and twenty VIP trailers built at the request of Iraqi officials). But since these items were authorized, they are wasteful but not illegal.[190]

The public perceives fraudulent cases to be widespread and common for almost all defense procurements. To the contrary, one analysis found that out of 330,000 procurements reviewed, only 372 purchases were even deemed questionable.[191] Out of the 15 million contract actions taken each year by the Department of Defense, one in a thousand might be considered questionable (not improper or illegal). In his annual report to the Congress in 1984, the Secretary of Defense noted that out of 24,380 cases investigated (which are equivalent to the questionable cases mentioned above), two out of three were found to involve no actual problem and were dropped, some required administrative action (such as changes in procurement procedure), and some were referred for prosecution.[192] That year, there were 657 convictions, so fewer than three out of every hundred questionable cases resulted in prosecution. By roughly generalizing these two sets of statistics, of the 15 million annual procurement actions, perhaps fifteen hundred involve some form of illegality.

The same ratio—of one in ten thousand—is found in the dollars involved. The Secretary's 1984 report to Congress stated that in fiscal year 1983, $5.2 million in penalties, restitutions, and recoveries had been collected by the Justice Department, and $9.6 million had been collected by the DoD. Thus, a total of $14.8 million was recovered out of an annual procurement budget of around $170 billion at that time—again, about one part in ten thousand. Although $14.8 million is not a small amount, in the same year, it cost the government far more (in the salaries of auditors, lawyers, and other employees in the Department of Defense and the Justice Department) to recover those dollars. The issue here is ethics and legality, but the economics do not argue for more auditors and lawyers.

The worst cases are those of bribery. The navy procurement scandal involved up to six officials out of approximately seventy thousand employees (also representing a ratio of about one in ten thousand). Similarly, in the case of the Iraq bribery sandals, fifteen to twenty examples were found out of 190,000 contractors in the region (again, a ratio of about one in ten thousand). As Norman Augustine observed, relative to the approximately 3 to 5 million people involved in the military-industrial complex, "Is there any city with even a small percentage of that number of people without a jail?"[193] Bribery is against the law, and offenders must be seriously punished. An example must be made of them to discourage others. Thus, after each of these periods of significant contracting increases and increases in waste, fraud, and abuse, a high-level commission was established to make recommendations for acquisition reforms, and in both cases, significant steps were taken to implement a series of broad, structural, corrective actions.[194]

To the average observer of the defense industry, it is surprising that with the huge dollar values of contracts put out by the Defense Department (particularly during periods of rapid budget increases), there are so few cases of illegal actions and that those that do exist tend to be relatively small. The high visibility (transparency) makes such actions difficult to commit. This is the result of both the constant review of all transactions by thousands of auditors and also the oversight by the press and the Congress. There is great sensitivity, both within the DoD and within the industry, to following the rules. As William Swanson, the Aerospace Industries Association's chair and Raytheon's CEO, stated about ethical behavior in defense corporations, "no company wants to get close to the foul line in this area."[195]

Despite the public perception and frequent headlines, cases of illegal actions in defense procurements are few, and the dollars associated with them also are also relatively few. A far greater problem is the billions of dollars of waste, which is actually caused by the processes used. Obtaining the maximum national security capability for the dollars received from Congress will require significant changes in how the government and the defense industry conduct their future business.

Summary of Conduct in the Defense Business
Defense is big business:[196]

- It contracts for over $450 billion per year (as of 2007).
- It implements 145.3 million pay transactions per year for nearly 6 million people (as of 2006).
- It posts 57 million general ledger transactions per year.
- It processes 13.8 million commercial invoices per year.
- It processes 7 million travel payments per year.
- It manages $255 billion in military retirement and health benefits per year.

The Federal Acquisition Regulations mandate the ways in which these processes are regulated. Although there are some potential advantages to detailed regulations, the focus is on compliance rather than on results. The uniqueness of the process and the visibility that it provides discourage many world-class firms from doing defense business. Some object to the publication of executive salaries and detailed company cost information; controls on exporting into the global market; the releasing of proprietary information; and the specialized nature of design, manufacturing, and logistics support. As Angela Styles (former administrator of the Office of Federal Procurement Policy) observed, "You have good, solid companies . . . looking at the situation and saying 'Gosh, the risk of doing something wrong or being perceived as doing something wrong in government contracts is so high that it's just not worth it for me to participate in this marketplace.'"[197] This problem is complicated by an incomplete understanding of government contracting. Congressman Tom Davis (R-VA), the ranking member of the House Oversight and Government Reform Committee, commented on colleagues' approach to contract reform: "They don't have any history of government contracting. It is done by anecdote. It is done by reaction to press reports. And so you get these very inconsistent contracting policies and practices and it's certainly not good."[198] Such excessive regulation also discourages government contracting personnel from applying management flexibility as they interpret the steps that should be taken in the interests of efficiency and effectiveness. As Christopher Dorobek argues, excessive oversight has put federal contracting officials in a precarious position in which they are afraid to use the available flexibilities: "procurement officials are running scared because they fear that any decision they make will be reviewed and reviewed and reviewed. If Federal employees make a mistake, they fear they will get called before Congress—or worse."[199] He believes that oversight is necessary and wrongdoing should be uncovered but that too many good federal officials and contractors are getting caught in the crossfire. He concluded by noting that the situation also harms the government's ability to attract new workers to public service—especially in the contracting area.

The government needs adequate numbers of experienced, smart buyers to handle the complexity of equipment and services purchased by the Defense Department, the large amounts of dollars involved, and the importance of the mission itself. These people must:[200]

- Have business and organizational savvy,
- Understand government procurement and program management,
- Understand economics and market forces,
- Understand and focus on the service area,
- Be familiar with technology, and
- Enjoy job stability and promotion potential.

Donald Winter, secretary of the navy, highlighted some key characteristics of an experienced government acquisition workforce.[201] He cited extensive domain knowledge, extensive business knowledge (including that of the commercial world), a good understanding of the cost aspects of their business, and knowledge of how competition can be used to improve performance and lower costs.

Given the size of the business of the Department of Defense, an integrated enterprise information system is needed to run the DoD's complex operations. Such a system should be capable of handling the finance system, personnel system, logistics system, and procurement system. All world-class enterprises have an integrated, modern information system, but the Department of Defense does not. In 2009, it had over four thousand different business systems that were neither integrated nor interoperable. Since 1995, the General Accountability Office has been flagging as high-risk the DoD's need for business systems modernization and the related area of financial management.[202] The DoD has gradually been addressing this problem, but institutional resistance and the relatively low priority assigned to it (the DoD views it as back-office stuff) have slowed down the process. Everyone agrees that it is desirable to have an integrated, enterprisewide system, but few want to give up their system (which they have used for many years).

The process by which the Department of Defense acquires goods and services (particularly, complex weapons systems) is highly detailed and complex. One of its most undesirable characteristics is the amount of time that it takes to field new equipment for the military—from the decision to initiate a program until the items are in the hands of the troops. First, a detailed process establishes agreement on what the requirement will be. Then this is put into a request for a proposal that often is hundreds of pages long. Next, the industry may spend six months or more putting together volumes of proposal responses (covering performance, cost, and management). Then six months (or so) are needed for proposal evaluation, source selection, contract writing, and award. If there are no protests, then the winning contractor goes through design reviews with the government, and detailed test programs are conducted (first by the company and then by the government separately). Finally, the initial production and fielding can begin, including setting up the support system for the program.

In general, this entire process tends to take ten to fifteen years for weapon systems, and during that time technologies change, requirements change, and quantities and budgets change. The program goes through constant revisions (a typical program goes through thousands of changes during this period), and many changes in personnel (senior government people rarely stay on a program for the entire process). Although this extended period may be tolerable in a peacetime environment, it is not in times of war. During periods of conflict, combat personnel frequently develop new urgent needs that have to be satisfied rapidly (in weeks, months, or at most one or two years). For a wartime situation, the government develops a parallel acquisition process largely ad-hoc) to have an acceptable (and legal) process for rapidly responding to urgent needs.

To purchase goods and services efficiently, the Defense Department's acquisitions system must address four critical issues:

1. What goods and services should be bought (within affordability and technology constraints),

2. How the goods and services should be procured (within the law and as efficiently and effectively as possible),

3. Who should do the acquiring (the quantity and quality of the government acquisition workforce and appropriate incentives), and

4. Who should provide the goods and services (this addresses the structure of the industrial base and questions about globalization, competition, innovation, health, and collaborations between industry and the military).

The combination of these four areas determines the results achieved.

Defense-Industry Performance: Results and Trends

In evaluating the effectiveness of the U.S. defense industrial base, perhaps the most important statement that can be made is that it provides the best weapon systems in the world. For the last fifty years, America's defense strategy has been based on technological superiority, and one of the greatest challenges for the nation in the twenty-first century will be to maintain that technological superiority. Maximum performance is a necessary result of the activities of the industrial base, but it is not a sufficient result. This equipment also must be affordable in sufficient quantities, delivered when needed, highly reliable, inexpensive and easy to operate and maintain, and a positive factor in the overall U.S. economy.

The U.S. aerospace industry is a leader in net exports. In 2005,[203] the aerospace and defense industry had a net export balance of $38.5 billion (out of a total of $65 billion of exports). This significantly exceeded the net exports of semiconductors, chemicals, and newsprint and exceeded the negative net exports of industries such as food, feeds, beverages, telecommunications equipment, household appliances, pharmaceuticals, and computers and computer accessories—all of which had negative net trade balances. The aerospace industry makes an outstanding contribution to U.S. exports because its weapons are recognized as being worldwide performance leaders. Since an increasing share of these exports are in the services sector, besides the benefits in the manufacturing sector this net of exports provides significant U.S. jobs in engineering, and support opportunities for equipment that is exported. The aerospace industry estimated that its net exports in 2006 generated between 1.4 and 1.9 million jobs.[204]

Trade balance and job creation are important, but the most critical issue for the defense industrial base is to create systems that provide maximum performance, are affordable, are delivered on time, and have high quality and reliability. In this area, the score card is less positive. A General Accountability Office (GAO) annual assessment of selected weapons programs[205] concluded that total acquisition costs for the fiscal year 2007 portfolio of major defense acquisition programs increased 26 percent from the first estimates. Development costs on these programs increased by 40 percent from the first estimates. In most cases, programs also failed to deliver capabilities when promised: current programs experienced an average delay of twenty-one months in delivering initial capabilities to the warfighter. Of the seventy-two programs assessed, none proceeded through system development by meeting best-practice standards for achieving planned costs, schedule, and performance outcomes. Several issues were identified:

- *Using proven technologies*   Data have shown that introducing both new technologies and a new weapon system at the same time introduced high risk, high cost, and schedule delays. The preferred approach was to use technology that has been demonstrated and insert new technologies into a subsequent phase (block) of the system (via spiral development).

- *Stable design*   The GAO found that 63 percent of the programs had requirement changes after system development began and that these programs encountered cost increases of 72 percent. Costs grew by only 11 percent among programs that did not change requirements. Again, the requirement changes should be brought into subsequent phases or blocks rather than introduced into the design as it is evolving.

- *Qualified and stable management and workforce* The government and industry workforce needs to be qualified and experienced. The GAO found that, since 2001, the average tenure for government program managers has been only seventeen months (less than half of what DoD policy prescribes), which undermines stability and accountability in the management structure. It also found that government acquisition departments were so understaffed that they either brought in outside contractors to compliment the program office (this happened in 48 percent of government programs) or counted on the industry contractors to do those management functions that should have been done by the government. Finally, it found that the government was not adequately managing the growing share of the business that was being done in the software area (on weapon systems) and that this was causing significant cost growth (more than a 25 percent growth in the expected lines of code since the systems started their development).

• *Planning in the early design and development phases* The GAO found that planning for the subsequent manufacturing and support of the products—at low cost, with high reliability, and with ease of maintenance—was inadequate.

These four areas must be dealt with efficiently, effectively, at an affordable price, and in a timely fashion if the DoD is to continue to have the best weapon systems in the world.

The above-noted cost and schedule performance information is quite damning, but it needs to be compared to how other organizations handle cost overruns and deliveries. Figure 4.4 shows how the DoD compares to other public-sector activities and to private-sector efforts in terms of development and production costs.

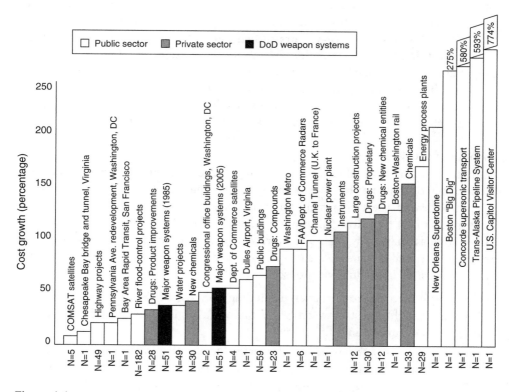

Figure 4.4
Cost growth in major military and civilian projects, *Source:* F. Biery, The Analytic Sciences Corporation (TASC), "Cost Growth and the Use of Competitive Acquisition Strategies," *National Estimator* 6, no. 3 (Fall 1985); RAND Corporation, "Cost Growth Study," November 2006; "Capitol Visitor Center," *Washington Post*, November 17, 2008. All data have been adjusted for quantity and inflation.

In 1986, the President's Commission on Defense Management (Packard Commission)[206] identified the average weapon systems' cost growth at about 40 percent, while a RAND Corporation study showed that for 2005 the average cost growth was about 55 percent. As shown in figure 4.4, the cost growth in defense weapon systems is comparable to or less than some of the major government construction projects (such as the Hart Senate Office Building, the Rayburn House Office Building, or Dulles Airport in Virginia) and dramatically less than enterprises like the Louisiana Superdome in New Orleans, the Big Dig underground highway system in Boston, the Trans-Alaska Pipeline System, the Concorde supersonic transport, and the recent U.S. Capitol Visitor Center in Washington, D.C. The Capitol Visitor Center was three years late in delivery. It began as a $71 million anteroom and rest stop for visitors, became a $265 million, more extensive Visitor Center in 1999, and when completed in 2008, had cost $621 million. It was a classic example of "requirements creep" but this time under congressional management. What started as a $71 million rest stop for visitors turned into a $621 million extension of the U.S. Capitol that looks like an underground football stadium.[207] These examples of congressionally controlled construction projects do not get brought out in the congressional hearings on defense weapon-system cost overruns. Nonetheless, the DoD has to change its acquisition process to control both the cost growth and schedule slippages that have historically been the result of defense procurements.

High and Growing Costs
If the total dollars available for the procurement of a weapon system is set, then the number of systems that can be bought is a function of the unit cost of each weapon. The Defense Department has been faced with two cost problems. One is the high unit cost of individual weapons (both as intended and with cost growths). The second is that as systems get more complex, the designed-in unit cost rises exponentially, and fewer systems can be procured year after year. Consider first the high unit cost of individual weapons:

- A new nuclear aircraft carrier (excluding the cost of the airplanes on it) has been estimated to cost between $11.7 billion (as estimated in 2003)[208] and $20 billion (as estimated in 2008).[209]

- Current nuclear submarines and larger surface combatants run between $3 and $5 billion each,[210] while the next generation are estimated at $7 billion or more.[211]

- Marine troop transport ships cost $1.76 billion each (almost three times its original projected cost a decade before).[212]

- The Stealth B-2 bomber cost about $1.2 billion each[213] (which was partially the result of reducing the quantity bought from the planned 128 aircraft to twenty-four).

- The numbers for stealthy modern fighter aircraft vary widely depending on the year and the quantities being produced. The F-22 is estimated to cost well over $200 million each, and the F-35 over $100 million each,[214] and both have grown dramatically in their cost relative to initial estimates. The F-35 was to have cost $35 million when produced in large quantities.[215]

- Army and marine mine-resistant, ambush-protected (MRAP) vehicles are produced in large quantities and cost over $1.6 million each (including outfitting them with communications, electronics, and spares).

Even the cost of providing protection to individual soldiers and marines has grown significantly since the Vietnam era, where 35 pounds of equipment per soldier cost about $1,941. In Iraq and Afghanistan, the individual protection had grown to 75.3 pounds at a cost of $17,442.[216]

The high costs of individual systems are only a part of the problem, since over time, each system tends to have new requirements for higher performance added to them, which causes them to grow in their unit costs. As might be expected, the biggest cost increases come from the larger programs. Between 2000 and 2007, six programs accounted for 56 percent of the total program costs. Out of a total program cost of $401 billion, the Future Combat System of the army cost $69.7 billion, the Joint Strike Fighter (F-35) cost $66.8 billion, the SSN 774 attack submarine cost $27.3 billion, the army's chemical demilitarization program cost $23.4 billion, the air force's evolved expendable launch vehicle (EELV) cost $18.3 billion, and the air force's C-17A aircraft cost $17.6 billion). These are extremely large numbers, but in many cases, large quantities of systems are being procured. The unit cost of a weapon system is critical because it is multiplied by the numbers being procured. Two important actions are required. First, the intent of the original design unit was the basis for the numbers that were needed and affordable, so making unit cost a design requirement becomes essential. Second, if the cost is maintained, then the number being bought will not decrease—(as long as the total dollars that are available for the system are maintained).

Consider the empirical data in each of these two cost categories—unit cost and cost stability. When the unit cost of tanks is plotted over time (after adjusting for inflation effects), the Sherman tank, in quantities of a thousand, cost $140,000, and if that cost is put on a curve with the M-60 tank and M-1 tank, then an exponential cost increase in the unit cost of a tank over time can clearly be seen. Similarly, if one starts the curve with the Midway aircraft carrier and moves up the curve for modern aircraft carriers, again it is an exponentially increasing cost curve. If one starts with the early jet aircraft (that is, the F-4 at $3.5 million for the hundredth unit) and then continues to add in the modern fighter planes up through the F-35 and F-22, then it is again an exponentially increasing curve.[217] And this exponential growth of unit cost in various weapons systems is repeated in all systems that have been analyzed. The growth rate varies as a function of the individual type of weapon system. For nuclear ballistic-missile submarines (in constant dollars after adjusting for inflation), the cost growth from generation to generation has been 3.48 percent per year, while for fighter planes, it has been 7.1 percent per year.

With each generation of new weapon systems, performance has also been exponentially increasing (in fighter aircraft, at an average rate of 5.6 percent per year). Many people will argue that you have to pay more to get more performance. However, the trends in computers, calculators, television sets, and cell phones show that from generation to generation, performance has improved dramatically while cost has declined. Considering that more weapon systems depend on electronics, one should be able to get higher performance at lower cost rather than accepting that it is a natural requirement to have to pay more to get more.

In the Defense Department, quantity of weapons matters greatly to overall force effectiveness, and the total dollars available for defense are finite. As a result, as unit costs of equipment go up, the numbers of systems that can be procured have declined dramatically. The overall phenomenon for defense procurement is an increase in unit costs, an increase in performance, a reduction in the numbers of weapon systems that are affordable, and therefore greatly reduced quantities procured each year. In fact, Norman Augustine has taken this reduced-quantity curve for fighter aircraft and projected it out. He found that in the year 2054, the Department of Defense will buy one fighter plane per year (to be shared among the services).[218] A similar shrinkage in the numbers of equipment in each service can be expected as the cost continues to rise for individual weapons. For example, the navy will have to shrink in terms of the number of ships unless it begins to buy far less expensive ships. Consider the Marine Corps tank program (known as the expeditionary fighting vehicle). The initial projection was to buy 1,025 tanks for $8.4 billion (according to a House Oversight Committee Report), but as the unit cost began to rise significantly, the Defense Department said that, instead, it will buy 593 of the amphibious assault vehicles, at a total cost of $13.2 billion. Similarly, in going from the navy's F/A-18A/D to the F/A18E/F, the average cost went from $38 million each to $82.6 million each. Although development costs and total procurement costs were comparable (each around $6 billion and $38 billion, respectively), the total quantity that the navy received went down from 1,021 to 462.[219]

The other significant effect of this growing unit cost is to slip the quantities procured further out into out-year budgets so that the time in which the troops get the equipment is delayed significantly. For example, in the above-noted expeditionary fighting vehicle, production slipped by eight years. Consider the following cost growths on individual programs:

- From 2003 to 2005, the army's future combat system grew from an estimated cost of $92 billion to $165 billion. This was a fiscally unconstrained program that grew as requirements grew and as the system became better defined[220]—until Secretary Gates canceled it in 2009.

• From 2005 to 2009, the presidential helicopter (which began as an off-the-shelf acquisition) grew from an initial version at $2.3 billion to $3.7 billion to a final version at $4.5 billion to $7.5 billion.[221] Again, requirements continued to grow, after the contract was awarded; ad until it was cancelled in 2009.

• From 1999 to 2005, the advanced spy satellite (the future imagery architecture project) grew from an estimate of $5 billion to $18 billion. It suffered from both technical difficulties and increased requirements; and was eventually cancelled.[222]

• From 2002 to 2004, the evolved expendable launch vehicle increased from $15.4 billion to $28 billion, even though the program was anticipating fewer launchings (138 instead of the 181 initially planned).[223]

• From 1998 to 2006, the costs for an information-gathering satellite program (the space-based infrared system) grew from $4.1 billion to $10.2 billion while the number of satellites decreased from five to three.[224]

The rising unit costs of the F-22 aircraft (from 1992 to 2006) and the declining numbers that were procured (from 1986 to 2005) are shown in figures 4.5 and 4.6. The causes of these cost increases have been known for decades, but the incentives within the system allow the practices to continue, and increasing costs, extended schedules, and reduced quantities continue to be seen.

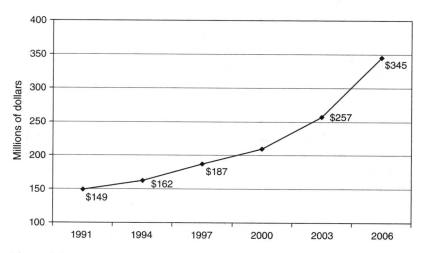

Figure 4.5
Average total cost per F-22 aircraft (millions), 1991 to 2006. *Source:* Data derived from U.S. Government Accountability Office (GAO), "Tactical Aircraft: Air Force Still Needs Business Case to Support F/A-22 Quantities and Increased Capabilities," March 2005.

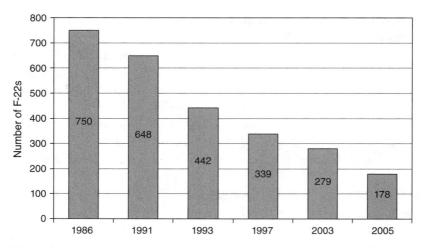

Figure 4.6
Procurement quantities of F-22s, 1986 to 2005. *Source:* Data derived from U.S. Government Accountability Office (GAO), "Tactical Aircraft: Air Force Still Needs Business Case to Support F/A-22 Quantities and Increased Capabilities," March 2005.

Often reports of high costs for defense systems are exaggerated because they do not specify the basis on which they are being described. As the data in figure 4.4 indicate, defense overruns are not insignificant but are dramatically less than many commercial and government acquisitions in other areas. In addition, to make the numbers look large, articles in the press often highlight the total costs of a weapon system without breaking down the details. In discussing the F-35 fighter plane, for example, one article noted that it eventually might cost $1 trillion to develop, but further down the article notes that this cost includes the procurement of 2,458 aircraft for the air force, navy, and marines; $650 billion to operate and maintain the aircraft for twenty years; and the twelve-year development costs of this state-of-the-art stealthy fighter.[225] Perhaps the most misleading use of numbers is when a highly successful program reduces the unit cost of a weapon system, which persuades the DoD to buy many more of them. In the commercial world, this is known as price elasticity—the lower the price, the higher the volume of sales. In this case, the quantity has increased significantly, but looking at the total costs of that individual program gives the impression that it has overrun. In the same way, some analyses state that the DoD doubled its planned investment in new systems from $790 billion in 2000 to $1.6 trillion in 2007, while the reality is that in 2000 seventy-five programs were considered major, while in 2007 there were ninety-five such programs.[226] Such comparisons are not apples to apples. Similarly, if unit costs grow and the DoD decides to buy fewer systems, the total cost can stay the same, but the military has gotten less overall capability because of the reduced quantities.

Nonetheless, even after adjusting for inflation, for quantity changes, and for performance increases, the cost of defense weapon systems is far too high and is continuing to grow.[227] This area requires significant attention by both the government and industry if the United States is to be able to maintain its national security posture in the twenty-first century.

Extended Cycle Times

For maximum military capability, the DoD needs to move high-performance systems out of development and into the field, and these systems need to be deployed in adequate quantities (not just one or two). This is particularly true when a wartime combatant commander discovers that the United States needs a certain capability and that it is needed right away. This problem is more prevalent in the twenty-first century than it was in the past as adversaries in Iraq and Afghanistan obtain advanced equipment on the world (commercial and military) market and often use it in unexpected ways—requiring a rapid U.S. response.

Short development and deployment cycles for new weapon systems also tend to minimize the cost of the program. As shown in figure 4.7, the shorter the time period to the first operational deployment of a new system, the smaller its cost growth will be. For these two reasons—shorter time to market and lowered development and unit costs—the auto industry, the electronics industry, and other commercial sectors have increasingly strived for and achieved much shorter

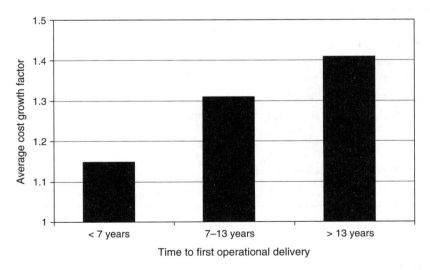

Figure 4.7
Average cost growth for three Department of Defense programs. *Source:* RAND Corporation, "Analysis of Selected Acquisition Reports," 1996.

product-realization cycles. Unfortunately, the DoD has not followed this trend. From 1969 to 1998, the average cycle time of a military product increased from approximately 80 months to 107 months, while the private auto industry reduced average cycle time from approximately 90 months to 24 months.[228]

An interrelationship between cost and schedule works in both directions. A short program yields less cost growth, and cost growth extends a program, and the longer schedule increases the cost. People are employed on the program longer, they make more charges to it, new requirements are assigned to the program, and new technology is introduced. The following examples illustrate how schedule can affect weapon systems:[229]

- In May 2000, the Future Combat System of the army had its program start, and its development program began in May 2003. The acquisition cycle time was expected to be 91 months. By August 2006, the cycle time had already grown to 139 months, and the system was not expected to have an initial capability in the field until December 2014.

- In February 1994, the unmanned aerial vehicle Global Hawk began as a demonstration program, and its development start and low-rate production decision were in March 2001. Its anticipated acquisition cycle time was 55 months. By September 2006, its acquisition cycle time had grown to 78 months, and its unit costs had grown from $78.6 million to $168.2 million.

- In September 1997, the joint tactical radio system (a software-based radio) had a program start, and its development start was in June 2002. The planned acquisition cycle time for this radio was 55 months. By 2006, the acquisition cycle time had grown to 117 months, and the quantity production decision was not expected until November 2012. This cycle time is dramatically different from commercial electronics equipment.

- Finally, table 4.4 shows the schedule delays for the F-22 program, which are consistent with the cost-growth data shown in figure 4.7.

Table 4.4
Schedule slippage in the F-22 program

Event	Number of months delayed
Critical design review complete	16
First flight	24
Initial production	58
First operational aircraft delivered	56
Initial operational capabilities delivered	27
Initial operation test and evaluating complete	63
Full production	63

Inadequate Reliability and Availability

Any weapon system must work when called on to perform its mission, and if it is not available, then backup systems must be available. When a system is unreliable, maintenance costs go up significantly—since every time a system fails, it has to be fixed and put back in working order. Thus, reliability and availability are critical both to warfighting capability and to the cost of weapon systems over their lifetime. Unfortunately, many DoD systems do not achieve the desired reliability or availability that was specified in their requirement. Between 2000 and 2003, the air force's B-2 bomber had a mission-capable (availability) rate averaging slightly above 39 percent, and in fiscal year 2005, it averaged a mission-capable rate of 31 percent.[230] At these rates, three bombers would need to be available so that one would always be ready. At their high unit costs, this is a prohibitively expensive ratio.

Similarly, the high cost of the air force's F-22 advanced fighter aircraft did not result in a reliable design. In fact, the DoD stated that the mean time between critical failures was only 1.7 hours[231] and that its availability was only 55.9 percent (besides having a cost of $49,808 per flying hour).

Consider the marine corps' amphibious expeditionary fighting vehicle (EFV), which transports troops to the battlefield at speeds of 30 knots on water and 45 miles an hour on land. By 2007, after ten years of development, tests showed that it breaks down, on average, every four and a half hours and also has significant software problems.[232] In 2009, the aging C-5 strategic airlift aircraft had a mission-capable rate of only 50 percent, and some claim it is lower.[233] A 2008 Pentagon review found significant reliability problems with the joint air-to-surface standoff missile (a $6 billion program). During tests in the prior year, four missiles that were designed for pinpoint accuracy and deemed combat-ready missed their targets by as much as 200 feet or failed to detonate on impact.

According to Pete Adolph, the former director of test and evaluation in the Office of the Secretary of Defense, "approximately 50% of the weapon system programs completing initial operational tests and evaluation have not been evaluated as operationally effective and operationally suitable."[234] The definition here depends on the stated requirement, and (as noted above) this frequently is an example of overspecification. After the littoral combat ship (which was based on existing and proven designs) was selected for use by the navy, fourteen thousand new technical requirements were added to what the ship had to do to comply with Naval Vessel Rules (such as operating under conditions of "sea-state 8" (wave heights of 27 to 42 feet).[235] Whether that requirement is really essential is not the issue. After it is made a part of the weapon's specification, it must be met—even if it is shown to complicate the system considerably, raise its costs, and lower its reliability.

Many large commercial or other government programs also have reliability problems. The Big Dig highway tunnel system in Boston had cost overruns much larger than the average DoD programs, was five years late in completion, and had falling ceiling tiles that killed an automobile driver and scared millions of others. Also in Boston, in the early 1970s the sixty-story John Hancock Tower became infamous for its unpredictable falling windows, which made walking in the area unsafe, and two total window replacements were needed before it was safe. Nonetheless, because of the implications of defense systems to both the nation's security and the lives of its service men and women, military equipment must work when it is needed. As Pete Adolph observed in 2008, the surprising thing is that "over the last fifteen years, reliability growth during system development was de-emphasized or eliminated by the DoD."[236]

Industry Performance

In their speeches, defense-industry executives state that they are measured by the quality, cost, and delivery schedule of the weapon systems that they supply. In reality, their stock prices and performance bonuses are based on their profits and annual revenue growth rates. Because they receive significant equity shares in their companies, they are also personally rewarded on the basis of the stock price itself.

As the Defense Department budget exploded after the terrorists attacks of September 11, 2001, and the basic budget was complimented by the wartime supplementals, by 2005 the U.S. aerospace and defense industry reached record sales and record profits,[237] and these results continued into 2006, when Lockheed Martin's stock was up 45 percent, General Dynamics' stock was up 30 percent, Raytheon's up 32 percent, and Northrop Grumman's up 13 percent.[238] In many cases, these records continued through 2008.

Industry profit can be measured in a number of ways, such as return on investment or return on sales. Prior to the post–cold war consolidations, the defense industry was extremely attractive (relative to the Standard & Poor's index of industries) in terms of return on equity. This was primarily because a large share of capital investments and of research and development investments were paid for by the government. During the consolidation period, however, the defense firms' return on equity declined significantly (relative to the Standard & Poor's indexes) because they were putting much of their equity into their acquisitions.[239] After the budget turned upward and the huge merger mania was cut back, the industry again returned to very favorable return-on-equity results (in the early twenty-first century).

The industry has traditionally been a low return-on-sales industry. Even though it is a highly regulated industry, its return on sales is significantly less than that of publicly regulated electric utilities. In fact, an analysis done by the Center for Strategic and International Studies (CSIS)[240] showed that defense-industry return on sales was lower than the Standard & Poor's 500 Index, its capital goods index, its Pharma and Bio index, its technical hardware index, and its software and services index. It was also significantly less than those private-sector firms known for their profit leadership. In 2005 (a very positive year for defense sales), the big five aerospace and defense firms had the following returns on sales—General Dynamics 6.9 percent, Lockheed Martin 4.9 percent, Boeing 4.7 percent, Northrop Grumman 4.5 percent, and Raytheon 4.3 percent. This compares with Exxon's 43 percent, Microsoft's 32 percent, Wells Fargo's 25 percent, and the Fortune 500s 14 percent.[241] The overall return on sales for 2005 averaged around 6 percent for the aerospace and defense industry, which was a five-year increase from the low of 3.9 percent in 2001.[242] Some of the largest contracts often have a relatively low percentage of profit on sales because they were awarded in a highly competitive environment. As noted above, the largest of the service contracts in the Iraq and Afghanistan war is the LOGCAP support contract (awarded to KBR), and this had a base-fee level of only 1 percent (with a maximum possible award of up to 9 percent).[243] The assumptions were that the contract was bid in a competitive environment, was a cost-based contract, was relatively low risk, and therefore entitled the company to only a small return on sales. From an incentive perspective, it motivated the contractor to maximize the work that it was authorized to do, since even at only a 1 percent or 2 percent (with some award fee)[244] return on sales, with low capital investment and high sales, it still represented a significant number of profit dollars.

From 2001 to 2007, the Standard & Poor's Aerospace and Defense Industry Index climbed 181.7 percent, while the broader market was up 17.6 percent. Wall Street was rewarding the defense stocks during this buildup period in the Iraq and Afghanistan war. Despite the large programmatic cost growths, the schedule slippages, and the often less than desired reliability of the equipment being supplied, the corporate executives (incentivized by profit, sales, and stock prices) were doing extremely well. In 2007, the Lockheed Martin chairman and CEO received a combined compensation package of $26 million, and five other company officers received between $6.8 million and $3.6 million;[245] the CEO of Boeing received $19 million;[246] the CEO and chairman of Raytheon received $19.3 million;[247] and the CEO of General Dynamics $15.7 million. That year, the government allowed (as chargeable contract expenses) executive compensation up to $597,912 for the share of those contracts that were cost-based. The rest of the compensation had to come out of corporate profits. Nonetheless, profit in that year was sufficiently high so that the additional executive compensation costs could easily be covered and the companies could still have record profits.

Corporate executives frequently will state that their job as managers is to maximize shareholder value. In the 1960s, when the average investor held shares for over six years, this was a valid consideration. However, as Steve Jobs of Apple

Computer observed, "today, 10% of all shares are owned by hedge funds, and their average holding period is just sixty days, while another 85% of the equities are owned by mutual funds and pension funds whose average tenure there is ten months. . . . I don't think it's right to think of these investors as shareholders of your company. They are investors who temporarily own securities in your company, at a particular point in time. They are responsible for maximizing the stock value of their investments. You, as the CEO, are responsible for maximizing the long-term health of your company."[248] The challenge for the Department of Defense is how to create sufficient incentives so that the executives of defense corporations see as their objective, and are rewarded for achieving, weapon systems that are of highest quality, at affordable costs, and with on-time deliveries. One way to do this is to use past performance (with regard to quality, cost, and schedule) in awarding contracts for future defense business and making the success measures based on the original claims made by the contractor when it submitted its bid. Unfortunately, this measure has not been proven effective (as discussed above). A second way is to reward the contractor with higher fees (award fees) when it meets the objectives. However (as also noted above), there has been much criticism by Congress, the GAO, and the DoD of government program managers who give high award fees when performance is far less than desired (even if the government was the cause of the problems). Another way to reward contractors is to exercise out-year options for purchasing the programs when the performance meets objectives and to decline those options (and then open the competition) when performance does not meet objectives. And still another way to reward contractors is to use the commercial practice of price elasticity. If the price of the weapon system falls and it becomes very attractive, then the government should use that money to reward the contractor by buying additional systems and thus increase its sales and resultant profits. Finally, there are many other techniques, such as sharing in the benefits, in which savings are split between the government and the contractor and both sides are ahead. All such incentives need to receive serious consideration in the future.

One final note in this regard has to do with whether defense firms are fully paying their taxes. A 2004 Governmental Accountability Office (GAO) study found that 61 percent of all American corporations, including 39 percent of large companies, paid no corporate income taxes between 1996 and 2000. In one case in 2008, KBR (the largest Iraq war contractor, admitted to reducing tax obligations through two Cayman Islands divisions, reportedly avoiding hundreds of millions of dollars in Medicare and social security taxes. Finally, a 2004 study by the GAO found that twenty-four of the largest federal contractors used the Cayman Islands to shave their tax bills.[249] When corporations receive most of their dollars from the federal government, it is appropriate for them to pay all of their taxes—and many of them do.

Military Logistics Support and Equipment Maintenance

According to a 2000 statement made by General Eric Shineski, the chief of staff of the U.S. Army, "We can not achieve a DoD transformation without a DoD logistics transformation." Since logistics is, by far, the largest area of contracting and has the greatest effect on force readiness, it must receive significant industry attention. *Logistics*, broadly defined, is the ability to project and sustain a combat-ready joint military force through current operations worldwide and to provide freedom of action for combat commanders to meet and sustain future mission needs. Its functions include transportation, maintenance, planning, ordering (replacements, repairs, spares), procurement, finance, inventory, and decision making. These functions— from factory to foxhole, from parts supplier to warfighter and all of those in-between—make up the DoD supply chain. This is a critical function for warfighting since if the bullets do not arrive in time, lives and wars are lost.

The numbers for the United States alone in fiscal year 2007 were staggering:[250]

• Annual expenditures for logistics (including supplementals), $172 billion

• Inventory, $94 billion

• Military and civilian government personnel, over 1.1 million (and at least as many contractors)

• Part numbers, over 5 million

• Requisitions each year, over 18 million

• Government infrastructure—13 maintenance depots, 3 arsenals, 212 major intermediate maintenance facilities, 21 distribution depots, 23 distinct working capital funds, and over 2,000 logistics information systems.

To be effective, this complicated system requires three things—(1) synchronization and total integration, (2) visibility throughout the supply chain to all elements, and (3) rapid, precise, and dependable response to needs. And it must do all three of these in a highly cost-effective way. In today's twenty-first-century world, synchronization and integration are required across all of its functions (finance, personnel, inventory, transportation, and maintenance), across all services (since most operations will be joint and must share required elements), across all involved agencies (for example, in Iraq, DoD should operate in an integrated fashion with the State Department, USAID, the intelligence community, and other agencies that need logistics support), with all allies (which also will need logistics support, and their readiness affects U.S. ability to conduct its integrated military operations), and with relevant industrial operations on a worldwide basis and at all tiers.

In Iraq (where an equal number of contractors and government personnel are in the war zone) and in Afghanistan (where there are about three times as many contractors as military personnel), the integration of the logistics system must include those personnel and their needs and must directly link the warfighters with the factories so that parts are delivered in a timely fashion. This system must be totally integrated and provide total asset visibility—real-time visibility into the status of all assets, including parts and systems flowing through the supply chain and also (and far more important) the results of that supply chain; in terms of the readiness of the weapon systems (the output measures).

Finally, the information must be accurate, and the supply chain must be totally dependable. General Douglas MacArthur once observed that "the history of war proves that nine of ten times an army has been destroyed because its supply chains have been cut off."[251] The most obvious of these potential breakdowns is from physical attack. In Afghanistan, about 90 percent of the U.S. goods destined for Bagram (the main U.S. military base in Afghanistan) make an eight-day road journey from Pakistan's Karachi Port (only weapons and ammunition are flown into Afghanistan). Not only are these convoys constantly under attack, but insurgents blow up roads and bridges to prevent the supply chain from coming through (in spite of NATO payments to local warlords to guarantee safe passage and in spite of the armed gunmen who accompany the large convoys). In June 2008, when a convoy of fifty trucks was attacked about forty miles south of Kabul, forty trucks were lost, and sixty personnel were killed.[252] In addition, the various nodes in the supply system (such as ports and storage areas) are highly vulnerable, and there are many other potential causes of a breakdown in the supply chain, including a fire at a factory or storage area, a strike at a factory or by transportation workers, a hurricane, a terrorist action, a company going out of business, or a foreign source that refuses (for political reasons) to supply certain goods. The combination of such events is surprisingly common and is seen in the commercial world as well. For example, Wal-Mart operates an emergency operation center that responds to a variety of such events, including hurricanes, earthquakes, and violent criminal actions, and this facility receives a call from at least one Wal-Mart store with a crisis virtually every day.[253] Finally, in the twenty-first century, the information systems themselves are vulnerable to cyberattacks. In 1996, the Defense Science Board conducted an exercise in which the National Security Agency broke into the DoD's global transportation system and sent (virtually) the planes to different locations. As soon as this vulnerability was exposed, it was immediately fixed. The following year, the National Security Agency conducted a large-scale exercise called "Eligible Receiver" that identified still more vulnerabilities. And the year after that, an exercise of large, extended cyberattacks (known as "Solar Sunrise") persuaded people that the vulnerability of information systems could disrupt supply chains. Unfortunately, all such attacks are not exercises, and the first large one of the twenty-first century was a widespread Internet worm attack (known as "Code Red"). In the first decade of the twenty-first century, the Department of Defense received over forty thousand attempted cyberattacks annually. In 2008, before the Russians invaded the country of Georgia, they flooded all Georgian government information systems with a widespread cyberattack.

Any future DoD supply chain that is based on an information system must worry about privacy and proprietary data (including pricing information and parts availability) and also about security protection.[254] Security must be designed in as a critical requirement, and frequently "red teamed" (by independent third parties), and tested to validate its security and accuracy.

Areas for Logistics Improvement
In spite of spending over $172 billion a year and employing over 2 million (government and industry) personnel, the DoD does not do a world-class job with logistics—by any measure (such as responsiveness, accuracy, readiness, or costs). Some of the following problems have been observed:

- The DoD has over two thousand noninteroperable logistics information systems and few links to the rest of the enterprise (such as finance, personnel, and procurement).

- DoD has little cost visibility (in terms of activities-based costing) and little performance accountability. It measures weapon-system readiness but does not link this to supply-chain responsibility.

- Some improvements have been made (the order-to-receipt time went from an average of forty-nine days in the first Persian Gulf war to twenty-two days in Iraq in 2003 and to sixteen days in 2008). But there have been numerous errors in the distribution and nothing close to world-class international performance (which would mean two days domestically to four days internationally, with almost no uncertainty, and with detailed, real-time visibility).

- There is a three-month deployment process going into Iraq (which is far longer than the military requirement of fourteen days).

- In 2008, more than 500,000 back orders remained unfulfilled in the logistics-supply system.

- The overall military equipment readiness was rated "unsatisfactory" 65 to 90 percent of the time (with some equipment significantly less ready; in 2005, the B-2 bomber had a mission-capable rate of 31 percent).[255]

- DoD could not account for more than fifty thousand shipping containers in theater.[256] And many individual items were unaccountable for in Iraq, due to poor tracking systems (including one reported case of 190,000 guns given to Iraqi forces).

- There has been an extremely slow implementation of radio frequency identification (RFID) technology to track supplies. A secretarial directive was issued to implement RFID by 2005, and four years later it still had not been done.

• According to the GAO, more than half of the air force's spare parts inventory (valued at $18.7 billion) was not needed to meet current requirements. About half of the spare parts on order from contractors ($1.3 billion) was not needed, and about $300 million of that would be marked for disposal after arrival. Excess inventory was accumulating, while shortages in needed items grew to $1.2 billion. In response to this report, one air force base observed that it had "only" approximately $1.3 billion in computer excess inventory.[257]

• Of the Defense Logistics Agency inventory, only 18 percent turned over in 2006. The rest was considered obsolete.[258]

• About 37 percent of the munitions inventory was rated obsolete, unusable, and unrepairable.

• The GAO commented, in another report, that the DoD lacked an outcome-focused set of performance and cost metrics for all of the individual initiatives in the supply-chain management-improvement plan, as well as for the plan's focused areas of requirements forecasting, asset visibility, and materiel distribution.[259]

• Finally, in another GAO report, it found that "achieving asset visibility has been difficult because of a lack of inoperability among information technology systems."[260]

Overall, the GAO has been highly critical of the DoD logistics system and has had it on its high-risk list since 1990. Many of these problems still persist. Unfortunately, most of the large expenditures for logistics and the personnel devoted to it seem to be focused on current operational problems rather than on the longer-term issue of fixing the system—transforming the DoD logistics system into a world-class system. The result has been that in the Iraq and Afghanistan wars, the United States has suffered from not having a modern logistics system.[261] This has been partially overcome through the use of excessive inventory and personnel, but the results are neither mission-effective nor cost-effective. And the problems probably will worsen as military equipment ages, is used extensively, and is not replaced at a high rate (primarily because of its high cost and the need for the defense dollars to be used in operations rather than modernization). In 2007, some average ages for equipment were B-52 bombers, C-135 tankers, C-130 transports, H-53 helicopters, thirty-six years; all TACAIR fighters (as a group), twenty years; U-2 Reconnaissance aircraft, twenty-four years; naval amphibious ships, twenty-two years; M-1 Abrams tanks, twenty-two years; HUMVEE Jeep fleet, eighteen years; army medium trucks, twenty-three years.[262]

Many of these weapon systems are electronic-intensive, and the electronics modernization cycle is typically eighteen months (in the commercial world). It is clear that many of these systems are no longer state-of-the-art. Yet not only are the systems wearing out from their extensive use in the extended conflicts in Iraq and Afghanistan and their training missions for these conflicts, but the cost of supporting and maintaining them will continue to grow—making even more urgent the need for modernizing the DoD logistics system (both to maintain readiness and to reduce costs).

In summary, the forces need to be modernized, and yet the rising costs of DoD personnel and maintenance costs on old equipment leave inadequate dollars for force, or even logistics, modernization. A death spiral is growing as old equipment requires more and more dollars to operate and maintain it, so less and less money is available for modernization, and the cycle accelerates downward. Budget reductions make the problem worse. And the problems with the logistics system compound both military effectiveness and overall cost problems.

Commercial Comparisons
There are significant differences between the requirements for a logistics system for a commercial firm and the DoD, and these differences must be recognized when designing a future DoD system. First, if the supply chain does not deliver, in the commercial case there is a financial loss or an unhappy customer, but in the Defense Department case, lives and battles are lost, so the DoD requirement for a greater supply buffer is real. Second, the commercial system operates under a largely peaceful environment, while the Defense Department system has to be designed to operate under dangerous conditions. Again, it needs greater built-in safety factors. Finally, the commercial system can operate to achieve maximum cost-effectiveness, while the DoD system is significantly hampered by politics and regulations (such as the legislated requirement that 50 percent of all depot maintenance work be done in government facilities by government workers). Nonetheless, modern logistics systems operating in the commercial world can provide the DoD with a large number of lessons learned and with many of the tools and techniques that allow them to operate effectively and efficiently.

In the commercial world, firms devote the resources that will help them achieve the desired performance. For example, United Parcel Service (UPS) is putting more than $1 billion a year into research and spent more than $600 million on package-flow technology to improve its logistic systems.[263] The DoD spends very little on research and development in this area. Also, commercial systems have moved into the domain of demand-pull systems. Using the techniques of sense-and-respond networks, a need is sensed either on the equipment itself (and a message is sent for repair) or from the retail or wholesale stores (with similar messages being sent), and significant efforts are made to do a better job in predicting and instantly responding (on a just-in-time basis). Wal-Mart and Dell distinguish themselves based on their sense-and-respond systems, and they respond within hours from order to delivery. By contrast, the dominant characteristic of the DoD system still is a supply-push system (requiring the above-noted large inventories). Although the DoD system is huge, many people are surprised to discover how much larger some of the commercial systems are:

- Caterpillar processes 28 million requisitions per year (in comparison to the 18 million of DoD).
- FedEx handles 9 billion packages a year. The FedEx Global Hub lands an aircraft every ninety seconds, and packages move through 300 miles of conveyer sorting belts.
- UPS handles an average of 15.7 million packages a day. Its Worldport sorts and routes 300,000 packages every hour, and UPS schedules some six hundred owned and chartered planes that cruise around the globe each day.
- Dell makes a desktop computer every five seconds to respond rapidly to tailored, Internet orders.
- Wal-Mart keeps its sixty thousand suppliers continuously informed about the variations in individual products within its $300 billion annual sales.
- Benetton dramatically revised its production process to respond rapidly to customers' changing demands. Instead of making many different colored sweaters for Christmas, they make them all white and then dip them into a color dye, depending on what color is fashionable for Christmas that year (as sensed at the sales counters).
- Most commercial firms have a procurement administrative lead time that is measured in minutes. The army used to take six months to a year to process a request and have now improved significantly down to fourteen days after the order is cleared by U.S. Central Command).[264]
- As shown in table 4.5, the response time for the DoD logistics supply chain (for distribution of in-stock items, repair of equipment, and administrative time for procurement) greatly exceeds that of world-class commercial firms.

Logistical Progress Being Made

For many years, the DoD has recognized the need to modernize its logistics systems. Finally, in 2004, the DoD established six pilot programs to test a performance-based logistics strategy (including contracting, programming, budgeting, and financial processes).[265] Also in 2004, the Joint Chiefs recognized focused logistics as a requirement and incorporated key sense-and-respond tenants.[266] To implement this, the DoD issued a directive requiring incorporation of RFID throughout the department, beginning in January 2005.

Besides these overall DoD initiatives, the individual services and agencies began their own logistics modernization activities. For example, although it took two years to win approval to initiate it, the army's Wholesale Logistics Information System (LOGMOD) replaced an old, government-operated, Cobalt-based system with a

Table 4.5
Department of Defense and commercial supply-chain response times

Process	DoD	Commercial companies		
Distribution (for in-stock items)	21 days (DoD average)	1 day (Motorola)	3 days (Boeing)	2 days (Caterpillar)
Repair (cycle times)	4 to 144 days (DoD average)	3 days (Compaq)	14 days (Boeing Electronics)	14 days (Detroit Diesel)
Repair (shop time)	8 to 35 days (army tank or truck)	1 day (Compaq)	10 days (Boeing Electronics)	5 days (Detroit Diesel)
Procurement (administrative lead time)	88 days (DLA)	4 days (Texas Instruments)	0.5 days (Portland General)	Minutes (Boeing, Caterpillar)

Source: Data taken from multiple Defense Science Board Task Force studies between 1996 and 2006.

modern, contractor-operated, commercial off-the-shelf (COTS) system (with Computer Sciences Corporation as the contractor). The following results were achieved:

- Performance was greatly enhanced, and annual costs were cut in half (from $200 million to $100 million) over five years.
- All four hundred government workers were guaranteed at least one year of employment with the contractor (with current salary and benefits at least maintained).
- All workers were to be trained in modern C++ software.
- The old system was to be maintained until switchover had been demonstrated.
- A multiyear (five-year) contract was competitively awarded.
- A survey of employees found that they were extremely pleased.

As another example, the air force (at the maintenance depot in Warner Robins, Georgia) competitively selected Hamilton Standard to be the prime vendor for the C-130 blade and hub engine parts:

- The time for the overhaul of engines was decreased by 50 percent.
- The parts availability increased by 30 percent.
- Assembly turn-around time was reduced on the prop by 20 percent and on the blades by 16.7 percent.
- The average material expenditure was 64 percent less than programmed.
- The quality was dramatically improved (there were zero returns in the first five years).

The Naval Air Systems Command (NAVAIR) established a logistics public/private partnership with Caterpillar commercial software and Honeywell Management on their auxiliary power units:

- The reliability of each carrier-based aircraft's auxiliary power unit has been increased by more than a factor of ten.
- The reliability exceeded the guarantees by more than 25 percent.
- Dramatic improvements were achieved in mean number of flight hours between unscheduled removals by 300 percent on the P-3 and by 45 percent on the F/A-18 A/B/C/D.
- For Afghanistan, the system surged by 50 percent to fill all demands.

The Defense Logistics Agency implemented a full business-systems modernization program and an industrial prime-vendor program. Their medical supplies prime vendor supplied deliveries directly to the hospital when ordered, rather than to a distribution center. The following results were achieved:

- The ordering cycle was reduced from 110 days to eight days.
- In the first five years, over $700 million was saved from inventory reductions, holding-cost reductions, product-cost reductions, and cost reductions.

Despite these outstanding experiments, there was still enormous resistance to changing the way that the DoD had historically done its logistics—that is, shifting from a supply-push (with lots of people and lots of material) to a demand-pull (sense-and-respond) system based on modern information technology. There were also problems in that many of the legacy systems had no baseline (of either activities-based costing or mission output measures) related to the supply chain. In 2007, a senior external review group (made up of logistician experts meeting at the Logistics Management Institute) concluded that "current DoD programs and initiatives will not achieve focused logistics by 2020."

Barriers to Moving to World-Class Logistics
Changing a culture is always difficult, and there are at least ten reasons for resistance at DoD:

1. The current system works and is believed to be a core competence of the Department of Defense ("if it's not broken, why fix it?"). This argument fails to recognize that the system is excessively expensive (in dollars and people) and that performance (in terms of responsiveness, reliability, and readiness) could be dramatically improved at much lower cost.

2. The desire to protect jobs is strong both for the civilian government employees (who make up a significant share of the government's logistics personnel) and for

the military (who feel they have more control over government employees than industrial workers).

3. There is strong political support for keeping things as they are. A government maintenance depot might employ twenty thousand voters in a congressional district; resulting in the legislative requirement for 50 percent of the maintenance work to be done by government workers in government depots (the largest single Congressional caucus on Capitol Hill [135 members] is the "depot caucus"). Similar congressional legislation has been passed against competitive sourcing of all work that is not inherently governmental but currently is being done by government workers. (In spite of the results that show such competitions save, on average, 30 percent—no matter who wins).

4. Contractors are distrusted for this critical function. There is a fear that they cannot be controlled on the battlefield, and that the government will be locked into a sole source.

5. There is resistance to multiservice sharing of logistics data for fear of lack of control in a crisis period.

6. There is resistance to using commercial off-the-shelf (COTS) logistics systems that satisfy only 90 percent of the requirements, and there is a reluctance to change the traditional DoD processes to match the modern COTS-based processes.

7. Some people distrust just-in-time delivery ("I want to see the inventory; I don't trust just-in-time delivery for satisfying the military need"). This objection does not recognize that for military applications, some buffer would be built into the system because of its criticality for warfighting.

8. Many people distrust the security of the information systems due to cyberwarfare (which, like all of the other concerns, needs to be addressed explicitly).

9. There are significant financial and controller issues. If working-capital pools are used to absorb all overhead, when one program makes a significant savings, then the overhead is simply shifted to another program. For example, in the late 90's when there was talk of outsourcing the Apache helicopter's logistics support to achieve significant program savings and improve performance, the response was that it would raise the cost of the M-1 A-1 tanks significantly, without improved performance. (The tank overhead rate would go up to absorb the fixed overhead that the helicopter had been absorbing.) Also, it was difficult to convince the comptrollers of the business case justification for a change when no baseline cost data were available. Finally, it was difficult to get R&D or procurement dollars to reduce operating and maintenance costs (due to different time periods and different congressional committees). Finally, the comptrollers were convinced that with congressional resistance, the savings would not be realized, so the investment should not be made (and wasn't).

10. "The transition will be just too hard." In many ways, this goes back to the first argument: if you know that it is going to be very hard to do it and you know you do not really have to do it, then why make such a big effort (given the expected resistance)?

Part of the problem has been that in the post-9/11 period, as the Defense Department budget was rapidly rising, there was not a perceived need to change. One could simply get the added money through a supplemental, and if there was enough money, one could pile up enough metal and put enough people on it so that the logistic system would work. The challenge will come as dollars are shrunk and people realize that they could make significant savings, with improved performance, by making the necessary changes.

The reality is that each of these ten items must be explicitly addressed to achieve the required successful transformation of the DoD logistic system. Overcoming this resistance will require a significant number of pilot demonstrations, extensive education and training on modern supply systems and on the dramatic results that are achievable, a clear set of proper measures and incentives for both government and industry, and significant socialization efforts among all key players in the services, the agencies, and industry. For all of this to happen, the senior leaders of the Department of Defense (both military and civilian) need to recognize the need and actively lead in supporting the vision and developing an explicit strategy for its implementation.

A Vision and Strategy for Implementing the Logistics Transformation

The vision of a transformed DoD logistic system is based on three key points. First, it is based on an integrated, agile, secure, and data-centric end-to-end enterprise information-technology supply system—with real-time, accurate, total asset visibility. Second, it is output-oriented, using performance-based logistics as the norm and with incentives for both government and industry personnel for achieving (or exceeding) the mission outputs desired. Finally, it achieves the optimum mix (based on cost and performance) of government and industry personnel and facilities with all work competitively awarded or with options to compete but with the options exercised only if the current awardees are not achieving the cost and performance objectives to which they committed in the competition (that is, continuing performance improvements with continuous cost reductions).

Based on commercial logistic system results, this vision should be achievable in a relatively short period, as soon as the above-noted ten barriers are significantly reduced. A major factor in making this transformation, however, is overcoming five incorrect perceptions that persist in spite of the existing empirical data that refute them:

1. To save money, performance will deteriorate. (This ignores the overwhelming data that show you can get higher performance at lower cost—as computers continue to demonstrate.)

2. Using contract employees will cost more than using government employees. (This false belief is partly based on the fact that contractors add on a fee and partly because their hourly rates tend to be higher. However, this does not recognize that with competitive forces comes increased productivity so that far fewer people can be used, and the small add-on for the fee, when the majority of the costs are reduced, still results in a significant total cost reduction. Additionally, as discussed below, the Congressional Budget Office, and others, have shown that, on a one-for-one basis, it is 90 percent cheaper to use contractors for maintenance then military forces.)[267]

3. The promised cost saving will not be realized. (This is believed in spite of the overwhelming data against it, as found in after-the-fact analyses of the cost reductions.)

4. Small businesses will be hurt. (This false perception is based on the fear that, as small parts of various contracts are put together to change the overall process, the large firms will be dominant in the awards. However, most of the large awards that are being made have an award requirement to have, for example, 35 percent of the total award set aside for small businesses, and the actual results indicate that small businesses are earning a larger share of the total dollars than they had before.)

5. A large number of government employees will be laid off. (This belief is based on the fact that if you can save 30 percent in costs, then there must be significant layoffs. But the actual data demonstrate very few layoffs since most of the government workers are either absorbed within the government in other positions or are hired at higher salaries by the winning contractors.)

The large amount of empirical data refuting each of these five points[268] must be made widely available (for example, in a DoD education course.). In addition, as many pilot programs as possible need to be implemented to demonstrate how it is possible to achieve higher performance at lower costs. Two stories from the Iraq and Afghanistan experiences illustrate the opposing positions being taken toward logistics transformation. The first relates to contract maintenance of army vehicles in Iraq.[269] In this case, forty-five contractor personnel were embedded in a Striker vehicle brigade, with the priorities for activities directed by the battalion commander. The results (according a GAO report) were that they "exceeded the Army-established goal of 90% operational readiness. . . . From October 2003 through September 2005, the Operational Readiness averaged 96%—despite 800% higher mileage usage than anticipated." And the army stated that "contractors were knowledgeable about maintenance," "provided timely information on status-and-spares," and "freed soldiers to perform military functions." Nevertheless, the army decided to replace the forty-five contractor personnel with seventy-one soldiers to be taken from military positions and trained on Striker maintenance. The army rationale was stated as "increased flexibility in different combat situations" (costs and readiness were not factors considered). Clearly, the army's mindset had not been changed by the superior contractor results.

The second case (which favors greater contractor use) was the recognition that as the buildup in Afghanistan began, there would be a need for significant contractor support.[270] In September 2008, the DoD issued solicitations for road construction and landmine clearance in and around the air force base at Bagram, Afghanistan and for the provision of airborne surveillance data. It also announced that it wanted a contractor to provide twenty-two medium- and heavy-lift helicopters to carry passengers and cargo in Iraq and Afghanistan. The army also announced a contract to provide maintenance and secure storage for 4,600 ground vehicles (expected to arrive in the coming months) to support the Afghan national police; and the Corps of Engineers announced a $50 million contract to design and construct a 1,000-person-capacity prison complex. Finally, the DoD announced that it is seeking intelligence contractors to screen detainees (to determine if they should be held as enemy combatants) and Islamic religious specialists to provide religious services for detainees and to act as interpreters in certain circumstances. The advantage of using contractors in all of these cases is that when the conflicts are over, the contracts are terminated and, unlike government employees or military personnel, only those few people who are required to maintain the activities are retained. The hope is that during the Afghanistan military operations, many of the lessons will have been learned and these activities can be done both effectively and efficiently in the future.

Actions That Can Achieve Logistics Transformation

Implementing the vision of a transformed DoD logistic system requires a seven-step strategy:

1. *Organization*   A single point needs to be responsible for end-to-end supply-chain performance and cost.

2. *Incentives*   The option for competition should be used throughout the system (public and private), and performance-based logistics should be used for legacy and new systems and for public and private workforces.

3. *Personnel*   Key government logistics leaders need to be trained and experienced in modern logistics (including the information systems).

4. *Business and finance rules*   Visibility and flexibility are essential.

5. *Infrastructure* Modern communications and a full enterprise resource planning (ERP) system are needed.

6. *Funding for technology* Funding for R&D and equipment is essential for rapid implementation.

7. *Focus on continuous improvement* Transformation is a process, not an event, so spiral development is the most cost-effective and quickest approach to higher and higher performance at lower and lower costs.

First, a dramatic cultural change nearly always requires a realignment of the organization that is consistent with the new direction. In the 1960s, under the leadership of Secretary Robert McNamara, the Department of Defense logistics landscape was significantly modified by ending the independent service supply systems (on common items) and creating what was then the Defense Supply Agency, which later became the Defense Logistics Agency (DLA). With the passage of the Goldwater-Nichols Act in 1986, the DoD consolidated the authority and management of transportation beyond the continental United States (which had remained under the authority of the services) and created the new Transportation Command (TRANSCOM). Modern supply-chain management, as practiced in the commercial sector, is based on the full integration of all of the logistics functions, whereas the DoD system is still highly segregated. The Defense Logistics Agency, the services, TRANSCOM, and the combatant commanders all play significant and often independent roles. There have been many recommendations for the creation of a single manager of DoD logistics. A Joint Logistics Command (LOGCOM) within the DoD could make clear the lines of authority and responsibility.[271] To have sufficient authority to overcome the institutional resistance that such a change would trigger, LOGCOM would have to have the full support of the Secretary of Defense and be staffed at a four-star level (as all other major commands are). It would also need the full support of the service chiefs since it would involve significant changes in the services' logistics operations. Here are several recommendations for this organization:

- The new organization would be responsible for global end-to-end supply-chain performance and costs.
- It would include the current organizations of TRANSCOM, the Defense Logistics Agency, and the service logistics elements as component commands.
- The joint theater commanders would retain operational control of the flow of in-theater logistics.
- On weapons systems, individual program managers would retain responsibility for life-cycle logistics support planning and configuration control.
- Implementation monitoring would focus on performance-based logistics metrics.

- An integrated logistics information system would be essential.
- The commander should appoint an external advisory board of industry experts to assist in the implementation guidance (including appropriate metrics).

Second, logistics transformation requires the proper incentives for making a cultural change. In this case, the incentives must be geared toward improved performance at lower costs. If a company achieves these objectives, then it should be rewarded with more work and not forced to continuously compete for the added work. If it does not continuously improve performance and lower costs, then it should expect to face competition for follow-on work. Similarly, if a company has provided a warranty and the reliability of the systems is continuously improved, then its profit will continuously go up. Again, this is an incentive for higher performance at lower total costs since less repair work is required and fewer spare parts are needed. Thus, using performance-based logistics, warranties, or other gain-sharing incentives on all systems (legacy and new) to drive up availability while lowering support costs should be a significant incentive. The continuous presence of the option for competition is maintained as an added incentive. In addition, the competition for this work can take various forms. It can be between the government's most efficient organization (MEO) and private-sector bidders, between teams of public-private partnerships competing for the work, or between an incumbent private-sector firm and alternative private-sector firms. The most important point is that it should not be done on a sole-source basis, either to the government, the private sector, or a single team composed of a public-private partnership. In any of these cases, it would be an award made to a monopoly that has no adequate incentives (under those conditions) to achieve the objective of higher performance at lower costs. Fortunately, the benefits of such performance-based logistics efforts are increasingly recognized. By 2008, more than two hundred performance-based logistics efforts were ongoing in the DoD.[272] They have demonstrated material availability above 95 percent, with commercial, world-class response times of two to four days (versus the DoD's average of sixteen days). In addition, they have had a documented average cost reduction (by 2008) of 11 percent.

Third, the current DoD logistic system is overly labor-intensive. When President George W. Bush planned to send 21,500 more combat troops into Iraq (as a surge in U.S. combat forces), the DoD said that as many as 28,000 additional troops would be required to provide critical support during the troops' extended deployment.[273] A transformed DoD logistic system would be much more information-based and less heavily labor-based. Additionally, there is the critical question of whether the work is to be done by government employees (civilian or military) or by temporary contractor employees. The question is not whether there should be public or private employment but whether all work that is not inherently governmental (such as truck driving, wrench turning, and computer software writing) should be competed to emphasize highest performance at lowest cost. These competitions might be won by organizations in the public sector because of their prior experience in this area, by a competitive team of public-private partners (taking maximum advantage of what each sector has to offer), or by an experienced private-sector competitor. But ensuring that all work that is not inherently governmental is competitively awarded will require legislative changes (to change the depot maintenance rule that requires work be evenly divided between public and private firms). Even with work that is inherently governmental, the government is facing significant personnel issues as a large percentage of the civilian workforce becomes eligible for retirement. The move toward having more of the work that is not inherently governmental done in the private sector may help to alleviate this problem (even if, for political reasons, some of this private-sector work is done at the government depot locations). To address both the labor and risk issues of supply disruption and loss of life, a significant share of the war-zone logistics supply system has recently been shifted to unmanned delivery means. In Afghanistan, for example, the Kaman Aerospace Corps' pilotless K-MAX helicopter is being used to airlift up to 6,000 pounds of supplies to remote mountain regions[274] (an adaptation from the logging industry).

Fourth, for logistics transformation to be achieved, far greater visibility and flexibility are needed in business and finance rules. The following recommendations apply to this step:

• Activities-based costing should be applied for maximum management visibility.

• Contingency contracting, finance, and administrative actions should be set up so that stand-by authority exists in terms of budgets, contracts, and working capital funds.

• There must be postransaction audits and adequate visibility to provide these rapidly.

• There must be an ability to do on-line work orders and to get approval for them.

• There should be broadening and deepening of the "prime-vendor" approach (where the single buyer is competing the multiple suppliers).

• There must be provisions for gain-sharing between the contractors and the government so that when costs go down, both gain.

• Nonproprietary and open systems must be used throughout.

• Expanded performance-based logistics (PBL) must be used and tracked for both new and legacy systems.

Fifth, an extensive infrastructure is needed to implement this integrated, information-based, data-centric system and to provide the necessary real-time and auditable visibility. The following recommendations apply to this step:

• Adequate bandwidth of communications must be available to handle radio frequency identification (RFID) of everything.

• The system must be wireless and able to handle all electromagnetic-interference concerns.

• It must use global commercial communications standards.

• Joint (multiservice) supply and maintenance data must be available.

• The system must link into logistic systems of other agencies involved in any particular event (for example, into Department of Homeland Security for domestic crises and into the State Department and USAID for expeditionary operations).

• The system must also be integrated so that it can tie together government and industry databases (while protecting proprietary information) and reaching down into the lower tiers of the industry to get adequate parts visibility information.

• The system should use commercial off-the-shelf (COTS) enterprise resource planning (ERP) systems and ensure that they are integrated and interoperable (but they need not be common).

• COTS-based middleware standards should be used.

• A major focus of the system should be on security and encryption (with privacy and proprietary information also fully protected but with a principal focus on the military sensitivity of the data).

• The system should be capable of being supported at a distance (with reach-back capabilities).

• The system should be user-friendly, and users should be provided with extensive training.

Sixth, a key driver of logistics transformation is technology, and modern information systems evolve rapidly as a result of commercial innovation. Nonetheless, there will be a need for R&D money (preferably in a separate line item) for DoD logistics-system developments (given some of its unique requirements). One of the key questions is the overall architecture to be used. Should it simply be a coordination of multiple approaches by the services, or should there be some form of top-down architecture? If the latter (which appears preferable), then what model should be used? In general, industry seems to be moving strongly toward a portal-based architecture (with a model similar to that shown in figure 4.8), where the system interfaces with various users and suppliers (including public and private maintenance facilities, original prime contractors and their suppliers, as well as service program

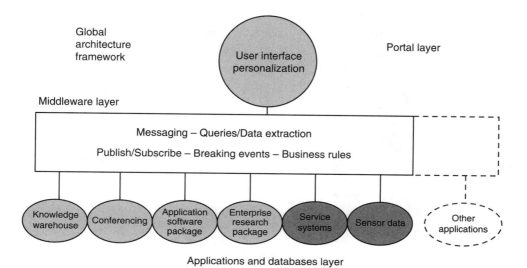

Figure 4.8
Portal-based architecture

managers, item managers, and many other users). The portal system will also have to allow monitoring and data aggregation by agencies and the DoD. The commercial world uses portal systems and bases them on Internet and commercial communication systems. The DoD could also compliment them with some special-purpose systems and adequate security (and testing thereof).

In general, the portal system provides an integrated approach and allows rapid spiral development. It has the following advantages:

- It is faster to deploy, since it uses proven commercial off-the-shelf technology.
- It is lower risk, since it demonstrates as it evolves.
- It leads to a highly collaborative system.
- It can build on current service initiatives.
- It can incorporate legacy systems (wherever desirable).
- It recognizes that technology and requirements will constantly change and can adapt to those changes as long as the standards are maintained.
- It keeps the users directly involved with its evolution.
- It recognizes the reality of cultural opposition to immediate, dramatic change.
- It provides high-level and detailed visibility to all users, at whatever level they would want it, and it is readily available to both public and private users in essentially real time.

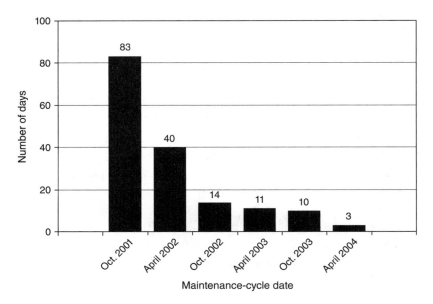

Figure 4.9
Continuous improvement: Maintenance-cycle days for F-404 engine repairs. *Source:* David Pauling, "Sustained Material Readiness via Continuous Process Improvement," 2006, Web page, accessed February 3, 2009, available at http://techcon.ncms.org/Symposium2006/presentations/2006%20Presentations/plenarySession/pauling%20ctma%20brief%20mar%202006.pdf.

Seventh but probably most important, logistics transformation requires a long-term focus on continuous improvement. Getting higher performance at lower cost requires continuous research and experimentation (which is why adequate R&D funding is important). Tracking the results over time is also important to show what is actually being achieved. Figure 4.9 illustrates a dramatic reduction in maintenance-cycle time on repairs on the navy's F-404 engines. Over two and a half years, the cycle time was reduced from eighty-three days to three days, which directly affects aircraft availability and the number of engines and spares that have to be procured. Savings are shown in direct labor dollars for maintenance, but even greater savings come from the indirect costs of the operation. Most important, much higher aircraft availability is gained at lower total costs.

Significant improvements also can be made by being constantly aware of what others are doing in your area of activity. In the case of jet engine maintenance, Snecma Services (a joint venture between the French company Snecma and General Electric) introduced a program called engine maintenance on-site (EMOS), which was aimed at avoiding engine removals for repairs or parts replacements. The company has specialized teams of experts who perform repairs in-situ and have special tools for on-wing machine repairs. In one case, it reported that a customer paid $5,000 for a repair and saved an engine shop visit that would have cost between $600,000 and $800,000, saved the additional time that would have been needed to ship and repair the engine in a shop, and also eliminated the need for a very expensive second engine during that period. Such lessons learned by others can prove valuable (as long as people are willing to observe and apply the experiences of others and not have a not-invented-here attitude).

Achieving the Vision

The commercial world has demonstrated what can be achieved in improving logistics performance at lower cost. Now the DoD must become a world-class player in the logistics area—both because it is critical to its military mission and because it has a very large cost (in an era in which the Defense budget may no longer continue to grow year after year and the supplemental dollars may disappear).

To achieve this transformation, strong leadership will be required to make modernization of the DoD supply chain a top DoD priority and to create the right incentives to achieve it. Demonstrations will need to be encouraged and funded, and success stories will need to be held up as examples. Finally, legislative and regulatory reform will be required in some of the financial issues discussed above, particularly reforming the way in which the competitive sourcing competitions are run and, most important, removing the mandate that 50 percent of the work be done on a sole-source basis.

For the logistics transformation to take place rapidly and effectively, five issues must be addressed:

1. The Secretary of Defense and the service chiefs must establish and adequately fund *management and organization integration* through a single Logistics Command (LOGCOM) and gain support for it throughout the DoD.

2. A detailed *transition plan* must be agreed to, it must evolve over time (using spiral development), and it must take full advantage of the incentives from competition. To ensure its full implementation, it must be continuously monitored, and actions taken as it evolves.

3. The information technology *architecture* that is established must evolve over time and must be portal-based, commercial off-the-shelf--based, focused on security and privacy, interoperable with enterprise resource planning systems, and must use standards that allow for continuous competition options (that is, nonproprietary standards).

4. The *tools and metrics* for continuous evaluation must include cost and performance baselines, a focus on force-readiness improvements, and initiation of

activities-based costing in government operations (to provide total cost visibility, which can be tracked along with performance improvements).

5. All *education and training* programs need to implement the vision, strategy, and results achieved and expected from the logistics transformation.

The point that must be emphasized throughout this logistics transformation (particularly in the education and training areas) is that the DoD can gain an enormous increase in total force effectiveness (through increases in readiness, mobility, flexibility, reliability, responsiveness, dependability, and error reductions) and accomplish it at significantly lower costs. The commercial world has demonstrated that this can be achieved, and the DoD must take maximum advantage of commercial experience and technology. But the key to success for logistics transformation is leadership action to overcome the anticipated barriers and institutional resistance. Logistics modernization must be a true leadership priority for it to succeed.

The Workforce: Industry, Government, and University

For America to have the strongest possible national security posture and for war-fighters to have the best possible equipment and support for that equipment, they need a capable and experienced acquisition workforce—in both government and industry. The government workforce consists of the military acquisition workforce, career civilian acquisition workforce, and senior political appointees. The industry workforce includes people from large, defense-industry firms as well as the small and midsized firms that often serve both military and commercial customers. This workforce is generally specialized by area, such as manufacturing, software, or services. Figure 5.1 shows total defense-related employment from 1965 through 2005. The figure shows wide fluctuations in the industrial labor force, building up dramatically in periods of the Vietnam War (the late 1960s), the Reagan buildup at the end of the cold war (the late 1980s), and the conflicts in Iraq and Afghanistan (after September 11, 2001). The variations in defense-industry employment go from a low of around 2 million people to a high of around 4 million, and these large variations take place over relatively short periods of time. The figure also shows that since the 1970s, both military and civilian government workforces have not been built up during periods in which the defense budget escalated. Instead, the budget increases were absorbed by defense-industry workers, who often performed many of the jobs that were not inherently governmental but that historically were performed by the government. This cyclical employment was achieved through outsourcing, which (as the figure shows) provides flexibility. If this had been done by insourcing, government workers would have remained on payrolls throughout the low periods.

Over the forty-year period shown in the figure and particularly since the information revolution of the 1990s, the nature of the work being done by this defense-related workforce has changed dramatically. In 1990, for example, 37 percent of the workforce was employed in the (broadly defined) aerospace industry, but by 2000 this was down to 28 percent, and by 2006 it was down to 16 percent.[1] There are two major causes for shifts in the workforce mix: (1) services have become a

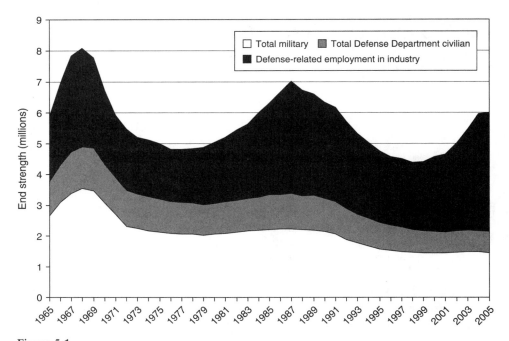

Figure 5.1
Total defense-related employment. *Source:* Office of the Undersecretary of Defense (Comptroller), "National Defense Budget Estimates for FY 2006," April 2005.

majority of the functions being performed in the defense industry (by 2007, over 60 percent of Defense Department procurements were for services), and (2) blue-collar manufacturing jobs have decreased significantly as the high cost of weapons systems and their increasing complexity have resulted in far fewer of them, both in types and in quantity.

Perhaps the single most important element in the weapons-acquisition process is the requirement for the government to have smart buyers, beginning with the government's career acquisition professionals. When the defense procurement budget plummeted at the end of the cold war, the acquisition workforce at the Department of Defense was correspondingly reduced significantly. In the mid-1990s, as procurement budgets flattened and started to expand, the Defense Department authorization act for fiscal year 1996 required the DoD to reduce its acquisition workforce by a further 25 percent by the end of fiscal year 2000. However, as acquisition budgets started growing (to compensate for the procurement holiday that the DoD had experienced in the post–cold war period) and skyrocketed after 9/11, the acquisition workforce continued to decline, causing a huge gap between the work that needed to be done and the people who were available to do it. This problem was further compounded by the fact that a significant share of the added work was in the difficult contracting area of services (rather than the traditional equipment procurements, for which the acquisition workforce had been trained). To make matters worse, much of this work was to be done in connection with an expeditionary operation, under extremely dangerous conditions (in Iraq and Afghanistan), with military who were doing the warfighting, and with government civilians who were there as volunteers. In the war zone, a large percentage of the requisitions for government contracting people were not filled, and of those that were filled, only 35 percent were certified for the positions they were in. No one there could do independent pricing or contract closeouts.[2] (In 2008, ninety cases of fraud were prosecuted as a result of questionable contracting actions in the area of expeditionary operations, which should not be surprising, given the shortage of government contracting people..) After the obvious shortcomings in the acquisition workforce that were highlighted by the problems in the Iraq and Afghanistan expeditionary operations, the secretary of the army (which was the executive agent for these operations) and the secretary of defense established a commission (known as the "Gansler Commision", after its chairman) to make recommendations for avoiding such actions in the future, and subsequently, took the commission's recommendations to initiate a series of actions to correct the problem in the future.

As recommended by the commission,[3] the corrective actions had to start at the top of the government acquisition workforce. Because these contracting activities were taking place in a war zone, senior people in uniform would be expected to oversee them. However, in the post–cold war period, when there was a significant draw-down of military personnel, the army chose to keep its general officer positions within the combat arms and to cut back significantly on those in the contracting field. In 1990, the army had five general officers with contracting background; and by 2007, all five of those positions had been eliminated. This also discouraged young military officers from going into the contracting field; since there were no longer general officer positions to which they could aspire. Additionally, in 1990, the Defense Contract Management Agency (which was responsible for contract management after awards were made) had four general officer (joint) positions, which by 2007 had all been eliminated. The overall personnel for the Defense Contract Management Agency was decreased from 25,000 in 1990, to 13,000 in 2000, and to 10,000 by 2007, which was typical of the cuts in the DoD civilian acquisition workforce in the last decade of the twentieth century—that is, a decrease of over 50 percent.[4]

When budgets began to skyrocket after 9/11, the government's acquisition workforce continued to decline (both in military and civilian personnel). In the army, for example, from 1995 to 2006, acquisition dollars increased by 382 percent, acquisition actions increased by 359 percent, and the workforce declined by 53 percent.[5] In essence, a vicious cycle was taking place. Military enrollments had been cut in the post–cold war period but now were badly needed as the nation went to war in Iraq and Afghanistan, so nonwarfighting military jobs were shifted to government civilians. But the government civilian workforce had also been cut dramatically, so for all positions that were not considered "inherently governmental" (for example, not at the decision-making or government commitment level), the support roles were contracted out to the private sector (see the right-hand side of figure 5.1—from 1998 to 2005). By 2007, over 190,000 contractors were operating in the war zone (over half of the total force operating there), but there were insufficient numbers of government personnel overseeing contract actions and checking on the implementation of the results. Fortunately, by 2008, these needs began to be recognized by the DoD and the Congress, and actions were initiated to correct them. The army was authorized to add five general officers to oversee contracting activities,[6] the army created a new Army Contracting Command (ACC),[7] and the Congress authorized funds and additional positions for the DoD to begin hiring and training additional acquisition personnel. But changes of the magnitude and nature required take effort and time—particularly in terms of DoD leadership and prioritization.

The Government Acquisition Workforce

At the top of the government acquisition workforce are senior political appointees in positions such as undersecretary of defense for acquisition, technology, and logistics; the corresponding assistant secretaries of the services; and the director of defense research and engineering. These Senate-confirmed positions should be filled with people who have extensive experience in the defense acquisition world, but often they are appointed more for their political (or other) backgrounds than their defense-related experience. Because these appointees receive extensive financial and security background checks (to satisfy both executive and legislative requirements) and go through the full Senate confirmation process, the appointments to top government jobs have been taking longer and longer. Figure 5.2 shows that recent administrations have taken over eight months to fill the top five hundred appointments.

Because people remain in these top positions for an average of only two and a half years, many career personnel in the department refer to them as "temporary employees" and simply wait them out if they disagree with their policies. Additionally, securing the right people for these positions can be difficult because they have to take a dramatic salary cut (assuming they came from senior positions in industry) and also agree to postemployment restrictions, which have become increasingly onerous. If government is going to have smart buyers—and it must to maximize the

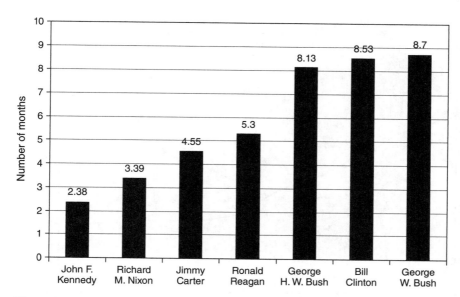

Figure 5.2

Time taken to fill the top 500 jobs in presidential administrations, 1961 to 2009. *Source:* Brookings Institution, "Staffing a New Administration: A Guide to Personnel Appointments in a Presidential Transition," Presidential Appointee Initiative, 2000.

efficiency and effectiveness with which it spends its hundreds of billions of dollars of acquisition resources—then it is going to have to address the problems of acquiring and retaining senior people with relevant experience at the top of the acquisition pyramid.

At the next level of the government acquisition workforce are the senior military officers. The numbers of these positions have been greatly reduced, and they have often been filled by people with little or no acquisition experience. As the cynics state, it is a way to keep combat officers in senior positions until they can find the correct spot for them in a combat role. This lack of acquisition opportunities for general officers has to be corrected so that younger officers can be encouraged to follow a career path in the acquisition area.

Most acquisition positions in the government are filled by career government civilians. A number of trends are clear. First, the federal government has experienced a dramatic reduction in acquisition personnel. For the DoD, the workforce fell by approximately 65 percent from 1990 to 2000; and this did not increase after 9/11. But as budget dollars (particularly in the Defense Department) have rapidly grown, the remaining acquisition workers have experienced greatly increased workloads. Figure 5.3 shows this clearly.

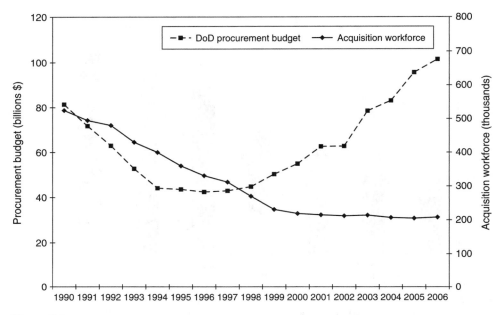

Figure 5.3
DoD acquisition workforce declined as procurement budgets increased service: Commission on army acquisition and program management in expditionary operations, "Urgent Reform Required: Army Expeditionary Contracting" (Washington, D.C., U.S. Government Printing Office, October 2007).

Even though in 2008 there was a decision to increase the number of acquisition personnel in the Defense Department, the competition for people with the relevant experience across the overall federal government (as well as in industry) became intense. For the DoD, the greatest need was in hiring people who were willing to go into the war zone to do contracting and acquisition management. Incentive bonuses for sign-up, extensive internship programs, and other benefits were used in the competition among various federal agencies (and with industry) for these key people.

The second major trend in acquisition personnel is that the overall government workforce (including those in the acquisition arena) is aging. The cutbacks in the post–cold war era primarily reduced the younger workforce (following the rule of "last in, first out"), thus increasing the average age of the workforce. In addition, because the baby boomers born after World War II were hired in large numbers, by the end of the twentieth century, many DoD civilian workers were in their fifties, and by 2005 more than half of the 124,400 civilian members of the DoD acquisition workforce were eligible to retire within five years[8] (and government retirement benefits were becoming very attractive). In fact, by 2006, 75 percent of the DoD's acquisition workforce was born before 1964.[9] The combination of this aging of the workforce, the difficulty of attracting and retaining new people with the requisite education and experience into the government, and the lack of middle management to supervise them presents a major problem. And it is compounded by the fact that the aging workforce often does not have modern, computer-based skills that match the DoD's twenty-first-century needs.

These government workforce problems have led to increased outsourcing of many critical government needs to the private sector. In some cases (for example, armed security personnel in the war zone or private contractors supporting government contracting or program-management activities), this has caused great concern in Congress about whether these functions are inherently governmental. But the need to fill these positions with contractors has been driven by the shortage of experienced government personnel to perform these functions, and with the upcoming retirements, the problem is anticipated to worsen unless significant corrective actions are taken. Numerous studies have shown that the government has not been taking adequate steps to address this pending crisis—for example, by shortening its lengthy hiring process, which commonly takes as long as five months,[10] and by taking other steps to become more competitive with the private sector for these key personnel.[11] The aging baby-boom workforce issue is not unique to defense, but defense has the additional problems of having to hire people who can gain security clearance (and therefore must be U.S. citizens) and of needing people with high-tech backgrounds (many of whom happen not to be U.S. citizens). By 2007, the Department of Defense and the Department of Homeland Security were understaffed in their procurement offices by 8,300 contracting officers,[12] and many of those in place were due to retire within a short period.

Eventually, outsourcing of many jobs previously done by government workers became the common practice. When done competitively, this has benefits (in terms of performance, costs, and flexibility), but it often results in a "blended workforce," with contractors and government workers sitting side by side and performing similar work. For example, in 2007, contractors accounted for 42 percent of the contracting specialists (i.e. people skilled in contracting) at the Army Contracting Agency's Contracting Center of Excellence.[13] There is nothing illegal, inefficient, or ineffective about this arrangement (in many cases, it was far more efficient and effective than the previous situation)—as long as the contractors are not doing inherently governmental work and they, or their firms, have no conflicts of interest. Yet this blended workforce has provided numerous operating (and even morale) problems for government workers (for example, around issues of management authority and pay disparities). So the practice of outsourcing began to receive significant executive and legislative branch visibility, and clearer definitions of roles, responsibilities, and potential areas for conflicts of interest were required. Nonetheless, the work has to be done, and the contractors have the required skills, so the practice has continued until the government workforce can be built up and additional specialized firms (with no conflicts of interest) can be established.

As the government brings in young employees to replace those who are retiring and as the numbers of middle-management workers who can provide guidance decrease (due to the post–cold war hiring freezes), it will be essential to provide extensive training and education to these new hires if the government is to become a smart buyer. This training will have to be in newer areas (such as expeditionary contracting, complex-systems acquisition, and the difficult area of sophisticated services acquisition and management) as well as in the modern techniques and tools used in the acquisition process (such as performance-based acquisition, strategic planning, effective resolution of contract disputes, independent pricing, requirements writing, and contract closeouts). Additionally, because the DoD civilian acquisition personnel may be increasingly asked to volunteer to travel into combat zones for expeditionary operations (to support the contracting and management of the many private-sector personnel in the war zones), the government will have to come up with greater incentives for these people to volunteer to put their lives at stake (such as greater incentive pay, enhanced life insurance, and other enhanced benefits). During the Iraq and Afghanistan conflicts, military people and private-sector contractors have received many of these benefits, but the government civilian personnel have not, and correcting this discrepancy was one the main recommendations of the army and Defense Department commission (described above) that looked into contracting problems in Iraq and Afghanistan. Finally, one solution for the government's acquisition personnel problems that needs serious consideration is enhancing the temporary rotation of people with specialized skills from industry to government (while avoiding conflicts of interest). Such programs proved to be effective in bringing in skilled workers in prior eras of need. Congress has recently begun to expand such provisions (for example, allowing the Defense Advance Research Projects Agency to hire, on a rotation basis, twenty people with exceptional scientific skills from industry), but this is a very small number compared to the government's needs, and such a program would have to be greatly expanded to cover many agencies and skills in order to satisfy the government's needs in the coming years.[14]

In partial recognition of the need for an "acquisition workforce-development fund" for the recruitment, training, and retention of acquisition personnel in the DoD, Congress (in section 852 of the fiscal year 2008 defense authorization act) provided some needed development resources, and Secretary Gates committed to hire twenty thousand new acquisition people for the DoD. But this cannot be seen simply as a quota challenge for the various services. Experienced people need to be hired, and new people must receive adequate training before being put into a decision-making position, and these people need be hired and trained to fill inherently governmental positions (not wrench-turning or other support roles).

The Defense-Industry Workforce

As noted at the beginning of this book, the defense industry (historically referred to as the "arsenal of democracy") supplies the weapon systems and services that the military warfighters count on to make the difference in conflicts. The essential elements in this industry are people—from the CEO down to entry-level positions. These people must turn out the highest-quality, highest-performance weapons and services at affordable prices. This business is a high-tech industry: it produces guided missiles, ships, planes, tanks, and complex logistics, analytic, and engineering software services. Unlike its commercial equivalents, it is an industry that is heavily influenced by politics, extensive regulation, and the unique characteristics of a single buyer. Chief executive officers and senior managers in the defense industry need to understand both the high-technology aspects of the business as well as the DoD's processes and culture. These CEOs have tended to come from engineering and program management backgrounds, but recently the focus has shifted toward the financial side. They have kept one eye on Wall Street and the other on mergers and acquisitions and have received multimillion dollar salaries and equity positions tied to the stock value of their company.

An even greater shift has taken place in the profile of the typical defense-industry worker. In the past, this was a heavily blue-collar, manufacturing industry. It was technology-based, with engineers doing significant design and prototype work, but the overwhelming share of dollars went into the manufacturing and maintenance of equipment. However, as equipment became more complex and expensive, fewer systems were built, and large amounts of contract dollars were shifted into professional services (which came to dominate the overall contract awards). As Mark Ronald (the then CEO and chair of a large defense firm) stated, "The nature of our workforce has dramatically changed. . . . this was a blue-collar industry. It's now almost exclusively white-collar. . . . the nature of our products has changed. . . . [Our company started with] airplane companies coming together, and today airplanes is only about 7% of our business. . . . we are electronics, we're software . . . which is what the other large aerospace companies are." [15] Today, a highly skilled workforce performs preliminary design work, prototype construction, systems engineering, system-of-systems architecture and implementation, extensive software, and significant professional services. In many cases, it is doing work that is not inherently governmental but that previously was done by government employees.

The industry workforce is suffering from many of the same problems that the government workforce faces. As a result of the major cutbacks in defense expenditures in the post–cold war period, very little hiring was done in the defense industry in the 1990s, and because both the government and private industry had built up their workforces at the same time, they were both facing an aging workforce. As these workers began to retire and as the demands from the post-9/11 budget buildups rolled into the defense industry, the competition for these workers—from the government and from the rapidly growing high-tech commercial sector—resulted in severe competition for these employees, and higher and higher salaries had to be paid. For example, computer-based simulation and modeling workers were badly needed in the defense area, and both Wall Street and Hollywood were paying high salaries to attract these people. Since 1995, when defense budgets began to increase and large defense-industry firms were consolidating, salaries for R&D scientists and engineers in the aerospace industry (broadly defined to include electronics and software) exploded—from just over $170,000 per year to over $370,000 per year.[16] The commercial world was free to hire non-U.S. citizens, so the defense industry was making special awards for people who were U.S. citizens and already had security clearances. The contractors offered signing and incentive bonuses and higher salaries for people who had security clearances or received them when they started work. In 2006, signing bonuses ranged from $3,900 to $11,400, and the increases for security clearances ranged from 3 percent for a confidential clearance up to 23 percent for a top-secret, polygraph clearance.[17] Many defense firms were also offering their own employees a bounty fee or finder's fee of up to $10,000 for every new employee that they suggested and the company hired.

By the middle of the first decade of the twenty-first century, America began to realize that its workforce was not keeping up to the demands of the growing science and technology needs of global competition (perhaps best exemplified by a National Academies 2005 report, *Rising above the Gathering Storm: Energizing and Employing America for a Brighter Economic Future*).[18]

But the problems were perhaps even greater in the aerospace and defense industry. Here, eight factors were leading to a crisis:

• *The post–cold war employment decline*   With the drop in government procurements and the defense-industry consolidations that took place after the cold war ended, there were massive layoffs accompanied by hiring freezes. By 2005, there were only 751,300 aerospace jobs—down 40 percent from a 1989 peak of more than 1.3 million aerospace employees.[19] Many of these losses were young workers, so the loss of young workers was disproportionately greater. The cutbacks extended to engineers and scientists, who from 1986 to 2003 declined from 144,800 to 32,500 in the aerospace industry.[20]

• *Retirement*   Thirty percent of the aerospace workforce was eligible to retire by 2008,[21] and this problem will dramatically worsen as the large group of baby boomers (who were the workers left after the cutbacks) continue to reach retirement age. The Labor Department has estimated that in the overall U.S. economy, baby boomers will retire at the rate of 7,918 a day from 2007 onward.[22]

• *A shift to a high-tech workforce*   As the nature of the work shifted from high-volume production of low-tech equipment to low numbers of systems that had heavy engineering and software content, the nature of the workforce correspondingly shifted. The demand for scientists and engineers as a percentage of the workforce grew significantly. In addition, blue-collar workers needed higher-tech skills, which caused many manufacturing jobs to go unfilled (primarily because the applicants lacked the necessary reading and math skills to fill these positions).[23]

• *Insufficient numbers of U.S. science and technology workers*   A major long-term problem for U.S. economic competitiveness and national security is that U.S. students are choosing not to enter the science and technology fields. For example, from 1997 to 2007, the number of engineering doctorates awarded by U.S. universities to U.S. citizens dropped by 23 percent; from 1987 to 2007, at the bachelor's level, the number of engineers, mathematicians, physical scientists, and geoscientists declined by almost 40 percent; and in 1956, almost twice as many bachelor's degrees were awarded in physics as were awarded in 2006.[24] Even in the field of computer science, enrollment in college computer science courses dropped 60 percent between 2000 and 2004, putting enrollment 70 percent below its 1987 peak.[25] These are the people that will be needed in the information-security area for the commercial world and the future world of cyberwarfare.

• *Competition from the growing high-tech commercial field*   Throughout most of the twentieth century, many of America's top scientists and engineers chose to go into the defense field because it represented the leading edge of technology. But as the commercial high-tech field exploded (both in the United States and globally), its demand for top students grew rapidly (even though the numbers of graduating U.S. students in these areas were declining). Many of these students were attracted to the innovative work being done in the commercial field. There was also the expectation that it was a long-term growth business, unlike the defense industry, which traditionally was viewed as a highly cyclical business and therefore riskier for long-term employment.

• *Declining industry and government investment in R&D*   As would be expected during a downturn, in the post-cold war period, the Defense Department significantly reduced its R&D investments, particularly long-term research. The same thing happened within the defense industry during this period, when an emphasis on the short term by Wall Street and corporate management similarly resulted in less money going into corporate-sponsored R&D. Then the Defense Department budgets rose dramatically after 9/11, money was poured into short-term, wartime needs, and again, research suffered. As this reduced demand continued over a significant number of years, young people who might have become scientists or engineers chose instead to follow the money and pursued careers in finance or law. As Norman Augustine observed, "in 2001 U.S. industry spent more on tort litigation, and related costs, than on research and development."[26]

• *Limited program experience*   As defense weapons-acquisition new-start programs have declined, the number of different programs that an individual within the industry can work on has dramatically declined (see table 3.1 for military aircraft program new starts from the 1950s to the 2000s). Engineers used to gain experience by working on many different programs, but more recently they have had to spend twenty or more years on a single program. This is both far less psychologically rewarding and much more limiting in terms of the experience base that they can build. This long-term commitment to a single program has tended to discourage people from entering the defense sector when they compared it to the commercial sector's explosion and rapid turnover of new products.

• *Lack of interest in aerospace and defense*   For many of the reasons noted above, the defense sector simply lost the appeal that it had during the Apollo and the cold war eras. Today's science and engineering graduates rank aerospace and defense low, if not last, on their lists of industries providing desirable employment.[27] A Bain study conducted at fifteen of the top engineering schools found that just 7 percent of students expected to pursue a career in aerospace and defense,[28] and a survey of five hundred U.S. aerospace workers found that 80 percent would not recommend that their children pursue aerospace careers because of workplace instability.[29]

The integrated effect of these eight factors is creating a crisis in defense-industry employment. Recruiting and retaining employees is now the number one priority for firms in the defense sector. The above-noted Bain study forecast a potential shortfall of tens of thousands of U.S. defense engineers over the next few years. If current trends hold, then the industry will be able to replace only about half of the 57,000 to 68,000 engineers who are expected to retire by 2010. This is a major problem for all of the large defense firms. For example, in 2006, one in every three of Lockheed Martin's employees was over age fifty, and the company was hiring fourteen thousand people a year. By 2009, it expected to need about 44,000 new hires, and yet Department of Education data stated that U.S. colleges and universities were producing only about 62,000 bachelor of engineering graduates a year (fewer than visual and performing arts graduates).[30] According to the Bain survey, there is likely to be (depending on demand) a potential shortfall of 41,000 to 87,000 defense engineers by 2010.[31] This represents a major problem for America's future national security and also (because these same people are needed in the commercial area) for future U.S. economic competitiveness. The industry will need to look to the universities to help solve this problem.

University Graduates

The science and engineering education story is equally concerning—particularly at the graduate-school level. For example, in 2005, U.S. universities awarded 41,000 master's and doctorate degrees in engineering, and just over half of these were earned by citizens of other countries.[32] This percentage has been increasing significantly as fewer U.S. citizens are interested in this field and as more foreign students enter the field. Even more troublesome is that 57 percent of scholars holding postdoctoral positions at U.S. universities in 2001 were foreign born.[33] This predominance of foreign-born scholars in the U.S. graduate-school programs extends to a wide variety of fields. For example, in the electrical engineering field, in 2007, 70 percent of PhDs went to non-U.S. citizens.[34] Similarly, in the information technology area, there are more foreign students than U.S. students in U.S. universities' graduate-level programs. Although the number of U.S. PhDs in science and engineering declined from 1996 to 2001, the number graduating in Asia and Europe each now annually exceeds the number in the United States by over five thousand.[35] This shortage of U.S.-citizen graduate students (which the defense industry requires) is mirrored by a shortage of U.S. undergraduates who simply are not choosing the science and engineering programs. Far more students in other countries are pursuing science and engineering career paths at the undergraduate level than U.S. students are (figure 5.4).

Thus, U.S. universities are faced with a dilemma: they are unable to interest U.S. students in science and engineering and are continuing to attract foreign students. But they are also pursuing a new direction—establishing U.S. universities abroad. For example, in Qatar, Carnegie Melon has a campus, Cornell University has a medical school, Texas A&M has an engineering school, and Georgetown has a computer science school. Michigan State and Rochester Institute of Technology have centers in Dubai. New York University is opening a campus in the United Arab Emirates and has one in Singapore; Georgia Tech has degree programs in France, Singapore, Italy, South Africa, and China and is planning one for India. As this trend continues, U.S. campuses will attract even fewer foreign science and engineering students, teachers, and scholars, and because in the past many of these people have stayed in the U.S. after their university affiliations have ended, they will no longer be available to be hired by U.S. industry (particularly the commercial sector). It is especially alarming to realize that one-third of America's Nobel Prize winners were not U.S. born and that most of the founders of Silicon Valley's high-tech firms were not U.S. born. The effect of the current trends on

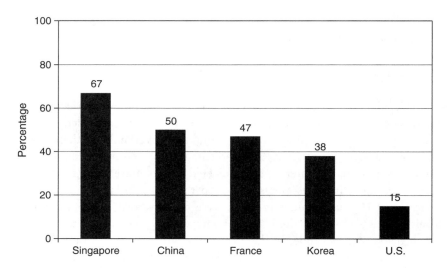

Figure 5.4
Undergraduate degrees in natural science and engineering in five countries, 2004. *Source:* Kenneth Cohen, "National Math and Science Initiative," November 2007, Briefing to the Committee on Science, Engineering and Public Policy, National Academies, September 4, 2008).

future U.S. competitiveness and security is significant, and yet U.S. policies tend to discourage foreign science and engineering scholars and students from coming to America for further research and study. For example, if they come here on a student or a temporary work visa, they must agree beforehand to return to their country when their studies or temporary work is completed (a policy that is counter to U.S. interests). Since September 11, 2001, the United States has tightened its visa-approval process for foreign scholars and students (for fear that they might be either terrorists or spies), another policy that is counter to U.S. interests.[36]

For the nondefense sector, the existence of the foreign students and scholars in the United States has been a great benefit. In fact, one-third of today's workforce of scientists and engineers were born outside of the United States.[37] But the post-9/11 immigration controls resulted in a 32 percent drop in the number of international student applications by 2004—so the long-term trend is clear.[38]

Equally troublesome is the fact that, to obtain the required labor force, American commercial firms are moving their research and development centers offshore. A survey by Booz Allen Hamilton and INSEAD found that between 1975 and 2005, the share of R&D sites located outside the country (for those with U.S. corporate headquarters) rose from 45 to 66 percent. The survey also found 77 percent of the new R&D sites planned over the next three years will be located in either China or India. Together, China and India are on the brink of overtaking western Europe as the most important locations for foreign R&D for U.S. companies. As a result, by late 2007, China and India "counted for 31% of the global R&D staff" of U.S. firms, up from 19 percent in 2004. The survey found that "the most cited reason for establishing a new foreign site was access to qualified staff."[39]

If the United States is to retain its technological leadership position in national security and in economic competitiveness, it must acknowledge these long-term trends. American-born scientists and engineers (particularly at the graduate-school level) are in short supply, and commercial technology companies are clamoring to hire qualified foreigners, particularly those trained at U.S. universities. Additionally, those who stay in the United States often start their own companies. During the ten years that ended in 2005, foreign-born entrepreneurs started a quarter of the new engineering and technology firms in the United States.[40]

In 2001, the United States granted 200,000 H1-B visas for highly skilled workers. Yet by 2004, the United States had reduced this allowable limit to 85,000 H-1B work visas (65,000 for foreign workers with bachelor's degrees and another 20,000 for foreign alumni of U.S. graduate schools). In 2008, there were 163,000 applicants for these visas, and the U.S. Citizenship Immigration Services was so swamped that it stopped accepting applications after five days. The numbers would have been dramatically larger if the application process had been kept open longer. These people are not replacing the blue-collar workers who are unemployed, and there is a shortage in the United States of U.S. citizens for these positions. It is in America's interests to increase the number of H-1B work visas rather than force these highly qualified scientists and engineers to move to other countries and compete with America. In addition, a significant number of these workers should be allowed to work in the defense industry. About 3 percent of U.S. military personnel are not U.S. citizens,[41] and after serving, they are allowed instant citizenship.[42] Similarly, some non-U.S. citizens should be allowed to work in defense plants in areas that are not classified and then obtain citizenship. (It also should be acknowledged that most famous spies operating against the United States were born here and lived here all their lives.)

Another change required is decreasing the wait time between receiving a visa and being hired. Today, even if a firm gets an employment acceptance from an H-1B visa applicant with an advanced degree from a U.S. university, it has to wait over a year to hire that person.[43] Additionally, the limits on obtaining green cards, especially for professionals from countries such as China, result in a wait of many years before residency status is granted. For example, a scientist from India or China would have had to apply in 2001 to be considered for a green card in 2006.[44] Yet according to one calculation, since the 1980s, three thousand technology firms (more than 30 percent of the total) were founded in Silicon Valley by entrepreneurs with Indian or Chinese roots.[45] Companies with one or more immigrant founders include Intel, Google, Yahoo!, Sun Microsystems, and eBay, and a 2006 survey of private, venture-backed startup companies in the United States estimated that 47 percent had immigrant founders. The study also found that two-thirds of those immigrant founders surveyed believed that current U.S. immigration policy hinders the ability of future foreign-born entrepreneurs to start American companies today.[46] It certainly appears that the United States has a vital interest in maintaining a more open, legal immigration system.[47] The Manhattan Project, a secret project to build the first atomic bomb, operated during World War II, and it provides an interesting perspective on the potential benefits of having non-U.S. citizens work in the national-security arena. Few U.S. citizens were involved. Most people working on the project were Europeans, and most had come from Germany or Italy, enemies of the United States at that time. In fact, Enrico Fermi did not get his U.S. citizenship until after the atomic bomb was dropped.

The problem of not allowing foreign skilled workers into the United States has been recognized for some time. In 2006, Bill Gates warned that the lack of visas and residence permits (green cards) for skilled workers was threatening American competitiveness "as other countries benefit from the international talent that the U.S. employers cannot hire or retain." Microsoft has a choice, however. It has four large research centers, and only one is in the United States. The others are in Bangalore, India; Beijing, China; and Cambridge, England.[48] Defense firms do not have this option (although they may be forced to, if these trends continue).

Increasing the number of H-1B visas will not allow foreign residents to take jobs that otherwise would go to U.S. citizens. Many jobs in science and technology need to be filled. One 2008 study noted that more than 140,000 job openings for skilled positions were available just within Standard & Poor's five hundred top companies. Major U.S. technology companies in 2008 averaged more than 470 U.S.-based job openings for skilled positions, and defense companies had more than 1,265 each. These all were jobs that require at least an undergraduate degree in the science and technology area. Examples of defense firms that had job openings in January 2008 include Northrop Grumman (3,925), Lockheed Martin (3,901), and Raytheon (1,694).[49] This problem is expected to grow significantly as a result of the aging workforce and the lack of U.S. students going into science and engineering. In fact, the Bureau of Labor Statistics estimates that "employers will have to fill more than one million new high-tech jobs between 2006 and 2016."[50] As Thomas L. Friedman said with regard to bringing in skilled foreign workers and the number of employment-based green cards given to high-tech foreign workers who want to stay here: "Give them all they want! Not only do our companies need them now, because we're not training enough engineers, but they will, over time start many more companies and create many more good jobs than they would possibly displace. Silicon Valley is living proof of that; and where innovation happens does matter. It's still where the best jobs will be located."[51]

6

The Criticality of Research and Development

After World War II and during the cold war, U.S. national security strategy was based on technological superiority. The secretary of defense from 1977 to 1981, Harold Brown, and the undersecretary of defense during that period, William Perry, decided to offset the Soviet Union's quantitative military superiority not by building bigger armies but—because the cost of DoD labor went up greatly with the end of the draft—by investing in technology.[1]

This policy has not been universally accepted (especially by many in the military, who would much prefer forces in being), but its effectiveness was demonstrated in the 1991 Gulf War when the technology that was developed during that prior period clearly worked and helped U.S. forces achieve a rapid victory. In the 2006 Lebanon war, fighters in Hezbollah (a paramilitary organization based on Lebanon) fired on northern Israeli towns. For thirty-four days, the group fought Israeli defense forces (the strongest army in the Middle East) in northern Israel and southern Lebanon, using technology to match its irregular tactics and recognizing that it could not confront Israel directly with conventional forces.[2] The insurgents in Iraq have been highly effective against the far more powerful coalition forces of the United States and its allies by using technology (such as secure communications, the Internet, and roadside bombs) with small forces and commercial technologies. Finally, small forces that acquire nuclear or biological weapons can dramatically affect future security—even with a limited number of forces.

Thus, the United States and its allies must develop advanced technology, anticipate how advanced technology (military and commercial) will be used in the future and who will use it, and develop technological and or operational counters to each of these. For example, as Russia demonstrated when its troops went into the country of Georgia in 2008, cyberwarfare can be used against adversaries in a significant way. U.S. research must devote significant attention to cyberdefense. Overall, as technology spreads rapidly and globally, the United States needs to stay ahead (offensively and defensively) to maintain its future security.

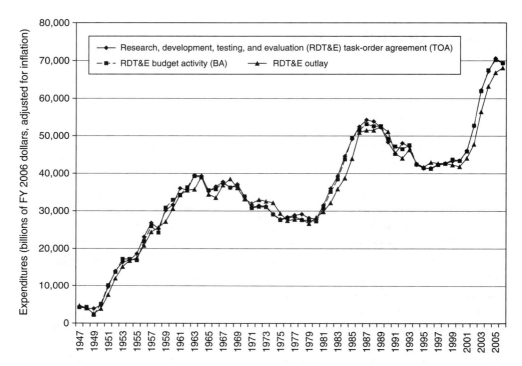

Figure 6.1
Research and development expenditures, 1947 to 2006 (adjusted for inflation). *Source:* National defense budget estimates for fiscal year 2006, Office of the Under Secretary of Defense (Comptroller), April 2005.

Fortunately, the importance of investing in research and development has been widely recognized since the end of World War II, and R&D investments have grown significantly since then (figure 6.1).

Large investments in defense research and development are possible only when the economy is healthy. In constrained economic periods, long-term investments (such as research and development, particularly fundamental research) are usually postponed so that near-term needs can be funded.

Not only do defense expenditures require a healthy economy, but R&D investments in defense and in nondefense have a synergistic relationship that is reinforcing in both directions. In the past, the U.S. economy has gained more from the spinoff of defense expenditures than the defense industry has gained from private R&D, but recently, defense has gained considerable benefits from commercial R&D expenditures (particularly, in the information-technology area). Because an increasing share of the U.S. national R&D expenditures are in the commercial world, the DoD needs to take full advantage of those investments (and not be hampered by regulatory or legislative restrictions).

There have been many spinoffs from defense technology to the commercial world:

• *Commercial aircraft* One of the Wright brothers' early planes was funded by the army as an R&D project. The Boeing 707 drew heavily on the Boeing military tanker (the KC-135) that was developed to provide in-flight refueling for strategic bombers. From 1945 to 1982, military R&D funding accounted for more than 74 percent of the total R&D investment in the commercial aircraft industry, and from 1985 to 2000, it never accounted for less than 70 percent of the annual R&D investments in this industry.[3]

• *Jet engines* Commercial aircraft engine technologies—the Pratt & Whitney Wasp of 1925, the high-bypass turbofans of the 1980s, and the large jet engines used in modern aircraft today—have benefitted from military procurement and military-supported R&D.

• *Semiconductors* Defense early procurements and continued R&D efforts played a major role in the development of this industry as the DoD moved toward a heavy dependence on electronics for technological superiority.

• *Computers* The ENIAC (Electronic Numerical Integrator and Computer), introduced in 1945 and generally considered the first electronic digital computer, was funded by the U.S. Army,[4] and the DoD has continued to be a major sponsor of the accelerating advances in the computer industry since that time.

• *Software* As the DoD's use of advanced computers exploded and as it moved toward its current heavy dependence on integrated electronic systems and systems-of systems, the development of advanced software became even more and more critical. For example, on the Joint Strike Fighter, over 50 percent of the development costs went into software development.[5]

• *Internet* In 1974, the Advanced Research Projects Agency (ARPA)—now the Defense Advanced Research Projects Agency (DARPA)—began the Advanced Research Projects Agency Network (ARPANET). ARPANET was funded as an open, nonproprietary set of standards that resulted in the architecture of the current, worldwide Internet. By allowing (and actually encouraging) small firms to take part in its development, ARPA could take advantage of the innovativeness of small firms.

• *Global positioning system (GPS)* Initiated by the DoD in 1972 as a three-dimensional navigation system for aircraft, ships, missiles, and vehicles, the global positioning system is now funded by the DoD and provided free to commercial users worldwide. Additionally, the nuclear clock on the GPS satellites is now used as the time standard for the international banking system.

• *Communication satellites*   With its need for global communications, the DoD played a major role in the development of communication satellites that are now used worldwide (both militarily and commercially).

• *Nuclear power*   Much of the development of the nuclear power industry— beginning with work on nuclear weapons but particularly on nuclear power plants for ships—was paid for by the Department of Defense.

• *Freeze-dried foods*   Much research and development work has been done on how to provide food to troops. This R&D has focused on packaging fresh food, maintaining it at room temperature for long periods, and rapidly heating it (including through packaging).

• *Standardized shipping containers*   Standardized shipping containers were developed so that large volumes of equipment could be rapidly packed and shipped when troops go overseas. This process quickly revolutionized the commercial shipping industry.

This list could go on, and a comparable list of process modernization steps have also been introduced by the Department of Defense—including program management, schedule-control techniques, modern manufacturing (which began with army-funded interchangeable rifle parts), and manufacturing technology projects. The above list indicates the dramatic effects that defense R&D has had on the growth and leadership of the U.S. economy. Although these spinoffs from defense R&D have been valuable, the large national investment in defense R&D is done for the nation's security, and the economic benefits are only a secondary consideration. Nonetheless, their value has helped to sustain congressional support for large defense R&D investments. In fact, defense-related R&D spending represented more than 80 percent of total federal R&D spending for much of the 1950s, and it rarely dropped below 50 percent of federal R&D expenditures from 1949 to 2005.[6] Although U.S. federal expenditures dominated overall national R&D until the mid-1970s, since the 1990s commercial R&D has dominated—accounting for almost 70 percent of the nation's total R&D expenditures in the twenty-first century (figure 6.2).

Thus, the DoD must take advantage of this commercial R&D—domestically and globally. This means removing many of the current legislative and regulatory barriers that prevent commercial firms from doing DoD R&D and prevent the DoD from using commercial products (in spite of both their higher performance and their lower costs).

For most of the past half century, industry (largely, the defense industry) has performed 60 to 70 percent of DoD-funded R&D, government laboratories have performed approximately 20 to 30 percent, and U.S. universities have performed 3 to 5 percent (primarily fundamental research).[7]

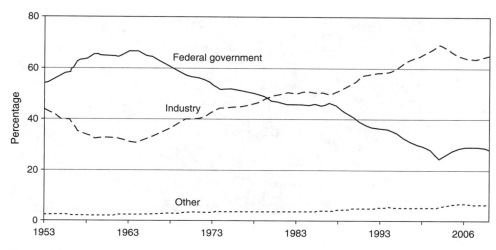

Figure 6.2
National R&D expenditures by funding sector, 1953 to 2007.

As the Defense Department maintains its objective of technological superiority, which requires a large R&D investment, its work in nanotechnology and cybersecurity will continue to have dramatic fallouts in the commercial arena. For example, it is estimated that by 2020, 15 percent of industry and 100 percent of the electronics industry will be based on nanotechnology.[8] But as the commercial world becomes more technology-oriented (particularly in terms of electronics and information technology), the DoD will draw increasingly from worldwide commercial technology (called *"spin-on"*). For example, as commercial systems increasingly demand cybersecurity (for example, in banks and hospitals) and as health care research (the second largest of the areas of government R&D investment) continues, the DoD is expected to benefit both in the cyberdefense and in the biodefense area (such as in broadband vaccines that are effective against bioengineered pathogens that might be used as weapons of mass destruction).

There are interrelationships between a strong U.S. economy and expenditures on national security and between R&D investments in defense spinning off into the commercial world and R&D investments in the commercial world affecting defense and the nation's economic growth. They provide an integrated interrelationship and a strong synergism between defense and the U.S. economy, between defense R&D and the U.S. economy, and between defense and the nation's security. Most twenty-first-century social concerns (such as energy, environment, health, and the economy as it affects employment and trade) and domestic and foreign security concerns will be shaped by the nation's ability to continue its R&D activities successfully.

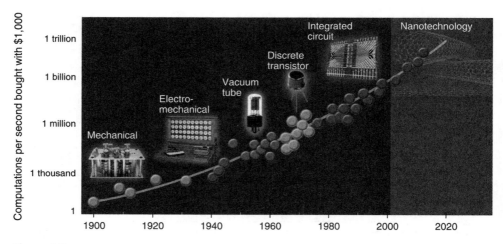

Figure 6.3
Accelerating advances in technology, 1900 to 2020. *Source:* Dave McQueeney and Gary Ambrose, "Use of COTS in DoD: An IT Industry Perspective," Defense Science Board Discussion, June 2008.

Throughout the second half of the twentieth century and into the twenty-first century, the two key characteristics of modern technology have been the speed of change (with its rapid deployment) and its globalization (in the military and, particularly, the commercial arenas). The obvious example of this speed of change is in the electronics field. As shown in figure 6.3 (which is drawn on a logarithmic scale because the changes have been so great that they cannot fit onto a linear scale), $1,000 could buy a few mechanical computations per second in 1900; successively more in the electromechanical era, vacuum tube era, discreet transistor era, integrated circuit era; and now billions of computations per second in the nanotechnology era.

Even as the processing power of microchips continues to double every eighteen months (following Moore's law), the cost of all that computing power has dropped precipitously. In 1978, Intel's 8086 cost 1.2 cents per transistor and $480 per million instructions per second (MIPS). By 1985, the 386 cost 0.11 cents per transistor and $50 per MIPS. Ten years later, the Pentium Pro's introductory price amounted to 0.02 cents per transistor and $4 per MIPS. And the prices are expected to continue to fall.[9]

On the globalization side, technology is rapidly moving around the world and being applied by adversaries and allies. There is also growing international recognition of the importance of doing basic research and moving it rapidly through the development and deployment cycle—to stay ahead. For example, the 2005 strategy document of the Chinese State Council stated that "basic research has become part of the international competition of overall national strength."[10]

Staying ahead—with continuous research and rapid transition of research to demonstration, system development, and deployment—requires significant resources at the front end of the defense acquisition process. During periods of wartime or periods of perceived military need, however, the tendency has been to shift money from research to the procurement of existing systems and increased personnel. This shift becomes even more pronounced in periods of national economic weakness. Thus, the challenge is not only to have people understand the need for research to stay ahead but also to provide adequate resources in the front end of the process— recognizing that significantly less money is required in this phase than in later phases.

The various stages of the research and development cycle and their funding levels for fiscal year 2006 are shown in figure 6.4. As can be seen from this figure, budget activity 1 (BA1), basic research (which is usually done by universities), is small. For fiscal year 2006, BA1 was $1.32 billion out of a total research, development, test, and evaluation (RDT&E) request of $69.36 billion. which represented only about 10 percent of the total expenditures for national security by the United States that year. In the next year's budget, the Congress passed a $250 billion farm subsidy bill

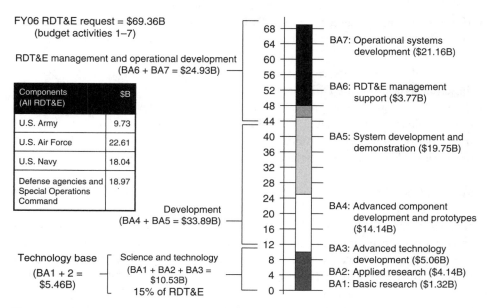

Figure 6.4
Budget request for research, development, test, and evaluation, fiscal year 2006.

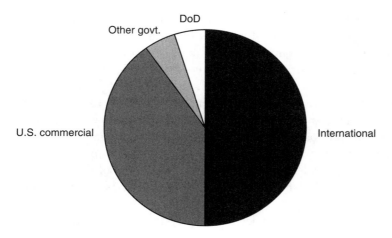

Figure 6.5
Science and technology investments, 2000. *Source:* National Science Foundation, "International Science and Technology Trends," *Science and Technology Pocket Data Book 2000.*

(over 3.5 times the total DoD budget for RDT&E).[11] With some slight variations since World War II, development expenditures have rarely accounted for less than 80 percent of DoD total R&D expenditures; while basic research has constituted significantly less than 5 percent of total DoD R&D spending.[12] As President George W. Bush observed, however, "It's research that will keep the United States on the cutting edge."[13]

Finally, DoD investments in science and technology need to be put in perspective. As shown in figure 6.4, the DoD spent $10.53 billion on science and technology in fiscal year 2006. This is comparable to the total amount spent in all other federal government departments (such as the National Science Foundation and the Department of Energy), but it is insignificant compared to the U.S. commercial sector or to international investments in science and technology (figure 6.5).

Making Defense Department R&D Investments Effective

To achieve its mission successfully, the Department of Defense has three objectives for its strategy of technological superiority: because it is a monopsony buyer, it must stimulate innovation; because other nations and individual organizations (such as terrorist organizations) are attempting to gain superiority, it must focus on avoiding surprises; and it needs to stay ahead.

To achieve these objectives, the Defense Department has four basic tools that it can use (in addition to spending research and development dollars): take advantage of competitive market operations to achieve increasing performance at lower costs;

partner with other organizations (such as industry, universities, and allies); do a great deal of experimentation, testing, and evaluation; and use its first-buyer market power to stimulate areas of technology that it needs but that also have considerable value in the commercial world.

Three Objectives for Defense Department R&D

Stimulate Innovation   Unlike the commercial market, in which there are many buyers with a wide variety of tastes and requirements, the defense marketplace has essentially a single buyer, the U.S. Department of Defense, and a few suppliers in each critical area. In this unique market, if the government wants to achieve a certain objective (in this case, technological superiority), the government must take a proactive role. This argument about government R&D was laid out by Vannevar Bush in his seminal 1945 report *Science: The Endless Frontier*.[14] The economic rationale for the government's funding of R&D was described by Richard Nelson in 1959 and by Kenneth Arrow in 1962.[15] In essence, the argument for having the government pay for military R&D is simple one. The government decides what it wants to buy, and companies cannot afford to spend billions of dollars doing research to determine whether their designs are something that the government might want to buy. The risk of failure is far too high for corporations to invest in this unique and specialized market. Defense firms often point to the decision of Tom Jones, president of Northrop Aviation, to invest corporate money in building an advanced jet fighter (the F-5) that the air force eventually decided was not the aircraft that it wanted. Jones's large investment was essentially wasted. To persuade industry to work on state-of-the-art weapon systems, the DoD puts out a request for proposals and awards the winning contractor a cost-based contract to develop the high-risk program.

Although this market-failure rationale remains central to DoD investment in research and development activities, this approach raises concerns:

- Bureaucracies are not known for picking "winners." Their tendency is to adopt low-risk, historic approaches

- Politically based organizations tend to be short-term oriented. They tend to modify current technology rather than proceed in new directions.

- Many innovative approaches to the DoD mission require multiservice (or even multiagency) cooperation, which is difficult to achieve in large bureaucracies.

- Technology moves rapidly in many areas (such as information systems and electronics), but the government's acquisition cycles are very long relative to modern technology cycles.

- The government tends to look in-house first for its innovation (since it has about one hundred DoD laboratories), and like employees in many large institutions, DoD personnel are most comfortable doing incremental improvements rather than suggesting and researching disruptive new directions.

Each of these concerns must be addressed through DoD policies and processes. Such efforts began in the late 1970s, when the federal government recognized that Japan was becoming a major economic competitor in autos, steel, computers, and electronics. In 1979, President Carter unveiled the president's industrial innovation initiatives, the result of an eighteen-month domestic-policy review led by Jordan Baruch (then assistant secretary of commerce for science and technology) and involving approximately five hundred private-sector participants and 250 representatives from twenty-eight federal agencies).[16] This initiative contained nine key proposals: (1) enhance the transfer of technological information to industry by expanding the National Technical Information Service (NTIS); (2) increase technical knowledge by creating technology centers at universities funded jointly by the National Science Foundation and industry; (3) improve the patent system; (4) clarify the federal antitrust policy, making it clear that collaboration on basic research is not an antitrust violation; (5) foster the development of small, innovative firms by increasing the National Science Foundation's Small Business Innovative Research (SBIR) program and expanding it to other government agencies; (6) open federal procurement to innovations by shifting to performance specifications instead of design specifications; (7) improve the regulatory system by encouraging innovation waivers; (8) facilitate labor and management adjustment to innovation through enhanced retraining programs; and (9) maintain a supportive climate for innovation by removing legislative and administrative barriers to innovation.

This set of initiatives resulted in legislation that significantly stimulated U.S. innovation. The Stevenson-Wydler Technology Innovation Act of 1980 authorized the Department of Commerce and the NSF to create centers for industrial technology at universities that would promote cooperative research with industry, assist small businesses and startups, and develop curricula. That same year, Congress passed the Bayh-Dole Act, which began the process of establishing a uniform federal patent policy. These laws (with some modifications) have remained on the books and have significantly stimulated U.S. innovativeness, particularly private-sector use of federally funded research, university-industry cooperation in research, and economic stimulation from government-funded university research. In addition, universities have received billions of dollars in royalty payments from the licensing of federally funded inventions, and well over a thousand companies have successfully started up based on federally funded patents. According to a 2002 article in *The Economist* entitled "Innovation's Golden Goose, the Bayh-Dole Act," this act has led to the creation of 2,000 new companies, 260,000 new jobs, and a $40 billion annual increase to the U.S. economy."[17] Another key piece of legislation was the National Cooperative Research Act of 1984, which reversed the burden of proof in joint-research antitrust cases (whether basic or applied). Large companies began to partner with many small, high-tech businesses, so they no longer were required to depend solely on their home-grown technology. Essentially, this act freed businesses first to do research together and then to manufacture together, thus speeding the rate of change. In 1986, the National Technology Transfer Act was passed to increase the flow of commercial ideas from government laboratories to the private sector. This established cooperative research and development agreements (CRADAs), which provided a legal means for government laboratories and outside parties to work together without trying to fit into the huge regulator framework of the Federal Acquisition Regulations. Instead, with a CRADA in place, agencies could work out an agreement quickly and begin collaborating immediately. This act also included permission for federal inventors to share in the profits from their inventions.

Perhaps the most important legislative change was the enactment, in 1982, of the Small Business Innovation Development Act, which changed the SBIR program from an NSF experiment (with an annual budget of around $5 million) to the federal government's largest source of funding for small, high-technology businesses. It now awards over $2 billion in grants per year in eleven agencies (the Department of Defense is by far the largest and has a funding level of around a billion dollars annually). Because 60 to 80 percent of all newly created jobs and much of the innovativeness of the nation currently come from small to midsize companies (with fewer than five hundred employees), the SBIR program has been critically important to both the nation's technological leadership and its economic growth.[18] As Jon Baron (who has had experience on both Capitol Hill and in the DoD) stated in congressional testimony, "In several instances, the SBIR program has spawned break-through technologies that have transformed their field and made a major contribution to the American economy."[19]

The SBIR program requires each agency involved to set aside a program for small business to engage in federal R&D with a specific objective of commercialization—that is, sales to either the commercial world or to the government for its mission needs. The law requires that 2.5 percent of all externally funded RDT&E budgets be set aside for this objective. In fiscal year 2007, this program received approximately $1.2 billion from the Department of Defense (with twelve DoD agencies participating). These Defense Department agencies put out multiple solicitations related to their current needs, and peer reviews are done (within the government) for selection among the many ideas submitted. It is a three-phase program: phase one is funded at $100,000 each for a six-month feasibility study; phase two is funded at approximately $750,000 each for a two-year research effort; and phase three is the transition into other funding for commercialization. Typically, most firms have under twenty-five employees, and about one-third are first-time phase one awardees. Because the basic solicitations are written around DoD mission needs, the phase three effort is often initially funded by DoD program offices. But often, because of this DoD support, venture capital funds quickly join in with additional resources (using the SBIR program and its government peer reviews as a filter to determine the projects that may have widespread commercial application). This is an attractive program for small businesses since it is the largest source of early stage R&D funding and comes with no strings attached (the company retains the data rights for five years). In addition, the company does not give up its equity to get started (as is the case with venture capital). But it is also an attractive program from the government's viewpoint since it is a safe way to try out high-risk R&D and a way to reach the small firms that often are the most cost-effective and innovative because of their far greater agility. Finally, a similar program known as the Small Business Technology Transfer Research Program (STTR) is a set-aside program that is similar to the SBIR (the objective is a potential for commercialization) but facilitates cooperative R&D between small business concerns and U.S. research institutions (particularly universities). The level is 0.3 percent of the externally funded RDT&E. Even though the program has a significantly smaller total dollar value than SBIR, it is appealing to university researchers, and it establishes an early and direct link with industry for the subsequent commercialization of ideas coming out of the universities.

Although government-funded R&D is a great source of innovation, other techniques allow researchers to take advantage of all possible incentives and opportunities. First, under the assumption that all good ideas do not originate with the government, industry is incentivized to spend a share of its authorized overhead dollars (fully covered by contracts) on independent research and development (IR&D). For example, a defense organization (large or small) might set aside 5 percent of its sales for a pool of IR&D dollars on which their scientists and engineers bid internally for research projects that could yield the company future new products of interest to the DoD. Typically, these are some of the most exciting projects to work on, and they are highly sought after by scientists and engineers. Because independent research and development is a way for any firm to stay ahead of its competitors on next-generation products, it is a focus of internal management attention and is controlled at a high level within each firm. Many advanced defense products have been the result of this industry-led IR&D activity.

IR&D for defense firms is somewhat like commercial firms' investments of their own resources in independent research and development. The government covers IR&D in the allowable overhead (of defense firms) on its major contracts with that company. In addition, although the government owns the data rights to research that it funds directly, the work that is done under IR&D belongs to the company, so the government cannot transfer it to one of the company's competitors. Companies that sell to both the private and public sectors are finding that they benefit when they allow their most creative scientists and engineers to explore areas that might yield significant benefit to the company without explicitly defining their work assignments. For example, Google allows its engineers to devote 20 percent of their work time to their own projects, provided it helps the company.[20]

A second approach to stimulating innovation, outside of government-directed efforts, attempts to learn from the venture capitalist. If a product can be dual-use (that is, have high-volume commercial applications but be designed to meet military requirements), then the DoD can benefit from the low cost and continuous product improvements of the commercial world. The result has been a series of government-sponsored venture-capital initiatives. The first was established by the Central Intelligence Agency (CIA) in 1999. In-Q-Tel is a private, independent, not-for-profit company that responds to the requests of the CIA and other intelligence community officials to work in their areas of interests (such as information systems, power systems, and virtual reality). In-Q-Tel invests CIA money in startups in these areas so that it can influence how the product develops. In 2007, its investment totals were approximately $60 million. Typically, In-Q-Tel has invested $3 to 3.5 million per startup company and also made some grants of $300,000 to accelerate development for ideas that were not yet ready to be commercially developed. The company's objective is to make these companies commercially viable and economically profitable, and it looks for third-party investments to compliment its own. The goal is that In-Q-Tel will become self-sufficient based on increased equity value as the companies in which it invests become successful. For example, the company points out that it initially invested in a satellite imaging program (known as Keyhole) in February 2003, which developed into Google Earth. This concept involves private-sector sharing of investments with government, so the army set up a private firm called On-point Technology (with an annual level of army investment of around $20 million), and NASA set up a similar venture-capital initiative known as Red Planet (now Astrolabe Ventures) with a NASA investment of about $75 million.

A third technique for stimulating innovation was introduced in 2005 by the Defense Advance Research Projects Agency (DARPA). DARPA offers a significant prize for the first company or individual to achieve a difficult scientific or engineering advancement—one that a particular government agency would like to realize. This first DARPA experiment was known as the Grand Challenge and was a prize contest to develop an all-terrain robotic vehicle for the army. In 2008, DARPA ran the Urban Challenge for autonomous vehicle operation in a city, with the winner receiving $2 million and the second- and third-place winners receiving $1.5 million. This competition for a prize is an old technique that was used when the British government offered an enormous prize for the person who could solve the most important and notorious technological problem of the eighteenth century—how a ship's navigator could determine the vessel's longitude position at sea.[21] According to Steve Kelman, former director of the Office of Federal Procurement Policy, contests are coming back into favor for two reasons. First, they are more performance-based than grants or contracts since they reward results and not just effort, and second, prizes often stimulate far more investment in finding a solution because many participants (not just the winner, as is the case with a grant or contract) put effort into solving the problem. Several agencies are starting to use this technique, and a number of industries are doing it by putting their problem on the Internet and offering a prize to anyone who can solve it.

Because it has been well documented that clusters of scientific and engineering organizations in a geographic region tend to increase the opportunities for innovation,[22] many states and even countries around the world are creating research parks. They offer companies significant incentives (such as tax benefits, use of incubator space, and cost sharing) to start up such parks and to take part in them. In some countries (for example, Indian, China, and Singapore), billions of dollars are being spent to set up vast research and science parks and innovation centers, while in the United States, regions and states are competing against each other to establish such science parks and clusters of high-tech companies (preferably in areas connected with university research and a high-tech labor pool). By locating these research parks near universities, there is a compounding effect of getting both the labor pool and the ideas that come from university professors who might want to start up a small company without having to move away from the area. A large share of the total federally funded basic research goes to the universities, and the DoD is a major funder in selected technology areas. In 2001, the DoD sponsored over 35 percent of the basic research in computer science and over 30 percent of the engineering research being done at universities.[23]

Avoid Surprises   As George Heilmeier, former director of DARPA, observed,[24] "the real difference between the surpriser and the surprised is usually *not* the unique ownership of a piece of new technology. . . . [Rather,] the key difference is in the recognition or awareness of the impact of that technology, and decisiveness in exploiting it." For example, when the Soviet Union launched the *Sputnik* satellite, the technology for doing so existed in the United States, but the army, navy, air force, and marines were focused on using technology in their traditional ways. In response and to overcome this institutional inertia, the Defense Advance Research Projects Agency (DARPA) was established in 1958 to "assure that the U.S. maintains a lead in applying state-of-the-art technology for military capabilities, and to prevent technological surprise from potential adversaries." Its job is to do work that is "not being done by the Services, but could have significant military application in unexpected ways." It has no internal laboratories but funds all of its work out to industry and universities at a level of approximately $3 billion per year. To stimulate original ideas, DARPA does not prescribe a specific solution for bidders to propose but instead issues broad area announcements (BAAs) to obtain proposals for R&D that is broadly generic but applies to the problems that it has identified. It also uses "other transactions authority (OTA)" to attract commercial firms that are not used to doing business with the government but that may have ideas that are applicable to military challenges. What is important about DARPA (and why it has been successful in helping the DoD avoid surprises) is that it searches out and hires the best people and gives them flexibility in what they do and how they do it. The objectives are to create disruptive products, surprise potential adversaries, and meet surprises that potential adversaries may introduce. It works across the spectrum from initial science to integrated systems and does it all in a highly competitive fashion. To avoid surprises, it does not count on basing its R&D activity on defined user requirements (since few people think about requesting things that they have not seen before).

As the result of the *Sputnik* surprise, in addition to establishing DARPA, the Department of Defense established an outside advisory board (the Defense Science Board) so that it could ask people outside of their institution to study areas of possible surprise (and ways to counter them) and to anticipate areas that the DoD could develop to surprise potential adversaries. Thus, for over half a century, the Defense Science Board has been providing suggestions on new directions for the Department of Defense that have proven to be of significant value for their nontraditional perspectives.

The importance of surprise is not new. In the sixteenth century, Niccolò Machiavelli in *The Art of War* wrote that "surprise is the most essential factor of victory . . . new and sudden things change armies by surprise."[25] Today, given the globalization of technology and industry and the growing commercialization of science and technology, the potential for technology surprises has never been greater. But similarly, the institutional resistance to dramatically new ideas (particularly if they are disruptive of the existing culture, organizations, or practices) will continue— even when the technology exists to make the changes. In one famous example, the navy refused to stabilize the guns on its ships, even though the technology was available, because it was more of a challenge to be able to shoot while rolling back and forth or up and down in ocean waves—in spite of the fact that the effectiveness of the gun, when stabilized, was orders of magnitude greater.[26] This resistance to change by the military was described by Admiral Alfred Thayer Mahan in his 1890 classic *The Influence of Sea Power upon History, 1660 to 1783*. In discussing resistance to change, he observed that even when the technology exists, the "changes in tactics have to overcome the inertia of a conservative class; but it is a great evil. . . . history shows that it is vain to hope that military men generally will be at the pains to do this, but that the one who does will go into battle with a great advantage—a lesson in itself of no mean value."[27] Another famous example of not admitting that something can be done and therefore being surprised when it happens is an October 9, 1903, article in the *New York Times* stating that "the flying machine which will really fly might be evolved by the combined and continuous efforts of mathematicians and mechanicians in from one million to 10 million years." On the same day, Orville Wright wrote in his diary, "We started assembly today" of the first airplane that he and his brother, Wilbur, flew shortly thereafter at Kitty Hawk, North Carolina.

The DoD also needs to be alert to surprises that take place in the commercial world but that might affect the military and would require significant government response. In the late 1970s, the Japanese were making dramatic advances in the semiconductor and computer memory fields (which would affect military electronics capability), so under President Carter's "Domestic Policy Review on Industrial Innovation," a road map was developed for optimizing U.S. innovativeness to respond to Japan's industrial policy. It took time to convince Congress of the need for such action (and its eventual response was undoubtedly based on fear of losing the overall electronics industry leadership, which the United States had counted on heavily for its economic growth). The Sematech initiative was undertaken as a combined public and private initiative (a precompetitive consortia of industry and university personnel) in which government and industry equally shared in an investment of $200 million per year. The result was a successful return of the U.S. semiconductor and computer industry to a significant position in this rapidly growing worldwide electronics market—and one that is equally significant for the military in the era of cyber-centric military operations. Today, there is growing concern about China's great emphasis on science and technology—in terms of personnel, research parks, and development and production of electronics equipment, all of which have considerable military value.

Stay Ahead   After World War II and throughout the cold war, the United States was able to stay ahead of other countries' technology through large investments in R&D. Both in magnitude and percentages, its technology investments were significantly more than all of Europe's combined. These large investments will still be required in the twenty-first century, but two other interrelated considerations become critical for the DoD to maintain technological superiority—globalization and high-tech commercialization.

As the National Academies stated in 2007, "although many people assume that the United States will always be a world leader in science and technology, this may not continue to be the case, in as much as great minds and ideas exist throughout the world. We forget the abruptness with which a lead in science and technology can be lost—and the difficulty of recovering a lead once lost, if indeed it can be regained at all."[28] As an independent study by the Center for Strategic and International Studies stated, "Globalization's most significant impact is the leveling of technological leadership."[29] The increased international mobility of highly skilled labor and the diffusion of technological know-how allow many countries to compete with the United States in producing cutting-edge research and innovation. As an example, the *London Times* of March 1, 2007, announced that "One-Atom Thick Material 'will revolutionize the world': It's the thinnest material ever and could revolutionize computers and medicine." It described a layer of carbon that had been manufactured in a film that was one-atom thick and that defied the laws of physics. It would take 200,000 layers to match the thickness of a human hair. This material was created by scientists at the University of Manchester in England working with the Max Planck Institute in Germany. Its main applications were expected to be in vastly increasing the speed at which computers could make calculations and in researching new drugs.[30] Figure 6.6 shows that R&D worldwide is growing more rapidly in countries outside of the United States and Europe—which has long-term implications for security and economic competitiveness.

In addition to the globalization of technology and industry, R&D spending is shifting away from the DoD and government funding to the commercial sector's

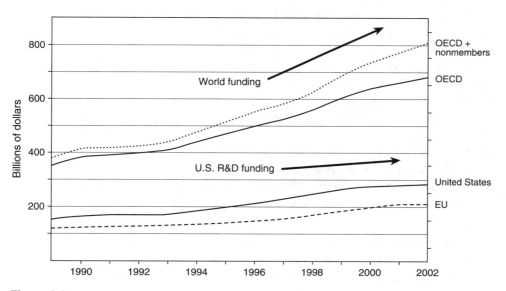

Figure 6.6
Estimated worldwide R&D expenditures, 1990 to 2002. *Source:* National Science Foundation, S&E Indicators 2006; OECD, Main Science and Technology Indicators database, November 2004. Billions of current dollars converted with purchasing power parities; EU data since 1998 include ten new member countries.

funding of R&D. As was seen in figure 6.2, the federal government sponsored about 70 percent of all U.S. R&D in 1966 and only about 25 percent in 2000 (the rest came from U.S. industry R&D). Moreover, the shift occurred in the areas that are most critical to the DoD. Information technology, telecommunications hardware and software, and biotechnology are all areas in which the Department of Defense is now a minor player—yet they are critically important to the DoD. The leading R&D investment activities by U.S. industry greatly exceed the DoD's investment, and most of the dominant players do not even take part in DoD R&D.[31] In 2006, the total nonfederal R&D in the United States was $246 billion, and the DoD's R&D was $37 billion. Many of the largest R&D investments by U.S. corporations were made by firms with no DoD R&D contracts—such as Intel ($5.2 billion), Ford Motor Company ($8 billion), Cisco Systems ($3.3 billion), Emgen ($2.3 billion), and Pfizer, ($7.5 billion). Some of the largest industrial R&D investments were also made by firms that receive very little DoD investment. Microsoft's internal R&D investment was $9.6 billion, and it received only $1.9 million in DoD R&D money; IBM's internal R&D was $5.2 billion with $12.7 million from the DoD; General Motors' internal R&D was $6.7 billion with $300,000 of DoD-sponsored R&D; DuPont's internal R&D was $1.3 billion with $3.6 million of DoD R&D. The message is clear: the DoD is not taking full advantage of large U.S. commercial R&D investments.

Putting these two broad trends together, it is clear that the Department of Defense needs to do a much better job of tracking and harvesting commercial and international R&D. One problem is the "not invented here" syndrome. This attitude is evident in DoD laboratories, the DoD buyer community, and the defense industry. The defense industry would be the primary transfer mechanism for a commercial or foreign technology, but its engineers and executives would prefer to use their own products. They thus have a disincentive to using either commercial or foreign designs or technologies since they were not built in their own factories and with their own designs.

In addition to these defense-industry barriers to using commercial and foreign technologies, there are government barriers in both categories. In the case of the commercial, a 2008 study[32] identified the five top barriers that the DoD has created for commercial firms doing R&D with the government:

- *Rights to technical data*   When the government pays for R&D, it feels entitled to the data rights (but commercial firms consider these to be their crown jewels).

- *Cost disclosure*   Companies consider their costs to be competitive information and therefore proprietary to them, but the government insists on full visibility because it does not trust the companies.

- *Full cost-accounting standards compliance*   The government wants full accounting for all costs (overhead included) and wants it done according to specific government-unique accounting practices. For a commercial firm to do government business, it has to set up a separate, totally unique accounting system (which is both expensive and burdensome).

• *Trade secrets* The government wants to be able to give one company's drawings to another company, so they can compete to make that part. However, commercial firms do not want to release that information since it is highly competitive and establishes their differentiation.

• *Export controls* Commercial firms aim for a worldwide market (not just a domestic one) and worry that if they develop a product (under DoD funds or even their own) that is used in a weapon, then any future sale of that product to the global market will fall under U.S. export controls. This inhibits foreign commercial sales (and also presents a considerable added expense).

• *Flow down of Federal Acquisition Regulations (FAR) clauses to the lower tiers* The subsystem or parts level of a system involves many commercial and foreign elements, and commercial firms would like to do this business in a commercial fashion. Under DoD FAR contracts, however, defense prime contractors are required to flow down all FAR terms and conditions to their suppliers. Commercial suppliers are unprepared, and find it undesirable, to deal with the burdens and expenses associated with the government-unique terms, conditions, and specifications of doing business with the government.

If the government is going to take advantage of the large R&D investments that are made by commercial firms (as potential adversaries are already doing), then it needs to remove these barriers and learn to do business in far more of a commercial fashion when dealing with these nontraditional, normally lower-tier, suppliers. "Other transactions authority," discussed in chapter 4, attempts to deal with some of these issues, but the "flow down" requirement of FAR prohibits prime contractors from using OTA's with its commercial subcontractors.

The DoD also faces significant barriers in dealing with worldwide high-tech suppliers. As one independent review group for the Defense Department wrote, "there are myriad barriers to the DoD doing business with the other global research sponsors."[33] These barriers include issues associated with domestic commercial firms (including intellectual property, proprietary data, and cost issues) and issues associated with foreign technology and production—including International Traffic in Arms Regulations (ITAR), Export Administration Regulations (EAR), buy-American laws, and security concerns. These barriers have been detailed in many studies.[34] If the Department of Defense wants to take advantage of commercial and military advanced technology from around the world, then it will have to revise its ITAR and other export-control regimes. As a Deemed Export Advisory Committee to the Department of Commerce stated in 2007: "It is the committee's principal conclusion that the existing . . . Export Regulatory Regime no longer effectively serves its intended purpose, and should be replaced with an approach that better reflects the realities of today's national security needs and the global economy. The obsolescence of the current regime has been brought about by profound developments in science and technology, the free flow of massive amounts of information, the mobility of the world's population, the burdening economies of other nations, and the change in the character of threats to America's security."[35]

Four Basic Tools for Defense Department R&D

Use Competitive Forces   Many authors have noted that the defense marketplace does not operate in a normal commercial fashion, particularly in the R&D phase. Commercial firms develop new products and put them into the market for potential users to evaluate. With defense firms, however, a fierce rivalry takes place at the beginning of the R&D phase as paper proposals from multiple defense firms are presented to the DoD, the government selects a winner, and the government provides funds to develop and subsequently deploy the product. This extremely expensive and time-consuming process tends to raise the cost of the products as they are developed and put into production on a sole-source basis. Because requirements continuously change and technology advances as the product develops (and the DoD usually wants to include these advances in their products), this development process often takes ten to twenty years prior to full-scale production. However, as the data in chapter 7 shows, this process is most effective when it is done with competition being maintained throughout the full process. Although it may seem that the DoD is paying twice for maintaining competition throughout the R&D phase, and then the production and support phases, continuous competition results in higher performance and overall (net) savings in money and time. Nonetheless, this model—competitive prototype awards, competitions for all critical subsystems, and competition between existing systems and next-generation systems—tends to be resisted within the military services because it requires some additional investments this year to make significant savings in future years. It is usually argued that "this year we can't afford the competitive source." Over time, the strong preference for competition within the U.S. economy, when applied by the DoD has resulted in a leadership position for the United States in its military equipment. By contrast the European model, where countries claim that they are not large enough to maintain multiple sources and instead turn to "preferred sources" within each country, results in a defense industry in each country that is sole-sourced and fully subsidized by the nation.

As discussed by Clay Christiansen, the most effective form of competition is disruptive competition.[36] It was described by Joseph Schumpeter as creative destruction: "The New Commodity, the New Technology, the New Source of Supply, the New Type of Organization . . . which commands a decisive cost-of-quality advantage . . . that incessantly revolutionizes the economic structure *from within*, incessantly destroying the old one, incessantly creating a new one."[37] Such disruptive competition represents a challenge to any existing culture. For example, remotely piloted vehicles were a disruptive technology to manned aircraft, and small personal computers were a disruptive technology to IBM's mainframe computers. Such changes are normally so fiercely resisted that they have to be set up in separate organizations and pushed from a top-down perspective, or they will be inadequately resourced and starved to prevent their being competitively demonstrated. If these disruptive ideas are coming from a high-tech development in another country, they are even less likely to be accepted—until their far superior effectiveness has been successfully demonstrated. The more that the United States can use competition throughout all of its programs (not just for an initial auction at the beginning of the R&D phase) and can open this competition to foreign and commercial sources, the more likely it is to maintain its technological superiority in the future.

Partner with Other Organizations   During the cold war, the Soviet Union placed rigid security controls on its defense workforce. Workers sitting literally next to each other often could not exchange information, and this greatly inhibited the evolution of new ideas.[38] Today, with technology spread widely around the world, sharing and openness are essential if new ideas are to progress rapidly. Such synergisms among people doing research in a given area have been greatly facilitated through the advent of the Internet and other key software developments that have changed the way that people work together in modern times.

But the openness of the policies of the nations involved will determine if benefits are to be realized. In the U.S. case, this partnering begins with sharing across military services so that maximum benefits can be realized from joint operations. Then it extends to the intelligence community (first working across the community itself and then working closely with the DoD). Finally, it extends to multinational R&D, where the United States shares with its allies its leading-edge technology R&D and where military forces who are working together in operations around the world can get maximum benefits from multinational activities. There are also significant economic (as well as military) benefits to be gained from such multinational R&D activities since it avoids duplication and both sides gain the benefits of economies of scale. But most important is the sharing of ideas, which maximizes the resultant innovations that come from the sharing of R&D activities.

Sharing is important at the product and process levels, but it is critical at the individual researcher level. As technology spreads rapidly to many countries, the best way that the United States can benefit from such worldwide research is by sharing it. For example, quantum computing is an area of great potential benefits in both computation speed and cryptology, and the United States is one of many countries (including Canada, France, Italy, Holland, and Australia) that are leaders in this field. U.S. researchers must work with these leading worldwide researchers to move this field ahead. (In fact, in some DoD awards today in the quantum computing field, subcontracts are being awarded to the Swiss, Japanese, and others.)

Recognizing the importance of such global sharing, President Reagan issued National Security Decision Directive (NSDD) 189 (which was later reconfirmed by National Security Council Director Condoleezza Rice in the George W. Bush administration), which stated that "basic research is to be open" (regarding publication and foreign participation). This is particularly important in the United States because of the many foreign-born undergraduate students, graduate students, postdoctoral students, and faculty at America's universities and because of the leading role that many of these people play in America's research. Larry Bock, executive chair of NanoSys, Inc., stated in congressional testimony that "the U.S. is far ahead of other countries in Nano Technology research, but the vast majority of researchers in the U.S. are foreign nationals, mostly from Asia."[39] Similarly, the share of U.S. postdoctoral scientists and engineers who are temporary residents has grown from 37 to 59 percent from 1987 to 2007.[40]

Even though national policy (as enunciated in NSDD-189) has clearly favored openness—to gain military and economic benefits from the sharing and synergism that come from it—actual practices by the Department of Defense and other government agencies have not followed this policy. In 2008, a congressionally mandated National Academies study addressed this question of foreign students and scholars at U.S. universities and the openness of the research being done there. A report titled "Science and Security in a Post 9/11 World"[41] found that many government agencies were not implementing this policy. Instead, security was used as the rationale for not sharing fundamental research information. Defense Secretary Robert Gates took the lead in reiterating to the Department of Defense the importance of the openness of such fundamental research.[42] The risks that terrorists or even a potential adversarial nation might benefit from such sharing is dramatically less than the risks (or losses) associated with having to use only U.S. citizens on such basic R&D and of not being able to share its work with researchers from other countries and thereby move the research more rapidly forward. This simple cost and benefit analysis is still widely resisted in many quarters for fear that a potential future enemy might be able to take advantage of such information. The challenge for the United States is to stay ahead, and in today's world, this cannot be achieved through isolation of basic research.

Experiment, Test, and Evaluate   One major shortcoming of much science and engineering work is to keep it in the laboratory far too long and to focus its application on a single objective. The way to overcome this kind of delay is to emphasize the importance of experimentation, particularly experimentation by potential users rather than the original designers. Novel ideas can come out of such experimentation in two directions—by modifying the technology (resulting in significant enhancements of performance) and by using the technology as-is in totally different ways, gaining advantages through nontraditional applications. A number of programs have been initiated to address such needs. For example, the DoD's advanced-technology demonstrations (ATDs) show the value of new technologies. Advanced-concept technology demonstrations (ACTDs) apply new technologies to different concepts to show their value in nontraditional ways. This valuable program has received significant funding. It is based on mission needs that come in from the combatant commanders, and the Office of the Secretary of Defense is responsible for coming up with new concepts that can be tested—based on new or existing technologies—to satisfy these combatant commander's needs. Finally, a specific program (also run out of the Office of the Secretary of Defense) is used for testing foreign military and commercial products to evaluate their potential application for U.S. Defense Department needs. Although these programs are done in conjunction with the military services, the presence of their management in the Office of the Secretary of Defense gives them high visibility and objective independence.

Similarly, a number of years ago, it was decided that the test and evaluation of new weapon systems needed to be done outside of the development community. After the development testing has been satisfactorily completed, there is a requirement for an operational test and evaluation (OT&E). The using community determines the value of these new products and makes recommendations on possible ways that they could be further improved to add even more military capability. (These OT&E tests are most valuable when not performed as a "pass-fail" test, but where they report on the capabilities and limitations: of the new system under test.)

Everyone agrees on the value of such experimental testing and evaluation, but frequently they are underfunded or stretched out, which is shortsighted in terms of gaining the maximum benefit from the large expenditures on defense R&D. The extreme in this area is the insufficient use of "red teaming"—having people try to defeat these new concepts so that their weaknesses can be highlighted early in the program. Again, this is valuable in the development of new weapon systems but also is normally greatly resisted because its objective is to find shortcomings, and most program-development people are not anxious to have these deficiencies highlighted early on. Nonetheless, the more that this red teaming can be done early in R&D programs, the more successful they will be in the long run.

Use First-Buyer Market Power   A major problem with most R&D projects (in the commercial world as well as the military) is getting the systems initially fielded after the idea has been demonstrated. (This is often referred to as "the valley of death.")

Defense Department procurements have very large dollar values, so the DoD can use its buying power to get the program started. As lead purchaser, it can place large orders for early versions of new technologies, such as items from the commercial world or the military world that have dual-use capability (for example, semiconductors or communication satellites in the past, and quantum computers and nanotechnology in the future). As long as the restrictions of security and export controls are not too rigid, the commercial world can improve the item's performance and lower its cost, which provides benefits for the military. This concept, of the military as the first buyer, can dramatically stimulate military and economic benefits if properly implemented.

Trends and Future Needs

Unfortunately, the United States and particularly the DoD appear to have lost sight of the overall importance of science and technology to their long-term future. In this area, the world is changing rapidly, but the DoD has not adjusted its policies, practices, or budgets to recognize these critical changes. It has significantly underfunded long-term research at the expense of near-term developments and production, not paid attention to the future science and technology workforce, and not acknowledged the importance of commercial and foreign science and technology to U.S. future security and economic competitiveness.

To quote from the 2001 Hart-Rudman Commission, "the inadequacies of our system of research and education pose a greater threat to U.S. national security, over the next quarter century, than any potential conventional war that we might imagine. . . . second only to a weapon of mass destruction detonating in an American city, we can think of nothing more dangerous than a failure to manage properly science, technology, and education for the common good."[43]

Consider the recent trends:

• Long-term research by the DoD has declined significantly. In the early 1980s, basic research accounted for nearly 20 percent of total DoD science and technology funding, but recently that percentage has dropped to 12 percent.[44]

• Over the past thirty years, the fraction of the DoD's overall research, development, test, and evaluation funds devoted to science and technology has dropped from 20 to 13 percent[45] (in government and industry spending).

• In the president's DoD budget requests, basic research has declined from a peak in fiscal year 1994 of $1.55 billion to $1.32 billion in fiscal year 2006 (both in constant FY 2006 dollars).[46] In the fiscal year 2008 budget submittal, overall federal funding for basic and applied research declined, in real terms, for the fourth year in a row.[47]

• Defense corporations' independent research and development (IR&D) is down 50 percent from the mid-1980s, and there has been a shift in the focus of defense industries' IR&D from innovation to support of major development programs.[48]

• Since fiscal year 2000, earmarks by Congress to the DoD's science and technology appropriations have dramatically increased. In fiscal year 2008 appropriations, Congress designated $2.2 billion of performer-specific science and technology projects (that is, "earmarks").[49] Many of the mission-specific DoD requests for science and technology funding were not included in order to fit in the congressional earmarks (even though the total S&T appropriations did go up significantly as a result of these earmarks). These earmarks are not peer reviewed, merit based, competitively awarded, or agency-sponsored. Approximately 40 percent of the military services' science and technology appropriations are earmarks.[50]

• Although the need is for significant innovation, the trend is toward risk minimization. Most research seems to be geared toward low-risk, incremental research on existing technologies and applications rather than toward the needed disruptive technologies. The general feeling seems to be that a "zero-defect" political culture in the Washington bureaucracy is minimizing risk- taking and creating disincentives for significant innovation. When a major study by the National Academies recommended that an energy equivalent to DARPA—ARPA-E—be established, it was resisted strongly by the Department of Energy's national labs and not initially approved by the Congress.[51] Numerous analyses and independent studies have shown that there are major disruptive needs of the Department of Defense that are not being fulfilled today. These include real-time, two-way language-translation devices (which have been badly needed in Iraq and Afghanistan); information security (as adversaries become more and more sophisticated in their understanding of communication systems); cyberdefense (as the Russians demonstrated when they went into the country of Georgia, cyberattacks have now joined kinetic attacks); advanced power sources (lightweight and long duration) as well as wireless power sources (for automatic recharging of mobile devices); microrobots (for air, land, and underwater use); biodefense (as biotechnology spreads worldwide and becomes available for undesired usages); oil-independent systems to save on logistics, cost, and vulnerability; biologically- inspired cognitive architecture (for software that mimics human brain functions); and many more disruptive needs that are as yet unclearly defined but likely to be developed by others, if not by the United States.

• Major defense weapon system developments are taking the overwhelming share of total R&D defense budgets. Major developments such as the air force's advance fighters and the army's Future Combat Systems are taking a larger and larger share of the DoD's R&D budget at the expense of the large number of smaller R&D projects required in many critical technology areas. Because these large programs are near-term oriented, long-term research is suffering. The DoD is eating its seed corn.

• Since the vertical integration of the industry that took place in the post–cold war era, prime contractors have increasingly maintained much of the subsystem and component work in-house, which significantly cuts back on the R&D of firms that would normally be competitive and innovative at the lower tiers of the defense industry (in products such as electronics and sensors).

When the primes do go outside for R&D at the lower tiers, they invariably pass along all of the defense-unique requirements of the Federal Acquisition Regulations and often pass along a requirement that the small firms do their research on a fixed-price basis (even if the prime has a cost-based contract). These practices greatly limit the amount of research done at the lower tiers, and often cut out many commercial, dual-use, and foreign firms from competing with new ideas (at the lower tiers). In reality, an innovation at the parts or components level (such as tubes, transistors, integrated circuits, and nanotechnology) often creates the breakthrough to allow new military technology.

• One of the greatest needs—which has been largely neglected—is for R&D that lowers costs for weapon systems and services (while maintaining or increasing performance). Cost as a design requirement (for both product and process)— and focused on manufacturing technology—has not been getting its share of R&D resources. Also neglected has been doing research into smart machines (that can think and quickly produce parts to exact specifications without unscheduled delays or extended work cycles); process techniques that can achieve efficient production in small quantities through advanced manufacturing technology; and other manufacturing technology research products. Even DARPA used to have projects for manufacturing technology and for lower-cost weapon systems, but these were dropped to focus on the near-term, higher performance objectives set out by the military services. Fortunately, they were reinstituted in 2010.

• The key element in future research (in addition to the lower cost objective) is developing process changes that can yield more rapid fielding of new ideas. Adversaries are obtaining more modern technology from the worldwide commercial market and using it in unexpected ways (such as the innovative explosive devices—or "roadside bombs"), and the United States must be capable of rapid response as these new technologies and applications appear on the battlefield.

• There is a growing shortage of qualified, defense-oriented S&T workers. There is a critical need for U.S scientists and engineers across the country, but even more so in defense, where U.S. citizenship is required. Government and industry need to address this problem if the United States is to achieve its desired twenty-first-century national security and economic competitiveness posture.

Summary of R&D

A different perspective is required on the importance of science and technology to America's future—both economically and in terms of its future security, since both require a strong technological leadership position. The United States cannot deny potential opponents or competitors access to most science and technology going on today. U.S. policy must be simply to stay ahead. To do so, requires four specific actions.[52] First, the United States needs to generate a supply of brilliant scientists and engineers who are capable of producing the new knowledge. There is a worldwide supply of brilliant students and scholars that can be tapped. Second, sufficient funds must be invested to support the research conducted by these scientists and engineers, and these funds must be applied to both short-term applications as well as long-term and disruptive changes. Third, engineers are needed who thoroughly understand fundamental laws of physics and yet are capable of the unconstrained, imaginative, creative thought that translates newly discovered scientific knowledge into new products and services (with higher performance but at much lower cost). Finally, an environment must be created that is highly conducive to innovation, particularly of the disruptive type—so that the institutional and cultural biases against change can be overcome by fully incentivizing and supporting innovation. This last goal requires risk capital, sound patent policies, a constructive tax policy, and reasonable liability laws. It also requires major revisions to U.S. export and import controls and a culture of openness to working on a global basis. The combination of these four actions can keep the United States ahead technologically and strengthen the integrated effect on its economy and its security.

7

Competition in Defense Acquisitions

Competition is the most important aspect of the Defense Department's acquisition strategy (for both goods and services) since it is a way to create incentives for innovations that result in higher performance at lower cost. Because a single (monopoly) source lacks such incentives, it tends to maximize its profits by raising costs and producing the same goods and services as it has in the past. Unlike in the commercial world, where the quantity of goods sold increases significantly as the price falls (this is price elasticity), in the defense world the quantities to be bought are usually fixed by the force structure (assuming the budget will allow it), and under those conditions, firms have few incentives to find ways to reduce costs.

Competition is the driving force in the U.S. economy, and as long as it is present, corporations continue to improve quality, innovate for improved performance, reduce costs, make product design and process improvements, and focus on satisfying changing customer needs. As table 7.1 points out, however, there are dramatic differences between the commercial market and the defense market, which is highly regulated and has a single buyer that demands state-of-art performance.

Even though Congress has recognized the benefits of competition and enacted the "Competition in Contracting Act," a significant share of Department of Defense dollars is still awarded on a sole-source basis. The normal practice has been to run an initial competition when a program begins. Then the selected winner becomes a sole-source supplier for the remainder of the development program, the production program, and the subsequent support program—for many years. The problem is that from the time the program is initiated until it is completed decades later, thousands of changes are likely to come along as a result of technological advances, developmental problems, threat changes, inadequate reliability, and performance shortfalls. Because all of these changes are quoted by the sole supplier on a monopoly basis, the typical program tends to have significant cost growth during its lifetime.

The critical distinction is between one-time competition and continuous competition. The latter is used in the commercial world, where there are multiple

Table 7.1
Commercial markets and defense markets

Aspects	Commercial markets	Defense markets
Products	Proven technology that is rapidly applied	Cutting-edge technology that is slowly applied
Market structure	Many buyers and multiple producers	One buyer; large items bought in small quantities
Demand	Competitive; sensitive to price and quality	Monopsonistic; rarely price-sensitive; driven by maximum performance
Supply	Competitive; adjusts to demand	Oligopolistic; large excess capacity
Entry and exit	Movement in and out of the market	Extensive barriers to entry and exit (such as unique requirements, perception of higher cost of two suppliers, special accounting, Congress)
Prices	Constrained by market competition	Cost-based and regulated
Outputs	Constrained by market competition	Determined by government
Risk	Borne by firm	Shared between firm and government
Profits	Constrained by market competition	Regulated by the government
Competition	In production	Usually for R&D

sellers and multiple buyers, but it is not traditionally the case in defense—despite the overwhelming data that show the clear advantages of forms of continuous competition (or at least the option of it) in improving performance and reducing the costs of defense goods and services. How the competition is conducted really does matter, and requiring an initial competition does not mean that the DoD has gained all of the possible benefits from continuous competition. For example, picking the low bidder on a high-tech product is the wrong way to make the source selection. Holding a "best-value" competition—which trades off performance and cost—results in the best combination of the various parameters. Similarly, having two suppliers in a team does not represent competition; it simply represents a monopoly team.

There are many forms of competition. It also can be achieved in different phases of an acquisition and should be done differently for the different items or services that are being procured. In addition, maintaining the option for competition (as long as it is a credible option) is effective in incentivizing the existing supplier. There can be formal or informal competitions. For example, the Defense Advanced

Research Projects Agency (DARPA) has a history of inviting known, qualified firms (or inviting others that might choose to come in) to have brief discussions about how they would approach the problem, which researchers they would assign to the problem, and what experience they have in the area. Based on those discussions, DARPA then limits the competition to two or three firms, which then move on to the prototype phase (this important step takes place after paper proposals and before demonstrated hardware, especially in advanced technologies). This "product competition" can be contrasted with competitions that are based on the desired "mission performance" results without specifying what product is being acquired. There is also a difference between "full and open competition" and "limited competition." Empirical research (conducted by a government procurement commission and reported on by Frederic Scherer)[1] has shown that bidders will try harder to be innovative in a limited competition (where they think they have a strong chance of winning) than in a competition with many others (that all have equal chances of winning). In fact, many firms will not bid unless they think they have a good chance of winning, because of the high cost of putting together the proposal.

Commodities that are well defined and that are listed on the General Services Administration (GSA) schedules can be bought at the previously negotiated prices, or purchasers can ask for bids from all potential suppliers and simply "open the envelop" (a process that is applicable only when products are totally interchangeable in terms of performance).

Besides these various forms of competition, different ways of approaching competition might be needed in a research and development program, a production program, or a support or services activity. Finally, in many complex high-tech systems, competition must be maintained at the level of the high-risk, high-cost subsystems (and not at just the prime-contractor level). For example, on an aircraft or a missile, the final assembly and test are very small portions of the total cost and risk, while the sensors, the guidance system, and the propulsion system often come out to be 70 to 80 percent of the total costs and are the high-risk, high-performance elements.

In the commercial world, a major consideration in competitive evaluations is the past performance that each supplier delivered: did the product work, was it delivered on time, was the service satisfactory, was the product reliable over its lifetime, was the firm responsive to the agency's needs. and did the firm live up to its cost commitments? The answers to these questions would help government procurement officers make their next source selections and perhaps even persuade them to pay a little more for a better product from a more reliable supplier.

The data overwhelmingly support the benefits of competition for obtaining higher performance at lower costs (due to product and process innovation). Despite the empirical data and the legal requirements of the Competition in Contracting Act, however, there is still enormous resistance to using full competition on many defense programs. Some procurement managers do not want to pay the small, up-front costs for the second supplier (even though the competition results in large, long-term cost savings), and the current producer always applies enormous political pressure (including through Congress) to avoid introducing a competitor. This chapter examines the data for five cases—competition in R&D, in production, for weapon support and maintenance, for services, and between public the and private sectors (for work that is not inherently governmental).

Competition in R&D

A typical weapon system is based on the technology that is embedded in the system's critical elements. On an aircraft, the system's critical elements include the aerodynamic design, stealth characteristics, propulsion system, radars, avionics and computing system, fire-control system, and weapons. Although each element goes through separate R&D efforts with various contractors, at the time of the proposal for the aircraft itself, each of the two or three bidding prime contractors assembles teams of suppliers (one for each critical subsystem) and submits proposals with thousands of pages describing technical characteristics, promised performance, delivery schedules, management plan, and a detailed cost analysis. Then the government establishes a large evaluation team. In the air force tanker competition, 150 government employees evaluated two proposals.[2] Based on this paper competition, a source-selection team evaluates and scores volumes of materials, and a winner is selected. After that selection has been done, all subsequent development and changes (and changes are frequent) are done in a sole-source environment. On the littoral combat ship, for example, there were seventy-five changes a week.[3] An alternative approach (which is the Defense Department's basic policy) is to have at least two bidders selected (depending on the product and its complexity and cost) and have them both build competitive prototypes. This approach has been used in a number of programs (such as the F-16 and F-35 fighter aircraft), and it has been proven to be a successful model. First, it creates enormous incentives for both producers to realize their proposal claims and to become the sole winner of the large production follow-on (assuming that will be done sole-source), and second, it provides a high probability that at least one of the two companies will achieve the needed results. Sometimes the initial feasibility contracts are given to three companies, and two companies are selected for the full development of the prototypes, thereby maintaining competition. DARPA used this model to develop the next-generation supercomputer. It initially funded IBM, CRAY, and Sun Microsystems and then awarded CRAY and IBM competitive contracts of around $250 million to develop the next generation of supercomputer.[4] The two firms were given about four years for prototype development in this competitive environment. If one failed, there would still be an existing alternative, but if both succeeded, then future customers would have choices (depending on cost and performance) and would not have to pay monopoly prices to a sole producer.

Because the R&D phases of programs are a small cost compared to the production and support phases, there are huge advantages to being able to maintain competitive prototypes—at both the prime-contractor level and the critical-subsystems level. One obvious disadvantage of competition is that two companies (rather than just one) must be funded, which means that in a resource-limited environment, some other program will have to be postponed. On the other hand, the benefits—in technological advancements and lower costs (particularly when unit production cost is one of the design considerations for the prototypes)—more than pay for the added cost of the second prototype (through the production and support savings that come from the R&D competition). Although there is often a tendency to do an early down-select, to save money, as soon as one of the two competing prototypes appears to be ahead. This temptation must be resisted to gain the full benefits of the competition into the production phase.

Competition in Production

Production competition can take many forms. If competitive prototypes are built, then there can be a down-select for either a single winner or a competition for the share of production that each will be awarded in the first and subsequent rounds. If it is an all-or-nothing competition, with a single winner, then both bidders will view it as a must-win and will apply extreme optimism to their bid (since there is going to be a multibillion dollar award to the winner, and the loser is basically out of the business for many decades). Both bidders also realize that it does not matter how poorly they actually do the job—in terms of cost, schedule, or even performance—since the customer must have the product to satisfy a mission need, and will continue to buy it and fund them for improvements or fixes. But they must win the initial competition—so their bid must be extremely attractive (in terms of proposed costs, schedule, and performance) The result is the typical cost growth and schedule slippage of defense weapon systems (after the winner is selected).

In an alternative model, the two developers are both declared winners, they are awarded a share of the business (with the share varying as a function of their bids and their performance on the prior round), and the results are a continuous improvement in performance with reductions in cost from both suppliers. Even if competitive prototypes are not produced, the government can still benefit from continuous production competitions in one of two ways. It can take the drawings from the single source (since the government paid for the R&D, it owns the drawings) and compete for a second source to "build to print." This has been done in the past for both subsystems and weapon systems, and it is an effective way to introduce competition. One disadvantage of this method is that it fails to maintain two engineering design teams in a given area since the winner of this second sourcing is usually a purely manufacturing operation that is focused on low-cost production. Since the key to innovation in advanced weapon systems is the presence of design competition in two companies, the alternative (and preferred) model (in cases where two prototypes were not built) is to introduce dissimilar competition for two products that can each satisfy the same military need but are different in design. If it is a subsystem, then the goal is to achieve standardized interfaces (as the airlines do with navigation equipment and other subsystems through standardized interfaces for form, fit, and function) or simply to have two products that each satisfy the mission need and that continuously compete for a share of the business. This was the case for the "great engine war" (when the two producers of dissimilar engines competed for a share of the air force fighter aircraft business).

Some costs are required for maintaining a competitive second source—the qualification costs for the second source, any nonrecurring engineering or tooling costs, the burden for the government of managing two sources (although the cost reductions from market forces help a great deal in managing the two suppliers), and the potential of having to support two different systems logistically in the field (although warranties by the contractors can be a big help in this area). But several potential benefits can come from continuous production competition. It gives companies incentives to achieve innovations in design and production processes (yielding higher performance, higher reliability, and significantly lower costs from both suppliers); it leads firms to assign their top people to the program because of its competitive nature (and there is abundant evidence that once a company has become a sole-source producer, it shifts its top people to the next competition); and it results in having two firms in the business rather than one, which allows future competitions and also provides the possibility of a surge in production (should it be required) in both facilities.[5]

There might appear to be a conflict between the potential benefits (in performance and costs) that come from competition and the learning-curve theory that says that splitting the production buy with competition allows each producer to build fewer systems and therefore not progress as far as possible on the declining learning curve. But the theory of learning curves comes from the commercial world, in which there is essentially continuous competition in almost all products, and therefore it is based on the presence of competition. In the defense model, when competition is not present, firms have a perverse incentive to increase costs (and the empirical data seem to confirm that they do it). In the absence of competition, the actual learning curves are either flat or ascending (rather than declining).

Table 7.2
Savings observed in production competition studies, 1964 to 1979

Study organization	Year	Number of systems	Observed net savings (percentage)
Frederick Scherer	1964	—	25%
Robert McNamara	1965	—	25%
RAND Corp.	1968	—	25%
Battle Memorial Institute	1969	20	32%
Army Electronics Command	1972	17	50%
Logistics Management Institute	1973	—	15–50%
Joint Economic Committee	1973	20	52%
Institute for Defense Analysis	1974	1	22%
ARINC	1976	13	47%
Army Procurement Research Organization	1978	11	12%
Institute for Defense Analysis	1979	31	31%
TASC Corp.	1979	45	30%

Source: Defense Science Board, "International Armaments Cooperation in an Era of Coalition Security," August 1996.

Consider the empirical data in this regard. First, table 7.2 shows a series of historic studies that were done from 1964 to 1979. They compared the net savings realized when production competition was introduced into a program with comparable results from programs that did not have competition.

These data are based on both prime contracts and subcontracts and include the costs of the second source to arrive at the net savings. The table shows that the projected net savings from having continuous production competition ranged from a low of 12 percent to a high of 52 percent, with an average around 30 percent.

Table 7.3 shows some aggregate information about actual results achieved on competitive aircraft production procurements versus sole-source aircraft production procurements.

Although this is not a one-to-one comparison in terms of aircraft types, the table shows that from 1971 to 2000, commercial aircraft were continuously in competition while military aircraft were produced in a sole-source environment. In the commercial cases, all programs had a decreasing cost of between 2 and 27 percent, with an overall simple average *decrease* of 16 percent over the program's life. By comparison, the actual costs (not the baseline projections) of the aircraft programs procured by the Defense Department showed that most programs had an increase between 25 and 104 percent (with two programs showing a very modest decrease)

Table 7.3
Program cost growth for aircraft with and without production competition, 1971 to 2000

Aircraft	Net cost growth (percentage)
A. Competitive commercial aircraft	
B737-400	0.76%
B757-200ER	0.80
A310-300	0.98
A320	0.92
A330-300	0.86
DC10-30	0.83
MD-11	0.73
Average	0.84%
B. Noncompetitive production DoD aircraft	
A-6E/F	0.96%
B-1B	0.98
C-17	1.70
EF-111A	1.62
F/A-18 A-D	1.54
F-14A	1.25
F-15A-D	1.47
F-16A-D	1.29
JSTARS	2.04
T-45	1.74
Average	1.459%

Source: Data for competitive commercial aircraft from "Historical Lease Rates/Values 1971–2000," http://www.aircraft-values.co.uk; data for noncompetitive commercial aircraft from John Birkler et al., "Assessing Competitive Strategies for the Joint Strike Fighter," RAND Corporation, Santa Monica, 2001.

and an overall simple average *increase* of 46 percent. The data in table 7.4 show how production competition affected seven missile programs in which competition was introduced after the first source started production.

In all of these cases, the second source began by having a steeper learning curve than the initial producer. As shown in figure 7.1, in all these cases, the first source had essentially a flat learning curve until the second source was introduced, the presence of competition caused both sources to lower their costs immediately through process or design changes, and both suppliers went down significantly steeper learning curves together while the competition continued.

What is actually happening is shown by the last of the cases, the Tomahawk missile program, in figure 7.2.

Table 7.4
The effect of production competition on seven missile programs.

Missile program	Cost improvement rate (percentage)		Percentage difference
	First source	Second source	
AIM-7F	0.87%	0.84%	3.00%
Bullpup	0.82	0.80	2.00
TOW	0.98	0.89	9.00
AIM-9L	0.90	0.83	7.00
AIM-9M	0.94	0.85	9.00
Hellfire	0.94	0.92	2.00
Tomahawk	0.79	0.71	8.00

Source: Defense Science Board, "International Armaments Cooperation in an Era of Coalition Security," August 1996.

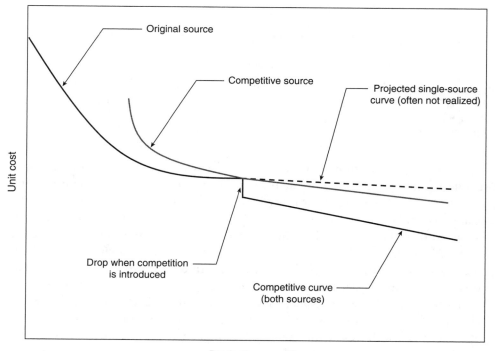

Figure 7.1
The effects of production-phase competition *Source:* Defense Science Board, "International Armaments Cooperation in an Era of Coalition Security," August 1996.

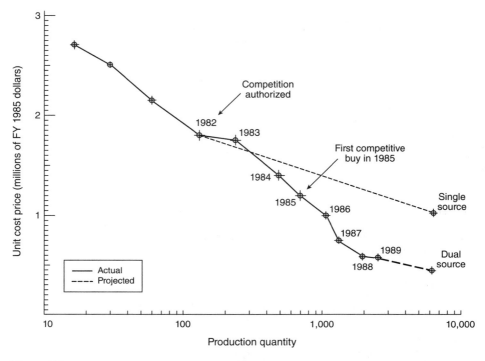

Figure 7.2
The Tomahawk missile competition experience, 1982 to 1990. *Source:* John Birkler, "Dual-Source Procurement in the Tomahawk Program," RAND Corporation, 1990; John Birkler et al., "Assessing Competitive Strategies for the Joint Strike Fighter," RAND Corporation, 2001.

In this case, the government wanted to shift the responsibility for achieving higher missile reliability onto the contractor, but General Dynamics/Convair (the prime contractor) was unwilling to warranty McDonald-Douglas's guidance system in this cruise missile. So the government decided to introduce competition (by forcing an exchange of technology) and to dual-source the missiles competitively (to get an improved weapon reliability). The cost of entry of the second source was low, and since there were large annual production quantities and General Dynamics had projected a relatively flat learning curve in its own studies, the risk to the government was low. The actual results, as shown in figure 7.2, were a significant cost reduction from both sources. System reliability improved from approximately 80 to 97 percent, which was attributable to the competitive pressure forcing design and production process changes by both companies. After the fact, both the government and the contractors felt that the introduction of production competition resulted in significant costs savings and performance improvements.

There are some startup costs for the second source—often between 1 and 6 percent of the production program's costs (with the Tomahawk, it was 2 percent), but in every program that has been analyzed (and there have been many), the second source (if it is a high-quality producer) has always had a significantly steeper learning curve than the first source. Thus, within a short time, the second source's costs have been reduced to below those of the first source. The first source then lowers its costs (shown in the figure as a downward shift in the solid curve), and both producers go down the steeper learning curve[6] and achieve the savings shown in table 7.2. For example, the Shrike anti-radar missile system was selling for $19,500 each when it was sole-sourced. After competition, the first producer's price dropped to $4,480 (a 77 percent reduction), and the second source's price dropped to $3,850.[7] Similar results were found when this acquisition strategy was used on critical subsystems of a weapon system. For example, the unit price of the computer on the HARM missile system dropped from $260,000 to $52,000.[8]

One of the best known of these production competition programs is the so-called "great engine war." In this case, a single supplier of engines for the F-15 and F-16 fighter planes was found to be unresponsive to government requests and was producing an engine with lower than desired reliability. Fortunately, there was a second engine alternative (which also had proven technology, although of a different design), and the startup costs would be minimal as long as the government was willing to accept two different designs for the aircraft (which could be handled by having different squadrons have different engines). Thus, the government decided to introduce competition using fixed-price contracts with warranties (where the warranty was an incentive for reliability improvements).[9] The result was that the reliability improved significantly. The shop visit rate for one thousand engine flight hours was half the precompetition engines, and the scheduled depot return increased from nine hundred cycles to four thousand cycles. The air force also found improved contractor responsiveness and contractor investments to improve efficiency, upgrade the manufacturing capability, reduce costs, and make other changes that would improve quality. They also found that by having competition that included warranties resulted in significant savings (of $53 million) compared to the original sole-source contractor's warranty costs. The lower tiers now had multiple suppliers, enhanced operational flexibility with an enlarged industrial base, and thus considerable protection from any production disruptions. Finally, the air force estimated that it saved a net of $3 billion to $4 billion over the twenty-year life cycle of the aircraft.[10] In general, both new engines proved to be more capable, more durable, more supportable, and less expensive than the original sole-source engine.

Another example of the benefits of competition is the Sparrow III anti-aircraft missile system, which was dual-sourced in production to improve its reliability (since the first source was having trouble in this area). The result was a dramatic improvement in reliability and a significant lowering of costs.

These benefits of continuous competition in defense procurement have been recognized for many years. In 1964, Frederick Scherer published findings that showed that during World War II, the learning curves for bomber production were much steeper when there was dual-sourcing (with cost visibility) than when there was single sourcing.[11] By the late 1970s, programs such as the navy's dual-sourced FFG-7 patrol frigates were known to have much steeper learning curves than any other ships being built (sole-source) for the navy. Yet there was still great reluctance to introduce the concept of competitive dual-sourcing in either development or production. It was believed that the quantities were not large enough or that sufficient contractual incentives already existed to ensure that the sole producer would achieve the results desired. There was always reluctance because of the startup costs and the difficulty of getting money for the initial investment. In fact, sometimes Congress supported the services (or the initial producer) in resisting the introduction of a second source.[12]

Finally, in 1984, Congress passed the Competition in Contracting Act (CICA).[13] It required a "competition advocate" to be established in each service with a general officer in charge. It also recognized that the use of sealed bids was inappropriate for most defense procurements and that negotiated competitions in which quality and price could be balanced ("best-value" competitions) would be an acceptable form of competition. It specified a limited set of conditions under which sole-source awards would be appropriate. However, one undesirable outcome of the act was that it greatly encouraged protests (of the government's decisions). Protests increased dramatically and have continued to the present.

Two arguments used against competition need to be addressed. The first argument claims that incentive fees can be used to manage the total costs on weapon systems instead of having to pay the extra cost of a second contractor. Here, part of the problem is that a typical program receives only a 5 to 8 percent fee on its total costs (since even with a fixed-price contract, the level of the fixed price is determined by the costs in the prior year, and the fees are applied to that estimate). Thus, the major share of the total price is the 92 to 95 percent basic cost, and there is a perverse incentive to try to maximize that and then simply add on 5 or 8 percent to it. The contractor would gain more if it significantly raised the basic cost—even if its percentage fee was slightly smaller. Also, the empirical results show (as noted above) that the actual award fees received tend to be high—even when the contractor overruns its costs and is late on its deliveries. The Defense Department needs to use its award fees (as incentives for meeting cost, schedule, and performance goals) more effectively, but those fees are not going to be a sufficient driving force in comparison to the overall benefits of competition. For example, after the Competition in Contracting Act was introduced and the amount of competition increased significantly, analysis showed that Pratt & Whitney had reduced its supervisory staff by 10 percent, Boeing said it had cut overhead costs by 25 percent, and General Dynamics said it was aiming for a 40 percent reduction in its overhead.[14] Even the threat of competition seems to reduce prices. For example, when Navy Secretary Lehman said that he might buy F-14 fighters instead of the F-18s, which had been significantly increasing in price, the price of the latter dropped dramatically.[15]

The second argument usually used against setting up a second source is that the efficiencies of the first source would have to be scaled back because of the reduced volume to be produced. There is some credibility to this argument if the initial production line has been scaled to a certain level (that is, full production by a sole source) and if the high overhead and inefficiencies of the initial source are allowed to continue. Under these circumstances, costs will go up—since those large overhead costs have to be absorbed by the smaller quantities being produced. However, if the production is initially scaled under the assumption that there will be a split buy, if after each bid the two firms scale their overhead to the size of their productions, and if the bids that each submits are based on efficient operations for economic production rates, then it is possible to have efficiency at smaller quantities. For example, when the navy decided to scale back on the production of the Trident D-5 strategic missile system[16] at Lockheed Martin from a rate of sixty per year to twelve per year, the unit cost of these large, sophisticated strategic missile systems fell. An explanation for this shift in the production efficiency curve is shown in figure 7.3.

This point is further illustrated by the competition for the navy's DDG 51 destroyer. In this case, very few ships were to be built each year, with one or two ships built in some years, and four or five ships built in other years. Despite these low production numbers, shipbuilding costs have remained fairly stable over time (in constant dollars).[17]

Given the overwhelming empirical data showing the large net cost savings from production competitions (whenever the volume is reasonable), competitions would be expected to be the norm. Some cases from 2007 are more typical of DoD practices, however. Perhaps the best known of these was the competition for an air force tanker program. The air force stated that this program was its number one priority because it had an aging fleet of tankers and an increasing need for long-range, long-duration flights that required in-air refueling. New tankers were needed, and the first buy of one hundred tankers (more were to be bought in the future to replace the aging fleet of six hundred) was budgeted for around $20 billion. The air force would hold an all-or-nothing competition between two commercial aircraft (either a Boeing aircraft or an Airbus aircraft, with the latter to be managed by Northrop Grumman and to be built in Alabama) that could be modified for this mission.

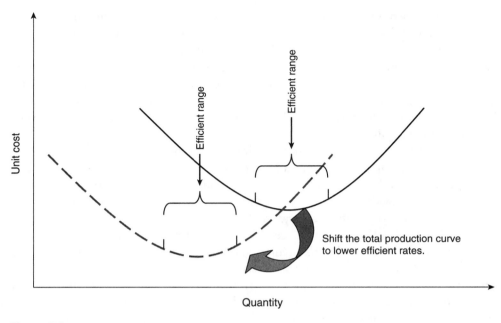

Figure 7.3
Shifting the production efficiency curve to adjust to smaller quantities

Originally, the air force was going to lease the aircraft from Boeing, but this approach was stopped by Congress. Then it was going to buy them sole-source from Boeing, but a political scandal (described above) caused this sole-source award to be abandoned in favor of an all-or-nothing competition. Both of these commercial aircraft use large numbers of U.S. and foreign subsystems, both already had world-wide logistic support, and both were in-production systems that were well down on their learning curves. So the startup costs for either system would be relatively small (although the Airbus system would have some startup costs involved in moving from France for final assembly in Alabama). If FedEx or UPS were making this choice, it would keep continuous competition for the first hundred aircraft as well as the larger number to be built in the future. It would have a competitive, dual-sourced acquisition strategy (not a sole-source award). However, the air force did not include in its requests for proposals the traditional clause that says, "The government reserves the right to pick one or more of the bidders." Instead, it stated that this would be an all-or-nothing competition[18] with the winner getting the first hundred orders and all of the follow-on orders as well. If the results of sole-source versus dual-source learning curves (see table 7.3) were compared for the first hundred aircraft alone, a competitive split-buy here (versus a total award to a sole source) would indicate a potential net savings of many billions of dollars (as the sole-source costs would undoubtedly grow from the initial bid as a result of changes in air force technical and/or mission requirements). In the dual-source case, reducing the costs would likely be a principal focus of the two firms since they would know that they were going to be competing again for the still larger follow-on buys. Additionally, if warranties were used for lifecycle support, then there would be added incentives for reliability improvements and significant air force benefits in availability and maintenance cost reductions.

When the extensive competition was run and the Northrop Grumman proposal was declared the winner, members of Congress objected to "buying a foreign design," and the Government Accountability Office (GAO) upheld a protest by Boeing on details of the procurement process itself. The overall program was further delayed, so this "urgent need" of the air force was delayed for at least two years. In early 2009, in a cost saving initiative, the new Obama administration initially proposed to delay the tanker program by five more years but then decided to go ahead with another winner-take-all competition. Northrop Grumman felt that the new request for proposals was biased in favor of Boeing and chose to "no bid."[19] If the DoD had chosen to dual-source this aircraft competitively and if the Congress agreed (based on the overwhelming empirical data regarding the benefits of competition and the fact that each firm would build the aircraft in the United States), there would have been significant savings, more timely deliveries, and high-quality, proven aircraft that satisfied a real national need—but there also would have been some up-front costs for setting up the second production line in the United States.

As a second example, consider the jet engines for the largest program in history— the F-35 Joint Strike Fighter, a multinational program requiring thousands of jet engines to be built for three variants of this aircraft, which will be used on a worldwide basis by 11 nations. This choice is similar to "the great engine war" described above. The air force chief of staff, General Michael Moseley, indicated that he backed the concept of a competitive alternate engine,[20] and a DoD independent cost analysis showed that, based on historical trends (including the great engine war), there would be significant savings from competitively dual-sourcing these engines. The GAO's independent study of the option of an alternative engine stated that, for 2,443 engines and their support, an estimate of $53.4 billion was the likely cost over the remainder of the F-135 engine program. It also stated that even if there was an additional investment for the second engine of between $3.6 billion and $4.5 billion, "given certain assumptions with regard to these factors, the additional costs of having the alternate engine could be recouped if competition were to generate approximately 10.3 to 12.3% savings. . . . according to actual Air Force data, from past engine programs, including for the F-16 aircraft, it is reasonable to expect savings of at least that much. Additionally, there are a number of non-financial benefits that may result from competition, including better performance, increased reliability, and improved contractor responsive."[21] The air force chose not to pay for this second engine's startup costs, but the Congress put in the money year after year to keep the competitive program going. Senator John Warner, then chair of the Armed Services Committee, stated that without competition the sole-source award would create "a $100 billion monopoly." Some believe that this was a case in which the navy and air force (the joint buyers of this aircraft) were simply leaving the money for the second engine source out of their budgets and counting on Congress to add it.[22]

As two final examples of the DoD's reluctance to seize the benefits of competitive dual-sourcing (versus either a sole-source or allocation to two sources that essentially are two sole sources), consider the army's need for armored vehicles in Iraq and Afghanistan, when many soldiers have been killed or maimed by roadside bombs. Two approaches were pursued to satisfy this urgent need for armored vehicles. The first was to build rapidly 15,274 mine-resistant, ambush-protected (MRAP) vehicles for the army and marines. Secretary of Defense Robert Gates declared that this was the Pentagon's highest-priority program, and the Department of Defense announced that it was going to award sole-source contracts to three different firms.[23] As these vehicles became increasingly heavy and increasingly expensive (over $1.5 million each), however, the marines cut back on their orders,[24] but the three sole-source contracts continued to have full congressional support. In addition, a study by the DoD inspector general found that sole-source awards were being made for armored vehicles and armored kits for a total of $2.2 billion and strongly recommended competition for future armored-vehicle contracts.[25] However, when the army and marine corps decided to solicit for a Humvee replacement to purchase 145,000 vehicles (at an estimated cost of $200,000 to $250,000 each), they again decided on a winner-take-all competition for the prototype of the joint light tactical vehicle (JLTV).[26] They could have either competitively dual-sourced the prototypes or competitively dual-sourced the full production quantities. Because roadside bombs are likely to proliferate in the future, this program, if successful, could have a large, worldwide market and a significant law-enforcement market.

These examples from 2007 and 2008 indicate the continued resistance on the part of the services to accept empirical data about the benefits of competitive dual-sourced production programs—in the belief that "this time we'll manage it better, and the costs won't follow the historic trends."

Competition for Defense Support and Maintenance

The largest single category of expenditures in the acquisition area for the Department of Defense is logistics support and equipment maintenance. In 2007, this cost $172 billion, and as the equipment ages and continues to be used, the cost of support

Table 7.5
Competitively awarded performance-based logistics (PBL): Availability and response-time comparisons

Navy program	Material availability (percentage)		Logistics response time (days)	
	Pre-PBL	Post-PBL	Pre-PBL	Post-PBL
F-14 LANTIRN	73%	90%	56.9 days	5 days
H-60 avionics	71%	85%	52.7 days	8 days
F/A-18 stores management system	65%	98%	42.6 days	2 days CONUS 7 days OCONUS
Tires	81%	98%	28.9 days	2 days CONUS 4 days OCONUS
APU	65%	90%	35 days	6.5 days

Source: Data for material availability from Paul Klevan, NAVICP, UID Program Manager Workshop Briefing, May 5, 2005; data for logistics response time from Lou Kratz, OSD, Status Report, NDIA Logistics Conference Briefing, March 2, 2004.
Note: CONUS refers to the forty-eight contiguous U.S. states; OCONUS refers to outside the contiguous U.S. states.

(including spare parts) and maintenance continues to grow. Thus, this area seems to be worth considering for the potential benefits of competition. The tradition in this area, however, has been that either the original equipment manufacturer supplies the support and maintenance or the government does it itself (this is known as "organic"). In either case, these are basically sole-source awards for the largest portion of the overall DoD acquisition dollars.

The potential benefits of competitively awarded performance-based logistics (PBL) on force readiness are shown in table 7.5.

Here, the columns labeled "Pre-PBL" show the actual sole-source performance that was obtained on these five navy programs, and the columns labeled "Post-PBL" show the enormous improvements that can be realized when a competition is won by the contractor that can supply the best availability and response time for the equipment. These performance results are achieved at lower costs than in the sole-source cases. As can be seen from the table, the logistics response time is approximately an order of magnitude better in the competitive environment, and this makes a huge difference in terms of military capability. Essentially, such results are being guaranteed either through fixed-price warranties or as the basis of the winning bidder's commitment. In this case, past performance can be used as one of the criteria for follow-on awards. In many cases, the costs of warranties offered in a competitive environment can be compared to those offered in a sole-source environment (this happened in the great engine war, where the sole-source warranty cost greatly exceeded that offered in the competitive environment).

Additionally, competitions in the logistics area frequently have been between a contractor (supplying the performance-based logistics) and the government (supplying it organically). It does not matter who wins the competition, since both obtain significantly improved results as long as they are being measured after the award (in terms of both their actual performance and their actual costs). As noted above, the Congress has strongly preferred that Defense Department maintenance work be done (sole-source) in government depots, since these are often the largest employers in a given congressional district and even in a state. Gaining the performance and cost benefits of competition in the logistics and maintenance area will require considerable administration leadership in overcoming congressional resistance (even to allow public and private competitors; which are frequently won by the public sector and with significant cost savings).

Competition for Services

Because 60 percent or more of Defense Department acquisitions today are in the services category and the barriers to entry and exit often are much lower for services than for large, military equipment contracts, more competition is to be expected in this area, and this is increasingly the case. However, there are a number of risks in this area. First, a service is sometimes treated as a commodity (because "anyone can do it") and therefore is awarded to the lowest bidder (rather than on the basis of "best value"). In one case a number of years ago, the navy was hiring engineering consultants on the basis of the lowest hourly rates and was flying them in from around the country to get the lowest hourly rate. But all engineers are not alike, and this service is not a commodity, so the proper evaluations must be based on best value. However, Congress (with pressure from public-sector unions) mandated that jobs that government workers are currently doing must be awarded based on the lowest bidder rather than best value. (Best-value bidding acknowledges that industry hourly rates include overhead and government hourly rates do not include overhead.) When some competitions between public-sector and private-sector bidders were won by the private sector (due to productivity enhancements), the Congress passed laws to stop the competitions.

Another shortcoming in contracts for services has to do with socioeconomic legislation. For example, Alaskan Native Corporations (ANCs) are allowed by law to receive sole-source awards (at any level and without competition). Congressional concerns were raised when the army did not renew two $100 million contracts with ANCs for security guards at numerous military bases around the country because the Government Accountability Office GAO reported that "competitively-bid, the private security contracts have cost about 25% less than the ANC 'no-bid' contracts."[27]

On the other hand, an equally undesirable result is too much competition. As Mike Scherer stated, "too much competition can discourage, rather than stimulate, vigorous effort."[28] There is a difference between allowing effective competition among a few highly qualified firms and simply throwing open all tasks on a broad services contract to many winners. The growing practice has been to allow nearly anyone who bids and has any kind of a track record in a given service area to be on the list of winners, so that every time there is a task under that service contract, all of those winners are allowed to bid on each task. For example, the navy's Seaport multiple-award contract—which was an indefinite delivery, indefinite quantity (IDIQ) contract—had over 2000 winning contractors put on the list as prequalified to compete for tasks for services such as modeling, simulation, training and analysis support, system design documentation, technical data support, software engineering and programming, and network support.[29] The navy could issue orders up to $5.3 billion a year under contracts with a two-year base period and up to eight option years. This type of approach—having many winners on the first phase to make the list and then recompeting every task that comes up—may appear to be fair, but it is far from efficient (either from the government's or the industry's perspective) since companies assign their best people and make their best efforts only when they have a reasonably good chance of winning in a competition. The effectiveness of a competition is far better when only two or three companies bid than when hundreds or even dozens of firms bid. Unfortunately, having many winners on the IDIQ contracts makes the government's job on the first round a lot easier simply because most people are winners (and there are few protests). But it is not in the government's long-term best interests to move in this direction. The number of winners should be kept to a relatively small number so that the government can benefit from the far more effective competition that takes place when additional orders are put in place under the contract.

One of the most difficult aspects of service contracting is defining the measures of performance to be used—determining whether the grass has been properly cut or whether a complex engineering job has been designed well. But measuring performance in supplying services and comparing the costs of those services are essential parts of effective defense procurement. As an example of competing for services, NASA's traditional approach used NASA employees to maintain desktop computational assets, and it had no way to track costs, no standards for comparison, and no tracking of service quality. When it decided to outsource its desktop initiative—Outsourcing Desktop Initiative for NASA (ODIN)—competitively, it transferred the responsibility for providing and managing most of NASA's desktop, server, and intracenter communication assets to the private sector. NASA's stated objectives were to cut down on desktop computing costs, increase their service quality, achieve inoperability and standardization across NASA, and focus NASA information technology employees on the core mission of NASA. After examining the winning contractor's results, it was found that the required service levels were exceeded (service delivery was 98 percent, availability 98 percent, and customer satisfaction in the 90 to 95 percent range), the hardware and software were standardized at each center, and inoperability and security were much improved. Although no cost comparisons were available, information technology costs could now be allocated to a firm fixed-price contract, and NASA was satisfied with both performance and costs.

Competition between Public and Private Sectors

It is U.S. economic policy that the government should not compete with the private sector and should perform only inherently governmental functions. Over the decades, however, the government has built up capabilities in many areas that are not inherently governmental. In 2001, when the government attempted to identify all jobs at the federal level that were not inherently governmental but were being done by government workers, it found 849,389 positions that could be subject to public and private competitions.[30] It has long been recognized that the rules for competitions between the public and private sectors had to be well defined, given the many differences between job descriptions and compensations in the two sectors. In the 1970s, the Office of Management and Budget issued circularA-76 to define how this should be done, and various administrations have attempted to emphasize or deemphasize this type of competition as a desirable management initiative. For example, when George W. Bush came into office, he made increasing the numbers of this type of competition one of his top five management initiatives.

Public and private competition is different from outsourcing (where work is taken from the public sector and given to the private sector without allowing the public sector to bid on it), and it is also different from privatization (where government facilities, equipment, and personnel are privatized). Either of these can be done on a sole-source basis or (preferably) in a competitive fashion. But these approaches are not fair options for government workers, who deserve the opportunity to bid on work that they have been doing for many years (on a sole-source basis). Competition between public and private sectors certainly differs from in-sourcing, in which work is brought from the private sector to the public sector (usually at the request of the government workforce, and supported by the Congress and, more recently, by the Obama administration). In-sourcing is totally noncompetitive and moves from a competitive environment to a sole-source environment.

Table 7.6
Results of competitions between public and private sectors under OMB's Circular A-76, 1978 to 1994

	Competitions completed	Average annual savings (millions of dollars)	Percentage savings
Army	510	$470	27%
Air force	733	$560	36%
Marine corps	39	$23	34%
Navy	806	$411	30%
Defense agencies	50	$13	28%
Total	2,138	$1,478	31%

Source: Office Of The Undersecretary of Defense for Acquisition, Technology, and Logistics, "Defense Reform Initiative Report," November 1997.

As is shown in table 7.6, from 1978 to 1994, over two thousand competitions between the public and private sectors were held using the OMB's Directive A-76 model. A wide variety of functions were competed, and a wide range of government-civilian positions were competed (from hundreds to thousands in each competition).

The table shows that it did not matter who won the competitions. On average, the savings were over 30 percent—with average annual savings across the DoD of around $1.5 billion per year.

In the post–cold war period, as DoD budgets plummeted and efforts were made to find savings, the number of A-76 competitions increased. As shown in table 7.7, over a thousand competitions were held from 1994 to 2003, and they involved over 65,000 civilian positions.

When government people bid on work that they had been doing for a long time and were required to create the most efficient organization (MEO), they proposed doing the same work, with higher quality, and with dramatically fewer people. As the table shows, when they won the competitions, they were going to perform the service with 44 percent fewer people than they had used in the past. In that period, contractors won 56 percent of the competitions, and the total average labor reductions, no matter who won the competitions, was 38 percent.

As the number of competitions increased, there was a consistency between the government bids without competition (the government's original number of positions) and the reductions that the government felt it could take in achieving its MEO of over 30 percent (as shown in figure 7.4) for the period from 1997 through 2001. As the number of positions being competed and as the government began to improve in its ability to compete on these programs, the results were even more dramatic.

Table 7.7
DoD competitive sourcing results, 1994 to 2003

Winning bidder	Number of competitions won	Civilian positions competed (excluding direct conversions)	MEO FTEs (excluding direct conversions)	Percentage decrease from civilian authorizations to government MEO FTEs
In-house	525 (44%)	41,791	23,253	44%
Contractor	667 (56%)	23,364	16,848	28%
Total	1,192	65,157	40,101	38%

Note: MEO refers to most efficient organization; FTE refers to full-time equivalent.
Source: Jacques S. Gansler and William Lucyshyn, "Competitive Sourcing: What Happens to Federal Employees?," October 2004.

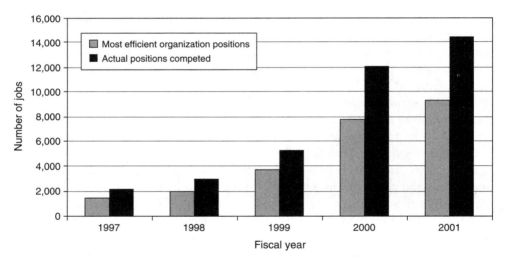

Figure 7.4
Comparison of government workforce bids (under OMB Circular A-76) with original positions, fiscal years 1997 to 2001. *Source:* Based on DoD Commercial Activities Management Information Systems (CAMIS) manpower data.

For example, when the IRS ran two competitions in 2004, the government won both of them. The first was for area distribution centers where 400 positions were competed and the winning MEO bid was for 160 positions (a reduction of 60 percent), and the second was for the IRS "Campus Center" operations and support, where 278 positions were competed and the winning MEO bid was for 60 positions to do the same work (a 78 percent reduction).[31]

As would be expected, considerable concerns were raised after each of these competitions about whether the promised results would be realized. A study by the Center for Naval Analysis looked at sixteen completed activities to determine whether the savings were realized.[32] It found that where the expected savings (as bid by the winner, whether government or private sector) averaged 35 percent, the actual savings realized (after adjusting for the scope changes and quantity changes that occurred during the execution of those projects) averaged 34 percent. In only one of the sixteen cases was there an increase in costs, and the overall observed savings realized (independent of the cost and quantity changes that took place) was still an average savings of 24 percent. Even when the scope or quantity was increased, there was still a savings in the overall program. It is noteworthy that a large share of these competitions was won by the public sector's MEOs. In fiscal year 2006, 87 percent were won by the public sector, and in fiscal year 2007, 73 percent were won by the public sector.[33]

Because a large share of the competitions was going to the public sector, private-sector bidders questioned whether they should continue to bid. As Stan Solloway, president of the Professional Services Council, which represented many of these professional service firms, stated in 2007, "A-76 Competitions are on its last legs. There are already very few people [in the private sector] willing to play."[34] Government workers also questioned whether huge layoffs would be required to take such large reductions from their current workforce to their MEO workforce. A detailed analysis of the actual workforce reductions looked at the overall government personnel database and found that, in spite of the large savings, only 5 percent of workers(on average) were actually laid off.[35] Similar results were found in a study of privatization affects on employment and wages in Eastern Europe and Russia, where the study looked at over thirty thousand initially state-owned manufacturing firms and found that "the results consistently reject job losses from privatization, and they never implied large wage cuts."[36] Many workers either found other government jobs or voluntarily left to take higher-paying positions with the winning private-sector firm. Also, many workers were eligible for government retirement and took advantage of that as well.

Given these statistics, it is surprising how much resistance there was to the competitions (particularly from the government unions and therefore the Congress) and how few actual positions were competed, compared to the number of not inherently governmental positions that were available. In fiscal year 2007, only 132 competitions were conducted across the overall federal government (involving 4,164 full-time equivalent positions), or about 1.5 percent of the positions that were identified for competition across the federal government (as not being inherently governmental functions).[37] Nonetheless, the Office of Management and Budget estimated that the cumulative savings from the competitions held from fiscal year 2003 to 2007 were projected to be over $7.2 billion and that the cost to run the competitions was $240 million—so there was a thirty to one return for every dollar spent in running the competitions.[38]

Despite the huge potential savings and the demonstrated results of obtaining equal or better performance, few competitions were held because the government unions strongly opposed any such competitions and were able to convince the Congress to resist them. Again, in many congressional districts, government employees were the dominant or at least significant voter population. For example, in fiscal year 2006, Congress passed Public Law 109-115, which mandates that government bidders must have a 10 percent or $10 million cost advantage in any OMB Circular A-76 competition involving more than ten jobs; even if the agency can demonstrate that an outside contractor provides the best value when both cost and quality considerations are taken into account.[39] In fiscal year 2008, the National Defense Authorization Act (section 325) prohibited the Office of Management and Budget "from directing or requiring the Secretary of Defense or Secretaries of military departments to undertake public-private competitions under OMB Circular A-76."[40] Finally, in the fiscal year 2008 Consolidated Appropriations Act (Public Law 110-161) and in the House version of the National Defense Authorization Act for fiscal year 2009 (H.R. 5658), there was a mandate to suspend all Department of Defense A-76 competitions for three years. A lobbyist for the American Federation of Government Employees even observed that Congress is considering in-sourcing as a mandate[41] and the Obama administration picked up this idea as one of its early initiatives—even though numerous independent studies (for example, by the Congressional Budget Office, the General Accountability Office, and so on)[42] all showed that "insourcing" of work (that was not inherently governmental) was more expensive, e.g., for equipment maintenance, logistics support, and security services around 90 percent more expensive than using competitively selected contractors.

Congress was giving mixed signals about competitions by passing some laws that require it and other laws that prohibit it—if public-sector workers are involved.[43] Steven Goldsmith, the former mayor of Indianapolis, experimented at the state level with competitions between private and public sectors and noted that the benefits are likely to be realized more at the state level than at the federal level "because

Table 7.8
Competitive sourcing of public transportation in five cities, 1979 to 1996

City	Years	Performance improvement
Denver	1988–1995	Service levels increased 26%
San Diego	1979–1996	Service levels increased 47%
Indianapolis	1994–1996	Service levels increased 38%
Las Vegas	1993–1994	Service levels increased 243%
Los Angeles	1980–1996	Service reliability increased 300%; complaints reduced 75%

Source: E. S. Savas, *Privatization and Public Partnerships* (New York: Chatham House, 2000).

Washington appears allergic to public-private innovation."[44] Many states and local governments have taken advantage of the benefits in improved performance and lower costs that can come from introducing competition for work that was previously done sole-source in the public sector. Table 7.8 presents an example in which five cities competitively sourced public transportation contracts. Service levels improved from between 26 and 300 percent, and the savings ranged from 20 to 60 percent, compared to the costs of the noncompetitive public services that were replaced.

And there have been many other examples of such savings.[45]

Increasingly, it is being recognized that some benefits can be provided by public-sector workers and some by private-sector workers. In some of the OMB Circular A-76 competitions, partnerships are being formed between the public and private sectors to bid together against other partnerships or against the private sector alone. In one competition for aircraft repair work that was won by the public sector, the prime contractor was the government depot, but it subcontracted out 70 percent of the work to the private sector. In an Army Corps of Engineers competition, the government teamed up with Lockheed Martin, and the winning bid required a workforce of about 520 government employees and 350 contract employees. The previous baseline had about 1,300 federal employees and 1,500 contract workers. This dramatic reduction in workforce was accomplished by making a variety of changes, such as moving the Corps of Engineers to a single location and consolidating much of the support work. This arrangement allowed the government to maintain its core competence and resulted in zero layoffs (since the government workers found other jobs within the Corps of Engineers).[46] Such public-private partnerships are important, but they must be done in a competitive fashion to gain the benefits of performance improvements with cost reductions. When done on a sole-source basis, they simply create a different monopoly.

Summary of Competition in Defense Acquisitions

The data overwhelmingly show that well-run competitions in Defense Department acquisitions result in improved performance and lower costs. The power relationship between the government and its suppliers also changes dramatically when competition is present, giving the government maximum leverage. Even competition between only two entities can be fierce and result in full benefits. But when the function is performed by a sole source (whether in the public or private sector), all of the benefits of competition are effectively lost, and the innovation and low cost incentives are removed.

Competition in Defense Department acquisitions is very different from purchasing in the commercial sector because of the limited number of suppliers and the singularity of the buyer. In effect, it is a power struggle between oligopoly suppliers and a monopsony buyer. But as long as there are at least two perceived viable competitors, the government can gain the benefits of increased innovation, performance improvements, quality improvements, and net cost savings. This combination represents the best value for the government, and it should be aggressively pursued. This competition model is one of the major distinctions between the U.S. defense industry and its foreign counterparts, whose dominant model is a single, domestic preferred source.

8

The Defense-Industry Strategies of Other Nations

U.S. security for the twenty-first century (both militarily and industrially) requires a global strategy. In the future, virtually all security scenarios that affect the nation will involve other nations, and technology and industry will themselves be global. Moreover, we can learn a great deal by looking at the strengths and weaknesses of alternative industrial models that have been tried for the defense industries of other nations.

The United States cannot by itself counter global terrorism, weapons proliferation, and regional instability. It also cannot depend solely on its traditional allies (like Europe, Japan, and Australia) but must develop strong alliances with countries such as Russia and China in addressing these issues (to which they are equally vulnerable).

The approach to defense industrial strategy that is taken by essentially all other nations in the world is much more planned than the U.S. approach. Even though the U.S. government is the sole buyer and its defense industry is almost totally regulated, the industry is supposedly laissez-faire. Other countries—whether capitalistic or socialistic—recognize the dominant role played by the government in its security industry. They may have different degrees of ownership and management participation by the government in the industry, but they all recognize the non-free-market conditions that exist. A few countries encourage internal competition, but most view the competition to be primarily with other countries (for foreign sales). Other nations are involved (in detail) in the planning of the structure, conduct, and performance of their defense industry—including its research and development, production capacity, and financing. They treat their defense industry as a valued national resource, and most have created financial incentives to lure high-tech defense firms (particularly from the United States) to their countries.

For example, the United States has an R&D tax credit of approximately 3 percent, but Singapore's is approximately 24 percent.[1] Similarly, overall foreign tax policies are a magnet, pulling U.S. capability offshore. The United States has a 35 percent corporate tax rate, but Ireland has a 12.5 percent rate, Israel a 10 percent rate with a two-year tax holiday, and China has a five-year tax holiday and then a half-normal rate for the next five years.[2] When such incentives are combined with a high-quality, low-cost supply of scientists and engineers (eleven qualified engineers can be hired in India for the cost of one in the United States),[3] U.S. firms find it extremely attractive to move much of their R&D offshore. When this work can be dual-use, it has benefits—(both militarily and economically)—for the sponsoring nation. This also can benefit U.S. security. Equipment that is designed and built offshore can be used in joint, multinational military operations if appropriate attention is paid to each country's security considerations and to appropriate controls on third-country transfers (of products or technologies); and if the United States still maintains a domestic capability in that technology area.

Historically, the industrial structure was thought of largely in terms of manufacturing jobs, for which labor location was the primary driver. Today a large share of the work is in the services area, and the labor force is only a "mouse click" away in India, China, Ireland, Australia, Singapore, or Brazil. Corporations around the world are taking advantage of the globalized workforce, which presents both an opportunity and a challenge for developing a nation's defense industrial strategy. The question is whether—from both military and economic perspectives—the nation gains more or runs higher risks by cooperating and sharing industrially in the national security area.

Because of the importance of advanced technology (in both commercial and military spheres), most nations are increasingly viewing research as well as science and engineering education as areas that are essential for their own economic and military development. But nations vary widely in terms of the share of government R&D spent on defense versus other objectives. For example, of total government R&D spending in 2003 to 2004, the United States spent 52 percent on defense, the United Kingdom 57 percent on defense, and France 43 percent on defense. Japan however, spent 47 percent on energy, and Germany spent 38 percent on industrial productivity. Similarly, there were wide differences in the share of government R&D spending devoted to mission-oriented efforts. The United States spent only 6 percent on non-mission-oriented R&D, but Germany and France devoted 28 percent, Japan 24 percent, and the United Kingdom 17 percent to non-mission-oriented generic R&D.[4]

A large share of the differences in approach here (between using the defense budget versus other government categories for R&D expenditures) can be attributed simply to the size of America's DoD budget. For example, as table 8.1 shows (for the so-called great powers of the twenty-first century), the U.S. defense budget swamps the budgets of Russia, China, and India, even when they are combined.

Europe has more than 300,000 defense-industry employees, but together its countries' defense budgets are still only half the size of the U.S. defense budget, and

Table 8.1
Military expenditures in India, China, Russia, and the United States, 2004

	Population (millions)	GDP per capita	Active military size	Estimated defense expenditure (billions of U.S. dollars)	Defense expenditures as percentage of GDP
India	1,110	$691	1,325,000	$19.6	2.6%
China	1,300	$1,462	2,255,000	$62.5	3.3%
Russia	144	$4,043	1,212,700	$25.1	4.3%
United States	294	$39,796	1,433,600	$465.0	4.0%

Note that by FY 2011 the total U.S. Defense Department appropriations (including the Supplemental for the Iraq and Afghanistan wars) was $725 billion.
Source: S. J. Flanagan and J. A. Schear, *Strategic Challenges: America's Global Security Agenda* (Washington, DC: Potomac Books, 2008), 188.

U.S. defense R&D investments are almost four times as large as Europe's. However, the United States and Europe have very different trends in basic research and in science and engineering education. There is a rapidly declining interest in the United States and a rapidly increasing interest elsewhere, which affects U.S. long-term national security and economic competitiveness and must be addressed as part of any twenty-first-century national strategy.

Although both U.S. future national security strategies and defense industrial strategies must be conceived of on a globalized basis, the discussion here—about Europe, Russia, China, Japan, India, Israel, Africa, and the Middle East—is regional and considers the approaches that have been taken to defense industrial strategies and the ways that these relate to the desired U.S. twenty-first-century defense industrial strategy.

Europe

Based on centuries of warfare, the historic tendency in Europe has been self-sufficiency in defense within each country. Even as the European Union moved aggressively into the development of a common market in the commercial world, Article 296 of the European Union charter allowed governments to avoid nonnational competitors in defense procurements.[5] As a result of this belief in the need for self-sufficiency, the small size of each country's domestic market, and its limited defense budget, each nation has moved simultaneously in two directions. They felt first, that they could afford to use only preferred sources (only one or two companies in any given sector of the defense industry) and second, that they needed to focus a major share of their national industries' and government's attention on foreign military sales to build up a sufficient scale to make their defense production efficient and to recover their R&D investments. Even though the nations each had essentially monopoly suppliers (or two oligopoly suppliers in some sectors), they still were driven to lower-cost designs to make the systems both affordable to their nation and attractive to foreign buyers. In France, for example, Dassault is essentially the only fighter aircraft firm, yet it produces a low-cost, high-performance military aircraft that is one of the world's most successful.[6] Dassault's organization has many desirable characteristics that are not found in U.S. aircraft companies—including small design teams, continuous emphasis on incremental improvement of existing designs, minimal paperwork, a maximum amount of subcontracting, continuous emphasis on low-cost designs for both domestic and international reasons, and a close working relationship with the government. Similar arrangements can be found in preferred sources in Germany, the United Kingdom, Italy, Sweden, and Norway. In each case of sole-source suppliers (at both the prime and the critical-subsystem levels), the government's involvement is limited mostly to the macro level, and it has a hands-off policy at the micro level (in the day-to-day operations of the firm). There also is considerable help from the federal government in terms of support for foreign military sales. In 2006, 75 percent of aerospace and defense sales in Europe were exports, and although significant sales were to other European countries, most, by far, were to foreign countries outside the European Union.[7]

By the end of the twentieth century, European nations recognized that they would not be able to play a role in the global security arena with their relatively small defense budgets (each of the big four of the European Union had a defense budget that was at least an order of magnitude less than that of the United States),[8] In addition, with the inefficiencies associated with each country's duplication of the other countries' preferred sources, they were not able to realize any benefits of competition or economies of scale. In 1996, France, Germany, Italy, and the United Kingdom created a four-nation armaments agency called the Organization for Joint Armaments Cooperation (OCCAR) to improve the efficiency of collaborative projects, and in 2004, the European Defense Agency (EDA) was created and open to all EU member states. Its charter was to develop defense capabilities in crisis management, promote European armaments cooperation, strengthen the European defense industrial and technological base, and create a competitive European defense equipment market.[9]

The competition referred to here is primarily competition with the U.S. defense industries in the worldwide arms market (not internal competition within the European community). As other EU organizations began funding Europe-wide efforts, they excluded U.S. participation. For example, the European Research Council stated that "funds are opened to any scientist (of any nationality) based in the E.U."

(by contrast, in the United States, the National Institutes of Health made 188 grants to researchers based outside of the U.S.—some for close to a million dollars).[10] As another example, the European Space Agency decided to build a competitor to the U.S. global positioning system (GPS), stating a concern that "the U.S. may turn the system off and Europe would be without the capability." However, most people believed that the $7 billion investment was being made primarily so that Europeans could have their own program. The United States has never shut down the GPS signal since it was open for civilian use in 1983, and all of the international banking system transactions are based on the atomic clock in the GPS system, so shutting it down would essentially turn off the international banking system. In addition, the worldwide commercial air transportation system is becoming increasingly dependent on GPS, so it is highly unlikely ever to be turned off. The U.S. military also has been willing to share its military GPS signals with its allies, and the U.S. government has been willing to provide presidential statements concerning the continuity of the system that would be a national commitment. Because the U.S. government is paying to supply the satellites, ground stations, and operation of the GPS system for all worldwide users to have available on a no-cost basis, it is hard to imagine how the European Space Agency thought that its competitive program (known as Galileo) would be paid for by commercial users. Nonetheless, it went ahead with Galileo.[11]

Europe also has gotten financial support from China, India, Brazil, and other countries that have sought to have an alternative to the U.S. system and also as a way to strengthen their ties to the EU. The question is whether it is in the interests of the United States and the European Union to compete in the national security arena—or to cooperate.

In the post–cold war era, as the U.S. defense industry went through dramatic consolidations, the European aerospace and defense industry consolidated into four major firms—BAE Systems (headquartered in London), Thales (headquartered in Paris), EADS (dual-headed in France and Germany), and Finmeccanica (headquartered in Rome). These four firms operate throughout the European Union: and, recognizing the R&D benefits and the large size of the U.S. market, they have made extensive acquisitions in the United States and operate essentially on a worldwide basis. By 2003, however, their average size was about half the average size of a large U.S. firm.[12] In many cases, they also moved from almost total government ownership to largely private ownership, but governments still had "golden shares" and a significant say in the operations of these large corporations. Increasingly, these companies began working together (and with other European companies). Additionally, as in the United States, European mergers continued in both horizontal and vertical directions throughout the EU and on a transatlantic basis. This has been particularly true further down the supply chain at the subcontract and critical-system lower tiers (for example, the merger of France's Snecma and SAGEM to create Safran).[13]

These collaborations continue to create even larger sole-source suppliers within the European context. The rationale (as stated by French Defense Minister Michele Alliot-Marie, in reaffirming her support for a merger of satellite makers EADS Astrium and Alcatel's Alenia)[14] was based on the argument that global competitiveness benefits would outweigh the disadvantages of having a single supplier. The world's global arms export sales are led by Russia and the United States, and this consolidation of the European defense industries has put them into the same category as the two leaders on exports. In that sense, the European consolidations can be said to have been a success.

One item of great concern in the competition for arms exports among the United States, Russia, and the European Union is the difficulty of reaching agreement on what items need to be controlled and to which countries. For example, the United States has refused to export critical military equipment to China but has imposed essentially no constraints on Russia. In June 1989, after the violence against demonstrators in Tiananmen Square, ministers attending the European Council's meeting in Madrid agreed to impose a number of EU-wide diplomatic and economic sanctions against China, including an arms embargo and interruption of military cooperation.[15] They were vague about what was banned and what punishments would be applied for violations. Many of the European countries fell back on a clause in the EU Code of Conduct that left the transfer of military equipment to the discretion of each member state. A large hole in the controls was opened by the fact that much equipment (such as electronics, helicopters, transport aircraft, and space systems) is dual-use. Because China's annual defense budget was estimated to be the world's third largest, it was an extremely attractive market. Many European nations balked at selling complete weapon systems, but the overall arms embargo was honored more in the breach than in the observance. Between 1993 and 2002, for example, France sold over $120 million in defense goods to China, and the United Kingdom sold China the Thales Skymaster (an airborne, early warning radar system) and the aeroengines for the Chinese JH-7 fighter bombers. Surrey Satellite Technology Limited (SSTL) cooperated in China's microsatellite development (a technology that the Chinese acknowledged was intended to be used in antisatellite weapons), German and French marine diesel engines power new Chinese submarine and surface combatants, Germany's MTU is coproducing marine diesels in China to power China's new SONG A-class submarines, and French-designed marine diesels power the new, very stealthy Chinese 054-class frigate.

The governments of the separate countries within Europe are in control of exports, and without clear EU guidelines and appropriate punishments, controls will be ineffective. Here, the growing power of the European Union (in a political and economic sense) must be exercised to achieve the appropriate, multinational controls (along with those of the United States and other countries) in the interests of worldwide peace and security.

As the European defense industries focus increasingly on the transatlantic relationship and as firms such as BAE Systems, EADS, Finmeccanica, and Thales make major investments in U.S.-based operations, the governments of their respective countries are still focused primarily on the export markets for their individual firms (and far less on a cooperative transatlantic industrial strategy). Because the U.S. firms are focused on the U.S. government market (with exports a secondary consideration) and the Defense Department's primary buying objective is technological superiority, the most distinguishing characteristic separating U.S. and European defense investments is research and development. In 2004, U.S. defense R&D spending totaled $67.5 billion (with most of this going to the large defense prime contractors), and the aggregate defense R&D spending for the EU big four was $11.9 billion.[16]

Such a discrepancy (unless the United States shared its technology with its European allies) would ensure that the U.S. will remain far ahead in all critical, future military technologies. This condition greatly limits U.S. military objectives when operating in a coalition environment and certainly limits the European military capability when the nations are operating alone or together. This does not reflect on the quality or quantity of European science and technology. In fact, the European Union and the United States have essentially the same number of people in these fields, and by 2007, the EU was outpublishing the U.S. in science research.[17] (The EU nations spend a significant amount on nonmilitary research and development.) What is lacking in the EU is an ecosystem where entrepreneurs thrive, and this is slowly being developed[18] (built around government, industry, university, and venture-capital partnerships). Additionally, since many new and creative ideas come from small firms or commercial firms and are applicable in defense, the European Union is going to have to break down the barriers to entry that exist for such firms in the defense area (where the large, preferred sources for defense supplies resist new entries and tend to resist changes in technology or equipment).

In the 1990s, the United States moved to a netcentric force and shifted from a primary focus on a central European scenario to a requirement for rapid mobility and response in expeditionary operations anywhere in the world. Europe was slow to pick up on these two shifts (resisting both the "revolution in military affairs" and the focus on expeditionary operations). As a result, European shortfalls began to appear (initially during the Kosovo war and subsequently in Afghanistan and Iraq) in smart munitions, all-weather and day-night capabilities, refueling, air transportation systems, and modern command and control systems that are integrated with intelligence, surveillance, and reconnaissance systems.[19]

Europe needs to determine whether it will continue to focus solely on internally integrating its defense structure or instead look to a new transatlantic compact. Within Europe, it has been moving toward the integration of new weapon systems across the continent. For example, the new European unmanned aircraft vehicle (known as Neuron) has many partners. A Dassault-IBM software tool is designing the vehicle; the overall program management and design is under Dassault; Thales is doing the primary and secondary data link; the French firm RRTM is doing the engine; Saab is a partner in program management and design; Volvo is doing the exhaust system; Alenia is a program management and design partner doing the electrical power system and the air data systems; Galileo Avionica is doing the electro-optical sensors and target classification algorithms; EADS CASA is doing the ground control station, the wings, and the data link management; the Swiss firm RUAG is doing the aerodynamic testing and the weapons loading and release system; and the Greek firm HAI is doing the rear fuselage, the exhaust pipe, the duct tail, and the integrated bench hardware.[20] As another example, the Norwegian F-310 frigate is being final-assembled in Spain, with a Spanish hull, an Italian gun, an electro-optic system from France, a navigation radar system from Norway, an antisubmarine warfare control system from Norway, an identification friend-or-foe system from the United Kingdom, an electronic countermeasure system from Denmark, and the AEGIS weapon system and vertical launch systems from the United States.

Both of these programs are examples of collaborative behavior (with the latter also representing a transatlantic collaboration). Although true collaboration can result in significant costs savings and performance improvements when the best-value system from each participating country is selected, actual collaborations tend to deviate widely from this ideal situation. They tend to be based much more on work-sharing arrangements that are based on political, equity, and bargaining criteria (such as *juste retour*, the principle that the proportion of contracts that firms in a country receive for a particular program should reflect the amount of funding that the country has invested in the program). This leads to inefficiencies in both development and production, since each partner nation tends to demand a share of the high technology involved in the projects and (often) a separate national final assembly line.

Critics also focus on the transaction costs associated with excessive bureaucracies, management by consensus, equal voting rights for all partner nations, and excessive delays in decision making that tend to be reflected in substantial time slippages and cost growths on the products. These inefficiencies are reinforced by the need to reach compromises in operational requirements and delivery schedules to satisfy the varying demands of each partner nation (including the varying budgetary environments).[21] An official UK National Audit Office study estimated that total development costs on collaborative projects were between 140 and 200 percent higher than for comparable national programs, depending on the number of partners.[22] A subsequent study on production costs found that collaboration programs achieved economies of scale in only half of those compared to national programs and that cooperation may cause an average delay of eleven months.[23]

This does not mean that nations should avoid collaboration, but improved methods of decision making and program management are required to realize the potential benefits. By 2007, there were still twenty naval shipbuilders and twenty-three separate yards in Europe,[24] demonstrating the enormous political resistance to moving toward increased efficiency and effectiveness. On the industrial side, this is far easier to work out. In the missile field, for example, the consortium of MBDA is made up of BAE Systems (37.5 percent), EADS (37.5 percent), and Finmecannica (25 percent). In the absence of political interference, these companies could work out the best-value solutions for maximum performance at lowest cost. But keeping politics out of these issues remains a challenge, and it is even more difficult to move to a transatlantic best-value operation—even though it is in the best interests of industry and the military.

Europe is not yet a single entity. Its major players—United Kingdom, France, Germany, and Italy—have historic differences (even among the broad similarities discussed above). The United States will have to address the future role of NATO and the relationship of both NATO and the United States to the European Union, and it will also have to evolve its bilateral relations (politically, militarily, and industrially).

United Kingdom

In December 2005, the UK Ministry of Defense (MOD) issued a far-reaching document titled "Defense Industrial Strategy."[25] In many ways, this was a shift from twentieth-century to twenty-first-century thinking. For example, it stated that the Joint Strike Fighter will be its last manned combat aircraft and that it would launch an unmanned combat air vehicle (a technology demonstrator) in 2006. The focus of the aerospace industry was to shift to through-life support of current systems via maintenance, upgrades, and integration of new weapons. Similarly, for land vehicles, it stated that "there is no absolute requirement to manufacture all of the constituent parts of an Advanced Fighting Vehicle in the U.K. An onshore capability to repair and overhaul AFVs is, however, required." The intent of this document was to shape the UK's defense industry and the government's relationship with U.S. and European companies—for decades to come. The strategy was aimed at keeping BAE Systems as the country's "national champion."[26] Arguing that foreign competition threatened the existence of BAE Systems, the company's chief executive, Mike Turner, stated that prior to the issuance of the "Defense Industrial Strategy," "there had to be a question mark about our future in the U.K." He further stated that the DIS established the company's "new position as partner of choice in land, air, and sea."[27] In essence, this guaranteed that a large share of the United Kingdom's total acquisition budget for weapon systems would go to BAE Systems.

This approach represented a dramatic shift in UK acquisition policy for weapon systems. For the prior twenty years, it had stressed the importance of international competition in achieving the desired benefits for the Ministry of Defense (maximum performance at lowest cost), but the new "Defense Industrial Strategy" instead focused on the importance of maintaining an indigenous defense industry—even if it cost significantly more.[28] BAE Systems was made the partner of choice for air, land, and sea weapons procurements,[29] and the DIS argued that the Ministry of Defense could achieve the same benefits from partnering as from competition—an assumption that flies in the face of historic data and that was questioned by many in the United Kingdom as well as in the United States. For example, Lord Levene of Bortsoken, the former defense procurement minister, told the Parliamentary Defense Committee that he had "a fundamental difficulty" with the notion that a partnering deal could be as effective as competition.[30] Nonetheless, the DIS guaranteed that a company would get a cradle-to-grave award for a weapon system—thus ensuring a sole-source business for R&D, production, and long-term support of that weapon system.

In its "Defense Industrial Strategy," the Ministry of Defense acknowledged that "U.K. companies still generally are seeking to secure a share of the larger and generally more profitable U.S. market. U.K. companies continue to invest in the USA, making a total of around 2 billion pounds of U.S. [corporate] acquisitions in 2004 alone, in almost forty separate acquisitions. British companies such as BAE Systems, Rolls-Royce, Smiths Group, VT, and QinetiQ have bought U.S. companies to overcome the high-entry barriers and secure progressive access to the U.S. market. . . . [This is] forcing difficult Boardroom decisions for U.K. companies on where to locate corporate capability and investment."[31] This was clearly the rationale for the shift from international competition in the United Kingdom to guaranteed domestic sole sources to ensure that firms would at least keep their headquarters in the UK even if a larger share of their business came from offshore. By claiming that partnering could achieve the same benefits as competition, the Ministry of Defense rationalized the decision to move to a national champion in most critical areas of defense equipment (a model that had been the norm in most other European countries but had been previously resisted in the United Kingdom).

Because UK investments in research and technology fell by 50 percent (in real terms) between 1991 and 2006[32] and because research received little attention in the "Defense Industrial Strategy," the following year the MOD released a document titled "Defense Technology Strategy." It stated the importance of research to the

MOD and acknowledged the shifts that had taken place in the way in which the MOD did its research. In 1991, the Defense Research Agency (DRA) absorbed the Royal Aircraft Establishment, the Admiralty Research Establishment, the Royal Armaments Research and Development Establishment, and the Royal Signals and Radar Establishment. In 1995, the Defense Evaluation and Research Agency (DERA) combined the DRA with the Defense Test and Evaluation Organization, the Chemical and Biological Defense Establishment, and the Center for Defense Analysis. Finally, in 2001, DERA was split into two organizations—QinetiQ (a private R&D organization) and the Defense Science and Technology Laboratory (DSTL), which remains a government research establishment but accounted for only slightly more than one-third of the staff of DERA at the time of its restructuring.[33] Essentially, these shifts privatized two-thirds of the previously nationalized Ministry of Defense research activities. Because QinetiQ was to be a preferred source for research in the United Kingdom, the hope was that privatization would encourage it to search for research efforts in other parts of the world as well. (QinetiQ has become aggressive in making acquisitions in the United States, since the U.S. research budget is more than an order of magnitude greater than the budget in the UK.)

The other aspect of UK defense research that differs significantly from the approach of many other countries is the fact that research funding in the United Kingdom is largely not based on a top-down establishment of priority mission needs but on a broad-based technology program that is administered by the UK Trade Department and that calls for bids (twice a year) for portions of the R&D dollars.[34] The other source of research funding is the UK's National Endowment for Science, Technology, and the Arts (NESTA), a $700 million endowment whose income is invested. However, NESTA's income is small compared to many programs in the United States, such as over $2 billion a year spent on the Small Business Innovation Research Program (SBIR) (almost one-half of which is the Defense Department's), $6.8 billion a year spent on the National Science Foundation program (NSF), and $3 billion a year spent on the Defense Advance Research Projects Agency. If the United Kingdom is to maintain its historic leadership position in many areas of research and technology, it needs to increase its investments significantly in this area and, most likely, restructure how it manages those resources to gain the maximum benefits for the Ministry of Defense in maintaining its technological strengths. A first step in this direction was made in 2008 when the MOD set up a Horizon Scanning Organization to search for worldwide technologies that it could apply (recognizing that technology is increasingly globalized and will not originate solely within the United Kingdom).

The final major change in UK defense business in the early twenty-first century has been a focus on private finance initiatives (PFIs). In the past, the United Kingdom used this approach for financing large civil capital projects (such as roads, prisons, and hospitals) in which contractors would build a facility and provide services with a guaranteed return over time. The Ministry of Defense has found that with a shortage of dollars and an increasing demand for military equipment, under PFI deals the state does not have to put up all the capital costs at the start and instead gets to spread its payments over the life of the contract (in much the same way as one might lease, rather than buy, a car). In early 2007, the MOD was committing tens of billions of future dollars to an aerial refueling contract for the private provision of airborne tankers, for refueling jet fighters and bombers on their way to the front line, and (on a separate contract) for private contractors taking over most of the training of its soldiers, airmen, and sailors (including the training of fighter pilots).[35] Although this looks attractive initially, as more and more of the business is done through the PFI route, a larger and larger share of the annual expenditures for defense equipment are precommitted, removing a great deal of the flexibility required for twenty-first-century security (given the greater uncertainty as to what the needs will be).

Perhaps the most difficult issue for the United Kingdom as it transforms its national security strategy and its corresponding defense industrial structure for twenty-first-century security operations is balancing west and east. It faces the dilemma of looking west (and maintaining its historic "special relationship" with the United States in uniquely sharing many areas of intelligence, technologies, and political/military relations) and of simultaneously looking east (and supporting the initiatives of the European Union, of which it is a critical member and which has declared itself to have an objective of strengthening the EU to more effectively compete with the United States). Both the United States and the United Kingdom will need to address these issues of technology-sharing and other activities in the coming years.[36]

France

Recognizing the dramatic changes in the twenty-first-century national security environment (and particularly the need for a more holistic perspective), in June 2008, the French president issued a "French White Paper on Defense and National Security."[37] It states that

The world has changed profoundly since the publication of the previous White Paper in 1994, in particular under the impact of globalization. The formidable acceleration of information exchanges, the increased trade in goods and services, as well as the rapid circulation of individuals have transformed our economic, social, and political environment in both positive and negative ways, as well as the paradigms of national and international security. The hierarchy of powers has changed and will continue to evolve. The world is not necessarily more dangerous, but it has become more unstable, more unforeseeable. New crises, in particular from the Middle East to Pakistan have come to the fore and have become more interconnected. Jihadism-inspired terrorism aims directly at France and Europe, which are in a situation of greater direct vulnerability. As we look to the 2025 horizon, France and Europe will fall within the range of ballistic missiles developed by new powers; new risks have appeared, be it intentional in the case of cyberattacks or nonintentional, such as health-related or environmental crises amplified by the deterioration of the biosphere. The White Paper aims at presenting the strategic appraisal for the next fifteen years to come, and consequences are drawn in order to draft together a new defense and security policy.

The White Paper goes on to state that France must "create an impetus and restructure the European Defense Industry":

Industry must be European. Individual European countries can no longer master every technology and capability at the national level. France must retain its areas of sovereignty, concentrated on the capability necessary for the maintenance of the strategic and political autonomy of the nation: nuclear deterrents; ballistic missiles; SSNs; and cybersecurity are among the priorities. As regards the other technologies and capabilities that it may wish to acquire, France believes that the European framework must be privileged: combat aircraft, drones, cruise missiles, satellites, electronic components, etc.; although procurement policy must include acquisitions on the world market.

Regarding electronic components in the defense sector, the report states that

The National and European Technological and Industrial Base for Defense Electronics is fragmented. In order to establish a more balanced relationship with countries which impose their own national regulations in this field (the United States and their ITAR Regulations). France will support a European approach conducive to the emergence of a European Industrial Base. The objective is to preclude situations of critical dependency which increasingly restrain our ability to export freely.

As in the past, France will continue to emphasize the importance of exports for its defense industry. Historically, it has incentivized this by paying 80 percent of the development costs of weapon systems and assuming that the remainder will be paid through exports of the products. This incentive also encourages the industry to make products that are competitive on the world market, and it discourages French firms from incorporating U.S. subsystems and components in their weapon systems—because of the ITAR restrictions that the United States places on third-party sales (thus, restricting the French from selling to many countries that the U.S. considers inappropriate). Although French firms are largely free to sell to any potential buyers, the United States, for example, objected when the French sold defense equipment to Iran because Iran was a known source of support of weapons to terrorists in the Middle East. The French also have been strong suppliers of submarines to both India and Pakistan.[38] And, in 2010, the French government began an aggressive sales effort of its Mistral power-projection warship to Russia; the first such major weapon system sale by a NATO country to Russia.[39] However, French policy is similar in this respect to that of the United Kingdom in stressing the importance of domestic production (even in a relatively small market) and in requiring a significant arms export market to produce military equipment efficiently (through achieving a reasonable volume). In 2007, President Nicholas Sarkozy stated that industrial policy would be a major goal of his administration and that the French defense industry has a significant say in the establishment of this policy.[40]

Finally, France recognizes the importance of research and development to its military posture and spends approximately 50 percent of its overall government R&D budget on defense. Additionally, it has recognized the synergistic benefits of clusters of research establishments,[41] and by 2007, it had established three research clusters (including an aerospace cluster in Provence that is led by Euro-copter, Thales, Alenia Space, Dassault Aviation, and the Defense Research Agency, Onera). It received over $685 million in public funds allocated for the cluster program. In addition, it is assumed that significant additional funds will be contributed by the corporations in each of these clusters.[42]

Germany

As many of its European military partners and many in the U.S. military have done, Germany resisted for some time the shift to netcentric warfare. However, its commitment to a joint EADS and Northrop Grumman team on the Euro-Hawk in 2007 was a signal that the Bundeswehr was transforming itself and acquiring capability for twenty-first-century netcentric operations. Germany has been second to the United States in the overall world market for R&D-intensive goods[43] and has always emphasized technological advancement. It is facing two important future concerns, however—its growing dependence on Russian fuel and its shrinking labor force. As many other nations are doing, Germany is reevaluating its defense and national security perspectives. Many of the comments made above about France (about taking a more holistic national security perspective and recognizing the importance of globalization in security) are equally applicable to Germany.

Historically, Germany has followed the European model of domestic preferred sources in each critical area of defense technology, and it has had strong representation in many areas. EADS (partially owned by Germany but registered in the Netherlands) is by far its largest; but Germany has many significant players in critical sectors (such as Zeiss in precision glass) and significant participants in many of the European consortia (such as in missiles). The trend in Germany is toward increased cooperative ventures—both within Europe and internationally.

Italy

Italy's Finmeccanica is the fourth-largest European defense firm (after BAE Systems, EADS, and Thales). The company has remade itself from a subsystem supplier to a prime contractor and systems integrator (with far greater emphasis on R&D and technology).[44] It has aggressively moved out from being an Italian European firm to a major international aerospace and defense firm. This has been done through major exports (for example, the C-27J tactical cargo aircraft was sold to the United States and Canada) and also through major acquisitions on a worldwide basis, so that it has a major presence in a wide variety of markets (for example, in 2008 it acquired DRS, in the U.S.). Also in the United States, Italy's Alenia North America operations have been making significant acquisitions in the large U.S. defense-industry market. Overall, the country is a strong international player in the aeronautics and space market, the helicopter market, and the defense electronics and systems markets, and it continues to be a world-class supplier at some of the lower tiers (such as composite space and aerostructures, sensors, and various defense electronics subsystems). Finally, Italy has greatly expanded its joint activities with other foreign companies and has been successful in this area as well. For example, MBDA, which is the number one missile company in Europe and the number two company in the world, combines BAE Systems, EADS, and Finmeccanica—all with equal governance rights. One highly publicized Finmeccanica success story was its winning (along with Lockheed Martin) of the U.S. presidential helicopter program (by its Agusta Westland subsidiary). Finmeccanica has put Italy on the world map of major defense-industry suppliers, and it continues to expand its worldwide presence.

Other European Countries

Other European defense firms—in Norway, Sweden, Denmark, Finland, the Netherlands, Belgium, Spain, Portugal, and Greece—play significant roles in Europe and elsewhere (both on teams and as direct suppliers). But the large firms—BAE Systems, EADS, Thales, Finmeccanica, Rolls-Royce, Safran, Dassault, Saab, DCN, and QinetiQ—are setting the direction both within Europe and globally for the European defense-industry sector.

Russia

The two most distinguishing characteristics of Russia in the early twenty-first century were its growing wealth and growing militancy. The booming Russian economy was due to the high prices paid for its oil, gas, and other export commodities (such as titanium sponge) as well as prudent fiscal policies instituted by the Russian government. There was a strong correlation between growth in the Russian gross domestic product (GDP) and the price of crude oil. From 1999 to 2005, the Russian GDP went from approximately $200 billion to $800 billion, and the price of crude oil went from $20 to $55 per barrel.[45] The Russian declared defense budget grew from $7 billion per year in the late 1990s to about $40 billion per year in 2008—with continued growth expected to over $58 billion by 2011.[46]

During the era of the former Soviet Union, the country's defense budget took one-third of GDP, but after the USSR collapsed, the budget similarly declined. Under President Putin, however, the wealth of the country grew, domestic spending on defense increased, and foreign military sales were reemphasized. In June 2006, Russia announced a new armaments program for 2007 through 2015, with a plan to spend $200 billion on rearmament of Russia's military[47] (which is only slightly less than China's long-term arms procurement plans). The message was that money was not a problem and that the oil and gas wealth would be spent in the defense sector, partly to stimulate the economy and partly to assert military strength. In 2007, the Kremlin stated a new industrial policy that combined state ownership with foreign technology and foreign investors—ito revive its heavy industry.[48] A major element of this strategy was the consolidation of various elements of key industries into single firms. This was a sharp deviation from the Soviet model, in which, for example, multiple firms would design different aircraft and compete for which one would go into production. In a sense, the Russians were moving from something closer to the American competitive model to the European sole-source model. In November 2006, the Russian United Aircraft Corporation (OAK is its Russian acronym) was formed. OAK integrated several Russian design and manufacturing companies in both the commercial and military areas (firms such as MiG, Tupolev, Irkut, Ilyushin, Sukhoi, and Yakovlev).[49] Other firms were consolidated in the missile area into the new Tactical Missile Corporation.[50] As Mikhail Pogosyan, Sukhoi's director general and OAK's first vice president stated, "We need to unite all our resources in order to succeed on the world market." The intent was to use foreign military sales as a stimulant for the defense sector and a mechanism for achieving greater efficiency through increased volume. Such foreign sales would have political implications as well. OAK was 90 percent owned by the state, and the other large defense firms were essentially under the control of the Russian government, even though there were minority outside owners (in the case of MiG, for example, there was a partnership with EADS in which MiG performed A-320 cargo conversions).

Exports were a major focus of these new consolidated Russian defense firms. For example, in 2006, only 10 percent of MiG's work was for the Russian air force (out of $2.5 billion of orders). MiG was exporting MiG-29s to Algeria and MiG-33s to India and upgrading MiG-29s for Slovakia—to bring Slovakia's fleet up to NATO standards.)[51]

Upgrading to NATO standards is important if Moscow plans on cooperating with NATO on common security concerns, including counterterrorism, weapons of mass destruction counterproliferation, missile defense, and aerospace management.[52] Because Russia and China represent future major military powers that can either aid or deter international efforts at world peace, all nations (especially the

United States) need to achieve a cooperative partnership with Russia in these areas. In 2010, France moved in this direction (as noted above) when it negotiated to supply a major naval ship (the Mistral) to Russia with follow-ons to be built in Russia. (and with the acknowledged Russian objective of technology transfer in the shipboard electronics area).

During the Soviet era, Moscow emphasized the importance of low-cost weapon systems both for domestic consumption and for exports, and it understood that incentives were required (particularly in a communist environment) to produce new innovation and lower costs. Thus, it offered monetary awards (often as much as $10,000 per year for three years) based on the savings that could be realized. This encouraged innovation for the sake of cost reductions[53] and achieved high performance at low cost through design approaches. For example, one 1976 study comparing U.S. and Soviet jet engines of similar performance found that the Soviet engines were between one-third and one-half the cost of comparable U.S. engines, even if the Soviet engines were to be built by U.S. personnel in U.S. factories with U.S. material.[54] The reasons for the far lower costs of the Soviet engines were design differences, maintenance philosophy differences, and specification differences. An example of a high-performance, low-cost system design is the Soviet MiG-25 aircraft:

It does not require advanced electronics, exotic materials, precise manufacturing techniques, or complex structures. Similarly, it used stainless steel and aluminum as the primary aircraft materials, instead of synthetic materials as used by the U.S. Rivet heads were left un-ground (except in aero-dynamically critical areas), and welding was said to be crude, but adequate. Larger engines were used to overcome the drag penalties. The radar, though based on technology that is out of date by American standards, is one of the most powerful ever seen in an aircraft, and therefore less vulnerable to jamming. The overall MiG-25 has been described by American aerospace analysts as "unsurpassed in the ease of maintenance and servicing," "a masterpiece of standardization," "one of the most cost-effective combat investments in history."[55]

These design practices are engrained into the culture of the Soviet system and carry over into Russia's twenty-first-century manufacturing processes, making them extremely attractive for export markets as well as for high volumes of domestic procurement. (For example, the next-generation stealthy Sukhoi T-50—now being prototype tested—is claimed by Prime Minister Vladimir Putin to sell for one-third that of the United States' F-22 and to be available on the world market.[56] Russia exports arms to over seventy countries[57] (including China, Iran, Venezuela, India, Algeria, the United Arab Emirates, Argentina, Jordan, Yemen, and Malaysia), and in 2008, it had worldwide sales of over $8 billion[58] (second only to the United States in foreign military sales). These exports have increased rapidly in the early twenty-first century. In May 2009, the Russian arms export monopoly (Rosoboronexport) stated that its arms export portfolio of orders was $35 billion, and Alexander Fomin (first deputy director of the Federal Service for Military Cooperation) said that the Russian defense industry had effectively "reached its ceiling" and could not take on any more contracts.[59]

Russia's defense exports include fighter and bomber aircraft, antisubmarine aircraft, diesel submarines, destroyers, naval air defense systems, short-range surface-to-air missile systems, antisubmarine and antiship missiles, military and civilian helicopters, air defense systems, and even production equipment (such as the equipment to produce AK-101 and AK-104 Kalashnikov guns in Venezuela). When Russia loaned Venezuela $1 billion for the purchase of Russian arms[60] to produce guns and to buy fighter jets, helicopters, armored personnel vehicles, and other equipment and when Russian bombers and warships go to Venezuela for training and joint exercises, there are significant political consequences for the United States (especially given the belligerent and anti-U.S. attitude of Venezuela's president, Hugo Chávez). Considerable concerns about regional stability are also raised in the United States and in countries around the world when Russia announced a $1 billion arms deal with Indonesia[61] or makes large arms sales to Algeria, Iran, or China (one of Russia's biggest markets). As Costa Rica's president, Oscar Arias (a Nobel Peace Prize winner), stated in 2006 about Russian arms going to Venezuela, "A new arms race has started in Latin America." Using its oil money, Venezuela has spent billions of dollars on jet fighters, frigates, submarines, and tanks, and President Chávez has stated that this equipment is needed to protect his population from a U.S. invasion of his country.[62] Other countries in South America have felt a need to counter this multi-billion-dollar buildup in Venezuela. Argentina, for example, began negotiations with Russia for arms, and Russia offered to trade for Argentine beef (of which Russia is the largest importer) in exchange for military helicopters and armor-plated patrol boats.[63]

Perhaps most surprising is that the Russian Deputy Defense Minister (responsible for arms procurement) Vladimir Popovkin announced (in 2010) that Russia intends to "shop in the West" for advanced weapons (including: unmanned aerial vehicles, etc.)—the French Mistral being the first.[64] He had previously (in 2008) announced that Russia was widely using foreign electronic components to make military satellites; and (in 2010) he announced that Russia was assembling, under license from Thales, French night-vision TV cameras for its tanks.[65]

However, one area in which the Russians have stayed ahead of the West is in cost-effective helicopters. And, as part of its effort to equip the militaries of Afghanistan, Iraq, and Pakistan, the United States has been buying Russian helicopters for them (for example, over $800 million was spent—by 2010—on Mi-17s).[66]

Russia's defense industry has come back from its post–cold war doldrums. It is building state-of-the-art military equipment for its over 1 million-member standing army and 20 million reservists. As it proved when going into the country of Georgia in 2008, it is willing to exercise its military strength and it also recognizes the importance of modern technology (it successfully used cyberwarfare before rolling its tanks into Georgia). Additionally, Russia is modernizing its intercontinental ballistic missile fleet to, as President Putin stated, make missile defense systems "powerless,"[67] and it is increasingly emphasizing its nuclear forces[68] (somewhat as President Eisenhower did in the United States when U.S. forces were believed to be tactically insufficient to counter Soviet forces). Finally, Russia has announced its military buildup intent with its seven-year rearmaments plan and with its plans for a Pacific fleet that will complement its more traditional, westward-looking military.

China

In the post–cold war period, there was a dramatic shift in the focus of world security from Europe to Asia. Some of this was based on the fear that the United States might be drawn in to defend Taiwan against mainland China's irredentist claims over Taiwan. There also was the possibility of a renewed attack by North Korea on South Korea (again drawing U.S. forces immediately into the conflict). China's growing economic and military strength as a potential future peer competitor—its fast rate of economic growth, its huge population, and its likelihood of becoming one of the twenty-first century's great powers—has been of increasing concern. For many, this was the rationale (prior to the terrorist attacks of September 11, 2001) for maintaining a strong U.S. national security posture. For others (this author included), the concern was that such actions would indirectly focus on making China an enemy rather than on creating a needed partnership with China (as well as Russia, Europe, and others) in addressing the mutual requirements for nonproliferation, control of terrorism, addressing energy needs, worldwide pollution, and health. The fact that China is a future economic rival need not lead to military conflict—but requires positive action on the part of the United States and others to ensure this peaceful outcome.

China has clear competitive advantages:[69]

• A very high savings and investment rate (about 40 percent) compared with the rest of the world (which is about 20-plus percent);

• Skill at tapping into global knowledge, accessing the Chinese diaspora, and allowing significant foreign investment and facilities within China;

• A critical mass in R&D that is increasingly deployed in a focused effort to increase its competitiveness and to make it dual-use, so that it is of value for both economic competitiveness and national security;

• A large and growing manufacturing base, advanced export-oriented logistics, and few export restrictions (in contrast to the U.S. export controls);

• Continuing strong investments in education and training to build a large and world-class Chinese scientific and technical workforce, focusing on R&D;

• A large supply of excess labor from the agricultural sector (some 150 to 200 million people) that continues to keep down labor costs;

• A government that has a strong sense of national purpose and that provides guidance and focus (and far less political interference) for the direction and funding of critical technologies.

China's long-term economic and security plans emphasize science and technology. The culture of the nation has always had a long-term focus—decades or even centuries (versus Wall Street's focus on quarterly earnings). The country's emphasis on science and technology is consistent with this long-term focus. By 2007, China had overtaken the United States as the world's largest exporter of information-technology products, and the United States was becoming a net importer of these products.[70] In 2006, the United States placed near the bottom of twenty nations in comparative testing in advanced math and physics, and ranked twentieth among all nations in the proportion of its twenty-four-year-olds with degrees in science and engineering. By contrast, it was estimated that within a few years, approximately 90 percent of all scientists and engineers in the world will live in Asia.[71] A study by Georgia Tech looked at the "high-tech indicators of technology-based competitiveness." It used four leading indicators that point toward future competitiveness prospects—national orientation, socioeconomic infrastructure, technological infrastructure, and productive capacity—and found that from 1996 to 2007 China grew faster than the United States by a factor of almost four to one and replaced the U.S. at the top of this technology standing (with Germany and Japan third and fourth).[72] Policies put in place by the Chinese government have resulted in this dramatic rise (in a little over a decade). In 1996, China was number fourteen in world investments in science, but by 2007, it was number two in the world.[73]

As the (U.S.) President's Council of Advisors on Science and Technology observed,[74] "China's overall Science and Technology Ecosystem is developing rapidly. This is all part of an explicit policy (as found in the strategy document of the July 2005 Chinese State Council) which stated 'basic research has become part of the international competition of overall national strength.'"[75] On February 9, 2006, China's cabinet restated the need for R&D spending to rise dramatically and listed sixteen key technologies that would receive more support from government and private industry, including computer software, telecommunications, nuclear energy, and a military-managed space program.[76]

This is all being driven on a top-down basis. At a 2006 national conference on science and technology, President Hu Jintao outlined the major strategic tasks for building an innovation-oriented country and stated that "innovation is the core of the nation's competitiveness and the strategic motive of China's future science and technology development. The practice of the world's scientific and technological development shows that only with strong capacity of innovation can a country win the initiative in international competition."[77]

This was followed (in October 2007) by the rollout of the results of a high-level workshop, organized by the Chinese Academy of Sciences, of a Science and Technology Roadmap for Priority Areas to 2050;[78] stressing the significance of research in China's future.

A report from the U.S. Office of Naval Research examined the Chinese investments in science and technology and noted the differences between Chinese investments and U.S. investments: "China emphasizes the hard sciences that underpin Defense and commercial needs. The United States emphasizes research areas focused on medical, psychological, and social problems."[79] In 2005, for example, China produced one hundred articles on missiles, and the United States produced twenty-four. China also produced a hundred articles on intrusion detection, and the United Stated produced twenty-three. (The ratios on medical research and microbiology are largely reversed, with the United States dominating.) The report further noted that "China's output of research articles has expanded dramatically in such critical future military technologies as nanotechnology and energetic materials, and it is among the leaders in these areas." Premier Wen Jiabao's 2007 annual report to the nation's People's Congress noted the country's determination to modernize its armed forces, stating that "We will intensify Defense-related research and efforts to advance weaponry and equipment."[80]

In addition, China has been carefully following the U.S. emphasis on netcentric warfare, and understand the importance of information flow for advanced command, control, communication, computing, intelligence, surveillance, and reconnaissance (C4ISR) and are hard at work on developing what they term an "integrated information electronic warfare" capability.[81]

In addition to large and increasing investments in science and technology, China is also emphasizing the importance of the scientific workforce. In China, 52 percent of all college degrees are awarded in science and technology. Between 1999 and 2003, the number of engineering graduates doubled in China but remained stagnant in the United States (in some cases, such as computer science and computer engineering,[82] the numbers of U.S. science graduates declined significantly).[83] China also sponsors students to study in the United States and other countries for their advanced degrees, but whereas most of these students used to stay in the United States (to take advantage of research and economic opportunities), China has been luring scientists home—with large salaries, the opportunity to build significant laboratories, and a great deal of freedom in the work that they do.[84] By 2008, more than 275,000 scientists had gone back to China. Known as "sea turtles," they returned with doctorates in science or engineering. At the Chinese Academy of Sciences—the government-affiliated research institute—81 percent of the members are returnees.

Multinational firms are now investing heavily in China, attracted by the country's large investments in R&D, its focus on developing a science and technology workforce, its enormous domestic market, and its ability to capture an increasing share of the world's export market. Many have opened research centers in Beijing and Shanghai, and others are setting up production operations linked to research centers (betting that future innovations and low-cost exports will come from China).[85] In 2007, Intel Corporation (the world's largest semiconductor maker), proposed and received approval for a $2.5 billion chip plant in China that will serve the booming Chinese demand for chips used in personal computers and mobile phones, as well as for possible exports of the next-generation, 25-nanometer chip technology (these chips are so small that 30 million of them can fit on the head of a pin).

China has also stated a desire to enter the aircraft business. Boeing estimates that over the next two decades, China will spend about $280 billion on aircraft and will become the world's second-largest plane market (after the United States). In 2005, Boeing set up an aircraft maintenance repair and overhaul base in Shanghai (the first such foreign-controlled facility in China). Its initial investment was over $100 million, and it holds a 50 percent stake (along with Shanghai Airlines and the Shanghai Airport Authority).[86] In response, Airbus, the other major supplier of large commercial aircraft, stated that it would build an assembly plant in Tianjin, and China announced a $10 billion deal to buy 150 Airbus A-320s. Then Boeing responded that it is buying an increasing number of parts from China for export to assembly plants in the United States, that it already had $600 million in supply contracts in China, and that major Chinese-made parts could now be found in roughly 34 percent of the twelve thousand Boeing planes in service around the world.

China, however, is eager to build its own aircraft industry and particularly to build large aircraft.[87] Besides the large aircraft facilities of both Boeing and Airbus, China's state-owned company, China Aviation Industry Corporation, is also entering the commercial aircraft market with a smaller plane to handle shorter routes. Currently, this company is mainly a defense contractor.[88]

Historically, the Chinese have depended on Russia for their military aircraft. They first agreed to buy the Russian Flanker (military aircraft) in 1991 and followed that with a licensed production contract in 1996. This provided a vehicle for Chinese industry to gain knowledge of fourth-generation fighter manufacturing. However, the Chinese J-11A fighter still uses Russian engines, radar, and weaponry.

Chinese defense plants are owned and operated by the People's Liberation Army (PLA), and although the plants' focus was initially on quantity of weapons, it is increasingly on the quality of the systems they build.[89] Along with developing key elements for fighter aircraft, these plants also build satellite-guided and radar-guided precision weapon systems and unmanned platforms. They are moving away from a heavy dependence on Russian systems, and their FC-1 light fighter is a joint development between China and Pakistan. In key areas of technology, they are using the incentive of competition between two Chinese firms (for example, the Luoyang laser-guided precision bombs are competing with the rival China Aerospace and Technology Corporation's satellite-guided weapons). Because of China's interests in protecting the sea lanes and the water area on the country's eastern shore, it is also focused on building submarines and ships.

Finally, because China recognizes the importance of space for both future commercial and military applications, it has been putting men in space, building independent earth observation and navigation systems, and exploring military applications. In response to the 1989 massacre in Tiananmen Square and U.S. concerns about losing its dominance in space, the United States imposed space-related export controls on China. As Luo Ge, the number two official of the Chinese National Space Administration, stated, "With the exception of the U.S., we are having extensive cooperation with the rest of the world in space."[90] He went on to describe joint satellite-development projects with the European Space Agency and with Brazil. In January 2007, China's attack on one of its own satellites (a five-foot square weather satellite) with a kinetic kill vehicle launched by a small ballistic missile had significant military potential.[91] Although not a technologically challenging incident (a nonmaneuvering satellite's path is predictable), it nonetheless was considered highly provocative and demonstrated Chinese military technological competence.

In recent years, China has made a policy decision to make its defense industry as dual-use as possible. This has allowed its defense investments to benefit the national economy (for commercial high-tech domestic goods and exports), which in turn has lowered costs for their defense goods (from the higher volume of the dual-use factories). This book has argued that U.S. policy should move toward civil and military industrial integration.

In 2004, the RAND Corporation released a 332-page report entitled *A New Direction for China's Defense Industry*[92] that suggested that parts of China's defense industry may be more advanced than had previously been assumed. The report noted that China's missile sector is doing well and that navy shipbuilding has benefited from the rapid growth in commercial sectors (since China is the world's third-largest commercial shipbuilder). The country also has produced turbo-fan fighters and has successfully formed a "digital triangle"—among booming commercial information technology companies, state R&D institutes, and the military's defense plants. Finally, the report found that China is no longer producing knock-offs of Soviet weapons that were designed in the 1950s but are becoming competitive on a global basis. The proliferation of its more capable weapon systems (including in the "grayer" market areas, such as Southeast Asia and Latin America) could significantly affect future U.S. military planning and U.S. foreign military sales potential.

Underlying this significant buildup in the Chinese defense industry is a dramatic increase in the Chinese defense budget. Declared defense expenditures grew from $15.21 billion in 2000 to $44.94 billion in 2007.[93] According to the Pentagon's estimates, however, that declared total represents only about a third of the actual military spending since it excludes purchases of foreign equipment, R&D investments, and industrial capital equipment.[94] Thus, the actual defense spending for China in 2007 was around $135 billion (still well below that of the United States but significantly higher than its potential regional adversaries, including Japan, India, and even Russia). If China continues this double-digit annual growth in its defense budget, it will be spending $400 billion a year by 2020 (double Europe's defense spending and four times as much as Russia).[95]

China is building up its military strength—as strong economic powers do—and its stated focus is on deterring its neighbors (Japan, Russia, and India) and the United States (because of its strong role in the Pacific). Even in a future world in which Washington and Beijing have an excellent partnership in addressing problems of world peace, energy, environment, and terrorism, the Chinese would continue to build up their military capability—consistent with the country's role as a global economic power in the twenty-first century.

The Chinese have a plan, described in their Defense White Paper of December 2004, to bring their military out of its perceived backwardness. The plan describes the modernization trajectory for the army in terms of a "revolution in military affairs with Chinese characteristics."[96] This involves "informationalization"—what in the United States is called command, control, communications, computers, intelligence, surveillance, and reconnaissance (C4ISR)—and emphasizes satellite and airborne sensors, unmanned aerial vehicles, information warfare, and strategic nuclear deterrence (by maintaining a force of ICBMs and SLBMs). Chinese officials continue to assure the United States that China will adhere to a no-first-use policy for nuclear weapons. Based on China's study of U.S. military doctrine and weapons acquisition, it is developing the capability, in many cases, to counter U.S. strength by exploiting vulnerabilities, such as using counterspace, countercarrier, counterair, and information warfare.[97] This does not mean that China is preparing for war with the United States, but since the literature produced during the George W. Bush administration seemed to focus the U.S. defense posture against China as a peer competitor, the Chinese are forced to take preventive measures—which then force the United States to take counter-countermeasures. At both political and military-to-military levels, it is desirable for the United

States to work at stabilizing the region and at avoiding an arms race or a new cold war in the twenty-first century.[98]

The Chinese have focused on countering adversaries' information systems and taking advantage of information warfare. They have run extensive exercises in this area (according to the Chinese News Agency, one exercise involved more than eight thousand personnel, including land, air, electronic warfare troops, artillery troops, and special operations troops). And the "twelve-day exercise was designed to root out any problems that exist among Chinese troops by exposing them to the most difficult electromagnetic environment." In another such exercise, Zeng Weihua, the director, stated, "The application of information technology is the main purpose of this drill. We want the troops participating in the drill to know that defeat in information techniques means defeat in actual combat. . . . [For Zeng, the] electromagnetic environment [was the] fifth dimension of warfare," and he stated that it was an integral element in modern military operations.[99]

China also has been moving away from its military isolation of the Mao years. It now participates in a number of multilateral military exercises with fellow countries of the Shanghai Cooperation Organization (a regional security organization established in June 2001 and consisting of China, Iran, Kazakhstan, Kyrgyzstan, Russia, Tajikistan, and Uzbekistan), and countries such as Pakistan, India, Belarus, and the United States have been seeking observer status.[100]

One area of great concern to American security is Chinese military equipment exports, particularly nuclear and tactical weapons. China has always been an export-oriented country, and in recent years, it has shifted dramatically from low-cost toys to the high-tech field. For example, about 80 percent of the world's laptop and desktop computers are assembled in China—often based on Taiwanese original designs.[101] Although China professes to have an export-control regime on weapons, U.S. policymakers have questioned the implementation of these controls.[102] It is known, for example, that China cooperated with A. Q. Khan (of Pakistan) in the early 1980s to further its own nuclear weapons program. China sold Khan a new nuclear bomb design in return for his centrifuge technology. Khan later sold his blueprints to Libya (and the same bomb design might have been sold to North Korea and Iran).

There is an inherent conflict within China between army-controlled defense plants (which desire extra money from export sales) and the central government's export-control regime.[103] For example, in 2007, when the Chinese arms company Xinshidai ("new era") displayed its latest weapons at the International Defense Exposition Arms Show in Abu Dhabi, it clearly was seeking to establish its place in the world's lucrative arms market, particularly its presence in the Middle Eastern market (which has ties to Iran). But the possibility exists that weapons sold in the Middle East could bleed into Iraq, especially given Xinshidai's prior record of flaunting international regulations on arms trafficking.[104] In the "gray areas" beyond the Middle East, Chinese military exports can add to instabilities in regions of interest to the Chinese. For example, China has become increasingly active in Africa, and its sale of twelve military aircraft to the repressive government of Zimbabwe (in 2005 and 2006) was of significant concern to U.S. interests in terms of worldwide stability.[105]

China is heavily dependent on oil, but as President Dou Xiaping once stated, "The Middle East has oil, and China has rare earth." China is increasingly establishing strategic alliances with Iran, Africa,[106] and other countries that have oil and would like to have arms and rare-earth materials (for their batteries and other requirements).

In future years, China will have the economic and military power to be either a cause for future conflicts or a partner with the United States, Russia, Europe, and others in maintaining a peaceful balance globally in the twenty-first century. Common multilateral concerns include antiterrorism, antipiracy, next-generation energy sources, environmental controls, and pressures that can be brought to bear against rogue nations. The United States and other countries need to work closely with the Chinese to help them arrive at the desired solution. In the short term, there will be issues over irredentist claims on Taiwan and some islands in conflict with Japan. But the long-term direction that China takes in the military and political arenas must be the focus of U.S. actions in the coming years.

Other Countries: Japan, India, Israel, Australia, the Middle East, and Africa

Although the major powers, in the military sphere, in the early twenty-first century will be the United States, Europe, Russia, and China, there are other significant players in the defense industry.

Japan

From the end of World War II through the 1980s, Japan essentially depended on the U.S. guarantee of defense for its strategic posture and therefore spent less than 1 percent of the Japanese gross national product on defense. But several events have led Japan to begin reassessing its need to develop further its own defense industry—growing concerns about the Chinese military buildup, North Korea's test launch of a missile that flew over Japan on October 9, 2006, the nuclear potential of North Korea, and the reliability of the U.S. security guarantees. When determining a direction for this move, the country chose the Japanese model that had been successful in the civilian sector—using government-based, informal, indicative planning. Estimates of likely demand were developed, and the work was allocated among a few large, private-sector companies—using a dual-use model. For example, in 2005,

Mitsubishi Heavy Industries (the largest Japanese defense firm) had over $2 billion in defense revenue, but each of the leading firms gained a very small percentage of their total business revenue from defense—Mitsubishi Heavy Industries, 9 percent; Kawasaki Heavy Industries, 10 percent; Mitsubishi Electric, 3 percent; and Capital EC, 2 percent.[107] Initially, much of Japan's military R&D came from the United States, but as it developed an indigenous capability through strong internal science and technology programs, it began to play an equal role in this field. For example, because of Japan's concerns about missile defense against China and North Korea, by 2000 the country was actively involved with the United States on antimissile defense technology work. The Japanese constitution limits the country's military activities to self-defense, and yet growing concerns—such as protection of sea lanes, the threat of nuclear attack, proliferation from China (including to nonstate actors), missile and nuclear threats from North Korea, and the weakening U.S. emphasis on nuclear forces (which were providing a nuclear umbrella for Japan)[108]—have caused Japan to reassess its national security posture.

In 2006, it upgraded its Defense Agency to a full-fledged ministry. As the chief cabinet secretary, Shinzo Abe, stated, "It is necessary and natural to give the Defense Agency ministry status in line with other countries, and to respond appropriately to any situation."[109] Japan also continued to upgrade its military, which are called the self-defense forces, but these activities were limited primarily to noncombat missions (because Japan's constitution renounced the use of arms to settle international disputes). Nonetheless, Japan was moving to a balance that would allow it to exist securely without being either too dependent on the United States or too vulnerable to threats from China.[110]

Its industrial model was clearly dual-use. To quote Mr. Abi from Mitsubishi Electric, "There is no 'civilian' or 'military' technology. All high-technologies are 'dual-use' technologies,"[111] and this dual-use approach applies to heavy industries as well as other areas in which Japan has been a leader in commercial systems but that are applicable to the military as well. For example, the United States needed Japanese technologies such as liquid crystal displays, fine ceramics, composite materials, voice recognition techniques, robots, computer-aided design, artificial intelligence, and supercomputers—all of which were developed by various Japanese corporations and fit into the category of dual-use technologies.[112]

Japan was a technological powerhouse in the late twentieth and early twenty-first centuries, and in 1995, it created a new energy and industrial technology development organization and a "Science and Technology Basic Law of 1995"—providing a framework to improve economic development, social welfare, and environmental sustainability. In 2001, Japan established the Council for Science and Technology Policy (CSTP), which is chaired by the prime minister and includes six cabinet ministers, five academics, and two industry representatives who are charged with developing a grand design for Japanese science and technology (including the country's five-year "S&T Basic Plan"). The council set aside $212 billion for the first of the five-year plans and continued to increase these budgets. The R& D budget of the well-thought-out plan focused on five key areas—nanotechnology and materials, information technology, life sciences, the environment, and aerospace technology. Other areas of a somewhat lesser research focus included fuel cells, robotics, and computing research.[113] Their objective was to link universities as collaborators with industry, and government. Since Japan has excellent universities and since 66 percent of their graduates are in the field of science and technology, they will remain a major technology leader for many years. For example, the Japanese earth simulator, a supercomputer designed for predicting the behavior of the earth and its atmosphere, was ranked as the fastest in the world from June 2002 to November 2004, and in a ranking based on the number of U.S. patents granted, five of the top ten companies are Japanese.[114]

Increasingly, the Japanese defense industry has been pressing to be allowed to export more of its equipment to keep its competitive advantage and to receive the income from the exports. For example, Japan's Keidanren (its defense-industry association) has sought a revision of three nonexport rules for military technologies.[115] Much of this is significantly dual-use and therefore ambiguous as to its end-use (even though it is clearly applicable to military use and therefore subject to export controls). There have been a few examples of improper exporting (through third countries) of some dual-use equipment, and this area is going to require significant attention on a multinational basis in the future. In the same way, as Japan plays a significant role in composite-based aerostructures (as the aerospace industry moves away from aluminum structures), this too becomes an important area of dual-use concerns. The three largest Japanese manufacturers (Mitsubishi, Kawasaki, and Fuji) account for 35 percent[116] of the 787 Boeing aircraft production, and they focus on key, large-scale composite components (such as the wing box, the outer wing, and fuselage sections). Because much of this dual-use technology is equally applicable to military aircraft, concerns about export controls are again raised.

The big question about Japan is whether its perception of the need to develop its own nuclear capability (as a deterrent to the nuclear threats of China and North Korea) will force it in that direction. It is estimated that the Japanese could build a prototype nuclear weapon in three to five years, at a cost of approximately $1.7 to 2.5 billion.[117] Even though deterrence is a defensive move, it has credibility only if the opposition believes that it would be used. Thus, it will be resisted by the passivistic Japanese population; and, based on Japan's constitution, it is officially banned. The United States needs to maintain the credibility of its nuclear umbrella over Japan for the future—and this credibility was losing its strength by 2008, when a series of events (the shipment of some nuclear material inadvertently to China and the unknown presence of two nuclear weapons flying across the United States on an air force plane) caused a reassessment of the importance of nuclear deterrence, not only to U.S. national security strategy but also (in terms of the nuclear umbrella) to our allies (particularly Japan and South Korea).[118] In the same way, there is concern about whether Japan will have to build a blue-water navy to ensure that its sea lanes can remain open as China greatly increases its investment in its blue-water navy.

India

India's economy is booming, and in spite of a relatively small investment in defense (approximately $22 billion in 2006), a worldwide market survey in 2005 stated that "The Indian Aerospace and Defense Industry is emerging as a key participant in the Asia-Pacific Aerospace and Defense market."[119] India possesses a major set of advantages, including a critical mass of capable, highly trained scientists and engineers (most notably in the chemical and software fields); world-class institutions (such as the Indian Institutes of Technology and the Indian Institutes of Management); a vibrant entrepreneurial class (which draw on more than 200 national laboratories and research institutes, 1,300 industrial R&D units, and over 300 universities with a strong student pipeline); an Indian diaspora that maintains strong linkages back to the home market from overseas; and a large English-speaking population—which make it an attractive place for multinational corporations to conduct R&D. India has tremendous cost advantages in human capital (eleven high-quality engineers for the cost of one comparable U.S. engineer) and relatively deep financial markets (better than many other developing countries).[120] These advantages have led firms such as Microsoft, Qualcomm, SAP, Google, General Electric, and IBM to set up R&D centers in India. For example, in 2007, IBM announced a $6 billion investment in R&D in India.[121]

These industry linkages between the United States and India are being complimented by government-to-government linkages. For example, in 2005, a strategic partnership was established through a bilateral agreement that discussed cooperation in civilian uses of dual-use technologies; a ten-year framework for U.S.-India defense relationships (including a joint defense procurement and production group); a binational science and technology endowment fund; a joint-knowledge initiative on agriculture (with a $100 million fund for research); a bilateral energy dialog (focused on civil nuclear energy cooperation); and a U.S.-India working group on civil space cooperation.[122]

On the defense-industry side, India has its own structure. Hindustan Aeronautics is the largest Indian defense firm and had over $1 billion in defense revenues in 2005 and over 90 percent of its total revenue coming from the defense area. However, the major share of India's defense equipment has been imported—first from Russia and more recently from Israel (including joint developments with Israel, such as on the advanced Barak-2 missile). By 2006, India had emerged as one of the largest buyers of Israel military equipment.[123] This includes a $1.1 billion contract to IAI for the Indian air force's Phalcon airborne early warning and control system, as well as high- and medium-altitude unmanned aerial vehicles from IAI. Israel is also upgrading the Indian air force's Russian MiG-21, MiG-27, and MiG-29 aircraft, and supplying much other equipment. India is simultaneously developing considerable linkages of cross-border investments and joint ventures with China (including some in which Singapore is acting as a middleman on economic ventures between India and China).[124]

With India's strong emphasis on knowledge-based industries (such as information technology and pharmaceuticals) and its strong, growing economy, the country can become a major player in establishing multinational partnerships to achieve peace and stability in the twenty-first-century global environment. It will need to overcome its one major disadvantage (in terms of its growing economy)—its bureaucratic burden, which significantly slows down and often hampers many of its economic activities. Transitioning from this overly burdensome bureaucratic structure to a rapidly responding and proactive structure is essential for India and will have many lessons that could be transferred to the U.S. structure as well.

Israel

Israel is a small country that—because of its history and unfriendly neighbors—has always focused on defense. It devotes approximately 8 percent of its gross domestic product to defense (the highest percentage of any developed nation—and even that is down from the 15 percent in 1991) and has mandatory military service (men serve for three years after secondary school, and women serve for two). Originally, Israel depended on the French for defense equipment; but after the Six-Day War in 1967, between Israel and three surrounding countries, the French stopped all arm shipments, and Israelis learned a bitter lesson about dependency. They vowed that from that point on, their defense sector would be self-sufficient, and since then they have built an impressive capability for military equipment development and production. By 2005, three of the top ten defense companies outside the United States and Europe were Israeli—Israel Aircraft Industries (IAI), Elbit Systems, and Rafael Armament Development Authority. The government owns a significant share of all three firms, and they all have a major share of their business in the defense sector (67 percent, 93 percent, and 100 percent, respectively).[125] The Israeli arms industry employs more than 57,000 people, and in addition to the three major firms, it has a thriving private sector of 150 firms whose products, particularly in the military electronics area, have been highly successful in the international market.[126] These firms design and produce tanks, military planes, missiles, ships, guns, and electronic warfare equipment that are equal to any in the world. With a small market, there are usually only one or two suppliers of each type of critical equipment. But these firms remain sensitive to price, high performance, and quality by continuous competition with alternative worldwide sources. In many cases, the firms are jointly owned by the government and the private sector, and there is a strong tie between the Ministry of Defense, the Ministry of Commerce, and the private sector—including explicit government responsibility for maintaining the defense industry. Additionally, many of the senior managers of the defense firms are former military leaders.

Israel is a country that requires a strong defense for periods of crisis and yet does not have the resources to pay for this without either external financial support or exports. The United States attempted to help Israel through financial aid to the defense sector in the mid-1970s by funding over $2 billion per year for military equipment. But instead of allowing Israel to use that money to build up its defense industry, the U.S. Congress required that the money be spent on U.S. military equipment that was shipped to Israel, forcing Israel to look even harder at arms exports to have a viable domestic defense industry.

Israel is a strong U.S. ally that operates in a dangerous portion of the world and has a highly skilled workforce that is capable of producing advanced technology and high-quality military equipment. The United States therefore needs to continue to work closely with Israel in the military and defense-industry areas and also in the political arena—to ensure a stable and peaceful Middle East in the twenty-first century.

From an industrial-base perspective, Israel's experiences demonstrate that a viable and advanced defense R&D and production industry can be maintained with a very small market—if it is properly scaled, managed, and planned. But it must be done in coordination with other countries—particularly in terms of export-control regimes and multinational counterproliferation policies.

Australia, the Middle East, and Africa

Most countries today are concerned about their security, and Australia, Singapore, South Korea, Taiwan, and South Africa have significant defense industries and plan them carefully from their governments' perspective. In 2007, for example, Australia published a "Defense Industrial Strategy" noting that, as a small country, it could not be self-sufficient but that a few areas required domestic capability. These areas included maintenance of equipment, capability to control the software for Australia's mission needs, and an encryption capability for its own equipment. All other systems were to be bought or jointly developed with allied nations.

Additionally, as oil money has flooded into countries such as Abu Dhabi, the United Arab Emirates, and others on the Gulf Cooperation Council, these countries have made huge purchases of foreign equipment.[127] But some of these countries also desire to develop their own capability. For example, Dubai Aerospace Enterprise (an organization dedicated to building a global aerospace manufacturing and services corporation) hired Robert Johnson as CEO after he had been president and CEO of Honeywell Aerospace and then chair of the $11 billion Honeywell Aerospace business.

Perhaps of greatest concern in the Middle East area is Iran, which has long supported science and technology[128] and is currently active in important future technology areas like nanotechnology, biotechnology, nuclear energy, and aerospace. The concern is that Iran has used its defense industry to supply Hezbollah (the Lebanon-based Shia Muslim paramilitary group) with long-range missiles, antiship cruise missiles, antitank weapon systems, and unmanned aircraft loaded with explosives—all of which were used in Hezbollah's 2006 war against Israel in Lebanon and northern Israel. Additionally, Iran has been supporting Shiite militias in Iraq with, for example, explosively formed projectiles (or shaped charges) that have been used in roadside bombs (improvised explosive devices) with sophisticated motion sensors against U.S. troops in Iraq.

Iran not only has the potential to develop nuclear weapons but is a considerable destabilizing force in the Middle East. The country is of great concern to the United States and to many other nations because it has gone beyond developing self-defense capability and is using its defense industry to support terrorism and instabilities around the world. For example, in 2010 (in a ceremony to mark national defense day) it unveiled its domestically-built unmanned bomber (capable of carrying a 200-kilogram bomb, with a range of 1,000 kilometers) and two high-speed naval vessels (one capable of launching missels and torpedoes).[129] This is the potential downside of defense industries and must be controlled by multinational agreements and pressures on the perpetrators.

9

Transforming the U.S. National-Security Industry

The Need for Change

According to the literature on culture change, the first requirement for achieving change is acceptance of the need for it. Widespread recognition of the need for change in the U.S. national-security posture began with the terrorist attacks on U.S. soil on September 11, 2001. At that time, then Secretary of Defense Donald Rumsfeld called for a total transformation of the Department of Defense, but the needed changes were delayed by widespread institutional resistance to change, the diversion of attention to the wars in Iraq and Afghanistan, and the large increases in available defense dollars.

In a February 2007 presentation at the Army War College, however, David Walker (the comptroller general of the United States and the Director of the General Accountability Office (GAO)) warned that "'the status quo' is not an option. The nation faces large and growing structural deficits, primarily due to known demographic trends (driving social security costs) and rising health care costs (Medicare and Medicaid). GAO's simulations show that balancing the budget in 2040 could require actions as large as cutting total federal spending by 60%, or raising federal taxes to two times today's level. . . . the federal government is on a 'burning platform' and the status quo way of doing business is unacceptable."[1] A fiscal crisis was coming, and the Defense Department (as the largest spender of discretionary dollars and an organization that has not demonstrated an ability to control its costs) needed significant across-the-board changes. Walker's warning of a coming fiscal crisis (driven by the rising costs of Medicare, social security, and the wars in Iraq and Afghanistan) was delivered before the dramatic global economic crisis that started on Wall Street in 2008 and spread throughout the world. The crisis compounded the previous economic problem by adding trillions of dollars of debt for corporate bailouts and economic stimulants—further limiting discretionary dollars for the DoD.

By early 2009, Secretary of Defense Robert Gates was offering a solution—"reprogramming the Pentagon for a new age."[2] In an article in *Foreign Affairs*, he stated that the DoD must prepare to use more limited resources to manage a broad spectrum of potential future conflicts—terrorism, expeditionary operations, regional conflicts, future peer competitors, and nuclear deterrence. Achieving what he termed a "balanced strategy" would require a major restructuring of the forces, the equipment being used, the acquisition workforce and its practices, and the industrial base that supports it.

By this point, a long list of negative DoD trends has been identified as needing urgent attention:

- Although the world is increasingly globalized, the trend in the DoD (and Congress) has been a shift toward isolationism. Rather than taking advantage of globalization (for example, through revised export controls, reduced import restrictions, and reduced restrictions on foreign students and scholars), the United States has been losing both its economic competitiveness and its national security advantages—especially through increasingly protectionist legislation (such as antiquated Buy American provisions). For political and flexibility reasons, both the Congress and the State Department have been reluctant to make the needed changes in International Traffic in Arms Regulations (ITAR), other export controls, and Buy American legislation.

Yet the need for change is increasingly recognized. In 2010, Senator Patty Murray stated, "U.S. national security and procurement policies represent some of the most burdensome restrictions affecting U.S. aerospace industry competitiveness." And, at the same meeting, National Security Advisor General James Jones announced the administration's intent to make "sweeping changes to modernize the U.S. export controls," in the interest of national security for the twenty-first century.[3]

- Rather than emphasizing the need to stay ahead and maintain its historic strategic posture of technological superiority (through "disruptive" R&D), the United States has been shifting its R&D to short-term and incremental developments.
- While the DoD (and the rest of the United States) has become increasingly dependent on advanced information systems, the DoD's 15,000 computer networks are under constant attacks. In fact, the DoD systems are probed by unauthorized users more than six million times a day![4] In addition, the civilian infrastructure on which the DoD is dependent (for power, banking, hospitals, and so on) is similarly vulnerable, making "cybersecurity" a crucial DoD and national need.
- At a time of significant future Defense Department budget reductions, increasing weapons costs and delayed weapon deliveries have been limiting the affordability of adequate quantities of weapons—thus greatly weakening the overall national security posture.

• In 2005, only 15 percent of U.S. military personnel were in jobs categorized as combat (and these combat positions include the chair of the Joint Chiefs and other senior personnel) (table 9.1). This is a poor ratio of "tooth to tail" (or in industry terminology, of direct labor to indirect labor).

In addition, the extended wars in Iraq and Afghanistan have overtaxed the military forces who are in a combat environment, increasing the need for sign-up bonuses and weakening the overall U.S. defense posture.

• The cost of maintaining and upgrading equipment has increased rapidly because of the extended conflicts in Iraq and Afghanistan and the age of much of the equipment. Combined with the increasing cost of fuel, the total cost of operations and maintenance (O&M) has risen rapidly, limiting the dollars available for other critical DoD needs.

• The share of the Defense Department's budget that is appropriated for health care has been increasing rapidly, as it also has been doing in other parts of the U.S. economy (General Motors was spending more on health care than on steel, and Starbucks was spending more on health care than on coffee).[5] By 2008, total health care costs for DoD (including costs for dependents and veterans) reached $93 billion annually and was growing.

• Combat commanders complain increasingly about slow responses to their urgent needs. For example, it took years to address the need to armor the army's personnel vehicles against roadside bombs, leaving soldiers to risk life and limb in the process.

• The aging workforce, in both the government and industry, presents growing long-term concerns, as do current skill-mix disparities.

• The DoD's supply-chain system has remained stuck in a twentieth-century model because of lack of funding and resistance to change. In the commercial world, world-class logistics operations use information technology to provide rapid, effective, and efficient logistic support as needed.

• The lack of an integrated approach to applying a combination of" hard and soft power" (in Iraq and Afghanistan and also around the world) has been increasingly recognized in the DoD and the State Department.

• The military services have been reluctant to modify their infrastructure, equipment, responsiveness, and budget distributions—despite widespread recognition of the changes that are required for many twenty-first-century equipment and scenarios. For example, despite the fact that, by 2010, 12,000 ground robots existed in the DoD inventory,[6] the infrastructure (operations, organizations, training, budgets, and so on) remains largely focused on twentieth-century equipment and scenarios.

Table 9.1
Distribution of the Department of Defense workforce

Occupation	Number of civilians (thousands)		Number of military personnel (thousands)		Total (thousands)		Percentage	
	1996	2005	1996	2005	1996	2005	1996	2005
Maintenance and engineering	233	198	445	402	678	600	27%	29%
Administration	262	270	119	207	382	476	16%	23%
Combat	12	8	324	296	336	304	14%	15%
Service, supply, and procurement (logistics)	132	92	152	127	283	218	12%	11%
Health and medical	28	28	131	112	159	140	6%	7%
Technical	114	76	91	50	205	128	8%	6%
Communications and intelligence	6	7	137	118	143	125	6%	6%
Other and unknown	50	8	180	60	229	69	9%	3%
Total	874	687	1,599	1,370	2,472	2,057	100%	100%

Source: Defense Science Board, "Summer Study," 2006.

• Planning policies have not been adjusted to reflect the fact that over 50 percent of the total force will be contractors in future expeditionary operations—even though the number of contractors in Iraq and Afghanistan has outnumbered military forces.

• The policies covering the enormous volunteer government civilian workforce—operating in a war zone—badly need to be revised. Areas that need to be addressed include life insurance, long-term medical insurance, and overtime pay.

• Even though competition yields great benefits in increased performance at lower costs, funding for even competitive prototypes has been strongly resisted because of the upfront costs (and the need to use "this year's money" elsewhere).

• The defense industry has not been agile and has grown increasingly less innovative and more resistant to change (particularly as a result of the augmented political power that it achieved through the large consolidations).

• By increasing its vertical integration (in both products and services), the defense industry has greatly reduced lower-tier competition and created significant conflicts of interest.

• Both Congress and the GAO have noted that the DoD lacks modern, integrated, enterprisewide information systems. It has over four thousand different business systems (for acquisition, finance, logistics, and personnel) that are not interoperable. This is highly unlike world-class commercial operations whose modern, enterprisewide information systems provide management and oversight visibility for rapid and effective decision making.

• Commercial and multinational firms have encountered significant barriers when they try to do to business with the Department of Defense, which greatly reduces the availability of advanced products and technologies to the DoD.

• There have been long delays in getting export license approvals for products to share with our allies. For example, by 2006, the annual caseload was around eighty thousand applications, and there was a two-month waiting period before the State Department could even send proposed technical assistance applications to the Pentagon to begin the deliberative process.[7]

• Most DoD acquisitions are labor-intensive services (including overseas stability operations, security, training, logistics, base operations, and reconstruction), but DoD acquisition rules and procedures were designed for buying products and purchasing sophisticated services is far more complex than purchasing products.

• Prime contractors have been experiencing growing conflicts of interest because they were forced to choose (in their "make or buy" decisions) between their own products and those of a competitor. This was the result of two factors—the move to netcentric warfare (with its focus on systems of systems) and the almost total decline of independent contractors who could objectively do the architecture and systems engineering associated with these systems of systems.

• As world opinion of the United States has grown increasingly negative, a greater investment in soft power has been needed, but there has been a reluctance to provide such national-security funds to the State Department.[8]

• Congress has continued to pass legislation prohibiting competitive sourcing between public agencies and private firms. This resistance ignores the very large costs savings (on average over 30 percent and recently far more) and the improved performance that come from public-sector/private-sector competitions for work that the government is currently doing and that is not inherently governmental.[9]

• There is growing concern that, because of a shortage of government acquisition personnel, contractors are doing many functions that should be performed by the government (those that are inherently governmental). In 2007, Secretary of the Navy Donald Winter stated that "the 'lead systems integrator' [that is, the organization performing the critical decision-making on systems of systems] should be the Navy—not the contractor."[10] This sentiment was echoed by the chief of naval operations, Admiral Mike Mullen, who stated that "We have taken a lot of our oversight capability out of the Navy and given it to the contractor. . . . the pendulum has swung too far, and we've got to swing it back."[11]

• According to a commission that examined the causes of fraud in Iraq contracting,[12] a severe shortage of acquisition personnel was caused by the dramatic budget reductions across the DoD in the post–cold war period and a subsequent absence of buildup in inherently governmental acquisition personnel when budgets increased exponentially after September 11, 2001.

• Finally, and most critical, the chair of the Joint Chiefs of Staff has stated that the likely future operating environment, for the DoD in the twenty-first century, will be characterized by "uncertainty, complexity, rapid change, and persistent conflict."[13] Certainly, it is a challenging period for the nation's security, and for both its military and the supporting industrial base.

In sum, the world is changing dramatically, but the DoD and its congressional oversight committees have failed to respond to these changes. As Jack Welch (former CEO of General Electric) stated, "When the rate of change outside your organization greatly exceeds the rate of change within your organization, the end is near." Or as Charles Darwin observed many years earlier, "It is not the strongest of the species that survives, nor the most intelligent, but the ones most responsive to change."

In light of growing concerns, the DoD asked the Defense Science Board to investigate the need for a possible transformation of the U.S. defense industrial base for the twenty-first century. The board's report concluded that not only did the industry have to be transformed but that such a change could not be brought about until there was significant transformation within the DoD itself.[14] The report made four key findings about twenty-first-century defense needs:

- DoD policies, processes, and management of the broad defense acquisition enterprise impede the transition to an effective, agile, and affordable overall, joint military force.
- U.S. government policies, practices, and processes do not facilitate the development, deployment, and support of innovative, affordable, and rapidly acquired weapons, systems, and services.
- DoD's acquisition workforce lacks many of the needed skills (such as systems engineering, biotech, and advanced information technology), large numbers of the workforce are nearing retirement age, and significant workforce reductions have taken place—all of which significantly impede the development, production, support, and oversight of military capabilities.
- Government acquisition policies and industry trends (such as further horizontal and vertical consolidations) will not produce the required competitive, responsive, efficient, and innovative national-security industrial base.

The Defense Science Board concluded that a total transformation of the DoD (including infrastructure, equipment, and acquisition workforce) and of the defense industry (in terms of what is bought, how it is bought, who does the buying, and from whom it is bought) is required to meet the country's national-security requirements in the twenty-first century—especially in the presence of reduced defense resources. The board also found that "the nation currently has a consolidated 20th century defense industry, not the required and transformed 21st century National Security Industrial Base it needs for the future."

With the demographic trends and ongoing economic crisis, it is clear that Paul Kennedy's projections in *The Rise and Fall of Great Powers: Economic Change and Military Conflict from 1500 to 2000* were correct[15]—that states need wealth to attain military power and need military power to acquire and protect wealth. If a state devotes too much of its resources to military purposes instead of to the creation of wealth, over the long term this weakens national power. Yet even during the financial crisis of 2008 and 2009, many in the military-industrial complex demanded that the government "protect" the defense industrial base. In contrast, Tom Jones (former president of Northrop Grumman) stated, in an earlier period of defense downsizing, that "the Defense industry has no natural right to exist."[16]

Instead of protecting the twentieth-century defense industrial base, government and industry need to transform it into a twenty-first-century industrial base that can justify its existence by providing needed military equipment at an affordable price. This requires an across-the-board transformation—including infrastructure, equipment, workforce, and the defense industry at large.

The Desired Industrial Structure

Before describing the changes that need to be made in government policies and practices (many of which have been described, or at least alluded to, in the previous chapters), we must first outline a vision for the twenty-first-century defense industrial base. As the United States moves from a mature twentieth-century defense-industrial structure to the new structures of the twenty-first century, certain requirements must be met:

1. The industrial structure must satisfy a broad range of mid-twenty-first-century national-security needs within the resources available.

2. To maintain the United States' historic defense posture of technological superiority, the structure must be technologically advanced (and remain so in the rapidly changing world of software, hardware, systems, and services).

3. The structure must be highly innovative (in architectures, products, processes, and applications), focused on game changers, and generate prototype demonstrations of these disruptive approaches.[17]

4. To implement the technological advances that rapidly take place globally in the commercial world, the industrial structure must remove the barriers that now exist to civil and military integration, and to globalization of the defense sector (while still recognizing that a few critical areas need to be protected).

5. To afford the equipment that will be required for potential future security scenarios (both domestic and worldwide), the industrial structure needs to reduce the unit costs of the equipment dramatically. The current costs of single ships and planes, for instance, are prohibitive To get the quantities required in the future, lower costs, through both product and process designs, must be a firm military "requirement" for all future weapon systems and systems of systems.

6. To achieve innovation and low costs while increasing the performance of each weapon system, the industrial structure needs to be highly competitive at all levels. There must be at least two firms in every critical area, but they need not all be domestically headquartered.

7. To meet the great uncertainties of the future national-security environment, the industrial structure must be agile and highly responsive. It must keep up with the adversary's changes and recognize that an adversary can acquire technology rapidly, on the global-technology market, and innovate in its use.

8. Finally, the industrial structure must be resilient enough to deal with the many forms of vulnerability that exist in today's environment (including physical and cyberattacks, natural disasters, fires, strikes, and changing geopolitical environments).

Achieving these eight desired characteristics will dramatically transform the current defense industrial structure, and this transformation of a unique market (with a monopsony buyer and a few oligopoly suppliers in each sector) is the responsibility of the government. The industry will respond to what its customer asks for and how it asks for it. For an industrial transformation to take place, the DoD must transform its business model, and to do this, it must have some vision of where it is trying to go and monitor progress toward its achievement.

Future DoD Businesses Practices

Unfortunately, there is no "silver bullet" that can achieve the required DoD culture changes. The solution must involve an understanding of four components:

- *What* equipment and services are purchased by the DoD: This is the requirements process and is the most important component, as it is pointless to acquire the wrong equipment or services. Someone must decide what equipment will be the most effective and in what quantities it will be needed for twenty-first-century security.
- *How* these systems are acquired: This must be done in a way that achieves the maximum performance at the lowest cost and in the least amount of time.
- *Who* does the buying and manages the development, production, and support of the acquired goods and services: The government must ensure that the acquisition workforce has the required skills and experience to manage these sophisticated acquisitions.
- *From whom* the goods and services are procured: This is the defense industrial base. To transform the defense industrial base so that it possesses the desired twenty-first-century characteristics, the government needs to change the first three areas. Then suppliers will respond to the changes that their customer has made.

Achieving the Transformation

It must be remembered that there is nothing more difficult to plan, more doubtful of success, nor more dangerous to manage, than the creation of a new system. For the initiator has the enmity of all who would profit by the preservation of the old institutions and merely lukewarm defenders in those who may do well under the new.
—Niccolò Machiavelli, *The Prince* (1513)

Making changes in government is difficult. And yet transforming the defense industry means changing the way that the government does its business. The Department of Defense needs to take nine interrelated actions to transform its business model and its industrial base, and each of these broad actions requires subactions for their achievement.

Action 1: Focus on netcentric systems of systems

To focus on netcentric systems of systems (rather than continue the current platform-centric approach), the DoD must shift available total resources (funding and top people) away from platforms and toward complex systems of systems. This is a significant change in outlook that will affect the budget, requirements, acquisition, organization, and management processes throughout the DoD. The government will need to have a systems architecture manager (or systems engineering manager) in all major areas, and it must provide experienced, government program management and systems engineering oversight on the systems-of-systems designs and evolutions.

This government-oversight structure must be established early (in the proposal process) so that it is well understood by industry. A key element in this regard is using independent systems architecture/engineering firms that will work with the government to optimize each system of systems. They must accept hardware and software contract exclusions to avoid any potential conflicts of interests (with regard to the selection of their own systems or subsystems within the overall architecture).

Interoperability will be a critical performance parameter when testing any new equipment, and it needs to be tested on a system-of-systems basis. Because interoperability is not primarily a technical issue (it is a governance issue), the only way to instill it within the contractors' culture is to have them realize that their system will fail its operational testing if it does not meet the interoperability requirements.

As the system evolves, to ensure that it will not be vulnerable to any unanticipated problems introduced by an adversary (who might use global technology in an asymmetric fashion), it will be necessary to establish small "red teams" (combining both government and industry personnel) that independently attempt to counter the system in nontraditional fashions.

Finally, because this new culture and focus on netcentric systems of systems is incompatible with the current budget and program approaches of the DoD and the Congress (which are platform-oriented), it will be necessary to move to mission-capabilities portfolio management, with the focus on specific mission areas (such as battle-space awareness and joint command and control). This is the direction advocated by the DoD in its February 2003 "Transforming the Defense Industrial Base: A Roadmap."[18] However, for it to be effective, other changes (such as an integrated, overall shift from platforms to netcentricity) are necessary.

Action 2: Achieve lower costs, faster to-field times, and better performance
Achieving lower costs, faster to-field times, and better performance is a paradigm shift from the old model of paying more to get more. The commercial computer world has shown that higher and higher performance can be obtained at lower and lower costs if modern product and process technologies are applied toward this objective. We can have performance superiority and affordability simultaneously.

Achieving this begins with a needed change to the weapon systems' requirements process. Cost and schedule must be part of a systems-analysis effort that precedes a firm set of requirements (from the Joint Requirements Oversight Council). In this way, fixed unit cost and time-definite acquisitions are equal partners with desired military performance—as overall design challenges for the contractors. This technique has been used effectively in the past on programs such as the joint direct attack munitions (where the requirement, as noted above, was "to hit the target with a weapon costing under $40,000"), but it has rarely been attempted and even more rarely has it been held to. Yet it can be achieved. The JDAM hits the target with great precision and costs around $17,000 each.

One way to understand the performance required from a system is to experiment extensively, with continuous user feedback on prototypes. This experimentation will yield the needed firm requirements for the development of the first "block" of the system. After the initial prototype phase, all weapon systems should use spiral development with a five-year cycle (or less) for each block (commitment, system development, and initial operational capability). Beginning with block one, each block of the system can use only fully proven technologies, but research and development (R&D) is funded, in parallel, for subsequent blocks. Once the new technology is proven, it can be phased in on the next block. When properly implemented, such spiral development will get higher-performance equipment more rapidly into the field and will do so (on average) at a savings of approximately 30 percent and with much lower risk.

Finally, some systems (particularly in wartime) must rapidly respond to situations that combatant commanders encounter on the battlefield. These require responses in weeks or months, not years. Today, this is done through a variety of ad hoc organizations that are thrown together every time an emergency situation requires a new piece of equipment, such as armoring the high-mobility multipurpose wheeled vehicles (HMMWVs) in Iraq. But these ad hoc organizations have no institutional memory and require constant approved deviations from the standard acquisition practices. To address this need (which is likely to grow in the environment of twenty-first-century security), the 2006 Defense Science Board Summer Study[19] recommended the creation of and adequate funding for a rapid fielding organization (beginning with combining the current, ad hoc organizations and their $3 billion annual funding).

Action 3: Stay ahead by funding engines of innovation

Over the last sixty years, the DoD's strategy for national security has been to maintain technological superiority; but despite the large DoD budget increases since September 11, 2001, the dollars going to research have declined. Additionally, with rapid changes in technology taking place globally, no organization can afford to focus solely on incremental change. Rather, some resources must be devoted to disruptive technologies that will result in game changers in the way that military operations are conducted in the future. The resources devoted to this must cover the research and analysis that goes into nontraditional technologies and applications and must also provide adequate resources to prototype and demonstrate these new ideas so that they can gain acceptance. So the budget for basic research must be increased, and the Office of the Director of Defense Research and Engineering needs to set aside a significant amount of money (perhaps 6 percent of the total research, development, test, and evaluation budget—around $4 billion per year) for disruptive systems demonstrations (in addition to the funding already given to DARPA for such nontraditional R&D).

As a complement to this and to encourage the defense firms to continue to innovate, the DoD should reestablish a separate allowable overhead expense for company-initiated independent research and development (IR&D). This prior practice had deteriorated because of congressional legislation that allowed IR&D to be mixed with bid and proposal (B&P) expenses, which encouraged companies to devote all of their resources to trying to win the next proposal (through elaborate B&P efforts) and to ignore the longer-term IR&D efforts. Returning to separate IR&D and B&P and providing government visibility into the companies' IR&D efforts should stimulate the firms to focus on staying ahead.

Additionally, the Congress and the executive branch must consider providing higher limits on the total size, the individual award amounts, and the duration of DoD small business awards, particularly through the Small Business Innovative Research (SBIR) program.[20] Small firms in the DoD's science and technology program can contribute innovations, and they should be encouraged to include a product-cost and manufacturing orientation to their efforts.

Finally, the United States is not taking full advantage of the scientists and engineers who are not U.S. citizens. A third of all U.S. Nobel Prizes have been won by people who were not originally U.S. citizens; and Silicon Valley was formed largely by people who were not originally U.S. citizens. Enrico Fermi was not a U.S. citizen when he contributed to the development of the atomic bomb, and over half of the current graduate students in science and technology in the top U.S. universities are non-U.S. citizens. As visa restrictions and other constraints (such as "deemed export control") continue to pile up, the numbers of non-U.S. citizens working in the defense arena are decreasing. It is national policy (as stated by Ronald Reagan in

National Security Decision Directive 189) that fundamental research be open to all and fully publishable, but this policy has not been implemented in practice—and it should be, if the DoD is to gain the benefit of these scientists and engineers.

Action 4: Conduct more best-value competitions

The empirical data overwhelmingly demonstrate that in a monopoly environment there is very little incentive for achieving either lower cost or higher performance (without cost increases). Thus, the DoD needs to make far greater use of best- value competitions—competitions that are not based on the lowest cost or the maximum performance but on the combination of these variables.

At both the prime and the critical-subsystems tiers, the primary objective of such competition must be to achieve innovation, and the secondary objective must be cost savings. It is not necessary to have two firms in production at all times in order to maintain a competitive industry in every sector of the defense area. But at least two design teams are needed in all critical areas, and each must go through funded prototyping so that they address technical feasibility, affordability, producibility, and supportability. If the quantities are sufficient, then it makes sense to have continuous production competition. This was held in "the great engine war" for the engines on the F-15 and F-16—where the presence of continuous production competition yielded higher performance and higher reliability yet with significant cost reductions.

Competition should not be a firm requirement—beyond the competitive prototype phase, where it always should be used. Rather, as long as the current producer is continuously improving performance and lowering costs, it should be rewarded by a continuation of the contract. A credible alternative must always be present, however, and an inexpensive way to maintain this option (and to encourage continuous innovation) is to fund a second source for interchangeable, next-generation, lower-cost, higher-performance prototypes (at either the system or subsystem level).

Even for sophisticated fighter aircraft (according to studies by the RAND Corporation),[21] this alternate source requires only one thousand to two thousand engineering and technical management personnel (at an annual cost of $100 million to $250 million) working on next-generation equipment. Significantly less will be required in critical-subsystem areas. The costs for the alternate source will be more than recovered because of the maintenance of a competitive option on multibillion dollar programs.

Finally, because historically the overwhelming share of the regulations and practices used in defense procurement were written to buy things and because today over 60 percent of DoD acquisitions are for services, the DoD needs to develop and fully utilize new regulations and practices that focus on competitive procurement of best-value services (particularly professional services and services provided by contractors on the battlefield).

Action 5: Understand and realize the benefits of globalization

For geopolitical reasons (perhaps even more than military reasons), future military operations are likely to be conducted in a coalition environment. Therefore, nations must learn to share technologies and train together to be prepared for such events. The needs in this area are for national sovereignty and military superiority—not for autarchy (self-sufficiency). Buying from foreign sources or codeveloping systems with them need not mean vulnerability, and each nation must take the necessary actions to ensure that this is the case. Similarly, commercial, off-the-shelf (COTS) systems—especially software—must be carefully tested to ensure that they are secure. Further research is required in this area in pursuit of new tools and techniques. The main change required in this area is a dramatic set of legislative and regulatory changes (for example, in International Traffic in Arms Regulations, export controls, the Berry amendment, and the specialty metals clause) to recognize the global defense market (again, with appropriate risk-based consideration of security and vulnerability concerns).

The required changes have been well defined by independent groups (such as the Defense Science Board, the Defense Business Board, the Center for Strategic and International Studies, and the National Research Council).[22] In general, there will be only a few areas for which controls should be applied. The DoD must actively take the lead with the Departments of State and Commerce and with the Congress in this critically important (but politically difficult) security area. The United States cannot afford the unintended consequences of laws that protect current U.S. technology. Laws cannot prevent the globalization of technology and of industry. The United States must learn to gain the benefits of such globalization—for both the nation's security and its economic competitiveness.[23]

Action 6: Build a high-quality, high-skill government acquisition workforce

Changes in process and structure will be largely ineffective unless the government also focuses on a high-quality, high-skill, government acquisition workforce. A combination of factors (including the dramatic reductions in the workforce in the post–cold war period and the large retirement wave of over 50 percent of the workforce who are eligible to retire by 2012) make it essential that the DoD focus on acquiring, training, and developing the best and brightest workers—particularly in acquisition management (of all inherently governmental functions such as management and decision making in finance, personnel, program management, procurement, logistics, engineering, and production).

For the DoD to compete with industry for the best and brightest, it will have to revise its salary policies. Pay-for-performance initiatives are a move in the right direction, but further steps are needed—for example, increases in starting pay for engineers to compete with industry. In addition, the DoD must develop and implement a personnel training and career-development program for the government civilian workforce that is comparable to the military program (where funds, time, and additional positions are allocated to provide for training and development). An added step that will be necessary (particularly due to the retirement of the senior people within the DoD acquisition core) is to increase the temporary rotations from industry to government (and visa versa).

For all functions that are not inherently governmental (many of which are currently being done by either civilian or military government personnel), these should be subjected to competitive sourcing—between the public and private sectors. Whenever this has been done, average costs have gone down by over 30 percent, no matter who wins (public or private sector), and performance has gone up significantly (since the measurement of performance now becomes an important consideration). This includes the many support services to the decision-making and management positions that are inherently governmental. All functions in the areas listed as acquisition are not inherently governmental (for example, wrench turning, analysis, and systems engineering). These support services should be filled competitively by industry personnel skilled in the required fields and terminated when the job is completed.

Action 7: Transform the DoD logistics systems to a modern, world-class, information-based supply chain

When he was chief of staff of the U.S. Army, General Rick Shinseki stated that "we cannot achieve a DoD transformation without a DoD logistics transformation." The current logistics system is the most expensive of the DoD acquisition processes (in 2005, it was budgeted for $90 billion but actually cost over $126 billion—including the supplemental appropriations), and it is also the most critical for sustained warfighting (since it affects readiness, responsiveness, and, in the long run, the capability to carry on the fight). Yet despite the fact that there are more people in the logistics area than there are in combat positions, despite the huge inventory (which grew, from 2005 to 2009, from over $67 billion to over $90 billion), and despite the annual expenditure for logistics of well over $100 billion, the current DoD logistics system is far from world-class. In fact, world-class systems measure their responsiveness in hours, while the DoD (at best) measures it in weeks. It has been improving. During the first Persian Gulf War, the average response, from shelf to soldier, was thirty-six days (with a large uncertainty, so parts were ordered three times). The average for the second Persian Gulf encounter moved down to twenty-one days and then sixteen days—again, with a large uncertainty. By contrast, world-class systems deliver domestically in twelve hours and internationally in twenty-four hours with 99.99 percent probability. Additionally, world-class operations provide "total asset visibility" at all times, while the DoD is far from achieving that—particularly in the last mile to the warfighter, who critically needs the delivery.

The data overwhelmingly support a shift to performance-based logistics (PBL) or warranties on all DoD systems (legacy and new). This would significantly drive up the equipment availability and lower support costs. If PBL or warranties do not show a continuous performance improvement, at continuously reduced costs, then the support work would need to be opened to competition among other contractors.

Finally, the traditional DoD approach to logistics has been to spend all of the money that is annually allocated to perform the current logistics support work—leaving no money available for improving the system. Therefore, it is strongly recommended that a new fund be established that would take a small share of the overall support budget (perhaps 1 percent or around $100 million per year) and use it for research and development on logistics transformation implementations. Since the commercial world has demonstrated that this is not a technological challenge, this is simply another area where cultural change must be achieved through determined leadership.

Action 8: Recognize that contractors will represent a major portion of the total force in future military operations

In Iraq, contractors have represented 50 percent of the total force, and in Afghanistan, they have been 75 percent of the force (in the theater, in 2010, there was a total of 239,451 contractors).[24] The DoD and the defense industry (with the support of Congress) need to plan for contractor involvement in future military operations, and this involves a wide range of considerations, including expeditionary contracting, security, education and training, readiness, exercises, and personnel policies. This area is too important to remain ad hoc, as it has largely been to date.

Action 9: Specify and achieve a twenty-first-century industrial structure

Although many of the above-noted changes can be done independently, the DoD—working closely with the Department of Homeland Security and the Director of National Intelligence (since all three organizations will need to draw on the same industrial base)—needs to have a clear vision of where the twenty-first-century national security industrial base needs to be, and to strive to achieve the needed transformation. In this unique market environment (with a monopsony buyer and a small group of oligopoly suppliers), the government has no choice but to play a significant role in achieving the industrial structure that it desires.

Because the commercial world has moved far ahead of the defense industry in many areas of technology and in production processes (such as flexible manufacturing), it is now possible to achieve the benefits of an integrated civil and military industrial organization (at the plant level). This allows the defense industry to benefit from the continuous process improvements that the commercial world makes (to increase performance and lower costs) and to gain the benefits of the economies of scale that are often present when the small volume of defense goods are mixed with the high volume of commercial goods. But significant regulatory and legislative barriers to such integration must be removed, including government-unique cost-accounting requirements, specialized military specifications, and unique government procurement regulations (which often are written for protectionist or socioeconomic considerations but are not applicable to the commercial world).

Additionally, DoD profit and overhead policies need to encourage the structural shifts, capital investments, lower cost initiatives, and incentives for entry by new and commercial firms. For example, in DoD profit policy, the regulation guidelines (as revised in 2000) allow added profit percentages for increased efficiency (specifically, in areas such as reduction or elimination of excess facilities, cost-reduction initiatives, incorporation of commercial items and processes, and contractor investment in cost-reducing facilities). Another mechanism by which industry can earn additional profit (which was also added in 2000) is using the category of technology incentives for cost reductions. Firms should receive significant added profit if their improvements resulted in reducing the costs or improving the reliability of either existing products or, with new products, of the products they replaced (recognizing that improved reliability reduces life-cycle costs). These added profit incentives for lower-cost and more reliable equipment have not received significant attention, but contracting personnel should be encouraged to make full use of them in the future.

In the same way, the government should be encouraged to create incentives for reduced vertical integration by getting more involved in the prime contractors' make-or-buy decisions. In the case of the Future Combat System, the program manager has played a significant role in the prime contractors' make-or-buy process, thereby ensuring that suppliers (other than the divisions of the prime contractor) have full access and are fairly treated in the evaluation. In future programs, the request for proposal should ensure that the government will have access and visibility into such decision making.

In the same way that the government should encourage civil and military plant integration, the government needs to remove the barriers (such as cost-accounting standards, export controls, and other defense-unique requirements) that prevent commercial firms from supplying their technology and equipment directly to the DoD, as well as from partaking in DoD R&D.

A major barrier to achieving efficient and effective business operations is the fact that, in 2009, the DoD had over 4,700 independent and noninteroperable business information systems. All world-class commercial corporations have integrated enterprise systems that tie together all of a firm's business systems and link it directly to its customers and suppliers. A new DoD organization (the Business Transformation Agency) was created to address this need. It was fiercely resisted, but was essential to building a twenty-first-century defense industrial structure. It was eliminated in 2010, but its function is critically required.

To implement a new integrated enterprise system, the DoD should work with the National Institute of Standards and Testing (NIST) to establish interface standards (as contrasted with common systems), security procedures, and protocols that allow and require full, enterprise-wide (all tiers of government and industry) network-centric industrial operations—fully utilizing commercial off-the-shelf software. This approach should be applied to all phases of the life cycle to provide all of the needed information for management decision making—again with the objectives of high performance at lower costs and more rapid fielding.

Finally, at least every three years, the DoD should perform a detailed sectoral analysis of each critical sector of the defense industrial base. This analysis should focus on the ability to have R&D competition in each sector, the potential for civil and military integration, and the potential for the establishment of a global marketplace in each area. Such analyses are not required when there are a large number of potential domestic suppliers for a critical technology (or even a large number of foreign suppliers from multiple countries and multiple firms). But in many critical defense sectors where there are only two or three firms, or (in some cases) only one, such analyses by the government are essential to maintain a highly competitive, innovative, low-cost, advanced-technology industrial base for the nation's long-term security.

In general, defense-industry transformation cannot happen simply by moving organizational boxes around or through increased regulation (which slows down the acquisition process and makes it even more unique and inefficient). However, one highly desirable organizational change can happen in information technology—in the weapon systems (particularly in the systems-of-systems arena) and internally (within the government and between the government and its suppliers). The Congress has legislated, in the Clinger-Cohen bill, that every agency hire a chief information officer (CIO) who reports directly to the secretary of that agency. The DoD has established an assistant secretary for networks and information integration (NII) who reports directly to the secretary. In 2008, the Congress established a new position of deputy chief management officer (DCMO), who is responsible for the acquisition of all business systems, reporting directly to the deputy secretary of defense, and with responsibility for the Business Transformation Agency. However, the Goldwater-Nichols bill mandates that there be a single acquisition executive who is responsible for all of an agency's acquisition activities, and in the DoD, this responsibility rests with the undersecretary for acquisition, technology, and logistics.

These three pieces of legislation are in conflict. Although the chief information officer, the assistant secretary for networks and information integration, and the undersecretary for acquisition, technology, and logistics can work out conflicts in a cooperative fashion, the critical importance of information technology for both warfighting and business operations suggests that the DoD acquisition executive (that is, the undersecretary) should be the individual responsible for information systems. The assistant secretary for networks and information integration and the deputy chief management officer should be moved to the organization of the undersecretary (acquisition, technology, and logistics). He/she is already the third-ranking person in the DoD. The title of the undersecretary also should be changed to undersecretary of defense for information, acquisition, technology, and logistics to emphasize the importance of information in the overall acquisition process. Such a change could help improve the effectiveness and efficiency of the overall DoD. And with a modification of the Clinger-Cohen bill, the assistant secretary for networks and information integration could still be the chief information officer for the DoD.

In summary, for an industrial transformation, there must first be a DoD business transformation. The direction of this transformation is clear (as described above), but for it to happen, both the DoD and the Congress must shift from a posture of maximum risk avoidance (through overregulation and protectionism) to an objective of achieving effective and efficient defense acquisition management. The model for this transformed industrial structure should be a government and industry partnership in a continuously competitive market and an industry that is flexible, adaptive, agile, innovative, resilient, low-cost, high-quality, and capable of satisfying the wide variety of twenty-first-century security needs. Achieving such a partnership will require frequent (at least semiannual) meetings among the CEOs of major defense firms (as well as some of the lower-tier suppliers), the secretary, deputy secretary, and undersecretary for acquisition, technology, and logistics, and the service chiefs (a practice that used to exist but has not taken place with much frequency in recent years).

Why, This Time, Change Can Be Achieved

Cynics might point out that there has long been a need for reform of the Defense Department's acquisition processes. Hundreds of studies, reports, and even entire books have been written about both the need and the actions required. Yet the costs of the weapons and services necessary for the nation's security have continued to rise, and the time to deliver them has been increasing. It is fair to ask, "Why will this time be different?" The answer is that the nation's security has reached the tipping point—the point at which covering the full range of national-security considerations (terrorism at home and abroad, expeditionary conflicts, regional wars, activities associated with stability and control in unstable areas of the world, potential peer competitors, and nuclear deterrence) has simply become unaffordable in an era in which the nation must spend an increasing share of its resources on Medicare, universal health insurance, social security for an aging population, the rebuilding of its deteriorating infrastructure, and the repayment of debts incurred during the economic collapse in the first decade of the twenty-first century.

As noted above, the literature on culture change states that two things are needed to achieve significant change. The first is a recognition of the need for change (the crisis). In this case, the economic reality is that if historic trends continue, the United States will not be able to afford to maintain its desired national security posture. This looming crisis is becoming more and more widely recognized within the executive and legislative branches and also by the public at large.

The second requirement for a successful culture change is leadership with a vision, a strategy, a set of actions, and the ability to align and motivate others to achieve the needed transformation. It is widely recognized (as Machiavelli indicated in the sixteenth century) that there will be fierce resistance to these needed changes, so strong, consistent, and sustained leadership is essential.

The DoD is facing a fiscal crisis, and change is required. Since the requirements for change (as described in this book) are generally recognized, the time is ripe to overcome resistance and achieve the necessary changes. U.S. taxpayers and the men and women in the armed services deserve to have these changes implemented. Most important, the nation's future security requires that it happen.

Notes

Chapter 1

1. Warren Zimmerman, *First Great Triumph: How Five Americans Made Their Country a World Power* (New York: Farrar, Straus, and Giroux, 2002).

2. Michael Signer, "A Scary World," *Washington Post*, February 24, 2008.

3. Paul Kennedy, *The Rise and Fall of Great Powers: Economic Change and Military Conflict from 1500 to 2000* (New York: Random House, 1987).

4. David Ignatius, "Wise Advice: Listen, and Engage," *Washington Post*, June 24, 2007.

5. Ibid.

6. Ibid.

7. Joseph S. Nye, *Soft Power: The Means to Success in World Politics* (New York: Public Affairs, 2004), as noted in Hans Binnendjik and Richard Kugler, *Seeing the Elephant: The U.S. Role in Global Society* (Dulles, VA: Potomac Books, 2007), 183.

8. For example, see John P. Kotter, *Leading Change* (Boston: Harvard Business School Press, 1996).

9. Jacques Gansler, Memo to the chair of the Defense Science Board, defining the terms of reference for a study on globalization and security from the Undersecretary of Defense, October 6, 1998.

10. Defense Science Board, Summer Study on Transformation, Subpanel Report on Defense Industry and Acquisition, "Assessment of the Current Situation and Recommended Actions," August 9, 2005.

11. "Military Culture Remains Rooted in Cold-War Era Mindset," *Inside the Army*, September 4, 2006.

12. Ibid.

13. Adm. Michael Mullen, "Navy Weighs Tank Maritime Strategy Options but Others May Immerge," *Inside the Navy*, April 23, 2007.

14. Ibid.

15. Abraham Lincoln, Second Annual Message, December 1, 1862, next to last paragraph.

16. David M. Walker, "America's Imprudent and Unsustainable Fiscal Path," *Defense Acquisition Technology and Logistics* (March–April 2006).

17. Robert Gates, Eisenhower Library Speech on Defense Spending, May 8, 2010, http://www.defense.gov/speeches/speech.aspx?speechID=1467 (accessed on October 21, 2010).

Chapter 2

1. This term was first used by President Franklin Roosevelt in December 1940, in connection with "Land Lease" to supply equipment to the U.K. and Russia who were at war with Germany. Then he used it in connection with production for U.S forces in WWII.

2. For a detailed discussion of the history of the U.S. defense industrial base, with numerous references, see Jacques S. Gansler, "The Diminishing Economic and Strategic Viability of the U.S. Defense Industrial Base," PhD dissertation, American University, 1978 (University of Michigan Microfilm International, 1978).

3. Lieutenant General Michael M. Dunn, U.S. Air Force, "The U.S. Defense Industrial Base: Past, Present, and Future Challenges," Paper presented at the Industrial College of the Armed Forces, June 2, 2005.

4. For a discussion of planning for surprise, see Defense Science Board, *Summer Study Final Report*, September 2008.

5. Naval Historical Center, "The Reestablishment of the Navy 1787–1801," online, June 22, 2007.

6. J. M. Blair, *Economic Concentration: Structure, Behavior, and Public Policy* (New York: Harcourt Brace Jovanovich, 1972), 380.

7. J. Houston, *The Provisioning of War: Army Logistics 1775 to 1953* (Washington, DC: U.S. Government Printing Office, 1956), 24.

8. Charles W. Freeman Jr., "National Security in the Age of Terrorism," Paper presented at the "National Security" Conference, Williamsburg, VA, January 6, 2006, and published in *Middle East Policy* (January 6, 2007).

9. Stephen Barr, "For Defense, Crunching the Numbers Is Half the Battle," *Washington Post*, May 12, 2008.

10. The $60 billion estimate comes from Sami Lais, "The Future of Intelligence," defensesystems.com, 2008. See also Walter Pincus, "2007 Spying Said to Cost $50 Billion," *Washington Post*, October 30, 2007; Walter Pincos, "ODNI Executive may have disclosed U.S. Intelligence Budget Amount," *Federal Times*, June 7, 2007. Bill Sweetman, "Blog: Black Budget Blows by $50 Billion Mark," *Aviation Week and Space Technology*, http://www.aviationweek.com/aw/blogs/defense, summarizes the data in the DoD's fiscal year 2010 budget for intelligence programs.

11. Walter Pincus, "DNI Cites $75 Billion Intelligence Tab," *Washington Post*, September 17, 2009, A7.

12. B. M. Blechman, E. M. Gramlich, and R. W. Hartman, "Setting National Priorities: The 1975 Budget," Brookings Institution Report, Washington, DC, 1974.

13. Wassily Leontief and Marvin Hoffenberg, "The Economic Effect of Disarmament," *Scientific American* (April 1961): 3–9 (and the ratios might be even greater for today's high-tech, high-cost defense sector).

14. For example, see Murray Weidenbaum, *The Economics of Peacetime Defense* (New York: Basic Books, 1974).

15. J. F. Lawrence, "Spending for Defense: Boom or Detriment?," *Los Angeles Times*, January 10, 1978, 1.

16. John T. Bennett, "Defense News," July 22, 2010.

17. *The Economist*, "Arming Up: The World's Biggest Military Spenders by Population," June 8, 2009.

18. Based on Department of Defense, *Green Book*, fiscal year 2005.

19. Tina Jonas, Paper presented at Jane's Defense Conference, Washington, DC, April 22, 2008.

20. Jim Greenwood, "Toward a More Accessible and Affordable Health Care System: Regulate or Innovate?," *Bio News*, February–March 2008.

21. According to the Social Security Administration's Office of the Chief Actuary, Centers for Medicare and Medicaid Services.

22. "Unified Military Medical Commands Studied," *Newport News Daily Press*, May 21, 2006.

23. "Schoomaker Expresses Concern Over FY '07 Army Budget," *Aerospace Daily and Defense Report*, July 17, 2006.

24. Paper presented at a Jane's Defense Conference, meeting, Washington, DC, April 22, 2008.

25. Government Accountability Office, *GAO Report 05647 on Military Health Care*, Washington, DC, May 2007.

26. Center for Strategic and International Studies, *CSIS Report*, June 13, 2007.

27. From Christopher Bowie and Karen Rodgers, Northrop Grumman, "Key Defense Policy Issues Facing the New Administration," briefing, September 18, 2007.

28. Norman R. Augustine, *Augustine's Laws* (Washington, DC: American Institute of Aeronautics and Astronautics, 1983)..

29. F. W. Lanchaster, *Aircraft in Warfare: The Dawn of the Fourth Arm* (London: Constable, 1916), chap. 5.

30. Gary Hart, *The Shield and the Cloak: The Security of the Commons* (New York: Oxford University Press, 2006).

31. John J. Hamre, "Realities of Today Demand a New Defense Acquisition Reform," *Aviation Week and Space Technology*, November 28, 2005, 74.

32. Barry Goldwater, "DoD Reorganization: Summary of the Problems," *Armed Forces Journal International* 123, no. 4 (October 1985).

33. Sam Nunn, "DoD Reorganization: An Historical Perspective," *Armed Forces Journal International* 123, no. 4 (October 1985).

34. RAND National Defense Research Institute, "Goldwater-Nichols Brief: Pre-Interview Information," RAND National Defense Research Institute, Washington, DC, 2008.

35. Some of the material in this section comes from a paper that the author presented at the Industrial College of the Armed Forces on June 2, 2005, and published as "U.S. Defense

Industrial Base: National Security Implications of a Globalized War," National Defense University Press, Washington, DC, April 2006).

36. James Langenfeld and Preston McAfee, "Competition in the Defense Markets: Meeting the Needs of Twenty-First-Century Warfighting," Institute of Defense Analysis, January 2001.

37. Raytheon, "The Consolidation of the Defense Industry," briefing, January 14, 2000, based on transaction closing data as of December 31, 1999.

38. Langenfeld and McAfee, "Meeting the Needs of Twenty-First-Century Warfighting," and JSA Partners, "Competition in the Defense Markets," both presented at the Institute for Defense Analysis Conference, January 14, 2001.

39. For a detailed discussion of this issue, see Jacques S. Gansler, *Defense Conversion: Transforming the Arsenal of Democracy* (Cambridge: MIT Press, 1995), 69–84.

40. Paul Blumhardt of Martin Marietta reported a 32 percent success rate from data from 1973 to 1993. Naval Research Advisory Committee, *Defense Conversion* (Washington, DC: U.S. Government Printing Office, November 1993), 55. A 1991 survey of 148 firms reported a success rate of 36 percent. Wiabridge Group, DRI/McGraw-Hill, the Fraser Group, "The Commercialization of Defense Technology: A Survey of Industry Experience," Lexington, Massachusetts, November 1991, 2.

41. David Ravenscroft and Frederick M. Scherer, *Mergers, Selloffs and Economic Efficiency* (Washington, DC: Brookings Institution, 1998).

42. McKenzie, "Defense Company Acquisitions of Defense and Commercial Businesses," 1986, as reported by Loren B. Thompson, in a presentation at a conference at Harvard University, April 21, 1994.

43. Jacques S. Gansler, "The Defense Industrial Structure in the Twenty-First Century," Paper presented at the American Institute of Aeronautics and Astronautics Acquisition Reform Conference, Washington, DC, January 27, 2000, and as reported by Lauren Thomson, *Defense Week*, January 18, 2000.

44. Bureau of Labor Statistics, as reported by Raytheon, at a conference on "The Consolidation of the Defense Industry," in Washington, DC, January 14, 2000.

45. Pierre Chao, "Structure and Dynamics of the U.S. Federal Professional Services Industrial Base, 1995–2006," Center for Strategic and International Studies, May 2007, 22, 33; see also Zachary Goldfarb, "Mid-Tier Contractors Getting Left Out: As Federal Contracts Grow, Medium-Size Firms Can't Keep Up," *Washington Post*, September 3, 2007.

46. John Harbison, Thomas Moorman, Michael Jones, and Jikun Kim, "U.S. Defense Industry under Siege: An Agenda for Change," Booze-Allen and Hamilton, July 2000.

47. Ibid.

48. Gansler, "The Defense Industrial Structure in the Twenty-First Century," Presented at the Aerospace Industries Association's "Acquisition Reform Conferences," Washington, DC, January 27, 2000. .

49. Ibid.

50. Department of Defense Report to Congress on the Adequacy of Defense Industry Capabilities, February 2005.

51. For example, see Jeff Cole and Thomas Ricks, "New Offer by Lockheed and Northrop on Merger Is Rejected by U.S. Officials," *Wall Street Journal*, March 18, 1998.

52. Anthony Velocci Jr., "Face-off over Merger Leaves Industry Riling," *Aviation Week and Space Technology*, March 16, 1998.

53. "Navy Breaks Up Destroyer Design Team," *Norfolk-Virginia Pilot*, June 6, 1998.

54. Lauren Thompson, "The Defense Industry's Winter of Discontent," *Defense Week*, January 18, 2000.

55. Jeff Cole and Ann Marie Squeo, "Defense Industry Questions Move by Pentagon to Spur Competition," *Wall Street Journal*, December 3, 1999.

56. Ibid.

57. Anthony Velocci Jr., "Merger Review Policy: Deciphering the Record," *Aviation Week and Space Technology*, December 3, 2001.

58. Langenfeld and McAfee, "Competition in the Defense Markets: Meeting the Needs of Twenty-First-Century War Fighting" (from data supplied by the Department of Defense, the Teal Group, industry publications, and JSA Partners Analysis).

59. "Arms Sales Monitor," *Federation of American Scientists* 21 (July 1993): 16; also see "Arms Sales Boom," *The Economist*, August 13, 1994, 24–28.

60. Richard Stevenson, "No Longer the Only Game in Town," *New York Times*, December 4, 1988.

61. R. Forsberg and J. Cohen, "The Global Arms Market: Prospects for the Coming Decade," Institute for Defense and Disarmament Studies, Cambridge, MA, 1993.

62. Department of Defense, *Inspector General Report D-2000–088*, February 29, 2000.

63. "Military Culture Remains Rooted in Cold War Era Mindset," *Inside the Army*, September 4, 2006.

64. Ashton B. Carter and William J. Perry, "China on the March," *National Interests* (March–April 2007): 21.

65. Lieutenant General Ross Thompson, Testimony before the House Appropriations Subcommittee on Defense, as reported in *GovExec*, February 12, 2009.

66. "Structure and Dynamics of the U.S. Federal Professional Services Industrial Base: 1995 to 2004," Center for Strategic and International Studies, May 2006, 10.

67. Ibid., 18.

68. "In Military Spending Boom, Expense of Pet Projects Prevail," *Wall Street Journal*, June 16, 2006.

69. Ibid.

70. Government Accountability Office, "Defense Acquisitions: Assessments of Selected Weapon Programs," GAO-08–467SP, March 2008.

71. "Congress Still Concerned about Affordability of Ship Building Plan," *Inside the Navy*, May 15, 2006.

72. "Defense Spending Set for Sharp Rise," *Wall Street Journal*, February 7, 2007.

73. Merrill Lynch, "Report on Aerospace and Defense," January 18, 2008.

74. Greg Grant, "Gates Tells Military Services to Prepare for Unconventional Wars," *Government Executive*, April 22, 2008.

75. Robert Gates, Defense Department Secretary, "Evening Lecture at West Point," Paper presented at the U.S. Military Academy, West Point, NY, April 21, 2008.

76. "New Top Spy Inherits an Office Still Finding Its Way," *Washington Post*, January 7, 2007, 10.

77. As of September 30, 2004, there were 1,426,836 active-duty personnel according to the DoD, Directorate for Information Operations and Reports.

78. Message from Deputy Secretary of Defense John White to Congress and then to reporters, April 5, 1996.

79. Herbert Meyer, "What in the World Is Going On? A Global Intelligence Briefing for CEOs," http://www.chosinreservoir.com/worldgoingon.htm.

80. "Outsourcing Market View," *INPUT*, January 12, 2006, 1.

81. Committee on Science, Engineering, and Public Policy, and the Committee on Policy and Global Affairs of the National Academies, *Rising above the Gathering Storm: Energizing and Employing Americans for a Brighter Economic Future* (Washington, DC: National Academies Press, 2007).

82. As quoted in Norman R. Augustine, *Is America Falling off the Flat Earth?* (Washington, DC: National Academies Press, 2007), 23.

83. For example, see Defense Science Board, *DSB Summer Study on Transformation, Subpanel on Defense Industry Acquisition: Assessment of the Current Situation and Recommended Actions*, Defense Science Board, August 2005, urging the exploration and exploitation of commercial and global technologies.

84. Robert Brodsky, "Former Defense Leaders Call for Simpler Acquisition System," *Government Executive*, June 3, 2009, governmentexecutive.com.

85. International Monetary Fund, "World Economic Outlook," May 1997, 45.

86. Terrence R. Guay, "Globalization and Its Implications for the Defense Industrial Base," Strategic Studies Institute, U.S. Army War College, February 2007.

87. Thomas Friedman, in *The World Is Flat: A Brief History of the Twenty-First Century*, categorized this Internet era of globalization as "Globalization 3.0."

88. World Trade Organization, "Selected Long-Term Trends," *International Trade Statistics 2005*, as quoted in Guay, "Globalization and Its Implications for the Defense Industrial Base," 3.

89. "Boeing Global's Strategy Takes Off," *Business Week*, January 30, 2006.

90. Leslie Wayne, "Boeing Not Afraid to Say 'Sold Out'," *New York Times*, November 28, 2006.

91. Wayne Arnold, "Where the Appetite for Aircraft Is Big," *New York Times*, November 28, 2006.

92. Augustine, *Is America Falling off the Flat Earth?*, 26.

93. Pierre Chao, "The Future of the U.S. Defense Industrial Base: National Security Implications of a Globalized World," Industrial College of the Armed Forces, June 2, 2005.

94. Augustine, *Is America Falling off the Flat Earth?*, 19.

95. Ibid.

96. Thomas W. Anderson and William J. Zeile, "U.S. Affiliates of Foreign Companies: Operations in 2004," *Survey of Current Business* 86, no. 8 (August 2006): 195–211.

97. Deborah Orr, "The Largest Foreign Investments in the U.S.," *Forbes Magazine*, April 10, 2008.

98. Jacques Gansler, "Trade War," *Foreign Policy* (March 2009), http://www.foreignpolicy.com.

99. The decision to use location is based on section 2500 of Title X of the U.S. Code, where it defines a member of the national technology and industrial base.

100. For a full discussion of this topic, see National Research Council of the National Academies, *Science and Security in a Post-911 World* (Washington, DC: National Academies Press, 2007).

101. According to data provided to the author by the undersecretary of defense for personnel and readiness in 2008.

102. For a full discussion of this topic, see National Research Council of the National Academies, *Science and Security in a Post 9/11 World*.

103. National Science Board, *Science and Engineering Indicators 2006* (2 vols.) (Arlington, VA: National Science Foundation, 2006).

104. Ibid.

105. Chris Nuttall, "Intel Chief Calls for Easing of Visa Curbs," *Financial Times*, February 8, 2006, 2.

106. "Early Intervention, Pentagon Eyes Ways to Encourage JSF Partners to Accelerate F-35 Buys," *Aviation Week and Space Technology*, April 2, 2007, 30.

107. Richard Kirkland, vice president, Lockheed Martin, February 2005, quoted in Michael Brewer, "An Aerospace Business Case for Transatlantic Cooperation," in Milton S. Eisenhower Symposium proceedings, conference on "American Mass Media: Redefining the Democratic Landscape" (Baltimore: Johns Hopkins University Press, 2005).

108. "Northrop Embraces the Small-Satellite Plan," *Wall Street Journal*, April 11, 2007, A9.

109. For example, Congressman Hunter stated that to hold the line on Buy American, we must block EADS bid to make Air Force tankers, .

110. Augustine, *Is America Falling off the Flat Earth?*, 17.

111. Robert Trice, senior vice president, Lockheed Martin, "Globalization in the Defense Industrial Base," briefing to the Defense Science Board, December 11, 2006.

112. Office of the Deputy Undersecretary of Defense for Industrial Policy, "Study on Impact of Foreign Sourcing of Systems," January 2004.

113. Ibid., v.

114. Ibid.

115. "Made in Mexico," *Aviation Week and Space Technology*, April 2, 2007, 67.

116. "Wiring the World," *Aviation Week and Space Technology*, July 30, 2007, 54.

117. "Made in Mexico," *Aviation Week and Space Technology*, April 2, 2007, 68.

118. "Oil Price Rise Fuels Leap in U.S. Arms Sales," *London Times*, August 21, 2006.

119. "Foreign Sales by U.S. Arms Makers Doubled in a Year," *New York Times*, November 11, 2006.

120. "MCS Announces Paveway II to the Czech Air Force," Prague, press release, October 12, 2005.

121. "Pakistan Seeks Three Subs from France," *Defense News*, February 27, 2006.

122. *The Economist*, December 24, 2005, 9.

123. "Agency Announces Surcharge Increase for Foreign Military Sales," *Inside the Pentagon*, March 22, 2006.

124. Frieda Berrigan, "Big Battles over Small Arms: But Progress at the United Nations Is Too Slow," World Policy Institute, January 23, 2006.

125. "Weapons Given by U.S. May Be Used against U.S. Troops," *Washington Post*, August 6, 2007, A14.

126. RIA Novosti, "Russian Arms Exports Break Records," March 8, 2007.

127. Tom Shanker, "Russia First in Selling Arms to Third World," *International Herald Tribune*, October 30, 2006.

128. "Russia, France Overtake U.S. as Top Arms Sellers," Agence France-Presse, October 30, 2006.

129. Kelly Hearn, "Russia Negotiating Arms Sales to Buenos Aires," *Washington Times*, August 9, 2006, 11.

130. RIA Novosti, "Russian Arms Exports Break Records," March 8, 2007.

131. Kelly Hearn, "Russia Negotiating Arms Sales to Buenos Aires," *Washington Times*, August 9, 2006, 11.

132. Robert Kimmitt, former deputy treasury secretary, Paper presented to the Atlantic Council, June 14, 2007.

133. Will Reese, paper presented to the Association of American Universities in La Jolla, CA, March 10, 2008.

134. "Defense Trade and Security Initiative," May 2000, http://www.fas.org/asmp/campaigns/control/dtsa17pts.htm.

135. Walter Pincus, "Taking Defense's Hand out of State's Pocket," *Washington Post*, July 9, 2007.

136. "Agency Announces Surcharge Increase for Foreign Military Sales," *Inside the Pentagon*, March 22, 2006.

137. "World Public Favors Globalization and Trade But Wants to Protect Environment and Jobs," WorldPublicOpinion.org, April 26, 2007.

138. "Buy American: A Roundtable Discussion," *Aerospace America*, September 2006, 28.

139. Ray Ann S. Johnson, "House and Senate Debate the Berry Amendment: Keeping the Focus on the Needs of a Twenty-First Century Military," Manufacturer's Alliance/MAPI, August 2006.

140. "Buy American Creates Hurdles for Pentagon's Business Plans," as stated by the Pentagon's deputy undersecretary for industrial base, *The Hill*, November 29, 2006.

141. J. C. Anselmo, D. A. Fulghum, and D. Barrie, "National Insecurity: Pentagon's Zealous Enforcement of Law Requiring Use of Domestic Metals Is Holding Up Deliveries, Threatening Corporate Profits," *Aviation Week and Space Technology*, March 13, 2006, 24.

142. As told to the author by the then-program manager of the activity in Iraq.

143. "Congressman Introduces Bill to Extend Berry Amendment," March 14, 2006, Government Printing Office, H.R.4946.

144. "ITAA Backs Relief from Berry Amendment for DoD," press release, June 26, 2006.

145. Ibid.

146. Kimberly Palmer, "Buy American Compliance Tricky in Increasingly Global Economy," *National Journal*, November 22, 2006.

147. Ibid.

148. Gordon Adams, Christoph Cornew, and Andrew James, "Between Cooperation and Competition: The Transatlantic Defense Market," Chaillot Paper 44, which was quoting from the *Blumberg News*, October 28, 1999.

149. "Boeing Fined $15 Million for a Chip," *Washington Post*, April 9, 2006.

150. Statement by the deputy undersecretary for acquisition, technology, and logistics, *International Affairs*, July 13, 2007.

151. International Traffic in Arms Regulation, "ITAR Summary: Definitions and Subchapters Pertaining to Non-tangible Items on Munitions List."

152. "High-Risk Series: An Update," *GAO Highlights* (January 2007).

Chapter 3

1. Alvin Toffler and Heidi Toffler, *War and Antiwar: Survival at the Dawn of the Twenty-First Century* (Boston: Little, Brown, 1993).

2. Gary Hart, *The Shield and the Cloak: The Security of the Commons* (New York: Oxford University Press, 2006), vii.

3. As quoted in Hans Binnendijk and Richard Kugler, *Seeing the Elephant: The U.S. Role in Global Security* (Dulles, VA: Potomac Books, 2007), 63.

4. Ibid., 167.

5. For an excellent discussion of the difficulty of achieving a paradigm shift, see Thomas S. Kuhn, *The Nature of Scientific Revolution* (Chicago: University of Chicago Press, 1996).

6. For an excellent discussion of this new environment, see Hart, *The Shield and the Cloak*, especially 11.

7. As reported by Greg Grant, "Gates Tells Military Services to Prepare for Unconventional Wars," *Government Executive*, April 22, 2008.

8. Chairman of the Joint Chiefs, "Capstone Concept for Joint Operations: Version 3.0," Department of Defense, January 15, 2009, 2.

9. As described by Thomas Friedman in *The World Is Flat: A Brief History of the Twenty-First Century* (New York: Farrar, Straus and Giroux, 2005).

10. Richard L. Kugler and Hans Binnedijk, "Future Directions for U.S. Foreign Policy: Balancing Status Quo and Reform," Working paper, Defense and Technology Papers 40, Center for Technology and National Security Policy, National Defense University, Washington, DC, May 2007, 10.

11. As described in Steven Flanagan and James Schear, eds., *Strategic Challenges: America's Global Security Agenda* (Washington, DC: National Defense University of Press, 2007), 111.

12. As quoted in Thom Shanker, "Gates Says New Arms Must Play Role Now," Paper presented at Heritage Foundation Conference, Colorado Springs, Colorado, May 14, 2008.

13. Flanagan and Schear, *Strategic Challenges*, 88.

14. Ibid., 89.

15. Graham T. Allison, *Nuclear Terrorism: The Ultimate Preventable Catastrophe* (New York: Times Books, 2004).

16. M. Schwirtz, A. Barnard, and C. J. Chivers, "Russia and Georgia Clash over Separatist Region," *New York Times*, August 9, 2008.

17. Bernard Lewis, as quoted in Binnendijk and Kugler, *Seeing the Elephant*, 96.

18. Greg Grant, "Gates Tells Military Services to Prepare for Unconventional Wars," *Government Executive*, April 22, 2008.

19. Moisés Naím, *Illicit: How Smugglers, Traffickers, and Copycats Are Hijacking the Global Economy* (New York: Doubleday, 2005).

20. As quoted in Binnendijk and Kugler, *Seeing the Elephant*, 154–155.

21. Robert D. Kaplan, *The Coming Anarchy: Shattering the Dreams of the Post-Cold War* (New York: Random House, 2000).

22. As described in Binnendijk and Kugler, *Seeing the Elephant*, 83.

23. Charles Lutes, Elaine Bunn, and Steven Flannigan, "The Emerging Global Security Environment," in Steven Flannigan and James Shear, eds., *Strategic Challenges: America's Global Security Agenda* (Dulles, VA: Potomac Books, 2007).

24. Samuel P. Huntington *The Clash of Civilizations and the Remaking of World Order* (New York: Simon and Schuster, 1996).

25. As described in Binnendijk and Kugler, *Seeing the Elephant*, 68.

26. Admiral Michael Mullin, Chairman of the Joint Chiefs of Staff, at the Atlantic Council, Washington, DC, April 21, 2008.

27. As discussed in Binnendijk and Kugler, *Seeing the Elephant*, 173.

28. Carl von Clausewitz, *On War* (London: Penguin Books, 1968 [1832]), chapter 1, book 1.

29. Rupert Smith, *The Utility of Force: The Art of War in the Modern World* (London: Allen Lane, 2005), 17, 269.

30. Major General Robert Scales, at the Joint War Fighting Conference, Virginia Beach, Virginia, June 17–19, 2008.

31. Walter Pincus, "Irregular Warfare, Both Future and Present," *Washington Post*, June 7, 2008.

32. Binnendijk and Kugler, *Seeing the Elephant*, 269.

33. Ashton B. Carter, "Defense Management Challenges in the Post-Bush Era," in *Defense Strategy and Forces: Setting Future Directions* (Newport, RI: Naval War College, 2008).

34. Lieutenant Colonel Richard Ellis, Major Richard Rogers, and Lieutenant Commander Brian Cochran, "Joint Improvised Explosive Device Defeat Organization (JIEDDO) Tactical Successes Mired in Organizational Chaos: Roadblock to the Counter-IED Fight," Joint Forces Staff College, March 13, 2007.

35. "Violence on the Rise" *Washington Post*, June 15, 2008, based on data released by NATO's International Security Assistance Force; Craig Whitlock, "IED Attacks Soaring in Afghanistan Stymie U.S. Counteroffensive," *Washington Post*, March 18, 2010.

36. David Eshel (reporting from Tel Aviv), "No Room for Maneuver," *Defense Technology International* (July–August 2007): 41.

37. Michael Moss, "Supply Gap in Iraq: What Went Wrong," *International Herald Tribune*, March 8, 2005 (originally published in the *New York Times*).

38. For a full discussion of this change, see Smith, *The Utility of Force*, 1.

39. Colonel T. X. Hammes, "Fourth-Generation Warfare Evolves: Fifth Emerges," *Military Review* (May–June 2007): 20.

40. Ibid., 14.

41. Lieutenant General Jeffrey Sorenson, army chief information officer, as quoted in Sandra Erwin, "Troops in the Digital Age, Disconnected," *National Defense Magazine* (December 2007).

42. David Bond, "Washington Outlook," *Aviation Week and Space Technology*, April 2, 2007, 27.

43. Government Accountability Office, "Defense Acquisitions: 2009 Is a Critical Juncture for the Army's Future Combat System," March 10, 2008.

44. "Network-Centric Warfare," *Aviation Week and Space Technology*, May 23, 2005, 50.

45. Martin Amis, "Terrorism's New Structure," *Wall Street Journal*, August 16–17, 2008, 101.

46. See Paul Boutin, "Biowars for Dummies," as discussed in Hammes, "Fourth-Generation Warfare Evolves."

47. For example, see Mark Mientka, "Dark Winter Teaches Bio-Lessons," www.usmedicine .com.

48. Binnendijk and Kugler, *Seeing the Elephant*, 270.

49. Bill Lambrecht, "Boeing among Defense Contractors Fighting Cyberterrorism," *Chicago Tribune*, June 28, 2010.

50. David E. Sanger, John Markoff, and Thom Shanker, "U.S. Steps Up Effort on Digital Defenses," *New York Times*, April 28, 2009.

51. "Second Fleet Releases Top Ten C-4 Requirements List for the Navy," *Inside the Navy*, December 18, 2006.

52. Sanger, Markoff, and Shanker, "U.S. Steps Up Effort on Digital Defenses."

53. "Fundforpeace.org and Foreign Policy Magazine," as noted in "States of Instability," *Washington Post*, June 24, 2008, which listed Somalia, Iraq, Nigeria, Kenya, Egypt, Iran, Ivory Coast, Liberia, Haiti, Pakistan, Bangladesh, and others.

54. Robert R. Tomes, *U.S. Defense Strategy from Vietnam to Operation Iraqi Freedom* (London: Routledge, 2007), 269.

55. As specified in the secretary of defense's August 2007 memo that established the transformation of the Southern Command as an integrated operation.

56. Noah Shachtman, "How Technology Almost Lost the War: In Iraq, the Critical Networks Are Social-Not Electronic," *Wired* (November 27, 2007).

57. Asharq Al-Awsat, May 2, 2007, as reported in *Terrorism Focus* 4, no. 13 (May 8, 2007).

58. J. C. Herz and John Scott, "COTR Warriors: Open Technologies in the Business of War," *DoD Software Tech News* 10, no. 2 (June 2007): 3FF.

59. "Rumsfeld Calls for More Spending on Non-lethal Weapons," *Inside the Navy*, May 22, 2006.

60. "Nano-Air Vehicle to Fly Like Seed," *Flight International*, August 1, 2006.

61. "Iraqi Translators High-Dollar Risk Can Mean Huge Payday," *New York Daily News*, May 6, 2007.

62. "Forward Observer: Bartlett's Not-So Familiar Quotations," *Congressional Daily*, May 1, 2006.

63. Robert Gates, secretary of defense, "Remarks to the Heritage Foundation," *U.S. Department of Defense Speeches*, May 13, 2008.

64. For example, I have argued for it in three prior books—*The Defense Industry* (1980), *Affording Defense* (1989), and *Defense Conversion* (1995). .

65. Government Accountability Office, "Contingency Operations: Army Should Do More to Control Contract Costs in the Balkans?," Washington, DC, September 2000, 9.

66. Congressional Budget Office, "Contractors' Support of U.S. Operations in Iraq," Washington, DC, August 2008, 1.

67. "Contractors Outnumber U.S. Troops in Afghanistan," *New York Times*, September 1, 2009 (based on a report by the Congressional Research Office).

68. Chairman, Joint Chiefs of Staff, Joint Publication 4–10, "Operational Contracts Support, Final Coordination," November 1, 2007, as quoted in *Atlanta Constitution*, MONTH DAY, 2003, II-1.

69. Government Accountability Office, "Military Operations: Contractors Provide Vital Services to Deployed Forces But Are Not Adequately Addressed in DoD Plans," Washington, DC, June 2003.

70. Renae Merle, "No Protection Policy for Overseas Contractors: Oversight 'Inconsistent' Report Says," *Washington Post*, June 26, 2003.

71. "U.S. Cannot Manage Contractors in Wars, Officials Testify on Hill," *Washington Post*, January 25, 2008.

72. Ibid.

73. "Army Manual Takes On Nation-Building," *USA Today*, February 29, 2008.

74. Robert Gates, "A Balanced Strategy: Reprogramming the Pentagon for a New Age," *Foreign Relations* (January–February 2009): 1–7.

75. "Truckers in Iraq," *New York Times*, September 27, 2004.

76. Warren Zimmerman, *First Great Triumph: How Five Americans Made Their Country a World Power* (New York: Farrar, Straus, and Giroux, 2002), 493.

77. Government Accountability Office, "Contingency Operations: Army Should Do More to Control Contract Costs in the Balkans," September 2000.

78. "Halliburton Successes: Improving the Lives of Soldiers and Iraqis," Halliburton Press Release, March 18, 2004.

79. Paul A. Brinkley, deputy undersecretary of defense for business transformation, "Restoring Hope: Economic Revitalization in Iraq Moves Forward," *Military Review* (March–April 2008): 8ff.

80. "Law Allows Contractors to Help Guard Military Bases," *GovExec.com*, December 5, 2002.

81. Steve Fainaru and Alec Klein, "In Iraq, A Private Realm of Intelligence-Gathering: Firm Extends U.S. Government's Reach," *Washington Post*, July 1, 2007, A-20.

82. "Contractor Personnel Authorized to Accompany the U.S. Armed Forces," *Department of Defense Instruction* 3020.41, October 3, 2005.

83. Dennis C. Colby, Lockheed Martin Orlando, remarks at DoD Conference in Annapolis, Maryland, as reported in Richard L. Dunn, "Contractors Supporting Military Operations," Center for Public Policy and Private Enterprise, School of Public Policy, University of Maryland, September 2006.

84. U.S. Army Material Command, Pamphlet 700–300, "Logistics Civil Augmentation Program (LOCAP)," August 2003.

85. Peter Higgins, "Civilian Augmentation of Joint Operations," Army *Logistician* 35 (January–February 2003), which describes each of these three programs.

86. Mark Cancian, "Contractors: The New Element of Military Force Structure," *Parameters* (U.S. Army War Colleges) (Autumn 2008): 61–77.

87. Congress Congressional Budget Office, "Contractors' Support of the U.S. Operations in Iraq," 1.

88. See George Cahlink, "Army of Contractors," *GovExec*, February 1, 2002; Claude M. Bolton, Jr., assistant secretary for acquisition, logistics, and technology, U.S. Army, Testimony before the Senate Armed Services Committee, April 19, 2007.

89. "Contractor Deaths in Iraq Nearing 800," *Houston Chronicle*, January 28, 2007, August 2009, page 1.

90. Ibid.

91. "Truckers in Iraq," *New York Times*, September 27, 2004, 1.

92. Steve Fainard, "Iraq Contractors Face Growing Parallel War: As Security Work Increases, So Do Casualties," *Washington Post*, June 16, 2007, A-1.

93. J. W. Anderson and S. Fainaru, "U.S. Confirms Killing of Contractors in Iraq," *Washington Post*, October 23, 2005.

94. Renae Merle, "Census Counts One Hundred Thousand Contractors in Iraq: Civilian Number, Duties Are Issues," *Washington Post*, December 5, 2006.

95. "Contractor Deaths in Iraq Soar to Record," *New York Times*, May 19, 2007.

96. Walter Pinkos, "Contractors in Iraq Have Become U.S. Crutch," *Washington Post*, August 20, 2007, A-13.

97. Steven Schooner, "Remember Them, Too: Don't Contractors Count When We Calculate the Costs of War?," *Washington Post*, May 25, 2009, A21.

98. David Phinney, "Dangerous Business: Sending Contractors to War Zones Poses New Problems for DoD," *Federal Times*, February 24, 2003.

99. Richard L. Dunn, "Contractors Supporting Combat Operations: Developing the Vision to Fill Gaps in Policy," Center for Public Policy and Private Enterprise, School of Public Policy, University of Maryland, January 2008.

100. A. E. Cha and Ellen McCarthy, "Prison Scandal Indicates Gap in U.S. Chain-of-Command," *Washington Post*, May 5, 2004, A-20.

101. Lieutenant Colonel Pamela Hart, as quoted in Leon Worden, "Army May Be Misusing Contractors," *The-Signal.com*, June 15, 2004.

102. Ibid.

103. David Bond, "Protecting Contractors," *Aviation Week and Space Technology*, September 6, 2004, 23.

104. "Bechtel Pulling Out after Three Rough Years of Rebuilding Work," *San Francisco Chronicle*, November 1, 2006, 1.

105. Gates, "A Balanced Strategy."

106. Joint Chiefs of Staff, "Operational Contract Support," Joint Publication 019, U.S. Government Printing Office, November 1, 2007, I-12.

107. Mark Lindemann, "Civilian Contractors under Military Law," *Parameters* 37 (Autumn 2007): 83–94.

108. Cancian, "Contractors."

109. Department of Defense Instruction No. 3020.41 issued by the Undersecretary of Defense (Acquisition, Technology and Logistics), October 3, 2005.

110. Renae Merle, "Pentagon Revises Contractor Rules," *Washington Post*, May 7, 2005, E-1.

111. Congressional Budget Office, "Contractors' Support of U.S. Operations in Iraq," 19.

112. Commission on Army Acquisition and Program Management in Expeditionary Operations (known as the Gansler Commission for its chair, the author of this book), "Urgent Reform Required: Army Expeditionary Contracting," October 31, 2007.

113. Paul Brinkley, "A Cause for Hope: Economic Revitalization in Iraq," *Military Review* (July–August 2007).

114. "Memorandum of Agreement between the Department of Defense and Department of State on U.S. Government Private Security Contractors," May 12, 2007.

115. Robert Brodsky, "New Direction Chartered for Wartime Contracting," *GovExec.com*, January 25, 2008.

116. "Official History Spotlights Iraq Rebuilding Blunders," *New York Times*, December 13, 2008.

117. Commission on Army Acquisition and Program Management in Expeditionary Operations, "Urgent Reform Required."

118. Mary Pat Flaherty, "Private Guards Status Outline by Pentagon: Number in Iraq Expected to Grow," *Washington Post*, May 5, 2004.

119. This material is drawn largely from Cancian, "Contractors," 61–77.

120. Mary Pat Flaherty, "Private Guards Status Outlined by Pentagon: Number in Iraq Expected to Grow," *Washington, Post*, May 5, 2004.

121. As a result of the adverse publicity, Whitewater changed its name to Xe Services LLC.

122. Jeremy Kahn and Nelson Schwartz, "Private Sector Soldiers," *Fortune Magazine* 149, no. 9 (May 3, 2004): 33.

123. Congressional Budget Office, "Contractors Support of U.S. Operations in Iraq," 2.

124. Congressional Budget Office, Logistics Support for Deployed Military Forces, Washington, DC, Congressional Budget Office, October 2005, 36–43.

125. Robert M. Gates, "A Balanced Strategy: Reprogramming the Pentagon for a New Age," *Foreign Affairs* (January–February 2009).

126. As quoted in Joint Chiefs of Staff, "Operational Contract Support," I-1.

127. John P. Kotter, *John P. Kotter on What Leaders Really Do* (Boston: Harvard Business School Press, 1999).

128. "Realignment of ACA and Establishment of ACC," Department of the Army, January 30, 2008.

129. Richard Lugar and Condoleezza Rice, "A Civilian Partner for Our Troops: Why the U.S. Needs a Reconstruction Reserve," *Washington Post*, December 17, 2007.

130. Joint Doctrine Pamphlet 4/01, "Contractors on Deployed Operations (CONDO)," Ministry of Defense, United Kingdom, December 2001.

Chapter 4

1. *The Government Contractor* 50, no. 16 (April 23, 2008): 1.

2. Pierre Chao, "Structure and Dynamics of the U.S. Federal Professional Services Industrial Base, 1995–2005," Center for Strategic and International Studies, Report, May 2007, 19.

3. Ibid., 21.

4. Steven Hall, "Defense M & A Trends and Issues," Office of the Deputy Undersecretary of Defense (Industrial Policy), 2007, based on data provided by the Department of Defense Directorate for Information Operations and Reports Procurement Statistics.

5. Tom Shoop, "Onward and Upward," *Government Executive*, August 15, 2007, 17.

6. "Carrier Industry Mounts Budget Defense," *The Hill*, April 12, 2006.

7. Tom Shoop, "Onward and Upward," *Government Executive*, August 15, 2007, 17.

8. DoD director for information operations and reports procurement statistics.

9. Anthony Velocci, "Lessons in Preparedness," *Aviation Week and Space Technology*, May 12, 2003, 47.

10. Chris Cavas, "LCS: Over Budget, But Still a World-Beater," *Defense News*, March 18, 2008.

11. "Pentagon Trims Armored Vehicles Due in '07 for Iraq," *Washington Post*, July 19, 2007; Committee on Armed Services, "Demand Improvement in Obtaining MRAP Vehicles," July 19, 2007.

12. "Stockpile Report," Federal Preparedness Agency, 1976, 1.

13. For a discussion of the abuses of the stockpile, see Walter Adams, "The Military Industrial Complex and the New Industrial State," *American Economic Review* 58 (May 1968): 655–661; also see Jack Anderson, *Washington Post*, December 14, 1976, B-13.

14. "Federal Funding Accountability and Transparency Act—Reporting," *Federal Register*, March 21, 2007.

15. Martin Bollinger, Booz Allen Hamilton, "Vertical Integration in the U.S. Defense Industry," Paper presented to the Defense Science Board, June 12, 2007.

16. For an extensive discussion of the benefits of smaller size in achieving innovation and growth, see F. M. Scherer, *Innovation and Growth: Schumpeterian Perspectives* (Cambridge: MIT Press, 1984), especially 224 and 237. In addition, see J. M. Blair, *Economic Concentration: Structure Behavior and Public Policy* (New York: Harcourt, Brace, Jovanovich, 1975); J. Jewkes et al., *The Sources of Innovation* (New York: Norton, 1971), 71–85; D. Mueller, *The Rate and Direction of Inventive Activity* (Princeton: Princeton University Press, 1962), 323–346. For example, see Department of Commerce, "The Role of New Technical Enterprises in the U.S. Economy," 1976.

17. National Academies, "Rising above the Gathering Storm: Energizing and Employing America for a Brighter Economic Future," October 2005, 15.

18. Created by the Small Business Innovation Development Act of 1982 (Public Law 97–219).

19. National Research Council of the National Academies, *An Assessment of the Small Business Innovation Research Program at the National Science Foundation* (Washington, DC: National Academies Press, 2007).

20. GAO, "Contract Management: Protégé's Value DoD's Mentor-Protégé Program, but Annual Reporting to Congress Needs Improvement," January 31, 2007.

21. Small Business Administration, "Small Businesses Garner $79.6 Billion in Federal Contracts in FY 2005: Another Record Year for Small Businesses," June 21, 2006.

22. "Second Small Business Scorecard Finds Dollars Rise but Percentages Decrease in FY 2007," *Washington Post*, October 23, 2008.

23. House Small Business Committee, "Manzullo: U.S. Small Businesses Secure Record Amount of Federal Prime Contracting Dollars," June 21, 2006.

24. GAO, "Alaska Native Corporations: Increase Use of Special 8(a) Provisions Calls for Tailored Oversight," June 21, 2006.

25. Griff Witte, "Alaska Native Firms Capitalize on No Bid Deals," *Washington Post*, April 12, 2006.

26. *Government Executive*, June 23, 2009.

27. Small Business Administration Office of Inspector General, "Participation in the 8(a) Program by Firms Owned by Native Alaskan Corporations," July 10, 2009.

28. "DoD Issues Seven Rule Changes to DFARS," *Federal Register,* June 16, 2006.

29. For example, refer to Defense Science Board, "Creating an Effective National Security Industrial Base for the Twenty-First Century," July 2008.

30. "Northrop and Lockheed Go to Court," *New York Times,* February 24, 2001.

31. Office of the Secretary of Defense, "Annual Industrial Capabilities Report to Congress," March 2008, 72.

32. GAO, "Report to the Chairman, Subcommittee on National Security and Foreign Affairs, Committee on Oversight and Government Reform, House of Representatives"; "Department of Defense: A Department Wide Framework to Identify and Report Gaps in the Defense Supplier Base Is Needed," October 2008.

33. For an example of an abuse, see Nathan Vardi, "The Spy in the Lab: U.S. Companies Need to Be Increasingly Careful about What They Tell Their Chinese Engineers," *Forbes Magazine,* July 21, 2008.

34. Office of the Deputy Undersecretary of Defense for Industrial Policy, "Study on Impact of Foreign Sourcing of Systems," January 2004.

35. Defense Science Board, "Final Report of the Defense Science Board Taskforce on Globalization and Security," Washington, DC, Office of the Undersecretary of Defense for Acquisition and Technology, 1999.

36. Jack Spencer, "The Military Industrial Base in an Age of Globalization: Guiding Principles and Recommendations for Congress," Heritage Foundation, 2005.

37. Kimberly Palmer "'Buy American' Compliance Tricky and Increasingly Global Economy," *National Journal,* November 22, 2006.

38. Ibid.

39. Capgemini, "Security and Offshore: Taking a Responsible Approach and Realizing the Benefits of Off shoring without Compromising Security," 2007.

40. Ibid.

41. "Booz Allen Weighs Splitting Operations," *Washington Post,* December 18, 2007.

42. For a detailed discussion of this topic, see Jacques S. Gansler, *Defense Conversion* (Cambridge: MIT Press, 1995).

43. Based on DoD reports to Congress and reported in "Creating an Effective National Security Industrial Base for the Twenty-First Century: An Action Plan to Address the Coming Crisis," Defense Science Board, July 2008, 25.

44. P. Chao, J. Gertler, and S. Seifman, "What Shipbuilding Crisis? These Are Bountiful Days in U.S. Shipyards, but the Industry May Be Steaming into Rough Seas," *Armed Forces Journal,* April 2006.

45. See "The Navy's Public/Private Competition Program" (parts A & B), Case study, Harvard Business School.

46. "Military Repair Work Booms," *Wall Street Journal* October 23, 2006, B8.

47. "Sir Janus: Sir Richard Evans, Chairman of BAE Systems, Is an Aerospace Boss Destined to Face Two Ways as His Company Grows outside Europe," *The Economist,* December 23, 2000, 106.

48. Gordon Adams, Christopher Cornu, and Andrew James, "Between Cooperation and Competition: The Transatlantic Defense Market," Chaillot Paper 44, Institute for Security Studies of WEU, January 2001.

49. Jacques Gansler, "Trade War," *Foreign Policy*, March 2009.

50. A. Butler, R. Wall, and A. Nativi, "Early Intervention: Pentagon Eyes Ways to Encourage JSF Partners to Accelerate F-35 Buys," *Aviation Week and Space Technology*, April 2, 2007, 30.

51. Bill Dane, "Fragmented Fighter Market: Euro Fighter Flexes Muscle as U.S. Eyes F-35, JSF Cuts," *Aviation Week and Space Technology*, January 15, 2007, 20.

52. "British Merchant Has Passport to Pentagon," *New York Times*, Aug. 16, 2006, C9.

53. Terrence R. Quay, "Globalization and Its Implications for the Defense Industrial Base," Army Strategic Study Institute, 22.

54. D. Barrie and J. L. Anselmo, "Cashing Out: General Electric Begins a Push Back into Systems Arena as Smith's Group Throws in Its Aerospace Hand," *Aviation Week and Space Technology*, January 22, 2007, 27.

55. "Europe Takes Offense as U.S. Buys Up Defense," *Financial Times*, July 10, 2003.

56. Ellen McCarthy, "Foreign Firms a Mainstay of Pentagon Contracting," *Washington Post*, March 18, 2006.

57. John Douglas, "Forty-First Annual Year End Review and Forecast Luncheon," Aerospace Industries Association, 2006.

58. "U.S. Army Poised to Restart Transport Aircraft Contest," *Flight International*, December 20, 2005.

59. "Euro Copter Wins First Major U.S. Military Contract," *Aviation Week*, July 16, 2006.

60. "BAE Systems Wins First U.S. Missile Contract as Prime," *Flight International*, April 28, 2006.

61. Merrill Lynch, "Thales Wins Large U.S. Order," June 19, 2007.

62. Aerospace Daily and Defense Report, "Navy, Air Force Maneuver to Save JSF Alternate Engine," January 5, 2006.

63. Walter Pincus, "Taking Defense's Hand out of State's Pocket," *Washington Post*, July 9, 2007.

64. "Agency Announces Surcharge Increase for Foreign Military Sales," *Inside the Pentagon*, March 22, 2006.

65. Derrick Johnson, "The $63 Billion Sham," *New York Times*, November 2006, as reported in the *Boston Globe*, August 1, 2007.

66. Dana Hedgpeth, "Sales to Navy Help Lift General Dynamics Profit Sixteen Percent," *Washington Post*, October 23, 2008.

67. "Arms Forced Stability: President Bush Re-Embraces the Middle East Strategy He Wants Repudiated," *Washington Post*, August 1, 2007, A16.

68. Simeon Kerr, "Oil Rich States Step Up Market Presence," *Financial Times*, September 10, 2007, 4.

69. Robin Wright, "House Members Say They Will Try to Block Arms Sales to Saudis," *Washington Post*, July 29, 2007.

70. "Arms Dealers Fight It Out for Sales in Booming Asia," *Los Angeles Times*, February 27, 2006.

71. David M. Walker, "Americans Imprudent and Unsustainable Fiscal Path: Fiscal Challenges Confronting DoD Will Necessitate Better Acquisition Outcomes," *Defense AT&L* (March–April 2006): 13.

72. "Lawmaker Calls Pentagon's Buying System 'Terribly Broken,'" *The Hill*, April 6, 2006.

73. Ibid.

74. This list comes from a GAO analysis of space systems acquisition entitled "Improvements Needed in Space Systems Acquisitions and Keys to Achieving Them," April 7, 2006.

75. As stated by Representative John Kline (R-Minn.) in "Lawmaker Calls Pentagon's Buying System 'Terribly Broken,'" *The Hill*, April 6, 2006.

76. Monitor Group, "Defense Acquisition Performance Assessment," 2007.

77. Daniel Terris, *Ethics at Work: Creating Virtue in an American Corporation* (Lebanon, NH: University Press of New England, Brandeis University, 2005).

78. Some of the material in this section comes from an earlier book by the author, *The Defense Industry* (Cambridge: MIT Press, 1980), 72–74.

79. Walter Adams, "The Military Industrial Complex and the New Industrial State." American Economic Review, LVIII no. 2, May 1968. 655–661.

80. James. W. McKee, "Concentration in Military Procurement Markets: A Classification and Analysis of Contract Data," Report RM 6307-PR, RAND Corporation, Santa Monica, CA, 1970, 16.

81. E. Raymond Corey, *Procurement Management: Strategy, Organization, and Decision-Making* (Boston: CBI, 1978.).

82. One exception to this was a 2003 case involving the Boeing Company and senior air force procurement officer Darleen Druyun. Druyun was found guilty of inflating the amount of a large contract to her future employer and giving Boeing information about a competitor's bid before she left the air force. Both Druyun and Boeing's chief financial officer served time in prison. This is considered a rare instance of corruption in the highly transparent defense marketplace.

83. For example, Adams, "The Military Industrial Complex and the New Industrial State," 10; or M. J. Peck and F. M. Scherer, *The Weapons Acquisition Process: An Economic Analysis* (Cambridge: Harvard University Press, 1962), 46.

84. David Ignatius, "Duplicating Uncle Sam," *Wall Street Journal*, December 18, 1978, 1.

85. Lt. Gen. Ross Thompson, Testimony before the Senate Armed Services Committee, January 24, 2008.

86. Commission on Army Acquisition and Program Management in Expeditionary Operations, "Urgent Reform Required: Army Expeditionary Contracting,," October 31, 2007; http://www.army.mil/docs/.

87. The basis for this is the Armed Services Procurement Act of 1947, which established the Armed Services Procurement Regulations (ASPRs). In 1978, the ASPRs were changed to the Defense Acquisition Regulations (DARs) by DoD Directive 5000.35.

88. Mark J. Green, ed., *The Monopoly Makers: Ralph Nader's Study Report on Regulation and Competition* (New York: Grossman, 1973), 8.

89. Adams, "The Military Industrial Complex and the New Industrial State," 10.

90. For a sophisticated presentation of this incorrect argument, see J. Kurth, Hearings before the Joint Commission on Defense Production, 95th Congress, September 29–30, 1977.

91. Vice Admiral Steve Stanley, director for structure, resources, and assessment of the Joint Staff, "Defense Budget Overview," March 25, 2008.

92. "Under PFI re: How Britain Is Managing to Fight Two Wars on a Peace-Time Budget," *The Economist*, January 13, 2007, 51.

93. This recommendation has been made in testimony by John J. Hamre, former deputy secretary of defense and president of the Center for Strategic and International Studies; "Realities of Today: Demand a New Defense Acquisition Reform," *Aviation Week and Space Technology*, November 28, 2005, 74.

94. For a thorough discussion of early systems engineering, see National Research Council of the National Academies, *Pre-Milestone A and Early-Phased Systems Engineering: A Retrospective Review and Benefits for Future Air Force Systems Acquisition* (Washington, DC: National Academies Press, 2007.

95. Susan Irwin and Grace Jean, "Heavy Duty: Marines: MRAP Impedes Operations," *Inside the Beltway*, 2008,.

96. Defense Science Board Taskforce on Integrating Commercial Systems into the DoD, Effectively and Efficiently, "Buying Commercial: Gaining the Cost/Schedule Benefits for Defense Systems," Office of the Under Secretary of Defense for Acquisition, Technology and Logistics, Washington D.C., February 2009.

97. Sydney J. Freeman, Jr., "Time to Fix Military Procurement—Again," *NationalJournal.com*, April 25. 2009.

98. John Paul Parker, "At the Age of Fifty, It's Time for DARPA to Rethink Its Future," *National Defense Magazine* (September 2009).

99. Government Computer News, "Incoming Army CIO Discusses Agenda," August 23, 2007.

100. Senator McCain's Remarks on Introducing S.32, Defense Acquisition Reform Act of 2007, September 22, 2007.

101. Senator McCain, Remarks at Senate Armed Services Committee hearing on the Weapon Systems Acquisition Reform Act of 2009 (S. 454), March 3, 2009.

102. Reuters, "Computer Sciences Corp. Wins U.S. Army Simulation and Training Contract," February 12, 2009; also Program Executive Office of Simulation, Training, and Instrumentation, Press Release, January 29, 2009.

103. Michael Moiseyev, assistant director of the Bureau of Competition for the Federal Trade Commission, Letter to Douglas Larson, deputy general counsel of the Department of Defense entitled "Proposed Joint Venture between the Boeing Company and Lockheed Martin Corporation (United Launch Alliance)," File No. 051–0165, July 6, 2006.

104. "Can Boeing and Lockheed Work Together?" *Wall Street Journal*, June 19, 2006.

105. "Management Weakness," *Aviation Week and Space Technology*, September 25, 2006, 27.

106. "Costly Fleet Update Falters," *Washington Post*, December 8, 2006.

107. Renae Merle, "Government Short of Contracting Officers: Officials Struggle to Keep Pace with Rapidly Increasing Defense Spending," *Washington Post*, July 5, 2007.

108. Eric Lipton, "A Twenty-four Billion Military Contract Had Become a Major Embarrassment," *Washington Post*, April 17, 2007.

109. Angie C. Marek, "Deep Trouble for Deep Water," *U.S. News and World Report*, March 12, 2007, 27.

110. "LM-NG Stripped of U.S. C.G. Lead Systems Integrator Role," *Aerospace Daily and Defense Report*, April 18, 2007.

111. "Congress Eyes Lead System Integrators," *Defense News*, January 9, 2006.

112. John Warner National Defense Authorization Act for Fiscal Year 2007, Public Law 109–364, sec. 807.

113. For an excellent historical overview, see James F. Nagle, *A History of Government Contracting* (Washington, DC: George Washington University Press, 1999).

114. M. Lovell and J. Graser, "An Overview of Acquisition Reform Cost Savings Estimates," in *Three U.S. Air Force Acquisition Reform Pilot Munitions Program Overviews* (chapter 4) (Santa Monica: RAND Corporation, 2003).

115. Coopers and Lybrand, "The DoD Regulatory Cost Premium: A Quantitative Assessment," 1994.

116. Department of Defense, Summary of Procurement Awards, October 2005–September 2006.

117. Neal Fox, "Despite Problems, GSA Still Provides Unbeatable Service," *Federal Times*, March 24, 2006; also see David Hoexter, "Purchase Cards: Strengthening Controls and Maximizing Potential," Acquisition Solutions Advisory, December 2005.

118. "Interior, Pentagon Faulted in Audits," *Washington Post*, December 25, 2006,.

119. Department of Defense, Office of the Inspector General, "FY 2005 DoD Purchases Made through the Department of the Treasury," December 27, 2006.

120. Robert O'Harrow and Scott Higham, "Interior, Pentagon Faulted in Audits: Effort to Speed Defense Contracts Wasted Millions," *Washington Post*, December 25, 2006.

121. "Acquisition Advisory Panel Recommends More Competition, Transparency in Federal Government Purchasing," *Earthtimes*, December 21, 2006.

122. Gundar J. King, "Army Flying Machine," Intercollegiate Case Clearinghouse, Soldiers Field, Boston, 1978.

123. Peck and Scherer, *The Weapons Acquisition Process*.

124. Subcommittee on Readiness and Management Support of the Senate Armed Services Committee, Hearings, January 31, 2007, 5.

125. Steve Kelman, "History Matters," *Federal Computer Week*, July 30, 2007.

126. The use of fixed-price developments has been frequently advocated by members of Congress and was a major initiative of the Obama administration (in spite of the historic data).

127. Government Accountability Office, "DoD Wastes Billions of Dollars through Poorly Structured Incentives," April 5, 2006.

128. Government Accountability Office, "Guidance on Award Fees Has Led to Better Practices but Is Not Consistently Applied," May 2009.

129. Federal Procurement Data System: Analysis by CSIS Defense Industrial Initiatives Group, 2007.

130. "Contracting in Perspective: DHS's EAGLE—Will It Fly?," *GovExec*, April 3, 2006.

131. Richard L. Dunn, "Feature Comment: Other Transactions—Another Chance?," *Government Contractor* 15, no. 5 (February 6, 2008).

132. Lt. Gen. James Stansbury, "Profit '76," DoD Publication, 1977.

133. Grant Thornton, "Thirteenth Annual Government Contractor Industry Highlights Book," February 19, 2008; and "Working for the Government Is Risky Business, Contractors Say," *Federal Times*, February 20, 2008.

134. Charles R. Babcock, "Big Rewards for Defense Firms: Extra Fees Paid Regardless of Performance, GAO Finds," *Washington Post*, April 17, 2006, D-1.

135. "Boeing Seeks Payment for Failed Job," *Wall Street Journal*, February 21, 2006, 6.

136. "Multi-Year Raptor Procurement Deal Nearly Complete," *Aerospace Daily and Defense Report*, May 4, 2007.

137. "Boeing Presses for a New Contract for Super Hornets," *The Hill*, March 19, 2008.

138. "Bell-Boeing Receives $10.4 Billion Osprey Contract," March 28, 2008, as reported in the *Aero-News Network*, March 29, 2008,.

139. GAO, "Defense Acquisitions: DoD's Practices and Processes for Multi-Year Procurement Should Be Improved," February 7, 2008.

140. Kim Hart and Renae Merle, "As Military Contracts Grow, So Do Protests," *Washington Post*, February 27, 2007.

141. Richard Lardner, "Do Defense Contractors Protest Too Much?," *Associated Press*, May 24, 2008.

142. "Aerospace Daily and Defense Report," *Aviation Week and Space Technology*, November 12, 2008, 1.

143. "Contract Award Protests Charging Conflict of Interests on the Rise," *GovExec*, March 21, 2008.

144. "Array of Evaluation Errors Prompts COFC to Set Aside Multiple Awards," Court of Claims Decisions, March 12, 2008.

145. Andrea Shalal-Esa, "Analysis—Losing U.S. Defense Firms More Likely to Protest," *Roeders News*, June 26, 2007.

146. Testimony before Congress, January 24, 2008.

147. Defense Acquisition Performance Assessment Project, "Defense Acquisition Performance Assessment Report," January 2006, Washington, DC, 25.

148. Commission on Army Acquisition and Program Management in Expeditionary Operations, "Urgent Reform Required: Army Expeditionary Contracting,".

149. "Defense IG Seeks Thirty-three Percent Increase in Staffing," *Federal Times*, May 28, 2008.

150. "Status Report on Acquisition Legislation," National Defense Industrial Association, June 5, 2007.

151. Steven Pearlstein, "What Smartphone Makers Can Teach Legislators," *Washington Post*, June 11, 2008, D-01.

152. "'Buy American' Disputes Stalls Delivery of 1,000 Military Trucks," *Government Executive*, September 28, 2007.

153. Dana Hedgpeth, "A Foreign Air Raid? Congress, Union Leaders Chafe at European Firms Winning Bid to Build Air Force Tankers," *Washington Post*, March 4, 2008.

154. Jeffrey Birnbaum, "Big Lobbying Spenders of 2007; K Street Hits Another Record," *Washington Post*, April 15, 2008, A-13.

155. Jen Dimascio, "Defense Donations Help Fuel Big-Money Campaigns," *Defense Daily*, November 8, 2006, 6.

156. "Long-Term Defense Plans Conflict," *CQ Today*, May 2, 2007.

157. "Mirtha Rules Out Adding DDG-51 Destroyers to Shipbuilding Budget," *Inside the Navy*, April 30, 2007.

158. Craig Mellow, "Directors to Lobbyists: Stop Picking Our Pockets," *Corporate Board Member*, November–December 2007.

159. Robert O'Harrow, "Earmark Spending Makes a Comeback: Congress Pledged to Curbs in 2007," *Washington Post*, June 3, 2008, A-1.

160. "Defense Appropriations Act Directs Earmarks to Largest Contractors," *Government Executive*, November 28, 2007.

161. "President Bush Signs H.R. 2764 into Law," White House, December 26, 2007.

162. "Republicans Ask Homeland Security to Report on Reports," *Federal Times*, May 30, 2007.

163. Richard F. Kaufman, *The War Profiteers* (New York: Anchor Books, 1972).

164. See *New York Times*, November 8, 1987; *Washington Post*, March 22, 1985; *U.S. News and World Report*, November 16, 1987; *Washington Post*, May 12, 1985, June 2, 1984, November 27, 1985. (all about the "spare parts scandal").

165. Packard Commission Survey of Public Opinion on Defense Procurement, 1986.

166. David M. Walker, comptroller general of the United States, "An Accountability Update from Washington," Atlanta, GA, October 1, 2007.

167. *Final Report of the President's Private-Sector Commission on Government Management (The Grace Commission)* (Washington, DC: Government Printing Office, March 1985), book 2, p. ES-9.

168. F. Hyatt and R. Atkinson, "To Pentagon, Oversight Has Become Overkill," *Washington Post*, July 4, 1985.

169. P. Earley, "Sherick Seeks to Plug Pentagon Dike," *Washington Post*, November 26, 1984,.

170. Brian Grow et al., "Dangerous Fakes: How Counterfeit, Defective Computer Components from China are Getting into U.S. Warplanes and Ships," *Business Week*, October 2, 2008.

171. "Manufacturer in $2 Million Accord with the U.S. on Deficient Kevlar in Military Helmets," *New York Times*, February 6, 2008.

172. "Employee of Aerospace Metals Company Ordered to Pay $213,402 in Restitution in Aerospace Parts Fraud Case," Department of Transportation, Office of the Inspector General, June 20, 2007.

173. Tony Capaccio, "Pentagon Paid $998,798 to Ship Two Nineteen-Cent Washers," *Blumberg.com*, November 30, 2007; also see "Creative Billing: If Your Scam Is Brazen Enough, You Can Still Hoodwink the Pentagon—for a While," *The Economist*, August 25, 2007, 31.

174. "KBR Pays Eight Million to Settle Overcharging Claims," *Federal Times*, November 29, 2006.

175. R. Atkinson and F. Hyatt, "The Arms Makers Ethics," *Washington Post*, September 15, 1985.

176. "Pentagon Fraud Unit Marches Slowly," *Washington Post*, February 10, 1987.

177. Robin Wright, "U.S. Military Technology Being Exported Illegally Is a Growing Concern," *Washington Post*, October 14, 2007.

178. Major General Dewey Low, at an Air Force Association Meeting on January 14, 1985 (this meeting was videotaped and used to educate air force personnel on the spare parts issue.).

179. H. Kurtz, "Meese Unveils Plan to Fight Defense Fraud," *Washington Post*, September 17, 1985.

180. R. Marcus, "The Case against General Dynamics Tripped over Two Little Words," *Washington Post*, July 30, 1987.

181. "Government Procurement Reforms: The Need to Consider Long-Term Effects," *Program Manager* (November–December 1987): 14.

182. J. Barry, "In Bureaucratic Splendor," *Business Month* (January 1988): 59.

183. "GSA Contract Specialists Could Get Temporary Duty at Pentagon," *Federal Times*, July 25, 2007; House Committee on Appropriations, "Summary: 2008 Defense Appropriations," July 25, 2007.

184. "U.S. European Defense Firms Push for Voluntary Ethics Code," *Wall Street Journal*, July 17, 2006, A-4.

185. "Former Tamimi Global Executive Admits Paying Kickbacks for Military Subcontracts in Kuwait," *U.S. News Wire*, June 23, 2006.

186. "Firm Charged with Bribing Military Contracting Officer in Iraq," *Federal Times*, January 29, 2008.

187. "Five Individuals Arrested, Two Contracting Companies Charged in Bribery, Conspiracy Related to Department of Defense Contracts in Afghanistan," Department of Justice release,, August 27, 2008.

188. Federal News Radio, "Iraq Contractor Fraud Said to Be Limited," June 19, 2007, lso see "Hearing On: War Profiteering and Other Contractor Crimes Committed Overseas," House Committee on the Judiciary, June 19, 2007.

189. Special Inspector General for Iraq Reconstruction, "Interim Report on Iraq Reconstruction Contract Terminations," April 28, 2008.

190. "U.S. Wasted Millions in Iraq Aid, Investigators Say," *New York Times*, January 31, 2007.

191. Jacques S. Gansler, *Affording Defense* (Cambridge: MIT Press, 1991), 196–197, based on "Defense Audit Uncovers 'Questionable' Purchases," *Washington Post*, July 19, 1985.

192. E. Luttwak, *The Art of War* (New York: Simon and Schuster, 1984), 265.

193. Norman Augustine, Paper presented at the Armed Forces Communications and Electronics Association National Conference, Washington, DC, June 22, 1988.

194. In the case of the Reagan buildup, it was the Packard Commission (named after the chair, David Packard), and in the case of Iraq buildup, it was the Gansler Commission (also named after the chair of the Commission).

195. David Bond, "Washington Outlook: Abject Lesson," *Aviation Week and Space Technology*, April 2, 2007.

196. Deputy Secretary of Defense, "DoD in Context: Work of the Enterprise," data as of 2005 (unless otherwise specified).

197. "Features: Oversight and Out," *Government Executive*, June 1, 2008.

198. Ibid.

199. Christopher Dorobek, "Editorial: Running Scared," *Federal Computer Week*, March 12, 2007.

200. "Attracting and Retaining the Right Talent for the Federal 1102 Contracting Workforce," Procurement Round Table, April 2006 (modified by the author).

201. Donald Winter, secretary of the navy, Paper presented at the Sea and Aerospace Exposition, Washington, DC, April 3, 2007.

202. David M. Walker, comptroller general of the United States), testimony before the Senate Subcommittee on Readiness and Management Support of the Committee on Armed Services, "Defense Business Transformation: Sustaining Progress Requires Continuity of Leadership and an Integrated Approach," February 7, 2008.

203. Bureau of the Census, Foreign Trade Division, 2006 (seasonally adjusted).

204. Aerospace Industries Association, June 14, 2007.

205. GAO, "Sixth Annual Assessment of Selected Weapons Programs," March 31, 2008.

206. President's Blue Ribbon Commission on Defense Management, "A Quest for Excellence," Government Printing Office, June 1986.

207. Michael Ruane and Joe Stephens, "Capitol Visitors Center Début Again Delayed," *Washington Post*, March 9, 2007; "The Capitol Visitors Center, *Washington Post*, November 7, 2008.

208. David Lerman, "Navy's Price Tag Hits $11.7 Billion for New Carrier," *Daily Press*, February 4, 2003.

209. Based on Congressional Budget Office Estimates from the fiscal year 2008 Defense Department budget.

210. Ibid.; for submarine costs, also see the Senate Armed Services Committee National Defense Authorization Bill for fiscal 2008.

211. Secretary Robert Gates, Speech to navy League Sea-Air Space Exposition, National Harbor, Maryland, May 3, 2010.

212. "USS San Antonio Has Drained off an Ocean of Money," *San Antonio Express-News*, December 22, 2005.

213. "Stealth Bomber Crashes on Guam; Two Pilots Safe," *Washington Post*, February 23, 2008, 2.

214. Dana Hedgpeth, "GAO Analyst Says Cost Overruns, Delays Continue to Plague F-35 Program," *Washington Post*, March 12, 2010 (GAO estimates unit cost of the F-35 at $112 million).

215. "Bad F-35 Message to Allies," *Aviation Week and Space Technology*, October 15, 2007, 8.

216. T. Lindeman, S. Hamblin, and J. White, "The Price of Protection," *Washington Post*, November 13, 2007, A-17.

217. Department of Defense, selected acquisition reports, 2000 to 2007 (second quarter) as reported to Congress.

218. For example, refer to J. S. Gansler, *Affording Defense* (Cambridge: MIT Press, 1989), 174–175; N. R. Augustine, *Augustine's Laws* (New York: Penguin 1986); or a set of data from the Defense Material Organization of Australia—Mark V. Arena, Irv Blickstein, Clifford Grammich, and Obaid Younossi, *Why Has the Cost of Navy Ships Risen? A Macroscopic Examination of the Trends in U.S. Naval Ship Costs over the Past Several Decades* (Santa Monica: RAND National Defense Research Institute, 2006); Mark V. Arena, Irv Blickstein, Clifford Grammich, andObaid Younossi, *Why Has the Cost of Fixed-Wing Aircraft Risen? A Macroscopic Examination of the Trends in U.S. Aircraft Costs over the Past Several Decades* (Santa Monica: RAND National Defense Research Institute, 2008.

219. Augustine, *Augustine's Laws.*

220. "Defense Buying Costs Doubled since 9/11 with Few New Weapons Added," *Inside the Pentagon*, August 17, 2006, 1.

221. "Cost Rises for Presidential Helicopter," *Washington Post*, March 5, 2008.

222. "In Death of Spy Satellite Program, Lofty Plans and Unrealistic Bids," *New York Times*, November 11, 2007.

223. "Pentagon Struggles with Cost Overruns and Delays," Produce, *New York Times*, July 11, 2006.

224. Ibid.

225. August Cole, "Pentagon to Review Lockheed Fighter," *Wall Street Journal*, March 26, 2008.

226. Government Accountability Office, "Defense Acquisitions: Assessment of Selected Weapon Programs," March 2008.

227. Jeffrey A. Drezner, Jeanne M. Jarvaise, Ron Huss, Daniel M. Norton, and Paul G. Hough, *An Analysis of Weapon System Cost Growth* (Santa Monica: RAND Corporation, 1993). An analysis by the RAND Corporation indicated that "no single factor explains a large portion of the observed variance in cost growth outcomes" and that "little improvement has occurred over time."

228. Dan Czelusniak, Briefing before the Defense Science Board, June 12, 1998.

229. Government Accountability Office, "Defense Acquisitions: Assessments of Selected Weapons Programs," March 2007.

230. "Air Force, DoD Move to Bolster B-2 Mission Capable Rates," *Inside the Air Force*, May 26, 2006.

231. R. Jeffrey Smith, "Obama Vows a Veto in Dispute over F-22s," *Washington Post*, July 14, 2009, A-2.

232. Renae Merle, "Marines Seek Fuse on Vehicle: General Dynamics Design Has Problems," *Washington Post*, February 17, 2007.

233. John J. Hamre, president of Center for Strategic and International Studies and former deputy secretary of defense, testimony before to the Senate Armed Services Committee, April 30, 2009.

234. Pete Adolph, "Developmental Tests and Evaluation, Defense Science Board Taskforce Study," March 12, 2008, .

235. "Acquisition Oversight of the U.S. Navy's Littoral Combat System," House Arms Services Committee, February 8, 2007.

236. Pete Adolph, "Developmental Tests and Evaluation, Defense Science Board Taskforce Study," March 12, 2008.

237. David Napier, "2005 Year End Review and 2006 Forecast: An Analysis," Aerospace Industries Association, Washington, DC, 2006.

238. Merrill Lynch, Report, January 3, 2007.

239. Based on a JSA analysis of Standard & Poor's and the defense industry's Returns on equity, 1975 to 1999.

240. Based on FactSet, S & P Compustat, U.S. Energy Information Administration data, company reports, and Center for Strategic and International Studies analyses.

241. Robert Trice, information about Fortune, Yahoo! Financials, and company reports for 2005 as presented to the Defense Science Board, December 11, 2006.

242. Douglas, "Forty-First Annual Year End Review and Forecast Luncheon."

243. Dan Baum, "Nation Builders for Hire," *New York Times*, June 22, 2003.

244. As stated at Naval Postgraduate School, Spring Conference, Monterey, CA, May 16, 2007.

245. Renae Merle, "Armaments and Investments: Stock in Niche Defense Firms Soars in Wartime," *Washington Post*, July 15, 2007.

246. "Who Got What in a Slowing Economy?" *Washington Post*, July 28, 2008.

247. Gary Weiss, "Are You Paying for Corporate Fat Cats?," *Parade Magazine*, April 13, 2008.

248. *Forbes Magazine*, June 25, 2008.

249. Weiss, "Are You Paying for Corporate Fat Cats?," 24.

250. Lou Kratz, vice president, Lockheed Martin, "Defining the Future of DoD Logistics," March 4, 2008.

251. From Air Force Logistics Management Agency, *Quotes for the Air Force Logistician* 1 (2006): 18.

252. Allen Cullison and Peter Wonacott, "Taliban Is Seizing, Destroying More NATO Supplies," *Wall Street Journal*, August 12, 2008.

253. L. V. Snyder and Z. J. Shen, "Managing Disruptions to Supply Chains," *The Bridge* (2006).

254. David A. Fulghum, "Cyberwar Is Official," *Aviation Week and Space Technology*, September 14, 2000, 54–55.

255. "Air Force, DoD Move to Bolster B-2 Mission Capable Rate," *Inside the Air Force*, May 23, 2006.

256. Government Accountability Office, "Defense Logistics: Efforts to Improve Distribution in Supply Support for Joint Military Operations Could Benefit from a Coordinated Management Approach," July 11, 2007.

257. Gene Rector, "Air Force, Robbins Dispute Findings in GAO Document," *Macon Telegraph*, May 24, 2007.

258. Vice Admiral Walter Massenburg, U.S. Navy (Ret.), former commander, Naval Air Systems Command, Paper presented to the Defense Science Board, in Washington, D.C., June 13, 2007.

259. Government Accountability Office, "DoD's High-Risk Areas: Progress Made Implementing Supply Chain Management Recommendations, but Full Extent of Improvement Unknown," January 17, 2007.

260. Government Accountability Office, "Defense Logistics: Efforts to Improve Distribution and Supply Support for Joint Military Operations Could Benefit from a Coordinated Management Approach," June 2007.

261. Ibid.

262. William M. Solis, Government Accountability Office, "Defense Logistics: Preliminary Observations on the Effectiveness of Logistics Activities during Operation Iraqi Freedom," House Government Affairs Committee, December 18, 2003, 4.

263. Sources include U.S. Department of Defense, "Fiscal Year 2009 Budget Requests Briefing to Aerospace Industries Association," March 3, 2008; President's Budget Fiscal Year 2008 (average fleet-wide age); U.S. Air Force headquarters; Robert Trice, senior vice president, Lockheed Martin, Briefing to the Defense Science Board, December 11, 2006 (data from Air Force Association, Association of the United States Army, and Navy League).

264. Claudia Deutsch, "UPS Obsession with Efficiency Spreads beyond Boxes," *International Herald Tribune*, July 7–8, 2007.

265. Department of Defense, Management Initiative Decision No. 917, October 20, 2004.

266. "DoD Logistics Transformation Strategy," December 10, 2004.

267. Congressional Budget Office "Logistics Support for Deployd Military Forces," October, 2005.

268. Jacques S. Gansler, "Moving toward Market-Based Government: The Changing Role of Government as a Provider," IBM Endowment for the Business of Government," Washington, DC, June 2003.

269. Government Accountability Office, "Defense Logistics: Stryker Vehicle Support," September 5, 2006.

270. "Defense Contracts Foretell Military Build Up in Afghanistan," *Washington Post*, September 14, 2008.

271. The creation of a LOGCOM was recommended by the 1995 Commission on Roles and Missions, numerous past Defense Science Board reports, and the Center for Strategic and International Studies report "Beyond Goldwater-Nichol's Report." For example, see Defense Science Board, *Transformation: A Progress Assessment* (vol. 2) (Washington, DC: Office of the Undersecretary of Defense for Acquisition Technology and Logistics, April 2006), 30.

272. Aerospace Industries Association, Draft Report on U.S. Defense Modernization, August 20, 2008, 32.

273. "Support Needs Could Double 'Surge' Forces," *Boston Globe*, February 2, 2007.

274. "Pentagon Pushes Non-Human Warfare in Afghanistan," *AIA Daily Lead*, March 24, 2009.

Chapter 5

1. Office of the Undersecretary of Defense (Comptroller), "National Defense Budget Estimates for 2006," April 2005. Statistics from the Aerospace Industry Association are available at http:\\www.aia-aerospace.org\stats\aero_stats\stat12.pdf.

2. Commission on Army Acquisition and Program Management in Expeditionary Operations, *Urgent Reform Required: Army Expeditionary Contracting* (Washington, DC: U.S. Government Printing Office, October 2007).

3. Ibid.

4. Acquisition 2005 Taskforce, "Shaping the Civilian Acquisition Workforce of the Future," October 2000.

5. Based on data supplied by the Army Materiel Command to the Commission (and found in the report listed at note 2 above).

6. Richard Lardner, "Army Adding Five Generals to Oversee Purchasing, Contractors," *Boston Globe*, July 3, 2008, A-11.

7. Elise Castelli, "Army Shaping Civilian Role in New Contracting Command," *Federal Times*, March 17, 2008, 6.

8. "The Future Acquisition and Technology Workforce," Office of the Undersecretary of Defense for Acquisition, Technology, and Logistics, April 7, 2000, 2–3.

9. "AT&L Human Capital Strategic Plan," version 3.0, 2007.

10. Bernard Rostker, "A Call to Revitalize the Federal Civil Service," RAND Corporation Report, August 2008.

11. "Graduating to Public Service," *Washington Post*, November 14, 2007; see also "Federal Agencies Called Unprepared for Future Wave of Retirements," *Government Executive*, November 13, 2007.

12. "Government Must Hire 193,000 by 2009," *Federal Times*, July 3, 2007.

13. Matthew Weigelt, "Debate Over Contractors Continues: Lawmakers Foresee No Easy Solutions to Concerns about Acquisition Outsourcing," *Federal Computer Week*, April 7, 2008.

14. For discussions of such exchange programs, see Cynthia Yee, "Developing Leaders: Industry-Exchange Pays Off," *Federal Times,* January 23, 2006, 21; Sally Ann Harper, "Trading Expertise: GAO's Public-Private Exchange Brings Fresh Ideas," *Federal Times*, January 30, 2006, 21.

15. Pierre Chao, "The Future of the U.S. Defense Industrial Base: National Security Implications of a Globalized World," Paper presented at the Industrial College of the Armed Forces, June 2, 2005.

16. Michael T. Brewer, "An Aerospace Business Case for Transatlantic Corporation," Paper presented at the Industrial College of the Armed Forces on June 2, 2005.

17. "Contractors Use Signing Bonuses, Higher Salaries to Lure Employees with Security Clearances," *Federal Times*, October 18, 2006.

18. *Rising above the Gathering Storm: Energizing and Employing America for a Brighter Economic Future* (Washington, DC: National Academies Press, 2005).

19. Aerospace Industry's Association Employment Facts, January 6, 2006.

20. Ibid.

21. Susan Pollack, "Human Capital Strategy and the Future of Nation's Space Industry Workforce," Industrial College of the Armed Forces, June 2, 2005.

22. "We Risk Mediocrity: Raytheon CEO Says Workforce Challenge Requires New Mindset, Focus," *Aviation Week and Space Technology*, February 5, 2007, 47.

23. Thomas Sheeran, "Manufacturing Jobs Go Unfilled," *Examiner.com*, May 26–27, 2007, 53.

24. Norman R. Augustine, *Is America Falling Off of the Flat Earth?* (Washington, DC: National Academies Press, 2007).

25. CRA Taulbee Survey, March 2006.

26. Norman Augustine, "U.S. Science and Technology Is on a Losing Path," *Aviation Week and Space Technology*, October 31, 2005, 70.

27. "Aerospace Needs Multi-Pronged Effort to Maintain Workforce for Future Growth"(Editorial) *Aviation Week and Space Technology*, May 3, 2004, 74.

28. Joseph Anselmo, "Vanishing Act," *Aviation Week and Space Technology*, February 5, 2007, 45.

29. Aerospace Industries Association Employment Facts, January 6, 2006.

30. Robert J. Stevens, CEO Lockheed Martin, "Social Engineering," *Wall Street Journal*, April 19, 2006, A-12.

31. Anselmo, "Vanishing Act," *Aviation Week and Space Technology*, 45.

32. Ibid.

33. Task Force on the Future of American Innovation, "The Knowledge Economy: Is the United States Losing Its Competitive Edge?," February 16, 2005, 4.

34. Engineering Workforce Commission, "2006 Engineering and Technology Degrees," American Association of Engineering Societies, 2007.

35. National Science Foundation, "National Science and Engineering Indicators," 2004.

36. For a full discussion of this issue of foreign students and foreign scholars, refer to National Research Council of the National Academies, *Science and Security in a Post-9/11 World: A Report Based on Regional Discussions between the Science and Security Communities* (Washington, DC: National Academies Press, 2007).

37. National Innovation Initiative Report, "Innovate America," December 2004, 19.

38. Ibid.

39. "Innovation: Is Global the Way Forward?," *Boozallen.com Media File*, 2006.

40. "A Recipe for Weakness: By Limiting Visas for Skilled Foreign Professionals, the United States Only Harms Itself," *Washington Post*, June 4, 2008, A-18.

41. "The 'Green Card Brigade': How to Become an American via Iraq," *The Economist*, January 20, 2007, 34.

42. Ernesto Londono, "Warriors of the U.S. Becomes Its Citizens, Too: In Baghdad, 159 Troops Take the Oath in Largest Overseas Naturalization Ceremony," *Washington Post*, April 13, 2008.

43. Competeamerica.org, 2007.

44. State Department Visa Bulletin, May 2006.

45. Taskforce on the Future of American Innovation, "Measuring the Moment: Innovation and National Security in Economic Competitiveness," November 2006.

46. National Venture Capital Association (NVCA), "Immigrants Have Founded One in Four of Public Venture Backed Companies in the U.S. since 1990, Finds First-Ever Study," November 15, 2006.

47. For a detailed discussion, see Stuart Anderson and Michaela Platzer, "American Made: The Impact of Immigrant Entrepreneurs and Professionals on U.S. Competitiveness," National Venture Capital Association, Arlington, VA, 2006, 41.

48. "Brains and Borders: America Is Damaging Itself by Making It Too Difficult for Talented People to Enter the Country," *The Economist*, May 6, 2006.

49. CNP Tech Web, "U.S. Tech Companies Add Five Workers for Each H-1B Visa They Seek," March 10, 2008.

50. Adrienne Lewis, "Giving Visas to Skilled Workers Bolsters Economy," *USA Today*, March 25, 2008, 10-A.

51. Thomas L. Friedman, "Laughing and Crying," *New York Times*, May 23, 2007.

Chapter 6

1. Paul Bracken, "Technological Innovation in National Security," Foreign Policy Research Institute, Philadelphia, June 2008.

2. Ibid.

3. National Science Board 2003, National Science Foundation, 2004.

4. David Mowery, "Military R&D and Innovation," University of California, Berkeley, 2007.

5. William Greenwalt, deputy undersecretary of defense, Jane's Conference, Washington, DC, May 1, 2007.

6. David Mowery, *Military R&D and Innovation* (Berkeley: University of California Press, 2007).

7. Ibid.

8. Mihail Roco, National Nanotechnology Institute, in a presentation to the National Research Council, Washington, DC, February 5, 2008.

9. Based on research by Charles Wessner, National Research Council, as communicated to the author, July 6, 2009.

10. Quoted by the New China News Agency, February 9, 2009, and included in National Research Council, *Innovation Policies for the Twenty-First Century: Report of a Symposium* (Washington, DC: National Academies Press, 2007), 35.

11. Craig Barrett, "Flagging Economy Needs Science Investments," *San Francisco Chronicle*, January 20, 2008, G-5.

12. Mowery, *Military R&D and Innovation*, 12.

13. Norman Augustine, *Is America Falling Off the Flat Earth?* (Washington, DC: National Academies Press, 2008), 54.

14. Vannevar Bush, *Science: The Endless Frontier* (Washington, DC: U.S. Government Printing Office, 1945).

15. As highlighted by David Mowery in *Military R&D and Innovation*, in reference to Richard Nelson's "The Simple Economics of Basic Research," *Journal of Political Economy* (1959), and Kenneth Arrow, "Economic Welfare and the Allocation of Resources for R&D," in R. R. Nelson, ed., *The Rate and Direction of Inventive Activity* (Princeton: Princeton University Press, 1962).

16. This discussion can be found in James Turner, *The Next Innovation Revolution: Laying the Ground Work for the United States* (Cambridge: MIT Press, 2006).

17. Ibid., 127.

18. National Research Council, *The Small Business Innovation Research Program: An Assessment of the SBIR Program at the Department of Defense* (Washington, DC: National Academies Press, 2009).

19. Jon Baron, Statement before the Subcommittee on Technology and Innovation, House Committee on Science and Technology, Hearing on the SBIR Program Re-authorization, April 26, 2007.

20. "The Rise and Fall of Corporate R&D: Out of the Dusty Labs," *The Economist*, March 3, 2007, 76.

21. Dava Sobel, *Longitude: The True Story of a Lone Genius Who Solved the Greatest Scientific Problem of His Time* (New York: Walker, 1995).

22. Michael E. Porter, "Clusters and the New Economics of Competition," *Harvard Business Review* (November–December 1998).

23. Mowery, *Military R&D and Innovation*, 19.

24. George Heilmeier, "Guarding against Technological Surprise," *Air University Review* (September–October 1976).

25. Niccolò Machiavelli, *The Art of War* (1520).

26. Elting Morison, *Men, Machines, and Modern Times* (Cambridge: MIT Press, 1995).

27. Admiral Alfred Thayer Mahan, *The Influence of Sea Power upon History, 1660–1783* (Boston: Little, Brown, 1890).

28. As reported in National Science Board, "Research and Development Essential Foundation for U.S. Competitiveness in a Global Economy," National Science Foundation, 2008, 3.

29. Center for Strategic and International Studies, "Globalization, Technological Leadership and Risks to the U.S.," June 2004,.

30. "One-Atom Thick Material Will Revolutionize the World," *London Times*, March 1, 2007.

31. The material in the following discussion comes from a presentation about integrated dual-use commercial companies by Bob Spreng to the Defense Science Board and titled "R&D Contracting by Non-Traditional Defense Contractors in 2008."

32. Ibid.

33. Independent Review Group, "Strategic Initiatives for Innovation and Transition," Phase One Report, done in support of the Office of the Assistant Deputy Undersecretary of Defense for Innovation and Technology Transition, February 2, 2008.

34. For example, the Defense Science Board Taskforce on the Technology Capabilities of Non-DoD Providers, 2000; Defense Science Board Report on Globalization and Security, 1999; and Defense Science Board Summer Study on Twenty-First Century Technology Vectors, 2007.

35. Deemed Export Advisory Committee, "The Deemed Export Rule in the Era of Globalization," Report submitted to the Secretary of Commerce, December 20, 2007.

36. Clayton Christensen, *The Innovator's Dilemma: When New Technologies Cause Great Firms to Fail* (Boston: Harvard Business School Press, 1997).

37. Joseph A. Schumpeter, *Capitalism, Socialism, and Democracy* (3rd ed.) (New York: Harper and Brothers, 1950), 83–84, as described in G. R. Simonson, "Missiles and Creative Destruction in the American Aircraft Industry, 1956–1961," *Business History Review* (Harvard College) 38, no. 3 (Autumn, 1964): 302.

38. Arthur Alexander, "Weapons Acquisition in the Soviet Union, U.S., and France," RAND Report P-4989, RAND Corporation, Santa Monica, 1973.

39. "Advisors to Examine Export Controls on Nanotechnology," *The Expert Practitioner* (Gilston-Kalin Communications, Rockville, MD), 18, no. 11 (November 2004).

40. Augustine, *Is America Falling Off the Flat Earth?*, 54.

41. National Research Council of the National Academies, "Science and Security in a Post-9/11 World: A Report Based on Regional Discussions between the Science and Security Communities," National Academies Press, October 18, 2007.

42. John J. Young Jr., Undersecretary of defense for acquisition, technology, and logistics, "Memorandum to Secretaries of the Military Departments; Chairman, Joint Chiefs of Staff; and Directors of Defense Agencies," June 26, 2008.

43. U.S. Commission on National Security (known as the Hart-Rudman Commission after the cochairs), "Roadmap for National Security: Imperative for Change," Washington, DC, 2001.

44. Association of American Universities, "Department of Defense Research," 2008.

45. Augustine, *Is America Falling Off the Flat Earth?*, 58.

46. Al Shaffer, Office of the Director of Defense Research and Engineering, "Fiscal Year 2007 President's Budget Request for Science and Technology," Briefing to the Defense Science Board, 2008.

47. American Association for the Advancement of Science, "Congress Wraps Up Another Disappointing Year for Federal R&D Funding," January 7, 2008.

48. Center for Strategic and International Studies, "Globalization, Technological Leadership and Risks to the U.S.," June 2004.

49. American Association for the Advancement of Science, "Congress Wraps Another Disappointing Year for Federal R&D Funding."

50. David Ignatius, "The Ideas Engine Needs a Tune-up," *Washington Post*, June 3, 2007.

51. National Academy of Sciences, National Academy of Engineering, and Institute of Medicine of the National Academies, *Rising above the Gathering Storm: Energizing and Employing America for a Brighter Economic Future* (Washington, DC: National Academies Press, 2007).

52. Augustine, *Is America Falling Off the Flat Earth?*, 67.

Chapter 7

1. "Report of the Government Commission on Government Procurement," December 1972; Frederic M. Scherer, *The Weapons Acquisition Process: Economic Incentives* (Cambridge: Harvard University Press, 1964), 48.

2. "Air Force Carefully Evaluating KC-X Proposals," *Air Force Link*, May 7, 2007.

3. Senator John McCain, Testimony before the Senate Armed Services Committee, March 3, 2009.

4. "IBM, CRAY Win Pentagon Funds to Develop Next Super Computers," *Wall Street Journal*, November 22, 2006, B-2.

5. James Richardson and James Roumasset, "Sole-Sourcing, Parallel-Sourcing: Mechanism for Supplier Performance," *Managerial and Decision Economics* (January 1995).

6. For detailed examples and historical data, see Lou Kratz and Jacques Gansler, "Effective Competition during Weapon System Acquisition," National Contract Management Association, 1987.

7. Fred Hiatt and Rick Atkinson, Years of 'Requirements Creep' send 'Silver' Bullet off its Mark *Washington Post*, May 19, 1985. p. A1 .

8. Ibid.

9. Robert W. Drewes, *The Air Force and the Great Engine War* (Washington, DC: National Defense University Press, 1987); David M. Kennedy, *The Great Engine War* (Cambridge: Kennedy School of Government, Harvard University, 1985); Frank Camm, *The Development*

of the F100-PW-220 and F110-GE-100 Engines: A Case Study of Risk Assessment and Risk Management (Santa Monica: RAND Corporation, 1993).

10. R. Ropelewski, "USAF Negotiating Contracts for F-100, F-110 Improvements," *Aviation Week and Space Technology*, May 20, 1985, 18; see also "Great Engine War," Cambridge Case Clearinghouse.

11. Scherer, *The Weapon Acquisition Process*.

12. Jacques S. Gansler, "Defense Spending: How About Some Real Competition?," *Washington Post*, April 4, 1982.

13. Public Law 98–92.

14. E. White, "Defense Industry Slims Down to Survive," *Wall Street Journal*, September 30, 1987.

15. John F. Lehman, "Command at the Seas," Naval Institute Press, 2001, Annapolis, MD.

16. The Trident D-5 is a three-stage, solid propellant, inertially guided missile that has a range of more than four thousand nautical miles and is armed with multiple, independently targeted reentry vehicles.

17. John Schank et al., "Acquisition and Competition Strategy Options for the DD(X)," RAND Corporation, Santa Monica, 2006.

18. Department of Defense, Office of the Inspector General, "Report on the Air Force KC-X Aerial Refueling Tanker Aircraft Program," May 30, 2007.

19. Tony Capaccio, "Administration Trims Supplemental Procurement, Eyes Big Weapons," *Defense News*, March 3, 2009.

20. "Air Force Now Supports Alternate Engine Program for F-35," *Government Executive*, March 11, 2008.

21. Michael Sullivan, director of acquisition and sourcing management at the Government Accountability Office, Testimony before the Subcommittee on Air and Land Forces of the Committee on Armed Services of the House of Representatives, "Defense Acquisitions: Analysis of Costs for the Joint Strike Fighter Engine Program," March 22, 2007.

22. "Navy, Air Force Maneuver to Save JSF Alternate Engine," *Aerospace Daily and Defense Report*, January 5, 2006.

23. Department of Defense, "Defense Department Contracts for 2,400 More MRAP Vehicles," October 19, 2007.

24. "Orders for Armored Vehicles to Be Cut," *Federal News Radio*, November 30, 2007.

25. Department of Defense, Office of Inspector General, "Procurement Policy for Armored Vehicles," July 18, 2007.

26. "HUMVEE Replacement Program to Begin Next Month," *GovExec*, January 18, 2008.

27. "Army Ends Deals with Native Contractors," *Anchorage Daily News*, April 22, 2006.

28. Scherer, *The Weapons Acquisition Process*, 49.

29. "Navy adds 556 contractors to Sea Port-e program, Washington Technology, July 19, 2010.

30. Many areas were defined by agencies as not included in the Federal Activities Inventory Reform (FAIR) Act, including military positions in jobs that were not inherently governmental. Thus, this excludes 320,000 DoD jobs that were being done by the military but were eligible for competitive sourcing (as of January 26, 2004). And this increased to 339,142 in FY09 (according to a Defense Business Board report "Reducing Overhead and Improving Business Operations," July 22, 2010.

31. Jacques S. Gansler and William. Lucyshyn, "Implementing Alternative Sourcing Strategies: Four Case Studies," IBM Center for the Business of Government, Washington, DC, October 2004.

32. Center for Naval Analysis, "Long-Run Costs and Performance Effects of Competitive Sourcing," Washington, DC, February 2001.

33. "Report on Competitive Sourcing Results, FY 2007," Office of Management and Budget, Washington, DC, May 2, 2008.

34. "Are They A-76 Winners or Second-Class Feds?," *Federal Computer Week*, August 20, 2007.

35. Gansler and Lucyshyn, "Competitive Sourcing: What Happens to Federal Employees?"

36. J. D. Brown, J. S. Earle, and A. Telegdy, "Does Privatization Hurt Workers? Evidence from Comparative Analysis of Enterprise Data," Upjohn Institute for Employment Research, January 2008.

37. "Report on Competitive Sourcing Results, Fiscal Year 2007," Office of Management and Budget, Washington, DC, May 2, 2008.

38. Ibid.

39. "Competitive Sourcing under Section 842(a) of Public Law 109-115," Office of Management and Budget, April 25, 2006.

40. "DoD IG Interim Report to Congress on Section 325 of the National Defense Authorization Act for Fiscal Year 2008," Department of Defense, April 22, 2008.

41. "Think Tank Calls Competitive Sourcing a Winning Tool for Taxpayers," *GovExec*, August 8, 2008.

42. Cost Comparison Studies for "in-sourcing":

• Congressional Budget Office: "Logistics Support for Deployed Military Forces," October 2005; "over a 20 year period, using army military units would cost roughly 90% more than using contractors."

• General Accountability Office: "Warfighter Support: A Cost Comparison of Using State Department Employees vs. Contractors for Security Services in Iraq," March 4, 2010; "using State Department employees to provide state security for the Embassy in Bagdad would cost approximately $858 million for 1 year; versus $78 M charged by contractor" (over 90 percent more for State Department employees); "For three out of four tasks comparisons, costs using State Department employees would be greater than using contractors; and, for that one lower cost case, when training costs for State Department were included, the costs were comparable."

• Congressional Research Service: "Department of Defense Contractors in Iraq and Afganistan: Background Analysis," December 14, 2009; "Using contractors can save DoD money";

"Hiring contractors only as needed can be cheaper in the long run than maintaining a permanent in-house capability"—also describes other advantages of contractors (versus in-house) in terms of available skills; rapid response; and so on.

• Congressional Budget Office: "Contractor's Support of U.S. Operations in Iraq," August 2008; "Comparable costs (over a 1 year period) for Blackwater Private Security Contractor Personnel and Army Personnel (but can get rid of contractor personnel when conflict ends)."

43. "Congress' Mixed Messages on Competition," *Washington Technology*, June 16, 2008.

44. Steven Goldsmith, "What's Left for Government to Do?," *The American*, January 1, 2008, Available at: http://www.american.com/archive/2008/january-february-magazine-contents/what2019s-laft-for-government-to-do (accessed on August 30, 2010).

45. E. S. Savas, *Privatization and Public Partnerships* (New York: Chatham House, 2000).

46. Stephen Barr, "A Challenge to ESPRIT at Army Corps," *Washington Post*, April 26, 2007, D-4.

Chapter 8

1. B. Anthony Billings, "Are U.S. Tax Incentives for Corporate R&D Likely to Motivate American Firms to Perform Research Abroad?," *Tax Executive* (July–August 2003): 291–315. These rates simulate three-year averages (1998–2000) for twenty U.S. multinationals, including IBM and Intel.

2. From Semi-Conductor Industry Association, "Keeping U.S. Leadership in Semi-Conductor Technology," September 2008.

3. Norman Augustine, "U.S. Science and Technology Is on a Losing Path," *Aviation Week and Space Technology*, October 31, 2005.

4. David C. Mowery, *Military R&D and Innovation* (Berkeley: University of California, 2007), figs. 1–2.

5. Robert Wall, "Opening Doors," *Aviation Week and Space Technology*, December 10, 2007, 36.

6. Edgar E. Ulsamer, "The Designers of Dassault: Men Who Take One Step at a Time," *Air Force Magazine* (August 1970): 32.

7. Robert Trice, "Globalization in the Defense Industrial Base," Briefing to the Defense Science Board, December 11, 2006, chart 21 (where the data come from company annual reports).

8. For example, in 2003, the U.S. defense budget was $455.3 billion, and at comparable prices and exchange rates, the United Kingdom's budget was $47.4 billion, the French $46.2 billion, the German $33.9 billion, and the Italian $27.8 billion (based on SIPRI data from 2005).

9. Keith Hartley, "Defense Industrial Policy in a Military Alliance," *Journal of Peace Research* 43, no. 4 (2006): 473–489.

10. Steven Pincock, "Could U.S. Scientists Get E.U. Funding?," *The Scientist: Magazine of Life Sciences* (April 19, 2007).

11. "Problems Run Rampant for Galileo Project: Rival to GPS System Faces Cost Overruns, Bickering Partners," *Wall Street Journal*, January 10, 2007.

12. Hartley, "Defense Industrial Policy in a Military Alliance," 477.

13. "Forecast 2007—Aerospace Industry Mergers: Mergers May Be off the Agenda for the Big Players, But There Are Stirrings Further Down the Supply Chain," *Flight International*, January 2, 2007.

14. Michael A. Taverna, "Togetherness; Germany Leads Looming Land and Naval Consolidation in Europe," *Aviation Week and Space Technology*, May 15, 2006, 32.

15. The material in this discussion of this embargo comes from Eugene Kogan, "The European Union Defense Industry and the Appeal of the Chinese Market," Studien und Berichte, zur Sicherheitspolitik, January 2005.

16. Hartley, "Defense Industrial Policy in a Military Alliance," 478.

17. As presented at the Bio-Science Research Building opening celebration at the University of Maryland's College of Chemical and Life Sciences, September 18, 2007.

18. Victoria Shannon, "A 'Third Way' on Fostering Research," *International Herald Tribune*, March 15, 2007.

19. Richard Kugler and Hans Binnendijk, *Seeing the Elephant* (Washington, DC: National Defense University Press, 2007), 224.

20. "Neutron Industrial Work Share," *Aviation Week and Space Technology*, January 8, 2007, 23.

21. Hartley, "Defense Industrial Policy in a Military Alliance," 486. Also refer to T. Sandler and K. Hartley, *The Political Economy of NATO* (Cambridge: Cambridge University Press, 1999), 144–151.

22. National Audit Office, "Maximizing the Benefits of Defense Equipment Cooperation," London, March 2001.

23. National Audit Office, "Major Projects Report, 2004," London, 2004.

24. Terence Guay, "Globalization and Its Implications for the Defense Industrial Base," Strategic Studies Institute, U.S. Army War College, February 2007, 13.

25. Secretary of State for Defense by Command of Her Majesty, "Defense Industrial Strategy (Defense White Paper)," December 2005.

26. "British Defense Industrial Strategy Secures BAE Systems as U.K. Champion," *Aviation Week and Space Technology*, December 17, 2005.

27. "Foreign Rivals Threaten Weapons Base," *Financial Times*, March 1, 2006.

28. James Boxell, "After the Battle of Britain: How BAE Can Call Itself Champion," *Financial Times*, June 23, 2006, 11.

29. Guay, "Globalization and Its Implications for the Defense Industrial Base," 64.

30. "Foreign Rivals Threaten Weapons Base," *Financial Times*, March 1, 2006.

31. "The Defense Industrial Strategy," 26.

32. "MOD to Unveil Wish-List for Technological Development," *Financial Times*, October 17, 2006.

33. Mowery, *Military R&D and Innovation*, 13.

34. "U.K. Plan for Slicing R&D Funding Pie Is Poorly Conceived," *Aviation Week and Space Technology*, July 11, 2005, 66.

35. "Defense Spending Under PFI: How Britain Is Managing to Fight Two Wars on a Peace-Time Budget," *The Economist*, January 13, 2007, 51.

36. Pierre Chao and Robin Niblett, "Trusted Partners: Sharing Technology within the U.S.-U.K. Security Relationship," Center for Strategic and International Studies, May 26, 2006.

37. President of the Republic, "The French White Paper on Defense and National Security," Paris, June 2008.

38. Pierre Tran, "Pakistan Seeks Three Subs from France: New Design Would Free DCN a Spanish Partnership," *Defense News*, February 27, 2006.

39. Jamestown Foundation, "Mistral Debate Unavoidable in NATO," *Eurasia Daily Monitor* 7, no. 70, April 12, 2010.

40. Michael Taverna, "Role Play: With French Defense White Paper Looming, Industry Produces a Wish List of Its Own," *Aviation Week and Space Technology*, June 16, 2007, 39.

41. Michael Porter, "Cluster and the New Economics of Competitions," *Harvard Business Review* (November–December 1998).

42. "More French Research Clusters," *Aviation Week and Space Technology*, July 16, 2007.

43. National Research Council of the National Academies, *Innovation Policies for the Twenty-First Century: Report of a Symposium* (Washington, DC: National Academies Press, 2007), 69.

44. "Finmeccanica Has Global Goals: A Strategy to Become a Key Player in the World's Two Biggest Defense Markets—and Has Put Its Money Where Its Mouth Is," *Flight International*, November 8, 2005.

45. James Schear, "Defusing Conflicts in Unstable Regions," in *Strategic Challenges: America's Global Security Agenda* (Washington, DC: National Defense University Press, 2007), 170 (and the source for their data was the International Monetary Fund's 2006 *BP Statistical Review*).

46. "Russian Defense Budget to Jump," *Washington Post*, September 20, 2008.

47. V. Ginodman and A. Rotkin, "The Spector of the Soviet Army: Military Reforms in Russia Are Still Following the Soviet Pattern," Moscow, June 20, 2006; also see Peter Finn, "Russia, Indonesia Set One Billion Arms Deal: Moscow Seen Trying to Boost Clout in Asia," *Washington Post*, June 7, 2007.

48. Andrew Osborn, "Russia Returns to Commercial Airline Market: Consolidation Key to Wider Strategy," *Washington Post*, June 26, 2007.

49. Ibid. Also see Alexey Komarov, "Russia's Roadmap: Aircraft Makers Target a Boost in Annual Production Rate," *Aviation Week and Space Technology*, March 12, 2007.

50. "Russia," *Aviation Week and Space Technology*, August 13, 2007, 24.

51. A. Komarov and D. Barrie, "Room for Expansion: MiG Targets Profit Growth through a New Military, Commercial Work," *Aviation Week and Space Technology*, May 15, 2006, 38.

52. Steven J. Flanagan, "Securing America's Future: Progress in Perils," in *Strategic Challenges: America's Global Security Agenda* (Washington, DC: National University Press, 2007), 331.

53. F. M. Scherer, *Industrial Market Structure and Economic Performance* (Chicago: Rand McNally, 1970), 398.

54. Internal DoD Memorandum, "Unclassified Summary of a Classified Study on Aircraft Engine Costs and Design," enclosure to S-5463-DE-4, released January 14, 1977.

55. A. J. Alexander, "The Process of Soviet Weapons Acquisition," Paper presented to the Europeans Study Commission, Paris, April 15–16, 1977, 4.

56. David Fulghum and Douglas Barrie, "Ministerial Review; Putin Observes Flight Tests of Next-Generation Multirole Fighter," *Aviation Week and Space Technology*, June 28, 2010, 34.

57. "Russia Intensifies Efforts to Rebuild Its Military Machine," *Christian Science Monitor*, February 12, 2007.

58. RIA Novosti, "Russian Arms Exports Break Record," March 8, 2007.

59. Sergey Safronov, "Russia Diversifying Arms Exports," *RIA Novosti*, May 28, 2009.

60. Phillip Pan, "Venezuela, Russia in $1 Billion Accord: Loan to Fund Arms Purchases; Two Leaders Also Consider Forming Gas Cartel," *Washington Post*, September 27, 2008, A-12.

61. Finn, "Russia, Indonesia Set a $1Billion Arms Deal."

62. "Latin American Defense Mins Eye Venezuela Arms Build-Up," *Wall Street Journal*, October 1, 2006.

63. Kelley Hearn, "Russia Negotiating Arms Sales to Buenos Aires," *Washington Times*, August 9, 2006, 11.

64. Jamestown Foundation, "Mistral Case Presages Russian Shopping Spree for Western Military Technology," *Eurasia Daily Monitor* 7, no. 71, April 13, 2010.

65. Jamestown Foundation, "Rearmament Declared the Main Issue in Russian Military Reform," *Eurasia Daily Monitor* 7, no. 122, June 22, 2010.

66. Nathan Hodge, "On Pentagon Wish List: Russian Copters," *Wall Street Journal*, July 8, 2010.

67. "Russia Intensifies Effort to Rebuild Its Military Machine," *Christian Science Monitor*, February 12, 2007.

68. Martin Sieff, "Tupolev Tu-95 M & S Bear-H Nuclear Bomber," UPI, Washington, DC, October 2, 2008.

69. Carl Dahlman, J.-E. Aubert, "China and the Knowledge Economy: In the Twenty-First Century," Washington, DC, World Bank, 2001, as quoted in National Research Council, *Innovation Policies for the Twenty-First Century: Report of a Symposium*, 11.

70. Senator Kay Bailey Hutchison, "Science Policy Matters," *Issues in Science and Technology* (Fall 2007): 5.

71. National Research Council, *Rising Above the Gathering Storm* (Washington, DC: National Academies Press, 2006).

72. A. L. Porter, N. C. Newman, X.-Y. Jin, D. M. Johnson, and J. D. Roessner, "High Tech Indicators: Technology-Based Competitiveness of Thirty-Three Nations, 2007 Report," Technology Policy and Assessment Center, Georgia Institute of Technology, Augusta, Georgia, January 22, 2008.

73. Conference on Grand Challenges in Twenty-First Century Bioscience, University of Maryland, September 18, 2007.

74. President's Council of Advisors on Science and Technology, "Leadership Under Challenge: Information Technology R&D in a Competitive World," August 2007, 14.

75. New China News Agency, February 9, 2006,.

76. "Chinese to Develop Sciences, Technology," *Washington Post*, February 10, 2006, A-16.

77. Fourth National Conference on Science and Technology, Beijing, January 9, 2006, as reported on Xinhua net.

78. Yongxiang Lu, *Science and Technology in China: A Roadmap to 2050* (Beijing: Science Press, 2007).

79. Ronald Kostoff, Office of Naval Research, et al., "The Structure and Infrastructure of Chinese Science and Technology," 2006, and reported in "O & R Report Highlights China's Investment in Military Science Research," *Inside the Navy*, April 3, 2006, .

80. Edward Cody, "China Boosts Military Spending: Senior U.S. Official Presses Beijing to Clarify Plans and Intentions," *Washington Post*, March 5, 2007, A-12.

81. Jacob Kipp, "Promoting the New Look for the Russian Armed Forces," *Eurasia Daily Monitor* 7, no. 113, June 11, 2010.

82. President's Council of Advisors on Science and Technology, "Leadership under Challenge: Information Technology R&D in a Competitive World," August 2007, 18 (the portion of first-year college students listing computer science as their probable major has declined from almost 4 percent in 2000 to 1 percent in 2006, which is the lowest rate for computer science since 1977).

83. Robert J. Stevens, "Social Engineering," *Wall Street Journal*, April 19, 2006, A-12.

84. Ariana E. Cha, "Opportunities in China Lure Scientists Home," *Washington Post*, February 20, 2008.

85. James Reynolds, "China's Drive to Promote Invention," *BBC News*, Beijing, July 24, 2007.

86. "Boeing Set to Establish Base in Shanghai," *Asia Pulse Business Wire*, December 21, 2005.

87. Wayne Arnold, "Where the Appetite for Aircraft Is Big," *New York Times*, November 28, 2006, C-1.

88. "China's Air Ambitions Face Obstacles: Beijing Hopes to Tap Lucrative Market Dominated by Boeing and Airbus," *Wall Street Journal*, March 20, 2007, A-12.

89. "Chinese J-11B Presages Quiet Military Revolution," *Aviation Week and Space Technology*, November 5, 2006.

90. "China Lays Out Its Space Ambitions before a U.S. Audience," *Asian Wall Street Journal*, April 7, 2006, 9.

91. Craig Covault, "Space Control: Chinese Anti-Satellite Weapon Test Will Intensify Funding and Global Policy Debate on the Military Uses of Space," *Aviation Week and Space Technology*, January 22, 2007, 24.

92. Evan Medeiros, Roger Cliff, Keith Crane, and James Mulvenon, *New Directions for China's Defense Industry* (Santa Monica, CA: RAND Corporation, 2005).

93. Schear, "Diffusing Conflicts in Unstable Regions," 155.

94. Edward Cody, "China Boosts Military Spending: Senior U.S. Official Presses Beijing to Clarify Plans and Intentions," *Washington Post*, March 5, 2007.

95. United Press International, "Here Comes China," December 18, 2006.

96. Ashton Carter and William Perry, "China on the March," *National Interests* (March–April 2007): 16–22.

97. Ibid., 18.

98. Ibid., 22.

99. United Press International, "Fighting an Asymmetrical Chinese War Machine," November 20, 2006.

100. Ibid.

101. President's Council of Advisors on Science and Technology, "Leadership Under Challenge: Information Technology R&D in a Competitive World," August 2007, 11.

102. Shirley Kan, "China and Proliferation of Weapons of Mass Destruction and Missiles: Policy Issues," Congressional Research Service, Washington, DC, January 31, 2007.

103. James R. Holmes, "Military Culture and Chinese Export Controls," *Non-Proliferation Review* 12, no. 3 (November 2005).

104. John C. K. Daly, "Fears That New Chinese Warhead Could Seep into Iraq," *Jamestown Foundation Terrorism Focus*, April 10, 2007.

105. Tony Hawkins, "Harare to Buy More Chinese Aircraft," *Financial Times*, August 24, 2006, 3.

106. Merrill Lynch, "Aerospace Update: Commodities and Gunboat Politics," May 15, 2008.

107. Terrence Quay, "Globalization and Its Implications for the Defense Industrial Base," Strategic Studies Institute, U.S. Army, February 2007, 16.

108. Report of the Secretary of Defense Task Force on DoD Nuclear Weapons Management, "Phase II: Review of the DoD Nuclear Mission," December 2008.

109. International Herald Tribune, "Japan Moves to Upgrade Defense Unit," June 10, 2006.

110. Richard J. Samuels, *Securing Japan: Tokyo's Grand Strategy in the Future of East Asia* (Ithaca: Cornell University Press, 2007).

111. "Militech Power," *Asahi Shimbun*, 1989, as quoted in a seminar on "Security Trade Control: Toward Regional Framework in Asia and Japan's Role," University of Tokyo, November 2007.

112. U.S. Department of Defense, "Electronics," July 29, 1985.

113. National Research Council, *Innovation Policies for the Twenty-First Century*, 22–23.

114. President's Council of Advisors on Science and Technology, "Leadership Under Challenge: Information Technology R&D in a Competitive World," August 2007.

115. "Japan Should Maintain Weapons Export Bar," *Mainichi Shimbun*, July 20, 2004.

116. Merrill Lynch, "Aerospace Update: Inside the Japanese Suppliers," February 15, 2007.

117. Agence France-Presse, December 25, 2006.

118. Report of the Secretary of Defense Task Force on DoD Nuclear Weapons Management, "Phase II: Review of the DoD Nuclear Mission," December 2008.

119. Frost and Sullivan, "Country Industry Forecast: The Indian Aerospace and Defense Industry," November 22, 2005.

120. National Research Council, *Innovation Policies for the Twenty-First Century*, 15.

121. Saritha Rai, "India Becoming a Crucial Cog in Machine at IBM," *New York Times*, June 5, 2006.

122. National Research Council, *India's Changing Innovation System: Achievements, Challenges, and Opportunities for Cooperation* (Washington, DC: National Academies Press, 2007), 7.

123. Neelam Matthews, "Middle Man Muddle," *Aviation Week and Space Technology*, October 23, 2006, 27.

124. Ambassador Devare, former Indian external affairs secretary, Paper presented at the University of Maryland, January 29, 2007.

125. Guay, "Globalization and Its Implications for the Defense Industrial Base."

126. "U.S. Provides Israel with 9 Billion £, Array of High-Tech Weapons," *London Daily Telegraph*, July 28, 2006.

127. Joris Janssen Lok, "Mature Market: Changing Threat Perception Leads to Rush for Defense of Capabilities," *Aviation Week and Space Technology*, March 12, 2007, 54.

128. Thomas Erdbrink, "Iran Makes the Sciences a Part of Its Revolution," *Washington Post*, June 6, 2008.

129. Farnez Fassihi, "Tehran Unveils Unmanned Bomber," *Wall Street Journal*, August 23, 2010.

Chapter 9

1. David M. Walker, comptroller general of the United States, "DoD Transformation: Challenges and Opportunities," Army War College, February 12, 2007 (GAO-07–500CG).

2. Robert M. Gates, "A Balanced Strategy: Reprogramming the Pentagon for a New Age," *Foreign Affairs* (January–February 2009).

3. Aerospace Industries Association, "New Export Control Proposals Announced at Senate Aerospace Caucus Lunch," press release, July 2010.

4. Ellen Nakashima, "New Cyber Command Chief Warns of Possible Attacks," *Washington Post*, June 4, 2010.

5. Norman R. Augustine, *Is American Falling Off the Flat Earth?* (Washington, DC: National Academies Press, 2008), 62.

6. Peter W. Singer, "How the U.S. Military Can Win the Robotic Revolution," Brookings, 2010.

7. Lincoln Bloomfield Jr., "Export Controls and Technology Transfers: Turning Obstacles into Opportunities," Hudson Institute, Washington, DC, September 11, 2006.

8. Richard Armitage and Joseph Nye Jr., "CSIS Commission on Smart Power: A Smarter, More Secure America," Center for Strategic and International Studies, Washington, DC, 2007.

9. "Hot or Not: Acquisition Was a Hot Spot," *Federal Computer Week*, December 17, 2007.

10. Donald C. Winter, "Remarks at the Sea Air Space Exposition," *Navy League Online*, April 3, 2007.

11. Greg Gant, "Launching a New Navy," *Government Executive Online*, May 15, 2007.

12. Commission on Army Acquisition Expeditionary Operations, "Urgent Reform Required: Army Expeditionary Contracting," October 31, 2007.

13. Joint Chiefs of Staff, "Capstone Concept for Joint Operations: Version 3.0," Department of Defense, Washington, DC, Jan. 15, 2009.

14. Defense Science Board Task Force on Defense Industrial Structure for Transformation "Creating an Effective National Security Industrial Base for the Twenty-First Century: An Action Plan to Address the Coming Crisis," Office of the Undersecretary of Defense for Acquisition, Technology, and Logistics, July 2008.

15. Paul Kennedy, *The Rise and Fall of Great Powers: Economic Change and Military Conflict from 1500 to 2000* (New York: Random House, 1987).

16. "For a Sound Defense Industry," *New York Times*, November 23, 1976, 35.

17. Joseph Bower and Clayton Christensen, "Disruptive Technologies: Catching the Wave," *Harvard Business Review* (January–February 1995).

18. Dawn Vehmeier, Michael Caccuitto, and Gary Powell, "Transforming the Defense Industrial Base: A Roadmap"; Office of the Deputy Under Secretary of Defense for Industrial Policy, February 2003.

19. Defense Science Board, *Twentieth-Century Technology Vectors*, 2006 Summer Study, Office of the Undersecretary of Defense of Acquisitions, Technology, and Logistics, Washington, DC, February 2007.

20. National Research Council, *The SBIR Program: A Reassessment* (Washington, DC: National Academy Press, 2009).

21. Jeffrey A. Drezner et al., "Maintaining Future Military Aircraft Design Capability," R-4199-AF, RAND Corporation, 1992; and John Birkler et al., "Competition and Innovation in the U.S. Fixed-Wing Military Aircraft Industry," RAND Corporation, 2003.

22. National Research Council, *Beyond "Fortress America": National Security Controls on Science and Technology in a Globalized World* (Washington, DC: National Academies Press, 2009).

23. In August 2009, President Obama ordered a review of U.S. export control systems, but results of this review were unavailable at the time of publication of this book.

24. Richard Fontaine and John Nagle, "Contracting in Conflicts: The Path to Reform," Center for a New American Security, Washington, DC, June 2010.

Bibliography

Abetti, Pier, and Jose Maldifassi. *Defense Industries in Latin American Countries*. Westport: Praeger, 1994.

Abramson, Mark, and Roland Harris. *The Procurement Revolution*. Maryland: Rowman and Littlefield, 2003.

Adams, Gordon. "Getting U.S. Foreign Assistance Right." *Bulletin of the Atomic Scientists* 64 (May 2008): 2.

Adams, Gordon, Christophe Cornu, and Andrew James. "Between Cooperation and Competition: The Transatlantic Defense Market." Chaillot Paper 44. Institute for Security Studies of WEU, January 2001.

Aerospace Industries Association. "A Special Report U.S. Defense Acquisition: An Agenda for Positive Reform." Washington, DC, November 2008.

Aerospace Industries Association. "The Unseen Cost: Industrial Base Consequences of Defense Strategy Choices." July 2009.

Alie, J. A., L. Bransercomb, H. Brooks, A. Carter, and G. L. Epstein. *Beyond Spinoff*. Boston: Harvard Business School Press, 1992.

Anderson, Roy. "Defense Research and Technology." Ministry of Defense, February 2007.

Anderson, Stuart, and Michaela Platzer. "American Made: The Impact of Immigrant Entrepreneurs and Professionals on U.S. Competitiveness." National Venture Capitalist Association, Arlington, VA, 2006.

Arena, Mark, Irv Blickstein, Clifford Grammich, and Obaid Younossi. *Why Has the Cost of Fixed-Wing Aircraft Risen? A Macroscopic Examination of the Trends in U.S. Aircraft Costs over the Past Several Decades*. Santa Monica, CA: RAND National Defense Research Institute, 2008.

Arena, Mark V., Irv Blickstein, Clifford Grammich, and Obaid Younossi. *Why Has the Cost of Navy Ships Risen? A Macroscopic Examination of the Trends in U.S. Navy Ship Costs over the Past Several Decades*. Santa Monica CA: RAND National Defense Research Institute, 2006.

Arendt, Michael, Jacques Gansler, and William Lucyshyn. "Competition in Defense Acquisitions." Center for Public Policy and Private Enterprise, January 2009.

Armitage, Richard, and Joseph Nye. *CSIS Commission on Smart Power: A Smarter, More Secure America*. Washington, DC: Center for Strategic and International Studies, 2007.

Association of American Universities. "National Defense Education and Innovation Initiative: Meeting America's Economic and Security Challenges in the Twenty-First Century." Association of American Universities, January 2006.

Augustine, Norman R. *Is America Falling Off the Flat Earth?* Washington, DC: National Academies Press, 2007.

Barma, N., E. Ratner, and S. Weber. "A World without the West." *National* Interest 90 (July–August 2007): 23–30.

Bialos, Jeffrey. *Ideas for America's Future: Core Elements of a New National Security Strategy.* Washington, DC: Center for Transatlantic Relations, Johns Hopkins University, 2008.

Bialos, J., C. Fisher, and S. Koehl. *Fortresses and Icebergs: The Evolution of the Transatlantic Defense Market and the Implications for U.S. National Security.* Washington, DC: SAIS, Johns Hopkins University, 2009.

Binnendijk, Hans, and Kugler, Richard. "Future Directions for U.S. Foreign Policy, Balancing Status Quo and Reform." Center for Technology and National Security Policy, National Defense University, May 2007.

Binnedijk, Hans, and Richard Kugler. *Seeing the Elephant: The U.S. Role in Global Security.* Dulles, VA: Potomac Books, 2007.

Binnendijk, Hans, and Richard Kugler. *Toward a New Transatlantic Compact.* Washington, DC: Center for Technology and National Security Policy, National Defense University, 2008.

Booz Allen Hamilton. "U.S. Defense Industry under Siege: An Agenda for Change." Booze Allen and Hamilton, July 2000.

Bowman, Marion. "Privatizing while Transforming." *Defense Horizons* 57 (July 2007): 1–9.

Brzezinski, Z. *The Choice: Global Domination or Global Leadership.* New York: Basic Books, 2004.

Bush, V. *Science: The Endless Frontier.* Washington, DC: U.S. Government Printing Office, 1945.

Cancian, Mark. "Contractors: The New Element of Military Force Structures." *Parameters* (U.S. Army War College) 38 (Autumn 2008): 61–77.

Carafano, James. *Private Sector, Public Wars: Contractors in Combat—Afghanistan, Iraq, and Future Conflicts.* Westport, CT: Praeger Security International, 2008.

Carter, Ashton, and William Perry. 2007. "China on the March." *National Interest* 88 (March–April): 16–22.

Carter, Ashton B. "Defense Management Challenges in the Post-Bush Era." In *Defense Strategy and Forces: Setting Future Directions.* Newport, RI: Naval War College, 2008.

Center for Strategic and International Studies. "Security Controls on the Access of Foreign Scientists and Engineers to the United States: A White Paper of the Commission on Scientific Communication and National Security." CSIS, October 2005.

Center for the Study of the Presidency. "Project on National Security Reform." November 2008.

Chao, Pierre. "Structure and Dynamics of the U.S. Federal Professional Services Industrial Base 1995–2004." Center for Strategic and International Studies, Report, May 2007.

Chao, Pierre. "The Future of the U.S. Defense Industrial Base: National Security Implications of a Globalized World." College of the Armed Forces, June 2, 2005.

Chao, Pierre, and Robin Niblett. "Trusted Partners: Sharing Technology within the U.S.-U.K. Security Relationship." CSIS, May 2006.

Commission on Army Acquisition and Program Management in Expeditionary Operations. *Urgent Reform Required: Army Expeditionary Contracting.* Washington, DC: U.S. Government Printing Office, October 2007.

Congressional Budget Office. "Contractors' Support of U.S. Operations in Iraq." Congressional Budget Office, Washington, DC, August 2008.

Costigan, Sean, and A. Markusen. "Arming the Future: A Defense Industry for the Twenty-First Century." Council on Foreign Relations, 1999.

Daalder, Ivo, and James Lindsay. *America Unbound: The Bush Revolution in Foreign Policy.* Washington, DC: Brookings Institution, 2003.

Defense Advanced Research Projects Agency (DARPA). "Bridging the Gap, DARPA, Powered by Ideas." DARPA, February 2007.

Defense Business Board. "Task Group on Best Practices for Export Controls." October 2008.

Defense Science Board. "DSB Summer Study on Transformation Sub-Panel on Defense Industry and Acquisition: Assessment of the Current Situation and Recommended Actions." Defense Science Board, August 2005.

Department of Defense. "The Acquisition 2005 Task Force Final Report, Shaping the Civilian Acquisition Workforce of the Future." Washington, DC, October 2000.

Department of Defense. "Annual Industrial Capabilities Report to Congress." Washington, DC, March 2008.

Department of Defense. "Creating an Effective National Security Industrial Base for the Twenty-First Century: An Action Plan to Address the Coming Crisis." Office of the Undersecretary Defense for Acquisition, Technology, and Logistics, July 2008.

Department of Defense. "Final Report of the Defense Science Board Task Force on Globalization and Security." Washington, DC, December 1999.

Department of Defense. "Quadrennial Defense Review." DoD, February 2006.

Department of Defense. "Report of the Secretary of Defense Task Force on DoD Nuclear Weapons Management. Phase I: The Air Force's Nuclear Mission." Washington, DC, September 2008.

Department of Defense. "Study on Impact of Foreign Sourcing of Systems." Washington, DC, January 2004.

Dombrowski, Peter, Eugene Gholz, and Andrew Ross. "Military Transformation and the Defense Industry after Next: The Defense Industrial Implications of Network-Centric Warfare." Strategic Research Department Center for Naval Warfare Studies, U.S. Naval War College, September 2002.

Douglass, John. "Forty-First Annual Year-End Review and Forecast Luncheon." Washington, DC: Aerospace Industries Association, 2006.

Drezner, Jeffrey, Jeanne M. Jarvaise, Ron Hess, Daniel M. Norton, and Paul G. Hough. *An Analysis of Weapon System Cost Growth.* Santa Monica, CA: RAND Corporation, 1993.

Dunn, Richard. "Contractors Supporting Combat Operations: Developing the Vision to Fill Gaps in Policy." Center for Public Policy and Private Enterprise, University of Maryland, January 2008.

Dyson, Freeman. *The Scientist as Rebel.* New York: New York Review Books, 2006.

Flamm, Kenneth. "Failures of Defense Industrial Policy Reform and Likely Consequences for the Bush Defense Build-Up." Technology and Public Policy Program, Lyndon B. Johnson School of Public Affairs, University of Texas, March 2002.

Flanagan, Stephen, and James Schear, eds. *Strategic Challenges: America's Global Security Agenda.* Washington, DC: National Defense University Press, 2007.

Flourney, Michele, and Tammy Schultz. "Shaping U.S. Ground Forces for the Future: Getting Expansion Right." Center for a New American Society, June 2007.

Freidman, Thomas. *The World Is Flat: A Brief History of the Twenty-first Century.* New York: Farrar, Straus & Giroux, 2005.

Frost, Ellen, James Przystup, and Phillip Saunders. "China's Rising Influence in Asia: Implications for U.S. Policy." *Strategic Forum* 231 (2008): 1–8.

Galama, Titus, and James Hosek. *U.S. Competitiveness in Science and Technology.* Washington, DC: RAND National Defense Research Institute, 2008.

Gansler, Jacques S. *Affording Defense.* Cambridge, MA: MIT Press, 1989.

Gansler, Jacques S. *Defense Conversion: Transforming the Arsenal of Democracy.* Cambridge, MA: MIT Press, 1995.

Gansler, Jacques. "The Defense Industrial Structure in the Twenty-First Century." Paper presented at the Acquisition Reform Conference, American Institute of Aeronautics and Astronautics, January 27, 2000.

Gansler, Jacques S. *The Defense Industry.* Cambridge, MA: MIT Press, 1980.

Gansler, Jacques. "Urgent Reform Required: DoD Expeditionary Contracting. Independent Assessment of the Commission on Army Acquisition and Program Management in Expeditionary Operations and Subsequent DoD Implementation Efforts." University of Maryland, October 2008.

Gansler, Jacques. "U.S. Defense Industrial Policy." *Security Challenges* 3, no. 2 (2007): 1–17.

Gates, Robert. "A Balanced Strategy: Reprogramming the Pentagon for a New Age." *Foreign Affairs* 88 (January–February 2009): 1–7.

Georgia Institute of Technology. "High Tech Indicators: Technology-based Competitiveness of Thirty-Three Nations." Technology Policy and Assessment Center, Washington, DC, January 2008.

Gholz, Eugene, Harvey Sapolsky, and Caitlin Talmadge. *U.S. Defense Politics: The Origins of Security Policy.* New York: Routledge Taylor & Francis Group, 2008.

Government Accountability Office. "Defense Business Transformation: Sustaining Progress Requires Continuity of Leadership and an Integrated Approach." GAO, February 2008.

Government Accountability Office. "Catastrophic Disasters: Federal Efforts Help States Prepare for and Respond to Psychological Consequences, but FEMA's Crisis Counseling Program Needs Improvement." GAO, February 2008.

Government Accountability Office. "Department of Defense: A Department-wide Framework to Identify and Report Gaps in the Defense Supplier Base Is Needed." GAO, October 2008.

Government Accountability Office. "GAO Forum: Managing the Supplier Base in the Twenty-First Century." GAO, October 2005.

Government Accountability Office. "Report to Congressional Committees, Defense Acquisition, Assessments of Selected Weapon Programs." GAO, March 2008.

Government Accountability Office. "Report to Congressional Committee, Defense Acquisitions of Selected Weapon Programs." GAO, March 2007.

General Accountability Office. "Report to the Chairman, Subcommittee on Readiness and Management Support, Committee on Armed Services, U.S. Senate, Contingency Operations: Army Should Do More to Control Contract Cost in the Balkans." GAO, September 2000.

Government Accountability Office. "Report to the Subcommittee on Readiness and Management Support, Committee on Armed Services, U.S. Senate, Military Operations: Contractors Provide Vital Services to Deployed Forces but Are Not Adequately Addressed in DoD Plans." GAO, June 2003.

Guay, Terrence R. "Globalization and Its Implications for the Defense Industrial Base." Strategic Studies Institute, U.S. Army War College, February 2007.

Hart, Gary. *The Shield and the Cloak: The Security of the Commons.* New York: Oxford University Press, 2006.

Hartley, Keith. "Defense Industrial Policy in a Military Alliance." *Journal of Peace Research* 43, no. 4 (2006): 473–489.

Hart-Rudman Commission. "U.S. Commission on National Security. Road Map for National Security: Imperative for Change." Washington, DC, 2001.

Hensel, Nayantara. "The Role of Trans-Atlantic Defense Alliances in a Globalized World." Naval Postgraduate School, Acquisition Symposium, May 13–14, 2009.

Joint Chiefs of Staff. "Operational Contract Support." Joint Publication 4-10. U.S. Government Printing Office, November 2007.

Kapstein, Ethan. *The Political Economy of National Security: A Global Perspective.* Columbia: University of South Carolina Press, 1991.

Kegley, Charles, and Gregory Raymond. *Multipolar Peace? Great-Power Politics in the Twenty-first Century.* New York: St. Martin's Press, 1993.

Kennedy, Paul. *The Rise and Fall of Great Powers: Economic and Military Conflict from 1500 to 2000.* New York: Random House, 1987.

Kotter, John P. *Leading Change.* Boston: Harvard Business School Press, 1996.

Kramer, Robert. "Antitrust Considerations in International Defense Mergers." Department of Justice, May 1999.

Langenfeld, James, and Preston McAfee. "Competition in the Defense Markets: Meeting the Needs of Twenty-First-Century Warfighting." Institute of Defense Analysis, January 2001.

Lebl, Leslie. "Advancing U.S. Interests with the European Union." Washington, DC: Atlantic Council of the United States, January 2007.

Ministry of Defense. "Contractors on Deployed Operations, Joint Doctrine Pamphlet." Chiefs of Staff, April 2001.

Moerman, Fiente. "Polishing Belgium's Innovation Jewel." *Issues in Science and Technology* (Fall 2007).

Mowery, David. *Military R&D and Innovation.* Berkeley: University of California Press, 2008.

Nagle, James F. *A History of Government Contracting.* Washington, DC: George Washington University Press, 1999.

National Archives. http://webarchive.nationalarchives.gov.uk/20060130194436/http://www.mod.uk/business/ppp/reserves.htm, 2005 (accessed March 30, 2005).

National Commission on Energy Policy. *Ending the Energy Stalemate: A Bipartisan Strategy to Meet America's Energy Challenges.* Washington, DC: U.S. Government Printing Office, December 2004.

National Research Council of the National Academies. *An Assessment of the Small Business Innovation Research Program at the National Science Foundation.* Washington, DC: National Academies Press, 2007.

National Research Council of the National Academies. *Beyond "Fortress America": National Security Controls on Science and Technology in a Globalized World.* Washington, DC: National Academies Press, 2009.

National Research Council of the National Academies. *Critical Technology Accessibility.* Washington, DC: National Academies Press, 2006.

National Research Council of the National Academies. *Innovation Policies for the Twenty-First Century: Report of a Symposium.* Washington, DC: National Academies Press, 2007.

National Research Council of the National Academies. *Pre-Milestone A and Early-Phase Systems Engineering: A Retrospective Review and Benefits for Future Air Force Systems Acquisition.* Washington, DC: National Academies Press, 2007.

National Research Council of the National Academies. *Science and Security in a Post-9/11 World.* Washington, DC: National Academies Press, 2007.

National Security Advisory Group. "Reducing Nuclear Threats and Preventing Nuclear Terrorism." NSAG, October 2007.

Nye, Joseph. *Soft Power: The Means to Success in World Politics.* New York: Public Affairs, 2004.

O'Keefe, S., and G. I. Susman. *The Defense Industry in the Post–Cold War Era: Corporate Strategies and Public Policy Perspectives.* New York: Pergamon, 1998.

Oliver, David. "Current Export Policies: Trick or Treat." *Defense Horizons* 6 (December 2001).

Packer, George. "A Reporter at Large, Knowing the Enemy." *New Yorker* (December 2006): 11.

Peck, M. J., and F. M. Scherer. *The Weapons Acquisition Process: An Economic Analysis.* Cambridge: Harvard University Press, 1962.

Philbrick, Nathaniel. *Mayflower: A Story of Courage, Community, and War.* New York: Viking, 2006.

President's Blue Ribbon Commission on Defense Management. "A Quest for Excellence." Government Accountability Office, June 1986.

President's Council of Advisors on Science and Technology. "Leadership under Challenge: Information Technology R&D in a Competitive World, an Assessment of the Federal Networking and Information Technology R&D Program." Executive Office of the President, August 2007.

PriceWaterhouseCoopers. "The Defense Industry in the Twenty-First Century: Thinking Global . . . or Thinking American?" http://www.pwc.com, 2005.

Ronis, Sheila, and Lynne Thompson. *U.S. Defense Industrial Base: National Security Implications of a Globalized World: The 2005 Dwight Eisenhower National Security Series Symposium.* Washington, DC: National Defense University Press, 2006.

Samuels, Richard. *Securing Japan: Tokyo's Grand Strategy and the Future of East Asia.* New York: Cornell University Press, 2007.

Sarkozy, Nicolas. "The French White Paper on Defense and National Security." Paris, 2008.

Sato, H., H. Shiroyama, K. Suzuki, and T. Suzuki, "Mini Seminar on Security Trade Control: Towards Regional Framework in Asia and Japan's Role." Science, Technology, and International Relations Project, November 2007.

Secretary of State for Defense by Command of Her Majesty. "Defense Industrial Strategy: Defense White Paper." December 2005.

Shorrock, Tim. *Spies for Hire: The Secret World of Intelligence Outsourcing.* New York: Simon & Schuster, 2008.

Singer, P. W. *Corporate Warriors: The Rise of the Privatized Military Industry: Cornell Studies in Security Affairs.* New York: Cornell University Press, 2003.

Smith, Rupert. *The Utility of Force: The Art of War in the Modern World.* London: Allen Lane, 2005.

Sperling, Richard, and Jino Choi. "Analyzing the Relationship between Navy Procurement and RDT&E." Center for Naval Analysis, October 2006.

Task Force on the Future of the American Innovation. "Measuring the Moment: Innovation, National Security, and Economic Competitiveness—Benchmarks of Our Innovation Future II." Washington, DC, November 2006.

Toffler, Alvin, and Heidi Toffler. *War and Anti-War: Survival at the Dawn of the Twenty-First Century.* New York: Little, Brown, 1993.

Trebilcock, Craig. "The Modern Seven Pillars of Iraq." *Army* (February 2007): 25–33.

Turner, James. "The Next Innovation Revolution, Laying the Groundwork for the United States." *Innovations* (Spring 2006): 123–144.

U.S. Congress, Office of Technology Assessment. *Building Future Security, Strategies for Restructuring the Defense Technology and Industrial Base.* OTA-ISC-530. Washington, DC: U.S. Government Printing Office, June 1992.

Walker, David. "DoD Transformation Challenges and Opportunities." Government Accountability Office, February 2007.

Walker, David. "DoD Transformation Challenges and Opportunities." Government Accountability Office, November 2007.

Walker, David. "U.S. Financial Condition and Fiscal Future Briefing." Government Accountability Office, August 2007.

Wulf, William. "The Importance of Foreign-Born Scientists and Engineers to the Security of the United States." Paper presented at the Subcommittee on Immigration, Border Security, and Claims, Committee on the Judiciary, U.S. House of Representatives hearing on Sources and Methods of Foreign Nationals Engaged in Economic and Military Espionage, Washington, DC, September 2005.

Zimmermann, Warren. *First Great Triumph: How Five Americans Made Their Country a World Power*. New York: Farrar, Straus and Giroux, 2002.

About the Author

The Honorable Jacques S. Gansler is a professor and holds the Roger C. Lipitz Chair in Public Policy and Private Enterprise in the School of Public Policy at the University of Maryland. Additionally, he is the Glenn L. Martin Institute Fellow of Engineering at the A. James Clarke School of Engineering, an affiliate faculty member at the Robert H. Smith School of Business, and a senior fellow at the James MacGregor Burns Academy of Leadership (all at the University of Maryland). He also served as interim dean of the School of Public Policy from 2003 to 2004 and as vice president for research for the University of Maryland from 2004 to 2006.

He is a member of the National Academy of Engineering and a fellow of the National Academy of Public Administration. He served as the chair of the Secretary of the Army's Commission on Contracting and Program Management for Army Expeditionary Forces. Additionally, he is a member of the Defense Science Board.

Dr. Gansler served as the Under Secretary of Defense for Acquisition, Technology, and Logistics from November 1997 until January 2001. In this position, he was responsible for all matters relating to Department of Defense acquisition, research and development, logistics, acquisition reform, advanced technology, international programs, environmental security, nuclear, chemical, and biological programs, and the defense technology and industrial base. His department had an annual budget of over $180 billion and a workforce of over 300,000.

Prior to this appointment, Dr. Gansler was executive vice president and corporate director for TASC, Incorporated, an applied information technology company. Earlier, he served in the government as deputy assistant secretary of defense (materiel acquisition), responsible for all defense procurements and the defense industry; and as assistant director of defense research and engineering (electronics), responsible for all defense electronics research and development.

His prior industrial experience included vice president, I.T.T. Avionics; program management, director of advanced programs, and director of international marketing, Singer; and engineering management, Raytheon.

Dr. Gansler holds a BE in electrical engineering from Yale University, an MS in electrical engineering from Northeastern University, an MA in political economy from the New School for Social Research, and a PhD in economics from American University.

Index